54

D0924133

# NIETZSCHE'S PRESENCE IN
# FREUD'S LIFE AND THOUGHT

# NIETZSCHE'S PRESENCE IN FREUD'S LIFE AND THOUGHT

## On the Origins of a Psychology of Dynamic Unconscious Mental Functioning

RONALD LEHRER

STATE UNIVERSITY OF NEW YORK PRESS

Library Resource Center
Renton Technical College
3000 N.E. 4th St.
Renton, WA 98056

Published by
State University of New York Press, Albany

© 1995 State University of New York

All rights reserved

Printed in the United States of America

No part of this book may be used or reproduced
in any manner whatsoever without written permission
except in the case of brief quotations embodied in
critical articles and reviews.

For information, address State University of New York
Press, State University Plaza, Albany, N.Y., 12246

Production by E. Moore
Marketing by Fran Keneston

Library of Congress Cataloging-in-Publication Data

Lehrer, Ronald, (date)
    Nietzsche's presence in Freud's life and thought  :  on the origins of a
psychology of dynamic unconscious mental functioning  /  Ronald
Lehrer.
      p.      cm.
    Includes bibliographical references and index.
    ISBN 0-7914-2145-7 (alk. paper). — ISBN 0-7914-2146-5 (pbk.  :
alk. paper)
    1. Freud, Sigmund, 1856–1939.    2. Nietzsche, Friedrich Wilhelm,
1844–1900—Influence.    3. Psychoanalysis and philosophy—History.
I. Title.
BF109.F74L44      1994
150.19′52′092—dc20                                                          94-571
                                                                                              CIP

10 9 8 7 6 5 4 3 2        150.1952092 LEHRER 1995

                         Lehrer, Ronald, 1943-

                         Nietzsche's presence in
                           Freud's life and thought

# CONTENTS

# A NOTE ON SOURCES AND CITATIONS

Quotations from and references to Freud's published writings are taken from *The Standard Edition of the Complete Psychological Works of Sigmund Freud*, translated and edited by James Strachey, et al. (London: Hogarth Press, 1953–74, 24 volumes). Volume number and page number will be indicated as follows: (SE 5:385), which refers to volume five, page 385, of the standard edition. In the bibliography, year and order of publication will be given with lowercase letters as provided by Strachey: (1905d) will refer to *Three Essays on the Theory of Sexuality*. The volumes of Freud's letters utilized, such as the letters to Fliess, Jung, Abraham, Andreas-Salomé, Pfister and Zweig, are listed under the names of the editors of the particular volume to which reference is made.

Quotations from and references to Nietzsche's writings are, with a few exceptions, taken from the translations by Walter Kaufmann and R. J. Hollingdale. These volumes are listed in the bibliography as are the sources of any quotations from or references to other volumes.

# ACKNOWLEDGMENTS

I would like to express my gratitude to editors Carola F. Sautter and Elizabeth Moore at SUNY Press. For their encouragement and/or helpful comments on various aspects of this study, I want to thank Carol Geisler, George Frank, Jeffrey Seinfeld, Wilma Heckler, Irvin Yalom, Emanuel Rice, John Kerr, Richard Kirkham, Maudemarie Clark, and Deborah Hayden. Rita Kozak was a great help in translating material and discussing the material on which she worked. Bill Parise, Rita Coleman and Sheree Worman of the Brooklyn College Library were able to locate and obtain virtually every book and article I requested. Debbra Lupien's skill and patience at the computer and word processor are greatly appreciated. Thanks to Carol Inskip for her work on the index. I want to thank Robert Bader for the many hours of conversation over many years. For their support during the years I worked on this study, I want to thank my mother, Dorothy Lehrer, and my many very helpful relatives, friends and colleagues. Most important, I want to thank my wife, Rhonda Lehrer, and our daughter, Ava Anne,—for everything.

Grateful acknowledgment is made for permission to reproduce excerpts from the following material: Sigmund Freud Copyrights, The Institute of Psycho-Analysis and The Hogarth Press for permission to quote from *The Standard Edition of the Complete Psychological Works of Sigmund Freud*, translated and edited by James Strachey. Selected excerpts from *The Interpretation of Dreams* by Sigmund Freud. Translated from the German and edited by James Strachey. Published in the United States by

Basic Books, Inc., 1956 by arrangement with George Allen and Unwin, Ltd. and The Hogarth Press, Ltd. Reprinted by permission of Basic Books, a division of HarperCollins Publishers, Inc. Selected excerpts from *The Interpretation of Dreams* by Sigmund Freud, translated and edited by James Strachey. Reprinted by permission of Routledge Kegan & Paul. From *Beyond the Pleasure Principle* by Sigmund Freud, translated and edited by James Strachey. Copyright © 1961 by James Strachey, renewed 1989. Reprinted with the permission of W. W. Norton & Company, Inc. From *The Future of an Illusion* by Sigmund Freud, translated and edited by James Strachey. Copyright © 1961 by James Strachey, renewed 1989. Reprinted with the permission of W. W. Norton & Company, Inc. From *Civilization and Its Discontents* by Sigmund Freud, translated and edited by James Strachey. Copyright © 1961 by James Strachey, renewed 1989. Reprinted with the permission of W. W. Norton & Company, Inc. From *An Outline of Psycho-Analysis* by Sigmund Freud, translated and edited by James Strachey. Copyright © 1949 by W. W. Norton & Company, Inc., renewed © 1976 by Alix S. Strachey. Copyright © 1969 by The Institute for Psycho-Analysis and Alix S. Strachey. Excerpts from *The Letters of Sigmund Freud & Arnold Zweig*, edited by E. L. Freud and translated by Professor William D. Robson, copyright © 1970 by Sigmund Freud Copyrights Ltd. and the Executors of the Estate of Arnold Zweig, reprinted by permission of Harcourt Brace & Company. From *Moses and Monotheism* by Sigmund Freud. Copyright © 1939 and renewed 1967 by Ernest L. Freud and Anna Freud. Reprinted by permission of Random House, Inc. From *The Birth of Tragedy* by Friedrich Nietzsche. Copyright © 1967 by Random House, Inc. Reprinted by permission of Random House, Inc. From *The Gay Science* by Friedrich Nietzsche. Copyright © 1974 by Random House, Inc. Reprinted by permission of Random House, Inc. From *Beyond Good and Evil* by Friedrich Nietzsche. Copyright © 1966 by Random House, Inc. Reprinted by permission of Random House, Inc. From *On the Geneology of Morals* by Friedrich Nietzsche. Copyright © 1967 by Random House, Inc. Reprinted by permission of Random House, Inc. From *Ecce Homo* by Friedrich Nietzsche. Copyright © 1967 by Random House, Inc. Reprinted by permission of Random House, Inc. From *The Will to Power* by Friedrich Nietzsche. Copyright © 1967 by Walter Kaufmann. Reprinted by permission of Random House, Inc. From

*The Portable Nietzsche* by Walter Kaufmann, editor, translated by Walter Kaufmann. Translation copyright 1954 by The Viking Press, renewed © 1982 by Viking Penguin Inc. Used by permission of Viking Penguin, a division of Penguin Books USA Inc. From *Untimely Meditations* by Friedrich Nietzsche, translated by R. J. Hollingdale, copyright © 1983 by Cambridge University Press. Reprinted with the permission of Cambridge University Press. From *Human, All Too Human* by Friedrich Nietzsche, translated by R. J. Hollingdale, copyright © 1986 by Cambridge University Press. Reprinted with the permission of Cambridge University Press. From *Daybreak: Thoughts on the Prejudices of Morality* by Friedrich Nietzsche, translated by R. J. Hollingdale, copyright © 1982 by Cambridge University Press. Reprinted with the permission of Cambridge University Press. From "Discussion: Towards a Social-Constructivist View of the Psychoanalytic Situation" by Irwin Z. Hoffman, *Psychoanalytic Dialogues: A Journal of Relational Perspectives*, vol. 1, no. 1 (1991), pp. 74–105. Reprinted with the permission of The Analytic Press. Some material in this book appears in the article "Freud's Relationship to Nietzsche: Some Preliminary Considerations" by Ronald Lehrer, accepted for publication by *The Psychoanalytic Review* in August 1993. Reprinted by permission of *The Psychoanalytic Review* published by the National Psychological Association for Psychoanalysis, Inc.

# INTRODUCTION

From the early years in the development of psychoanalysis up until the present day, there has been substantial discussion and debate regarding the extent to which Nietzsche discovered and elaborated upon ideas generally ascribed to Freud as well as the extent to which Freud may have been influenced by Nietzsche in his development of a number of fundamental psychoanalytic concepts. In 1929 Thomas Mann, a great admirer of Freud, wrote: "He [Freud] was not acquainted with Nietzsche in whose work everywhere appear lightning-like gleams of insight anticipatory of Freud's later views."[1] Mann considered Nietzsche to be "the greatest critic and psychologist of morals."[2] In an early study of the development of Freud's thought, Wittels, a member of the psychoanalytic community, mentioned Nietzsche at numerous points. He suggested that Freud was not aware of certain philosophical influences on his thought,[3] that Nietzsche "must perhaps be looked upon as the founder of disillusioning psychology,"[4] that "Nietzsche's division into Dionysian and Apollonian . . . is almost completely identical with that of the primary and secondary function [process],"[5] and that Nietzsche and certain other writers "were aware that the dream had a hidden meaning and significance for our mental life."[6] In a 1932 study of Freud and psychoanalysis, Maria Dorer mentioned Freud's debt to Nietzsche.[7] Karl Jaspers, who contributed to the fields of psychiatry, depth psychology and philosophy, frequently commented on Nietzsche's psychological insights and discussed Nietzsche in relation to Freud and psychoanalysis. In his text, *General Psychopathology*, only Freud appears

1

more frequently than Nietzsche. He went so far as to state that Freud and psychoanalysis have used ideas pertaining to the "meaningfulness of psychic deviations . . . in a misleading way and this blocked the direct influence on [the study of] psychopathology of great people such as Kierkegaard and Nietzsche."[8] He wrote of Freud popularizing "in cruder form" certain ideas related to Nietzsche's concept of sublimation.[9]

Much earlier in the development of psychoanalysis, at a 1908 meeting of the Vienna Psychoanalytic Society devoted to the discussion of one of Nietzsche's works, Paul Federn stated that Nietzsche had come so close to the views of these early analysts, "that we can ask only, 'Where has he not come close?'"[10]

There have been a number of studies over the past twenty-five years or so concluding that Nietzsche did in fact anticipate certain central psychoanalytic concepts.[11] It is important that these studies do not follow the characterization of Freud and some authors, such as Mazlish and Gay, who regard any insights Nietzsche had in the domain of dynamic psychology as flashes of intuitive brilliance to be contrasted with the laborious procedures and accumulation of knowledge characteristic of psychoanalysis as a science.[12] These studies argue that Nietzsche seriously and extensively discussed and elaborated upon a number of ideas which were to be central to the development of psychoanalysis.[13]

One can look to the most ardent admirers of the originality of Freud's achievement and find acknowledgment of Nietzsche's anticipation of aspects of Freud's thought. For example, Jones notes "a truly remarkable correspondence between Freud's conception of the super-ego and Nietzsche's exposition of the origin of the 'bad conscience,'"[14] Another analyst, Anzieu, offers the following summary of Nietzsche's anticipation of psychoanalytic concepts:

> It was Nietzsche who invented the term das Es (the id). He had some understanding of the economic point of view, which comprises discharge, and transfer of energy from one drive to another. But he believed that aggression and self-destruction were stronger than sexuality. On several occasions he used the word sublimation (applying it to both the aggressive and the sexual instincts). He described repression, but called it inhibition; he talked of the super-ego and of guilt feelings, but called them resentment, bad conscience and

false morality. Nietzsche also described, without giving them a name, the turning of drives against oneself, the paternal image, the maternal image, and the renunciation imposed by civilization on the gratification of our instincts. The "superman" was the individual who succeeded in transcending this conflict between established values and his instinctual urges, thus achieving inner freedom and establishing his own personal morality and scale of values; in other words, Nietzsche foreshadowed what was to be one of the major aims of psychoanalytic treatment.[15]

In his study of Freud's anthropological writings, Wallace states that Nietzsche "anticipated, one can almost certainly say influenced, a chain of ideas central to *Totem and Taboo*."[16] Wallace goes on to demonstrate the intimate relationship between Freud's anthropological writings and the central concepts of psychoanalysis. Regarding Nietzsche's relationship to anthropology, in a recent study Shweder has written: "Friedrich Nietzsche is not an acknowledged founding father of cultural anthropology, yet far more than is realized, his way of thinking propagated and took over modern anthropology."[17] In his biography of Nietzsche, Hayman writes of Nietzsche's recognition of ambivalence[18] and that "Freudian psychology is prefigured in his analysis of forgetting; in his recognition that only a small part of the mind's functioning is conscious, and that consciousness is pathological; in his discovery of abreaction and repression, and in his understanding of the sexual and sadistic instincts, and of the retreat into illness."[19] Hayman writes of Nietzsche's enormous influence on the twentieth century, "in which almost every major writer in the German language has been profoundly indebted to him—Rilke, Kafka, Mann, Musil, Benn, Heidegger and Freud, for instance."[20]

Ernest Gellner, in his book on psychoanalysis (which has not been published in the United States), has written of the "Nietzschean Minimum" (N.M.). This refers to ideas basic to Freud's development of psychoanalysis that were taken over by Freud from Nietzsche. These ideas include, among others, the following:

1. *Instinctuality*. "Our real satisfactions and needs are closely linked to our basic instinctual drives."

2. *Trauma and Gestalt.* "Perception, formation of permanent pictures and attitudes, is by *trauma.*"

3. *Covertness.* ". . . these . . . crystallizations [are] not generally conscious or accessible to the consciousness. . . ."

4. *Surrealism.* "The . . . principles . . . which govern these crystallizations, are strangers . . . to all the normal rules of time, space, logic and causality. . . ."

5. *Cunning.* ". . . these inner reactions are . . . cunningly functional, and at the service of our persistent instinctual drives. . . ."

6. *Fraud.* "These attributes [cunning, camouflage, etc.] . . . apply . . . to the activities traditionally considered to be furtherest removed from our beastliness: conscience, reason, pursuit of ideals, etc."[21]

The analyst Hans Loewald has written that Nietzsche's "direct and indirect influence on Freud and his early followers has been generally underrated."[22] Surprisingly, Loewald does not mention Nietzsche in his monograph on sublimation,[23] a concept to which Nietzsche gave considerable attention.

While there is a growing body of literature examining the relationship between the writings of Freud and Nietzsche, there has appeared no detailed, comprehensive study on the extent to which Freud may have been influenced by Nietzsche through the course of his life and the complex nature of Freud's personal and intellectual relationship to Nietzsche. In part this may be attributed to Freud's assurances that he had never studied Nietzsche, had never been able to get beyond the first half page or so of any of his works due both to the overwhelming wealth of ideas and to the resemblance of Nietzsche's ideas to the findings of psychoanalysis.[24] In other words, Freud avoided Nietzsche in part to preserve the autonomy of the development of his own ideas. In 1908 he assured members of the Vienna Psychoanalytic Society "that Nietzsche's ideas have had no influence whatsoever on his own work."[25] One also might get the impression from Freud's letter to Wilhelm Fliess of February 1, 1900, that he had just acquired Nietzsche's writings for the first time. He adds that he has as yet been too lazy to open them.[26] On this last point Ticho comments: "Freud lazy? I would rather assume that he was conflicted."[27]

Although Freud expressed admiration for Nietzsche on a number of occasions, acknowledged his "intuitive" grasp of concepts anticipating psychoanalysis, placed him among a handful of persons he considered great[28] and stated in 1908 that "the degree of introspection achieved by Nietzsche had never been achieved by anyone, nor is it likely ever to be reached again,"[29] he never acknowledged studying specific works of Nietzsche and never expressed at any length or in any detail what his own thoughts were in regard to specific works or ideas of Nietzsche.

In recent years, sources have become available and studies completed which make it clear that Freud was familiar with the ideas in some of Nietzsche's early writings while a student at the University of Vienna[30] and that Nietzsche's influence on the world of young Viennese intellectuals surrounding Freud, including some of his closest and most admired friends and acquaintances, was immense.[31] Nietzsche also had an enormous impact on the entire intellectual and political life of the German-speaking world and beyond from 1890 on, that is, soon after he became insane in early 1889. There are Freud scholars such as Trosman who acknowledge the pervasive influence of Nietzsche but suggest that Freud may have avoided reading Nietzsche and may have avoided significant influence during the years he was first formulating the basic tenets of psychoanalysis.[32] Other authors suggest that with Nietzsche's ideas saturating the intellectual life of the German-speaking world in the 1890s (and we can add Freud's exposure to Nietzsche as a university student), it was virtually impossible for Freud to avoid being influenced by Nietzsche.[33]

Regarding the period after publication of *The Interpretation of Dreams* (1900) and *Three Essays on the Theory of Sexuality* (1905), we know that in 1908 Freud read (and discussed with members of the Vienna Psychoanalytic Society) sections of *On the Genealogy of Morals* and *Ecce Homo* and that his development of the concept of the superego as well as ideas expressed particularly in *Civilization and Its Discontents* bear striking similarity to ideas expressed in *On the Genealogy of Morals*.[34] It would also appear that the *Genealogy* was among the works of Nietzsche likely influencing *Totem and Taboo* and Freud's other anthropological writings.

What is not at all clear includes the following matters: What else did Freud read of Nietzsche or hear discussed besides early works (such as *The Birth of Tragedy* and the first two or three essays in *Untimely Meditations*), likely read and/or discussed when

Freud was a university student, and *On the Genealogy of Morals* and *Ecce Homo* read in 1908 and discussed at two meetings of the Vienna Psychoanalytic Society? What evidence is there that the early works of Nietzsche had any bearing on the development of Freud's thought? What evidence is there that between the mid-1870s and 1900, that is, the period that includes those years in which he matured and then developed the foundation concepts of psychoanalysis, Freud read Nietzsche or came into contact with his ideas? Is there evidence that can shed light on the nature of Freud's complex relationship to Nietzsche throughout his adult life?

It is the aim of the present study to fill a gap in Freud studies by attempting to address these and related questions. While important studies such as those by Ellenberger and McGrath clarify the nature of Nietzsche's impact on the world around Freud, these studies do not offer a detailed and comprehensive examination of the nature of Freud's relationship to Nietzsche through the course of his life. An attempt will be made to examine material that has a direct bearing on Nietzsche's anticipation of and possible influence on Freud as well as material that illuminates the nature of Freud's thoughts and feelings regarding Nietzsche. Although it is of course possible that Freud had a highly emotionally charged personal relationship to Nietzsche while being only minimally influenced by him in regard to his own intellectual development, an attempt will be made to determine how the nature of Freud's thoughts and feelings, as they pertain to Nietzsche, may shed light on the question of influence.

Freud's genius was such that he struggled with and absorbed, both consciously and unconsciously, a remarkable range of influences from diverse personal, historical, social, cultural, religious and scientific sources. Various studies have focused on one or more of these influences. The present study is an examination of yet another important influence without implication of minimizing any of the many other important influences on the development of Freud's thought, or for that matter the originality of much of Freud's work. Freud's development of psychoanalysis as a theory and therapy moved far beyond anything envisioned by Nietzsche. In addition, even in the more strictly philosophical sphere, Nietzsche was only one, though an exceptionally important one, of a number of important figures (for example, Feuerbach,

Schopenhauer, Brentano) exerting a significant influence on the development of Freud's thought.

Since this study focuses on the similarities of the two thinkers, when ideas and passages are compared it is similarities that are usually emphasized. It should be understood that when Nietzsche's ideas are found to be similar to or a possible influence upon a particular work of Freud's, consideration is not given to the ways in which the work in question may move into areas in which Nietzsche is of little or no relevance. At certain points differences between Freud and Nietzsche are also discussed. In addition, it will be evident that at times similar interests, concerns and ideas are discussed without any implication of Nietzsche having influenced Freud on the matters under consideration.

Nietzsche and Freud were influenced by many of the same currents of nineteenth-century thought. Both were interested in ancient civilizations, particularly Greek culture. Both were interested in Greek tragedy (and debates about catharsis), both particularly drawn to the figure of Oedipus. Both were interested in and attracted to heroic figures and regarded themselves as such. Both held Goethe in the highest regard. Of course they were influenced by Darwin, evolutionary theory, contemporary theories of energy, anthropology and studies of the origins of civilization. They were influenced by earlier psychological writings, including, possibly, those of Hippolyte Taine (1828–1893). They were also influenced by a basic historical sense, "the sense of development and change [which] was now permeating thinking in nearly every sphere."[35] They wanted to understand, so to speak, the animal in the human and, as unmaskers, were concerned with matters pertaining to the relation between instinct and reason, conscious and unconscious, rational and irrational, appearance and reality, surface and depth. Both attempted to understand the origins and power of religion and morality. They were influenced by the Enlightenment and the hopes for reason and science while at the same time being influenced by Romanticism's preoccupations with the unconscious and irrational. While beginning their careers in other fields, both came to regard themselves, among other things, as depth psychologists.

One has to keep in mind the extent to which Nietzsche and

Freud were both influenced by forces at work in the German-speaking world of the latter part of the nineteenth century and the extent to which similarities in their thought might be attributed to such factors rather than Nietzsche having a direct influence upon Freud.

For example, both Nietzsche and Freud were interested in anthropology. Both read Sir John Lubbock (1834–1913) and Edward Tylor (1832–1917), and both were influenced by these authors. However, an examination of the similarities between Nietzsche and Freud would seem to indicate that there is also the direct influence of Nietzsche upon Freud; so that Wallace, while examining the specifically anthropological influences upon Freud, still writes of Nietzsche's anticipation of and influence upon Freud.[36] Also, Thatcher, while writing of Nietzsche's debt to Lubbock, writes specifically of Nietzsche's, not Lubbock's, "remarkable" anticipation of an idea central to Freud's *Future of an Illusion*.[37]

In regard to broad cultural changes and paradigm changes, Nietzsche was one of the thinkers that heralded and effected such changes. In his book on Freud's social thought, Berliner writes of the changes in intellectual orientation that occurred around 1885, stating that such changes were "reflected in the work of Friedrich Nietzsche."[38] (Ellenberger makes the same point.[39]) Berliner goes on to mention some of Nietzsche's contributions to understanding the human mind, conscience and civilization's origin and his being a representative of "uncovering" or "unmasking" psychology. (Ellenberger credits Ludwig Klages with characterizing Nietzsche as an "uncovering" or "unmasking" psychologist.[40]) Berliner concludes, as have others, that "the generation of his [Freud's] young maturity was permeated with the thought of Nietzsche."[41]

It should also be noted that since this is a study of Nietzsche's influence on Freud, there is virtually no discussion of influences on the development of Nietzsche's thought. Like Freud, Nietzsche came to his groundbreaking explorations with the help of those who came before him, such as Spinoza, Boscovich, Rousseau, Kant, Hegel, Schopenhauer, Emerson, Darwin, Julius Robert von Mayer, Lubbock, Hartmann, F. A. Lange, and others. Since whenever an idea of Nietzsche's that may have influenced Freud is discussed without tracing the influences and development in Nietzsche, and it possibly appearing as if it is being suggested that Nietzsche formulated his ideas without the great help of his forerunners, perhaps it would be useful at this point to take note of the following words of Stephen Jay Gould regarding our discomfort with evolutionary explanations: "One reason must reside in our social and psychic attraction to creation myths in preference to evolutionary stories—for creation myths . . . identify heroes and sacred places, while evolutionary stories provide no palpable, particular object as symbol for reverence, worship or patriotism."[42] Or as Nietzsche put it, "Whenever one can see the act of becoming [in contrast to 'present completeness and perfection'] one grows somewhat cool."[43]

It may be that the place of myth in our lives, in this instance the myth of the hero (with implications for our relationships to Nietzsche and Freud, their relationships to themselves as heroes, and Freud's relationship to Nietzsche), is not so readily relinquished even in the realm of scholarly pursuits, a notion Nietzsche elaborated upon on a number of occasions.

In addition to the published works of Nietzsche and Freud, material utilized for this study includes a number of letters written by and written to Freud as well as the *Minutes of the Vienna Psychoanalytic Society*, particularly volumes 1 and 2.[44] There is also an examination of letters written by Freud's friend Joseph Paneth to his fiancé regarding his meetings with Nietzsche in 1883–84.[45] Paneth was writing to Freud of Nietzsche at the same time, although these letters appear to have been destroyed by Freud.

Part one of this work covers Freud's years at the university through 1900. Part two covers the rest of his life, in particular the two 1908 discussions of Nietzsche at the Vienna Psychoanalytic Society meetings, the period of Freud's work on *Totem and Taboo*, implications of his relationship with Lou Andreas-Salomé and the period of his work towards the end of his life on *Moses and Monotheism*. In the earlier sections of this study, Nietzsche is often quoted to demonstrate in a general way the relevance of his writings to Freud and psychoanalysis. As the study progresses, passages in and ideas of Nietzsche are compared to specific passages and ideas of Freud. At certain points, such as in the discussion of Nietzsche's ideas on dreams, eternal recurrence and truth and the feminine, consideration is given to Nietzsche's relationship to contemporary psychoanalysis.

While the significance of this study rests to a substantial

degree on the extent to which it demonstrates some things about the origins of Freud's development of psychoanalysis, it is also hoped that those who understand themselves and others to a significant extent through psychoanalytic theory will find an enhanced understanding of the origins of their depth psychology; perhaps for some who are not very familiar with Nietzsche, also a hint at ways in which engagement with Nietzsche may enrich their understanding of Freud, themselves and others. I hope that even those who remain unconvinced of Nietzsche's substantial impact on Freud will gain some appreciation of Nietzsche's great achievements as a psychologist. (And in exploring the extent of Nietzsche's psychology of dynamic unconscious mental functioning, I hope to make some contribution to Nietzsche studies.) It has been my experience with analytically oriented colleagues and students as well as with psychoanalytically oriented writings generally, that there is very limited awareness of the ways in which Nietzsche anticipated Freud, not to mention the matter of influence. It is striking that acknowledged Freud scholars who have examined all manner of possible influence upon Freud, for the most part pay very little attention to Freud's relationship to Nietzsche.

Although throughout the study material is presented to support conclusions reached, it will be evident that certain passages are more speculative than others. I hope that even these more speculative passages will provoke useful discussion of the matters under consideration. It should be kept in mind that while at a few points I speculate along the lines of "If Freud read these passages in Nietzsche . . . ," such speculations or imaginings are not of importance regarding the central findings and arguments of the study. I hope that they will not deter readers from appreciating the firm linkages between Nietzsche and Freud that are established.

# PART I

# 1872–1900

Library Resource Center
Renton Technical College
3000 N.E. 4th St.
Renton, WA 98056

# Chapter 1

## THE UNIVERSITY YEARS

*The journal founded by the three, and later four, of us, namely myself, Paneth, Loewy Emanuel, Lipiner, has passed peacefully into the keeping of the Lord . . . From now on I shall have to keep my philosophical ideas purely to myself or pass them on unrefined to Paneth.*

—Freud to Eduard Silberstein, January 1875

We know from Freud's correspondence with his friend Eduard Silberstein that while a university student he was familiar with Nietzsche. In one of the letters of 1875 Freud refers to and quotes from a passage from Nietzsche's essay, "David Strauss, the Confessor and the Writer" (1873), the first essay to be later included in the volume *Untimely Meditations.*[1] Nietzsche was well enough known to Freud and Silberstein for Freud to mention nothing about Nietzsche. A phrase (taken by Strauss from Goethe and included in Nietzsche's essay) is quoted and Nietzsche and Strauss mentioned without any further elaboration deemed necessary. Freud is quite aware that in regard to the passage quoted and its context, "Nietzsche took David Strauss to task . . . for this philistine dictum in 1873."[2] If Freud was familiar with Nietzsche's writings of this period, he would possibly have read *The Birth of Tragedy* (1872) and the first three essays in *Untimely Meditations,* all published in 1873 and 1874. However much Freud actually read of these works, we know that those around him were intensely discussing these early writings of Nietzsche.

Friedrich Wilhelm Nietzsche was born in 1844 in Röcken, a village in Prussian Saxony. He grew up in Naumberg, which was not far from Leipzig where Freud briefly lived after moving from Frieberg (at about the age of three) and before moving to Vienna. Nietzsche began his career as a classical philologist and studied in Leipzig. (Philologists of the time generally believed that important truths regarding the nature and history of ancient civilizations could be revealed through historical and comparative research into the development of language and literature.[3]) His abilities were recognized early, and he was granted his Ph.D. without his meeting the requirement of completing a dissertation. At twenty-five he was awarded a professorship at the University of Basel which he left in 1879 due to health problems as well as his concerns about moving into the areas of philosophy and psychology. While he was well known and much discussed in the German-speaking intellectual world of the mid-1870s, his fame diminished in the 1880s. His productive life ended in January of 1889 when he became insane (probably due to the contraction of syphilis earlier in his life, although there is no consensus on this matter). By 1890 his fame and influence were growing rapidly. Nietzsche died on August 25, 1900, in Wiemar. His great impact on a variety of disciplines has continued throughout the twentieth century with articles, books and anthologies on his work still being produced in great numbers.

Some of Nietzsche's writings criticizing Jews and mixed races as well as writings glorifying war, domination, aristocratic values, breeding, the will to power, destruction as prelude to creation and the superman or overman became associated with Nazi ideology and slogans. Nietzsche certainly bears some responsibility for how certain of his ideas were used or misused, but his emphasis on the individual and his attacks on nationalism, glorification of the state, hero worship, Germany and Germans and antisemitism were all contrary to Fascist and Nazi ideology. Not only were his writings distorted (including by his sister), but writings were invented in his name to support Nazi ideology. This had to be done because there is so much in Nietzsche that is so clearly hostile to antisemitism and currents leading to Nazi ideology.[4]

Freud was almost twelve years younger than Nietzsche, having been born in 1856 in Moravia. His family moved to Leipzig and then to Vienna in his early childhood. (Freud lived in Vienna until 1938 when he emigrated to England due to Nazi persecution. He

died in England in 1939.) At the time Freud was completing his education at the Gymnasium and afterwards during his years at the
university, Nietzsche exerted an enormous influence on young
German-speaking intellectuals. McGrath, in his study of the intellectual life of Austria during the latter part of the nineteenth century, describes Nietzsche as an intellectual father figure for certain
groups of students at the University of Vienna in the 1870s.[5] Or he
may have been seen as an older brother figure, given that he was
not yet thirty when Freud entered the University of Vienna.

The early writings of Nietzsche permeated the lives of many
Viennese university students. Freud and a number of his admired
friends and acquaintances were members of a reading society in
Vienna, the Leseverein der deutschen Studenten Wiens. Freud remained a member until 1878 when the government dissolved the
society. The intellectual figures the members of the group particularly admired were Schopenhauer, Wagner, and Nietzsche.[6] Among
the friends and acquaintances of Freud who were deeply impressed
by Nietzsche's writings were Siegfried Lipiner, Heinrich Braun,
Viktor Adler and Joseph Paneth.

McGrath writes of Freud's somewhat deferential attitude towards Siegfried Lipiner, a poet and student two years behind him.
Lipiner was an articulate young man who spoke impressively on
matters of interest to the young Viennese intellectuals. He was
deeply involved in the study of Nietzsche, corresponded with him,
and eventually established a relationship with him. While still a
university student, he enjoyed the esteem of Wagner and the young
Mahler as well as Nietzsche.[7] He was a member of the Rede Klub,
a discussion society within the Leseverein, and he presented a report to this society in 1877 on Nietzsche's essay, "Schopenhauer as
Educator." Aschheim describes Lipiner as among the significant
early interpreters and popularizers of Nietzsche.[8] Regarding
Lipiner, Freud wrote to Silberstein in 1877: "I . . . have a very favorable opinion of him."[9]

Heinrich Braun, two years older than Freud, was a close friend
of Freud's at the Gymnasium and during the early years at the university. According to Shorske,[10] Braun was the school friend Freud
most idolized. He later became one of Europe's most prominent
Socialist intellectuals. McGrath portrays their close friendship at
the Gymnasium as including passionate discussion and sharing of
ideas.[11] Braun too immersed himself in the study of Nietzsche, and

along with Lipiner, Adler and others signed a letter to Nietzsche in 1877 declaring devotion to his outlook. "Schopenhauer as Educator" is specifically mentioned in the letter.[12]

Viktor Adler, a few years older than Freud, became a leading political figure by the late 1880s. He is described by one historian as "the remarkable man who, abandoning his medical practice, had united Austria's splintered Socialist movement in the late 1880s."[13] By the late 1890s he was the revered leader of Austrian Social Democracy.[14] Shorske points out that Freud acknowledged strong feelings of envy and rivalry towards Adler.[15] As a university student, Adler was an avid reader and admirer of Nietzsche's work. It was Adler along with Paneth who lectured to and co-led the first formal discussion of Nietzsche's work in the Leseverein in 1875.[16] An interesting turn of events involved Adler and Braun later becoming brothers-in-law, and it being Braun who in 1883 took Freud to Berggasse 19 which was then Adler's residence, the place where, among other endeavors, in 1889 he created the idea and plans for the first May Day parade.[17] Aschheim writes that a kind of "Nietzschean socialism . . . informed Viktor Adler's infusion into Austrian social democracy of Dionysian impulses designed to arouse the nascent proletariet to a willful consciousness of its own power."[18] It has been suggested that Freud's admiration for Adler was a factor in his choosing to move into the dwelling in 1891.[19] It is certain that the atmosphere of Berggasse 19 was infused with the ideas of Nietzsche before Freud's move there, and more generally, it is certain that among Freud's friends in the early 1880s were those with a strong interest in and involvement with the field of philosophy.[20]

Joseph Paneth was a close friend of Freud at the university, and the two men remained friends until Paneth's death in 1890. Freud respected Paneth and in *The Interpretation of Dreams* refers to "my brilliant friend P., whose whole life had been devoted to science."[21] In 1882 Freud left the satisfying environment of the laboratory of the highly esteemed Ernst Brücke (1819–1892) to enter medical practice after it became clear that no promotion was in sight and that his income would not reasonably allow for marriage and family. It was Paneth who replaced him in Brücke's laboratory and later received the promotion that Freud had hoped for before deciding to leave the laboratory. Paneth also gave Freud money during a time of financial difficulty while he was engaged to

Martha Bernays. Paneth knew Joseph Breuer, and he may have been the person who introduced Freud to Breuer.[22]

Freud and Paneth studied philosophy together at the university and took a number of philosophy courses with Franz Brentano (1838–1917). On a few occasions they met with Brentano at his home. Although Brentano embodied what some might regard as a more empirical or scientific approach to philosophy than did Nietzsche, Freud's interests and concerns included those of a metaphysical nature. One of the courses he and Paneth took with Brentano was on the topic of the existence of God.[23] (From early on, Freud was strongly drawn to both the more speculative-metaphysical concerns of philosophy and a more empiricist and materialist world view.)

Paneth was an avid reader of Nietzsche and retained an interest in him after leaving the university. Paneth was the co-lecturer and leader along with Adler of the first formal Leseverein meeting specifically devoted to Nietzsche.[24] Freud and Paneth (along with Lipiner) were also involved in the establishment of a journal for which Paneth wrote on philosophy.[25] After the journal expired, Freud wrote to Silberstein of now having to keep certain philosophical ideas to himself or share them only with Paneth.[26] Freud and Paneth together read Ludwig Feuerbach whom Freud greatly admired at the time.[27] Feuerbach anticipated some of Freud's and Nietzsche's ideas on religion.

Paneth corresponded with Nietzsche and, as will be discussed in greater detail below, had the opportunity to meet and talk with him on a number of occasions over a three-month period from December 1883 through March 1884. He wrote to Freud of these meetings. Later in this study, when we come to Freud's self-analysis (after the death of his father in October 1896) and his work on *The Interpretation of Dreams*, consideration will be given to the possibility that Paneth's appearance in Freud's famous "Non Vixit" dream may in part reflect Freud's ambivalent feelings regarding the influence of Nietzsche on his work and the link between Paneth and Nietzsche. Further on in the study mention will be made of the fact that towards the end of his life, in correspondence with Arnold Zweig—who was considering the possibility of writing a fictionalized biography of Nietzsche just before the time Freud was giving thought to *Moses and Monotheism*—Freud recalled Paneth's writing to him of Nietzsche.[28]

When we appreciate the great influence Nietzsche had on a substantial number of Viennese university students in the 1870s and in particular on a number of admired student friends and acquaintances of Freud, and when we then add to this our knowledge of Freud's interest in philosophy and his having possibly read (and certainly having heard discussed) *The Birth of Tragedy* and the first two or three essays of *Untimely Meditations*, it would appear to be a reasonable conclusion that the ideas of these early works had significant impact upon Freud, at least during this particular time of his life. In the correspondence with Arnold Zweig, Freud wrote regarding Nietzsche: "In my youth he signified a nobility to which I could not attain."[29] An alternative translation is: "In my youth he was a remote and noble figure to me."[30] As Freud was fantasizing about his own future greatness,[31] Nietzsche's greatness was being proclaimed all around him.

We will next consider the extent to which these early works of Nietzsche may have had any bearing on Freud's later intellectual development and the origins of psychoanalysis.

# Chapter 2

## NIETZSCHE'S EARLY WRITINGS

> *I mean by plastic power the capacity to develop
> out of oneself in one's own way, to transform and
> incorporate into oneself what is past and foreign,
> to heal wounds, to replace what has been lost, to
> recreate broken moulds.*
> —Nietzsche, "On the Uses and Disadvantages
> of History for Life"

### THE BIRTH OF TRAGEDY

Interpretations of Greek drama and myth, particularly pertaining to the figure of Oedipus, were common in nineteenth-century German literature. Both Nietzsche and Freud drew from and contributed to that tradition. Although Nietzsche has not been a force in mainstream classical philology, contemporary scholars writing on Greek philosophy and literature continue to draw inspiration from him. In a recent study of our relation to the Greeks, Bernard Williams has written of "Nietzsche, a writer with whom my inquiry has relations that are very close and necessarily ambiguous . . . Nietzschean ideas will recur in this inquiry, and, above all, he set its problem, by joining in a radical way the questions of how we understand the Greeks and of how we understand ourselves."[1]

*The Birth of Tragedy* was Nietzsche's first major work and one which continues to receive a great deal of attention. It is an innovative work in form as well as content. Some have regarded it as much a work of art as a scholarly study. Traditional standards of philological studies had emphasized the attempt at objective understanding of the past. While Nietzsche naturally attempts to uncover the past, he also believes that many human cognitive and interpretive activities, including scholarly pursuits, are influenced by the personal motivations and interests of the individual scholar. The past is approached in terms that reflect the needs of the present, or as Nietzsche put it in *Human, All Too Human:* "It is only *our* blood that constrains them [works of earlier times] to speak to *us*." He also writes of the special role of the genius-hero, in particular the artistic genius and specifically Wagner, as the hope for the renewal of a culture in crisis.[2] (Nietzsche had a close relationship with Wagner at this time and highly idealized him.) Even though Freud's ambitions were to a great extent scientific in nature, Nietzsche's overturning of tradition, breaking new ground and emphasis on the role of the genius-hero may have resonated strongly with, and perhaps served to some degree as a model for, his own ambitions.

Nietzsche discusses the origins of Greek tragedy in the creative integration of what he refers to as Dionysian and Apollonian forces, named for their representation in the gods Apollo and Dionysus. (While I use the term "Apollonian," some writers and translators use the term "Apollinian.") Apollo is associated with law, with beauty and order, with reason, with self-control and self-knowledge, with the sun and light. Dionysus is associated with orgiastic rites, music, dance and later drama. He is a god who is torn to pieces, dismembered (representing individuation), and whose rebirth is awaited (the end of individuation).[3] Religious rituals associated with him enact and celebrate death, rebirth and fertility. He is also associated with crops, including the grape (and wine and intoxication), and with sexuality. Frenzied, ecstatic female worshippers (maenads) are central to the rituals and celebrations. Both gods have a home in Delphi, Dionysus reigning in the winter when his dances are performed there.[4]

In a note from *The Will to Power* Nietzsche defines the Apollonian and the Dionysian:

The word *"Dionysian"* means: an urge to unity, a reaching out beyond personality, the everyday, society, reality, across the abyss of transitoriness: a passionate-painful overflowing into darker, fuller more floating states; . . . the feeling of the necessary unity of creation and destruction. [One contemporary classical scholar writes of "the unity of salvation and destruction . . . (as) a characteristic feature of all that is tragic."[5]]

The word *"Apollinian"* means: the urge to perfect self-sufficiency, to the typical "individual," to all that simplifies, distinguishes, makes strong, clear, unambiguous, typical: freedom under the law.[6]

Apollo is also described as the dream interpreter.[7]

The Apollonian refers to those capacities for measure, restraint, and individuation, particularly as they pertain to the visual arts, especially sculpture, while the Dionysian refers to the capacities for and experience of union with others and the natural world, ecstasy, intoxication, and the unleashing of savage instincts (including fused sexuality and aggression), particularly as they are reflected in the realm of music. With its rootedness in the body, its bridging the divisions between mind and body as well as subject and object, music best symbolizes the primal unity prior to and beyond individuated phenomena.

Nietzsche attempted to demonstrate that classical Greek culture and drama had accomplished the great achievement of recognizing and creatively integrating the substratum of the Dionysian with the Apollonian. As Siegfried Mandel has indicated:

> Nietzsche destroyed widely held aesthetic views, inspired in 1755 by the archaeologist-historian Johann Winckelmann, about the "noble simplicity, calm grandeur," "sweetness and light," harmony and cheerfulness (Heiterkeit) of the ancient Greeks and posed instead the dark Dionysian forces that had to be harnessed to make possible the birth of tragedy.[8]

Nietzsche also writes of the conflict of opposing forces within the psyche and of the possibility of creative integration. He is concerned with what he regards as the current overvaluation of reason and consciousness and the need for integration of what is unconscious, emotional and primitive. He writes of the "Apollinian consciousness which, like a veil, hid this Dionysian world from . . .

vision."[9] The Dionysian, including its most primitive and savage dimensions, is regarded as necessary for creative existence. It is an integral substratum of Apollonian consciousness at its most creative and not something to be denied its important place. We have here the beginnings of Nietzsche's interest in matters pertaining to sublimation: "The Apollinian Greek . . . had to recognize [that] . . . despite all its beauty and moderation, his entire existence rested on a hidden substratum of suffering and of knowledge, revealed to him by the Dionysian . . . The 'titanic' and the 'barbaric' were in the last analysis as necessary as the Apollinian."[10]

It is also important to consider that Nietzsche takes dreams, the value and function of dreaming, seriously. He discusses dreams on the first page of this work and relates the creation of the illusions of dreams to Apollonian-inspired art forms. He writes of the need for pleasurable illusion as provided by dreams, that dreams, among other things, serve this needed reparative function.[11] Perhaps what is most important, Nietzsche places the realm of the dream and the unconscious closer to who and what we most deeply and fundamentally are in contrast to the realm of waking consciousness:

> Though it is certain that of the two halves of our existence, the waking and the dreaming states, the former appeals to us as infinitely preferable, more important, excellent, and worthy of being lived, indeed, as that which alone is lived—yet in relation to that mysterious ground of our being of which we are the phenomena, I should, paradoxical as it may seem, maintain the very opposite estimate of the value of dreams.[12]

Nietzsche also writes that in dreams "there is nothing unimportant or superfluous."[13]

It is also evident, however, that with illusion-creating form and the realm of the dream as pertaining to the domain of the Apollonian, there can be no absolute equation of the Apollonian with rational, analytical consciousness. Therefore, the Apollonian is not to be thought of as identical to the rational ego and secondary process thinking. For Nietzsche the realm of the Dionysian would have to be a substratum of the dream state since the dream is closely related to "that mysterious ground of our being of which we are the phenomena." What Nietzsche emphsizes as Apollonian is a kind of artistic creation of form, the creation of the individu- ated phenomena, so to speak, of the dream which is linked to artis- tic creation that offers beautiful deception in the service of making life bearable in the face of its horrors. Julian Young suggests that Nietzsche's connecting of the Apollonian with the metaphor of a dream has the functions both of "capturing the merely phenome- nal status of everyday reality . . . [and] the idea of the pleasurable contemplation of the beautiful."[14] The dream is like Apollonian art in that, in Nietzsche's words, it "simplifies, distinguishes, makes strong, clear" in its creation of form. Young also suggests that the Apollonian component of dreams refers in particular to the lucid dream, "the dream one spectates rather than lives."[15] Neitzsche writes of lucid dreams in the very first section of *The Birth of Tragedy*.

It is also important to consider that it is through the dream's Apollonian images that the Dionysian reality can be manifested and known, as it is through the individuated actors on stage that the underlying Dionysian reality is manifested in Greek tragedy. At its most creative the Apollonian can allow an infusion of and can harness the Dionysian. But we should also note that Nietzsche is quite explicit that when the splendor of the Apollonian impulse first stood before "the ecstatic sound of the Dionysian festival,"[16] it stood before an art that in its frenzy, rapture and excess "spoke the truth . . . *Excess* revealed itself as truth."[17] (So there is a truth here revealed *before* its integration with the Apollonian.) The Apollonian splendor was "overwhelmed by the influx of the Dionysian; and . . . against this new power the Apollonian rose to the austere majesty of Doric art and the Doric view of the world."[18] For Nietzsche, "the Dionysian and the Apollonian, in new births ever following and mutually augmenting one another, controlled the Hellenic genius."[19]

We can also note that rational consciousness of a Socratic na- ture, the "faith that thought using the thread of logic, can pene- trate the deepest abysses of being,"[20] is distinguished from the Apollonian as well as the Dionysian. In his study of *The Birth of Tragedy*, Lenson suggests that Socratic rationality is as hostile to the Apollonian as it is to the Dionysian:

Even the Apollonian, as Nietzsche describes it, devolves upon a mystery as profound as dreams themselves. What makes the

Socratic so different from the Apollonian and the Dionysian is its need to know before it can respond to beauty. For the Socratic, the mystery cannot cause aesthetic fascination; only the resolution of the mystery can bring a sense of beauty in its wake.[21] [At a later point we will consider Freud's "Socratic" comment regarding his own experience of music.]

Nietzsche writes of the quest for power and the desire inherent in the quest for Socratic insight:

> Socrates . . . ascribes to knowledge and insight the power of a panacea, while understanding error as the evil *par excellence*. To fathom the depths and to separate true knowledge from appearance and error, seemed to Socratic man the noblest, even the only truly human vocation. . . .
>
> Anyone who has ever experienced the pleasure of Socratic insight and felt how, spreading in ever-widening circles, it seeks to embrace the whole world of appearances, will never again find any stimulus towards existence more violent then the craving to complete this conquest and to weave the net impenetrably tight.[22]

Here the quest for insight, for knowledge, is prompted by violent, and perhaps lustful, cravings for conquest.

However, for Nietzsche, when optimistic Socratic rationality and science reach their limits, they prompt a regeneration of art and mythology as protection and remedy in the face of the new form of insight that breaks through, tragic insight or Dionysian insight.[23] In other words, for those who have had the faith that science "can penetrate the deepest abysses of being," science itself cannot resolve the crisis engendered with the dawning recognition of its limits.

While Nietzsche writes of Dionysian *insight*, he also writes of what would seem to be the specifically Dionysian "metaphysical comfort [and illusion] that beneath the whirl of phenomena eternal life flows on indestructibly." This Dionysian comfort is discussed along with the Socratic delusion of being able "to heal the eternal wound of existence" and "art's seductive [Apollonian] veil of beauty fluttering before [one's] eyes." Nietzsche concludes that "these three stages of illusion are actually designed for the more

nobly formed natures" who must be "deluded . . . into forgetfulness of their displeasure," and that "all that we call culture is
made up of these stimulants."[24]

Julian Young suggests that if there is Dionysian illusion here
it is not in the distinction between the Dionysian primal "One"
and the Apollonian principal of individuation, but may be the illusion that "the being of the one constitutes the 'eternal life' of any
person."[25] We can also note that a *belief* is not necessarily equivalent to the Dionysian *experience* or consciousness as Nietzsche describes it. This experience or state of consciousness includes "the
*feeling* of the necessary unity of creation and destruction" (emphasis added). Also, the truth or falsity of one's belief may tell us little,
if anything, regarding how that belief functions for one psychologically. Experiencing momentarily the truth and reality of Dionysian
becoming, of primordial being, *is* a metaphysical comfort, as is the
illusion that beneath the flux of phenomena eternal life flows on
indestructibly. It appears, therefore, that Nietzsche writes of tragic
or Dionysian insight into the essential (and in part horrific) nature
of things as well as the need of even "the more nobly formed natures" for the stimulant that will enable them to forget their pain.
He goes so far as to state that "all that we call culture is made up
of these stimulants." Reaching painful truths and developing illusions that are a stimulant to creative life which will find new
painful truths and new creative illusions appear here to be inextricably intertwined for Nietzsche. One may see the truth of things
but then require creative illusions for action or redemption.
Nietzsche will move on from this position, but he will struggle
with and play with related concerns throughout his productive life.

Nietzsche also discusses the Oedipus myth as presented by
Sophocles. He asks what we are to make of the mysterious triad of
Oedipus as murderer of his father, husband of his mother, and
solver of the riddle of the Sphinx:

> How else could one compel nature to surrender her secrets if
> not by triumphantly resisting her, that is, by means of some-
> thing unnatural? It is this insight that I find expressed in that
> horrible triad of Oedipus' destinies: the same man who solves
> the riddle of nature—that Sphinx of two species [lion and
> human]—also must break the most sacred natural orders by
> murdering his father and marrying his mother. Indeed, the

myth seems to wish to whisper to us that wisdom, and particularly Dionysian wisdom, is an unnatural abomination; that he who by means of his knowledge plunges nature into the abyss of destruction must also suffer the dissolution of nature in his own person.[26]

Rudnytsky points out that Nietzsche anticipated Freud in placing incest in a central role for his understanding of the myth, and also, in a sense, laid down a fundamental thread of the path Freud would have to find and face as discoverer of the Oedipus complex;[27] that is, what he would have to face in his self-analysis after the death of his father in 1896. Lieberman points out how in the *Introductory Lectures on Psychoanalysis*, Freud compares the development of psychoanalysis to Sophocles' *Oedipus*.[28] One might also consider that, with his later notion of the theory of instincts as psychoanalysis' mythology and the central place of the life and death instincts, Freud ultimately followed Nietzsche in finding mythology at the boundaries of, and generated from, science.[29] In a passage from a later work, to be discussed below, Nietzsche connects the truth of wishes expressed in dreams explicitly to the Oedipus myth and to oedipal wishes as understood in the psychoanalytic sense. We will return to *The Birth of Tragedy* when we discuss *Totem and Taboo*.

## "DAVID STRAUSS, THE CONFESSOR AND THE WRITER" (1873)

The first essay to be included in the volume *Untimely Meditations* is "David Strauss, the Confessor and the Writer" (1873), and it is a brutal attack on Strauss' book, *The Old Faith and the New* (1872). This is the essay to which Freud referred in a letter to Silberstein. Strauss (1808–1874) was the author of a much admired and discussed earlier work, *The Life of Jesus Critically Examined* (1835), in which he analyzed the Gospels of the New Testament with a focus on their inconsistencies in their portrayals of Jesus. He utilized such analysis in the service of challenging belief in a supernatural, divine Jesus and in demonstrating that the needs of the period called for such a hero.[30] Nietzsche was a university student when he read this book and was apparently among those impressed by it. J. P. Stern states that Nietzsche's reading of it "completed a process begun during his last year at Schulpforta [secondary school]; it led to his rejection of the Christian faith and his refusal, at Easter 1865, to take Communion."[31]

What Nietzsche found particularly offensive, even dangerous, in Strauss' new book was Strauss' unwillingness or inability to face the discomfort and pain that accompany the renouncing of important, deeply held, security-providing beliefs. For Nietzsche, although Strauss was writing of rejecting the idea of a personal God and the Christian faith, he was replacing such belief with a scientific materialism and Darwinian cosmology in such a way as to offer comfort and not disturb the peace and complacency of the educated classes. Strauss maintained a place for religious feeling and a dependence on the "All" as well as the notion that there were, despite appearances of moral relativism, moral standards that hold for the entire human race.[32] As Nietzsche put it: "He announces with admirable frankness that he is no longer a Christian, but he does not wish to disturb anyone's peace of mind."[33] Nietzsche writes of Strauss' view of the new scientific man and his "faith" that "the heir of but a few hours, he is ringed around with frightful abysses, and every step he takes ought to make him ask: Whither? Whence? To what end?"[34] However, rather than facing such frightful questions, Strauss' scientific man "seems to be permitted to squander his life on questions whose answer could at bottom be of consequence only to someone assured of an eternity."[35]

During the early years of the development of psychoanalysis and even afterwards, Freud regarded himself as the bearer of painful truths that people, at least upon first hearing or reading, did not want to face. Psychoanalytically oriented therapy involves facing great pain in giving up certain deeply held, personally important beliefs. If read, Nietzsche's words would have touched a sympathetic chord in Freud when he wrote that "anything truly productive is offensive."[36] Nietzsche insisted, as did Freud, on resisting the temptations towards easy answers and superficiality in the face of painful truths. In concluding the essay, Nietzsche writes of his present age that it has more need than ever of what continues to count as untimely—"I mean: telling the truth."[37] (Even during this early period of his life Nietzsche believed, at least regarding some things, that truth can be reached and communicated. This is a matter to which we will return.)

Another aspect of this essay likely to have impressed Freud is Nietzsche's psychological analysis of the disguised, defensive maneuvers and ploys utilized by Strauss to conceal the underlying, latent if you will, agenda of offering comfort and consolation rather than uncertainty and anxiety to educated Europeans. Nietzsche looks to the possible origins of unconscious motivations for Strauss' ideas and his manner of presentation, sometimes with implications for group psychology:

> Strauss himself gives us to understand that the confessional book is not intended to offer instruction *only* to scholars and the cultivated, but we adhere to the view that it is directed at these in the first instance[38] and particularly at the scholars, and that it holds up to them the reflection of a life such as they themselves live. For this is the trick of the thing: the Master affects to outlining the ideal of a new philosophy of life, and now he hears himself praised on every side, since everyone is in a position to think that this is precisely how *he* thinks and that Strauss would see already fulfilled in him that which he has demanded only of the future.[39]

This passage has affinities with Freud's idea, presented in *Group Psychology and the Analysis of the Ego*, of the leader of a group functioning as a shared ego ideal for members: "A number of individuals . . . have put one and the same object in the place of their ego ideal."[40]

Of additional interest regarding the possible impact of this essay on Freud is the fact that he had read Strauss' book and apparently responded favorably, even enthusiastically.[41] One wonders how the sting of Nietzsche's criticism might have affected him, keeping in mind that he and his fellow students had already been reading and discussing the much admired Nietzsche.

One might raise the question of whether or not Freud might have wondered, as did Strauss, about Nietzsche's own motivations, anxieties, defenses, etc., in writing such a ferocious attack on Strauss.[42] We might wonder about Strauss' disillusioning role in regard to Nietzsche's Christian faith and the relationship between this loss and the death of his father when he was four-and-a-half years old. Strauss died about six months after publication of the essay, and Nietzsche wrote to a friend, "I very much hope that I have not aggravated the end of his life."[43] At the end of his productive life, in *Ecce Homo*, Nietzsche wrote: "I never attack persons; I only avail myself of the person as of a strong magnifying glass with which one can render visible a general but creeping calamity which is otherwise hard to get hold of. Thus I attacked David Strauss."[44] (This statement may be, in part, defensive in nature, but it may be worth considering its relevance to another recipient of Nietzsche's scathing attack, the Apostle Paul, to whom we will return.) Perhaps, as suggested by Pletsch, the most important factor motivating the brutality of the attack is the fact that Wagner had spoken harshly to Nietzsche regarding his recent work on Greek philosophy (*Philosophy in the Tragic Age of the Greeks*, 1873) and proposed that instead of continuing work on it he write an attack on Strauss who had been critical of Wagner. Pletsch suggests that while Nietzsche attempted to please the master, he likely had a great deal of rage and frustration to vent.[45]

## "On the Uses and Disadvantages of History for Life" (1874)

This second essay in *Untimely Meditations* was the essay discussed in 1875 at the Leseverein meeting led by Paneth and Adler.[46] (I have not seen any information indicating whether or not Freud was present at the meeting.) Although the essay addresses the study of history, historiography, and different types of and approaches to historical studies, Nietzsche also addresses the individual and his or her own life history in ways that have relevance for Freud and psychoanalysis. One reads passage after passage dealing with memory, remembering, forgetting, and the relationship between reason and emotion. Nietzsche criticizes what he regards as a prevalent overvaluation of the power of reason and writes of the need for the integration of reason and emotion. He also writes of the need to incorporate and digest from the past in such a way as to make the past truly one's own and in this way to enhance one's own unique development, a major goal of psychoanalytic therapy:

> I mean by plastic power the capacity to develop out of oneself in one's own way, to transform and incorporate into oneself what is past and foreign, to heal wounds, to replace what has been lost, to recreate broken moulds.[47]

> The most powerful and tremendous nature would . . .
> draw to itself and incorporate into itself all the past, its own
> and that most foreign to it, and as it were transform it into
> blood. That which such a nature cannot subdue it knows how
> to forget.[48]

Knowledge, memory, and history are to serve life. Transforming
and incorporating the past involves replacing what has been lost.
Serving life also requires forgetting. An excess of knowledge, memory and history can impair spontaneous, creative living. For Nietzsche, there is a place for both facing painful truths and the ability
to forget or repress what cannot be incorporated and made one's
own. Later in his career Nietzsche will write of the "correct idea of
the nature of our subject-unity, namely as regents at the head of a
communality . . . The relative ignorance in which the regent is
kept concerning individual activities and even disturbances within
the communality is among the conditions under which rule can be
exercised."[49] While emphasizing the value of creative conflict,
Nietzsche also indicates that by transforming what is foreign into
one's own blood it is possible to make it a part of one's self in such
a way as to be or feel almost instinctive.

In the following passage one might say that Nietzsche is contrasting intellectual knowledge with emotionally integrated knowledge and pointing out the power of resistance to change:

> A historical phenomenon, known clearly and completely and
> resolved into a phenomenon of knowledge, is, for him who
> has perceived it, dead: for he has recognized in it the delusion,
> the injustice, the blind passion, and in general the whole
> earthly and darkening horizon of this phenomenon, and has
> thereby also understood its power in history. This power has
> now lost its hold over him insofar as he is a man of knowl-
> edge: but perhaps it has not done so insofar as he is a man in-
> volved in life.[50] [In *On the Genealogy of Morals* Nietzsche
> refers to the belief "that pain is *bound* to vanish as soon as
> the error in it is recognized; but behold! it refuses to van-
> ish."[51] Nietzsche is very cautious about the possibilities of
> self-transformation through knowledge or recognition of
> error. He is acutely aware of the powerful obstacles to such
> transformation.]

In his discussion of truth and objectivity in historical interpretation, Nietzsche points to underlying motivational factors which may be involved even in the striving for truth:

> Only insofar as the truthful man possesses the unconditional will to justice is there anything great in that striving for truth which is everywhere so thoughtlessly glorified: a whole host of the most various drives—curiosity, flight from boredom, envy, vanity, the desire for amusement, for example—can be involved in the striving for truth.[52]

If any theme of this essay as well as the following one, "Schopenhauer as Educator" (also published in 1874), would have been particularly prominent in the discussions around Freud, it very likely would have been Nietzsche's description of and discussion of the superior man, the true hero. In this second essay Nietzsche specifically writes of the superior man as a person equipped to creatively interpret the past:

> *If you are to venture to interpret the past you can do so only out of the fullest exertion of the vigour of the present:* only when you put forth your noblest qualities in all their strength will you divine what is worth knowing and preserving in the past.[53]
>
> History is written by the experienced and superior man. He who has not experienced greater and more exalted things than others will not know how to interpret the great and exalted things of the past. When the past speaks it always speaks as an oracle.[54]

Freud quite early on had notions of himself as a future hero and in particular a hero who one day might interpret oracles or solve profound riddles.

"Schopenhauer as Educator" was much discussed in Freud's circle of friends and acquaintances. The essay was mentioned in an October 1877 letter to Nietzsche signed by a number of former and current fellow students, including Lipiner, Adler, and Braun,[55] and Lipiner gave a report on it at a meeting of the Rede Klub.[56] There is little exposition of Schopenhauer's philosophy in the essay. The focus is on Schopenhauer as genius, as hero who "*voluntarily*

*takes upon himself the suffering involved in being truthful,*"[57] including the suffering involved in facing rejection and hostility.
Schopenhauer is an idealized mentor and father figure as well as a
role model of the genius, the intellectual hero. We don't know the
extent to which Freud may have learned more of Schopenhauer's
philosophy through his readings or through discussions with his
friends and acquaintances. Paneth's letters to his fiancé in late
1883 and early 1884, the period during which he was meeting with
Nietzsche and also writing to Freud, indicate familiarity with
Schopenhauer's writings. It is possible that Paneth would have discussed Schopenhauer as well as Nietzsche with Freud.

It is of interest that Freud's destruction of letters and records
(which he did in 1877, 1885 and 1907[58]) which might have shed
light on his intellectual origins, seems to have been connected in
his mind to notions of himself as hero. In April of 1885 he wrote to
his fiancé Martha Bernays:

> I have destroyed all my notes of the past fourteen years, as
> well as letters, scientific excerpts, and the manuscripts of my
> papers . . . As for biographers, let them worry, we have no de-
> sire to make it too easy for them. Each one of them will be
> right in his opinion of "The Development of the Hero," and I
> am already looking forward to seeing them go astray.[59]

In February of 1900, in a gloomy mood regarding reception of *The
Interpretation of Dreams,* Freud described himself to Fliess as "not
at all a man of science, not an observer, not an experimenter, not a
thinker. I am by temperament nothing but a conquistador—an ad-
venturer."[60] Later in the same letter he wrote: "I have just acquired
Nietzsche, in whom I hope to find words for much that remains
mute in me, but have not opened him yet. Too lazy for the time
being."[61] We will return to this letter.

We find in these early writings of Nietzsche a valuing of the
function of dreams, a recognition of the instinctual and revelatory
substratum beneath individuated form, recognition of the importance of incest in the Oedipus myth as portrayed by Sophocles,
how even the quest for truth can be prompted by the "drives," and
how scholarly inquiries are influenced by the needs of the scholar.
We also read of ideas pertaining to idealization of a group leader,
ideas pertaining to the concept of resistance, the importance of cre-

atively integrating the more primitive aspects of our nature, the importance of integrating our past and making it our own as well as the importance of forgetting, and ideas pertaining to the nature of the intellectual hero. All of these ideas have relevance for Freud's future development, although in and of themselves they clearly cannot be regarded as absolutely critical influences on the development of Freud's thought.

# Chapter 3

## 1878–1884

*He [Nietzsche] is completely convinced of his mission and of his decisive importance. In this faith he is strong and superior to all misfortune, physical suffering, and poverty.*
—Paneth to Sophie Schwab, 1884

While we can see in these earliest works of Nietzsche[1] a number of ways in which he anticipated certain psychoanalytic concepts and may have influenced Freud, Nietzsche's following three works, *Human, All Too Human* (vol. 1, 1878; vol. 2, pt. 1, 1879; vol. 2, pt. 2, 1880 and included in the volume in 1886), *Daybreak* (1881) and *The Gay Science* (1882), contain passage after passage explicating certain fundamental concepts very close to ones later developed by Freud. (After these three volumes, Nietzsche began writing a work of a very different kind, *Thus Spoke Zarathustra*,[2] which is generally regarded as one of the greatest lyric works in the German language and which exerted an enormous influence in the German-speaking world and beyond from the early 1890s on into the twentieth century.)

Before turning to a discussion of matters pertaining to Freud's interest in psychology and philosophy during this period and his possible continued interest in or contact with the ideas of Nietzsche, it will be helpful to present a few pages of quotations from the three volumes just mentioned. This is not to be regarded as a mini anthology of Nietzsche's psychological ideas in these works. Rather, it is hoped that these particular passages will convey some idea of the extent and depth of Nietzsche's thought on matters specifically pertinent to the development of psychoanalysis. (Any other extensive quotations cited in this study should be understood as serving similar purposes.) Other pertinent passages could have been presented. At later points in this study a number of these passages as well as others will be specifically related to writings of Freud. The earliest of these works was published the last year Freud was still a member of the Leseverein, and its opening passage includes a discussion of sublimation.

From *Human, All Too Human:*

*Chemistry of concepts and sensations—*
There exists, strictly speaking, neither an unegoistic action nor completely disinterested contemplation; both are only sublimations, in which the basic element seems almost to have dispersed and reveals itself only under the most painstaking observation . . . what if . . . the most glorious colours are derived from base, indeed from despised materials?[3]

*Logic of the dream—*
In the dream this piece of primeval humanity continues to exercise itself . . . the dream takes us back again to remote stages of human culture and provides us with a means of understanding them better . . . the dream is a relaxation for the brain which has had enough of the strenuous demands in the way of thinking such as are imposed by our culture during the day.[4]

*Morality as the self-division of man—*
A soldier wishes he could fall on the battlefield for his victorious fatherland . . . A mother gives to her child that of which she deprives herself . . . are these all unegoistic states? . . . Is it not clear that in all these instances man loves *something of himself,* an idea, a desire, an offspring, more than *something else of himself,* that he thus *divides* his nature and sacrifices one part of it to the other? . . . The *inclination for something* (wish, impulse, desire) is present in all the above-mentioned instances; to give in to it, with all the consequences, is in any

event not "unegoistic." —In morality man treats himself not as *individuum* but as *dividuum*.[5]

*The innocent element in so-called evil acts—*
All "evil" acts are motivated by the drive to preservation or, more exactly, by the individual's intention of procuring pleasure and avoiding displeasure . . . Morality is preceded by *compulsion,* indeed it is for a time itself still compulsion, to which one accommodates oneself for the avoidance of what one regards as unpleasurable. Later it becomes custom, later still voluntary obedience, finally almost instinct: then, like all that has for a long time been habitual and natural, it is associated with pleasure—and is now called *virtue.*[6]

*Unaccountability and innocence—*
We are torn back and forth by conflicting motives until we finally choose the most powerful of them—as we put it (in truth, however, until the most powerful motive chooses us). But all these motives, whatever exalted names we may give them, have grown up out of the same roots as those we believe evilly poisoned . . . Good actions are sublimated evil ones . . . It is the individual's sole desire for self-enjoyment (together with the fear of losing it) which gratifies itself in every instance . . . whether his deeds be those of vanity, revenge, pleasure, utility, malice, cunning, or those of sacrifice, sympathy, knowledge.[7]

*Origin of the comic—*
If one considers that man was for many hundreds of thousands of years an animal in the highest degree accessible to fear and that everything sudden and unexpected bade him prepare to fight and perhaps to die; that even later on, indeed, in social relationships all security depended on the expected and traditional in opinion and action; then one cannot be surprised if whenever something sudden and unexpected in word and deed happens without occasioning danger or injury man becomes wanton, passes over into the opposite of fear: the anxious, crouching creature springs up, greatly expands—man laughs. This transition from momentary anxiety to short-lived exuberance is called the *comic.*[8]

*Deception in love—*
We forget a great deal of our own past and deliberately banish it from our minds: that is to say, we want the image of ourself that shines upon us out of the past to deceive us and flatter our self-conceit—we are engaged continually on this self-deception.[9]

*Interpreting by dreams—*
That which we do not know or feel precisely while awake—whether we have a good or a bad conscience towards a particular person—the dream informs us of without any ambiguity.[10]

*Content of the conscience—*
The content of our conscience is everything that was during the years of our childhood regularly *demanded* of us without reason by people we honoured or feared. It is thus the conscience that excites that feeling of compulsion ("I must do this, not do that") . . . it is . . . the voice of some men in man.[11]

*The dream—*
Our dreams are . . . chains of symbolic scenes and images in place of the language of poetic narration; they paraphrase our experiences or expectations or circumstances with such poetic boldness and definiteness.[12]

*Do not want to see prematurely—*
For as long as one is experiencing something one must give oneself up to the experience and close one's eyes: that is to say, not be an observer of it while still *in the midst* of it. For that would disturb the absorption of the experience: instead of a piece of wisdom one would acquire from it indigestion.[13]

From *Daybreak:*

*Experience and invention—*
However far a man may go in self-knowledge, nothing however can be more incomplete than his image of the totality of *drives* which constitute his being . . . suppose a drive finds itself at the point at which it desires gratification—or exercise of its strength, or the saturation of an emptiness—these are

all metaphors—it then regards every event of the day with a view to seeing how it can employ it for that attainment of its goal . . . my supposition is . . . that the meaning and value of our *dreams* is precisely to *compensate* to some extent for the chance absence of "nourishment" during the day . . . These inventions . . . give scope and discharge to our drives . . . when we are awake [as well as in our dreams] our drives . . . do nothing but interpret nervous stimuli and, according to their requirements, posit their "causes" . . . all our so-called consciousness is a more or less fantastic commentary on an unknown, perhaps unknowable, but felt text.[14]

*Alleged conflict of motives*—
What here comes into play is the way we habitually expend our energy . . . there come into play motives in part unknown to us, in part known very ill, which we can *never* take account of *before-hand* . . . *Probably* a struggle takes place between these . . . a battling to and fro, a rising and falling of the scales—and this would be the actual "conflict of motives":—something quite invisible to us of which we would be quite unconscious . . . though I certainly learn what I finally *do*, I do not learn which motive has therewith actually proved victorious. *But we are accustomed* to *exclude* all these unconscious processes from the accounting and to reflect on the preparation for an act only to the extent that it is conscious: and we thus confuse conflict of motives with comparison of the possible consequences of different actions.[15]

*"No longer to think of oneself"*—
In the feeling of pity—I mean in that which is usually and misleadingly called pity—we are, to be sure, not consciously thinking of ourself but are doing so *very strongly unconsciously* . . . it is *only* . . . *suffering of our own* which we get rid of when we perform deeds of pity. But we never do anything of this kind out of *one* motive; as surely as we want to free ourselves of suffering by this act, just as surely do we give way to an *impulse to pleasure* with the same act.[16]

*Empathy*—
To understand another person, that is, *to imitate his feelings*

*in ourselves,* we do indeed often go back to the *reason* for his feeling this or thus and ask for example: *why* is he troubled?—so as then for the same reason to become troubled ourselves; but it is much more usual to omit to do this and instead to produce the feeling in ourselves after the *effects* it exerts and displays on the other person by imitating with our own body the expression of his eyes, his voice, his walk, his bearing (or even their reflection in word, picture, music). Then a similar feeling arises in us in consequence of an ancient association between movement and sensation, which has been trained to move backwards or forwards in either direction. We have brought our skill in understanding the feelings of others to a high state of perfection and in the presence of another person we are always almost involuntarily practicing this skill.[17]

If we ask how we became so fluent in the imitation of the feelings of others the answer admits of no doubt: man, as the most timid of all creatures on account of his subtle and fragile nature has in his *timidity* the instructor in that empathy, that quick understanding of the feelings of another (and of animals). Through long millennia he saw in everything strange and lively a danger: at the sight of it he at once imitated the expression of the features and the bearing and drew his conclusion as to the kind of evil intention behind these features and this bearing.[18]

*The forgetful—*
In outbursts of passion, and in the fantasising of dreams and insanity, a man rediscovers his own and mankind's prehistory: *animality* with its savage grimaces; on these occasions his memory goes sufficiently far back, while his civilised condition evolves out of a forgetting of these primal experiences.[19]

From *The Gay Science:*

*Consciousness—*
Consciousness is the last and latest development of the organic and hence also what is most unfinished and unstrong.[20]

*On the doctrine of the feeling of power—*
Benefiting and hurting others are ways of exercising one's power upon others . . . the state in which we hurt others . . . is a sign that we are still lacking power, or it shows a sense of frustration in the face of this poverty.[21]

*Laughter—*
Laughter means: being malicious but with a good conscience.[22]

*As interpreters of our experiences—*
We . . . who thirst after reason, are determined to scrutinize our experiences as severely as a scientific experiment—hour after hour, day after day. We ourselves wish to be our experiments and guinea pigs.[23]

*The meaning of knowing—*
What else is this *intelligere* [knowing, understanding] than . . . [o]ne result of the different and mutually opposed desires . . . Before knowledge is possible, each of these instincts must first have presented its one-sided view of the thing or event; after this comes the fight of these one-sided views . . . only the last scenes of reconciliation and the final accounting at the end of this long process rise to our consciousness.[24]

*Long live physics—*
Why do you *listen* to the voice of your conscience? . . . Your judgment "this is right" has a pre-history in your instincts . . . "*How* did it originate there?" you must ask, and then also: "What is it that impels me to listen to it?"[25]

*Two kinds of causes that are often confounded—*
I have learned to distinguish the cause of acting from the cause of acting in a particular way . . . The first kind of cause is a quantum of dammed-up energy that is waiting to be used up somehow . . . while the second kind is, compared to this energy, something quite insignificant, for the most part a little accident in accordance with which this quantum "discharges" itself in one particular way . . . the tremendous quantum of energy that presses, as I have said, to be used up

somehow. The usual view is different: People are accustomed to consider the goal (purposes, vocations, etc.) as the *driving force*, in keeping with a very ancient error; but it is merely the *directing* force—one has mistaken the helmsman for the steam. And not even always the helmsman, the directing force . . . Is the "goal," the "purpose" not often enough a beautifying pretext, a self-deception of vanity after the event that does not want to acknowledge that the ship is *following* the current into which it has entered accidentally? that it "wills" to go that way because it—*must?* that is has a direction, to be sure, but—no helmsman at all?[26][This section was published in the second edition of 1887.]

These passages demonstrate that as regards general or overarching concepts and the territory being explored, Nietzsche was explicitly discussing material directly related to Freud's formulations of psychoanalytic concepts. Nietzsche discusses the nature of instincts and drives, the relationship of consciousness to unconscious processes, dynamic psychic conflict, the development of conscience, sublimation, the nature of dreams, that our actions are determined by multiple motives, including gratification, defense, and assuaging of conscience, and so on.

One can also note Nietzsche's inclination to use medical terminology in relation to psychological observation and "dissection":

At its present state as a specific individual science the awakening of moral observation has become necessary, and mankind can no longer be spared the cruel sight of the moral dissecting table and its knives and forceps. For here there rules that science which asks after the origin and history of the so-called moral sensations.[27]

Freud wrote of analysts modeling themselves on the surgeon "who puts aside all his feelings, even his human sympathy, and concentrates his mental forces on the single aim of performing the operation as skillfully as possible."[28] (However, on the preceding page Freud wrote that "the most successful cases are those in which one proceeds, as it were, without any purpose in view, allows oneself to be taken by surprise by any new turn in them, and always meets them with an open mind, free from any presuppositions"[29]; cf. *Human, All Too Human*, 2, pt. 2, sec. 297, "Do not want to see prematurely," quoted above.)

During the years these works were published Freud was working in the laboratory of Ernst Brücke, creatively pursuing his anatomical and physiological researches. It was in 1882, the year of publication of *The Gay Science*, that Freud left Brücke's laboratory for medical practice due to the fact that promotion and greater earnings did not seem likely in the near future (since those he would have replaced had no plans to leave), and Freud had marriage and family on his mind. However much Freud may have been immersed in his anatomical and physiological work, there are a number of factors to consider pertaining to likely continued interest in the humanities, philosophy and psychology at around this time in his life. Certain of these factors are particularly relevant to his relationship to Nietzsche.

First, Freud was a member of the Leseverein, with all of the implications discussed above, until 1878, the year of publication of the first volume of *Human, All Too Human*. In the opening passage of this volume sublimation is discussed, and a few pages further along the logic of dreams is discussed. Freud's friends and acquaintances had written to Nietzsche only the year before. (We can also note, more generally, the highly cultured sensibilities and interests of the scientists Freud admired.[30])

Second, in the summer of 1882 Freud wrote to Martha Bernays of his continuing and growing interest in philosophy: "Philosophy, which I have always pictured as my goal and refuge in my old age, gains every day in attraction."[31] Trosman suggests that in addition to matters pertaining to finances and family, ultimately the work in the laboratory failed to satisfy Freud's more humanist concerns and interests.[32]

Third, in 1882 Freud's interest in psychology was likely stimulated by discussions with Breuer (steeped in philosophy) of the latter's work, terminated in 1882, with Bertha Pappenheim, better known as Anna O.[33] It is here that a "talking cure" had its origins.

Fourth, mention can also be made of the fact that Martha Bernays, to whom Freud became engaged in 1882, had an uncle, Jacob Bernays (1824–1881), who was a well-known and highly regarded classical scholar and professor of classical philology in Breslau and Bonn. Nietzsche knew of him and read and valued his work.[34] Nietzsche drew on Bernays' conception of catharsis in tragedy and possibly other ideas for *The Birth of Tragedy*.[35] Nietzsche even alludes to a dispute surrounding an 1857 essay by Bernays in section twenty-two of *The Birth of Tragedy*.[36] Freud would have known that Bernays would have been well aware of *The Birth of Tragedy*. In fact, Bernays had some positive things to say about the book.[37]

Also, at the time of Nietzsche's appointment to a professorship at Basel in 1869, Bernays published a study on Heraclitis, a pre-Socratic philosopher Nietzsche held in the highest regard.[38] Nietzsche mentions Heraclitis a few times in *The Birth of Tragedy*, including in the penultimate section:

> Again and again it [the Dionysian] reveals to us the playful construction and destruction of the individual world as the overflow of a primordial delight. Thus the dark Heraclitis compares the world-building force to a playing child that places stones here and there and builds sand hills only to overthrow them again.[39]

Late in his life, in 1932, Freud would have a hand in editing a book of Bernays' letters.[40] He mailed a copy of the book to Arnold Zweig with whom he was corresponding and who earlier in the year had written Freud of his plans to write an essay comparing Freud and Nietzsche.[41] (Zweig originally wrote to Freud about this planned essay in December of 1930.[42]) Zweig wrote to Freud that he was having the introduction of the Bernays book read to him (his vision was very poor) and mentioned the light shed on "Nietzsche's teacher Ritschl."[43] Friedrich W. Ritschl (1816–1876) was professor of classical philology in Halle, Breslau, Bonn and Leipzig. Both Bernays and Nietzsche were his students. One wonders how Freud may have had Nietzsche and Bernays linked at various points in his life given that Bernays was such a highly esteemed member of his wife's family. Bernays' influential conception of catharsis and the idea that psychological relief is derived from discharge of aroused emotion probably influenced Breuer and Freud[44] as well as Nietzsche.

Fifth, in 1883 Freud worked under Theodor Meynert (1833–1892) in the psychiatric division of the General Hospital. Meynert, who had lectured a number of times to the Leseverein and was a close friend of Brentano, was a well-known and influential figure. He openly acknowledged being influenced by Schopenhauer in his understanding of mental functioning. McGrath suggests that "Schopenhauer's conception of a primary will versus a secondary intellect, which led to Meynert's primary ego–secondary ego system, pointed forward to Freud's distinction between id and ego, between the primary and secondary process levels of mental activity."[45] Trosman suggests that "psychoanalytic notions, such as loss of ego defences, wish fulfillment, primary and secondary processes, reality testing, cathexis and repression can also be considered fruits of Meynert's primitive theory of the mind."[46] Meynert also developed a theory of mental associations from which causal relations could be inferred, this being another important influence on Freud. At this time Schopenhauer's name was closely linked to Nietzsche, given Nietzsche's building on, and later moving beyond, Schopenhauer's work and the attention Nietzsche's essay "Schopenhauer as Educator" had received among young Viennese intellectuals. Schopenhauer anticipated and influenced both Nietzsche and Freud in, among other things, his understanding of the nature of repression and the prevalence of unconscious sexual motivation.[47]

Sixth, Freud would have had no special reason not to read Nietzsche at this time in his life. As mentioned, later in life Freud stated more than once that he avoided Nietzsche in order to preserve his own independence of thought. However, during this period, while Freud appears to have continued to have an interest in philosophy and psychology, he wasn't yet close to approaching the psychological explorations that would lead to the development of psychoanalysis. This was still a few years away. Therefore, there would have been no particular reason for Freud to avoid Nietzsche at this time.

Finally, mention can be made of the fact that Nietzsche was directly brought to Freud's attention in late 1883 and early 1884. From late December of 1883 through March of 1884, Freud's friend Joseph Paneth spent time near Nice where Nietzsche was staying. (Later in life, Freud mistakenly thought that the location had been the Engadine.) During this time Paneth was able to speak with Nietzsche on a number of occasions. Late in his life Freud recalled that Paneth wrote a great deal about Nietzsche in letters to him during this period.[48]

One should keep in mind that Freud and Paneth were close friends who had seriously studied philosophy together. Although we do not know what Paneth wrote of to Freud since Freud, it would appear, destroyed all the letters in his possession a year later, it is difficult to imagine, given the nature of their relationship and the fact that Freud specifically states that Paneth wrote a great deal about Nietzsche, that Paneth wouldn't have written to Freud about aspects of Nietzsche's thought as well as about personal impressions of the man. We do have some idea of what Paneth thought of Nietzsche since letters he wrote to his future wife and others at this time do survive. Passages on Nietzsche from these letters, which are included in Nietzsche's sister's biography, come to about thirteen pages.[49] The letters of Paneth have also been published in a more carefully edited edition in *Nietzsche-Studien*.[50] This more recent edition reveals that Paneth, while having great admiration for Nietzsche's work and for him as a person, also had reservations about and criticism of his work, such as ideas about sacrificing humanity for the sake of great men or the overman. He seems to have been put off somewhat by *Zarathustra* and to have had some difficulty understanding the first two parts that had been published. Like many others, he did not appear to appreciate the humor in this work. This edition also reveals that in Paneth's view Nietzsche did not have great hopes for moral or psychological means of self-transformation, although such a view is in tension with much in Nietzsche's writings. (Recall that from his early writings Nietzsche was acutely aware of the powerful obstacles to self-transformation.) This edition also makes it clear that Nietzsche and Paneth discussed antisemitism and issues specifically pertaining to Jews. Paneth came away from these discussions writing that Nietzsche was clearly above antisemitism.[51] Paneth also discussed his own ideas and his work at Brücke's laboratory. It is not impossible that in passing Freud was referred to or even mentioned by name. We do know that Nietzsche was reading John Stuart Mill and probably read a volume translated into German by Freud.[52]

It is particularly important to understand that the letters (in the Krummel edition) indicate the interest in Nietzsche of those close to Paneth in Vienna. Paneth's fiancé, Sophie Schwab, was familiar with Nietzsche (and did not care for his ideas on women).[53] She may have visited Paneth and met Nietzsche.[54] Paneth also wrote to others about his meetings with Nietzsche, including, it appears, his fiancé's uncle, Samuel Hammerschlag who had been Freud's revered religious instructor in childhood. (Paneth had been a border with the Hammerschlags after the death of his parents.[55]) Paneth had hopes of continuing to have contact with Nietzsche and to be able to discuss his work with friends and family with greater knowledge.[56] Nietzsche asked his publisher to mail Paneth a copy of the most recently completed part of *Zarathustra*.[57] Paneth even asked Nietzsche if he wanted him to write something (to publish in Vienna) on *Zarathustra* when the third part was published, although Nietzsche did not respond enthusiastically.[58]

We should also note that the letters indicate that Paneth was quite familiar with Nietzsche's writings prior to *Zarathustra* and that he offered Nietzsche some interpretations of these earlier writings to which Nietzsche responded favorably.[59] Nietzsche also asked Paneth for his ideas on the nature of consciousness.[60] It is of interest that Paneth and Nietzsche discussed Schopenhauer[61] and Meynert's ideas on moods[62] and agreed that the unconscious life of a person is so much richer and more important than the conscious.[63] Paneth also commented on the depth of Nietzsche's self-knowledge (with which Freud will later agree) and his ability to formulate another person's deeper thoughts.[64] He saw Nietzsche as an optimist in the sense of attempting to locate the good that can be found even in the mishaps of life.[65] One also gets the impression that Nietzsche had high regard for Paneth.

A few passages from these letters follow:

> There is not a trace of false pathos in him or the prophet's pose in him, as I had rather feared after his last work. Instead his manner is completely inoffensive and natural . . . He told me, but without the least affectation or conceit, that he always felt himself to have a task and that now, as far as his eyes would permit it, he wanted to go out of himself and work up whatever might be in him. [Nietzsche had numerous medical problems, including very poor eyesight.]
>
> He told me that through his physical pains he had got rid of his pessimism—from defiance, in order not to let himself be tyrannized by pain . . .
>
> There are many contradictions in Nietzsche, but he is a thoroughly honest human being . . .

He is completely convinced of his mission and of his decisive importance. In this faith he is strong and superior to all misfortune, physical suffering, and poverty. Such a contempt for all external instruments of success, such freedom from all that smacks of cliques or advertising, is impressive.[66]

We can, therefore, be quite certain of the estimation of Nietzsche as a person that Paneth conveyed to Freud, this from a man Freud later described as "my brilliant friend P., whose whole life had been devoted to science," "my friend P., who was very greatly my superior."[67]

We don't know what, in the context of his friendship with Freud, Paneth may have discussed or written about as regards Nietzsche's writings or what he may have stimulated Freud to read. However, given Paneth's interests (the letters indicate his familiarity with the field of philosophy), Freud's interests, the nature of their relationship, and that family and friends of Paneth in Vienna (including those around Adler at Berggasse 19) were discussing Nietzsche, it would seem very likely that Nietzsche had been discussed with Freud during the years preceding, as well as after, Paneth's meetings with him. We can recall that the friendship between Paneth and Freud included sharing of their deepest philosophical interests and their sharing of the greatly admired Brentano. (On the other hand, Freud does not get to share Nietzsche with Paneth.) It would seem quite possible that in 1883 and 1884 Paneth and Freud were discussing the relationship between conscious and unconscious aspects of mental life in a context that included Nietzsche. That Paneth's meetings with Nietzsche, and his writing to Freud of these meetings, were significant to Freud is attested to by the fact that he recalled these meetings and letters fifty years later in the correspondence with Zweig regarding Zweig's plan to write a fictionalized biography of Nietzsche.[68] (For Freud, Zweig's regard for Nietzsche may have been a reverberating echo, fifty years later, of Paneth's correspondence.)

In light of this recollection, it would appear that Nietzsche was an impressive figure to the young Freud, a "remote and noble" figure who had been the intellectual father or older brother figure to young Viennese intellectuals. Now here is Paneth actually meeting with him, spending time with him in intellectual, philosophical discussions. In addition to the possible impact on the development of Freud's thought, one might wonder about the emotional impact of this meeting on Freud, particularly in light of the fact that it was also Paneth who in 1882 replaced Freud in the laboratory of the revered Brücke. In 1889 Paneth received the promotion that Freud had so greatly desired, only to die a year later of tuberculosis.

While we do not know with certainty what Freud may have read of Nietzsche from the late 1870s through 1884 (or, for that matter, up until 1900 and even beyond), it is a distinct possibility that he read some parts of the three volumes preceding *Zarathustra* as well as parts of *Zarathustra* itself during the period of their publication or afterwards under the impact of and stimulation from Paneth's interest or the interest of other friends and acquaintances, as well as his own. If Freud did not read Nietzsche at this time, he would likely have been exposed to aspects of his thought through Paneth and others. It is hard to imagine that Paneth would not have discussed his meetings with Nietzsche with Freud upon his return to Vienna. Increasing this likelihood is the fact that Nietzsche wrote to Paneth after Paneth returned to Vienna.[69] It should come as no surprise that in a recent article on Freud's exposure to philosophy and philosophical discussions in the 1870s and 1880s, Gunter Godde writes of Paneth as the mediator of Nietzsche for Freud. Godde concludes that while Freud may not have systematically studied Nietzsche during this period, he most definitely was exposed to his thought. (Godde also makes it abundantly clear that there were quite a number of philosophical influences on Freud that had a direct bearing on the development of his thought.)[70]

While we never learn from Freud himself just what he read of Nietzsche, when he read it, and what he thought of what he read (excluding the *Minutes of the Vienna Psychoanalytic Society* and a few brief comments scattered through his works and letters), Freud did, many years later in 1911, in "Psychoanalytic Notes on an Autobiographical Account of a Case of Paranoia," refer to a section from part 3 of *Zarathustra*, the part Nietzsche was completing when he and Paneth met:

> One of my patients, who had lost his father at a very early age, was always seeking to rediscover him in what was grand and sublime in Nature. Since I have known this, it has

seemed to me probable that Nietzsche's hymn Vor Sonnen-
aufgang (Before Sunrise) is an expression of the same longing.[71]

In a footnote Freud writes: "Also Sprach Zarathustra, Part III. It
was only as a child that Nietzsche too knew his father." Nietzsche
was four when his father died. (Both Freud and Nietzsche had
younger brothers die during their early childhood, Freud at almost
two, and Nietzsche at five. Both families moved to new communities not long after these deaths.) Rediscovering longed-for, idealized
father figures at critical points in their careers was a need of both
Nietzsche (Schopenhauer, Wagner) and Freud (Brücke, Breuer,
Charcot, Fliess).

It would appear that for Freud to have known of this particular section within part 3 and to make such a comment on it, he
was, at this later time, familiar with at least parts of this work and
had given this section some thought. It should also be kept in mind
that by 1890, Thus Spoke Zarathustra[72] was a very popular book.
Included in Zarathustra are the popular concepts of eternal recurrence of the same, the overman, and the will to power, all of which
Freud mentions or alludes to in a number of published works. Of
additional interest to Freud would have been the fact that
Zarathustra places a focus and positive value on the body, explores
fundamental riddles of life via a depth psychology and presents
dreams for interpretation. Also, part 1 of Zarathustra contains a
section, "On the Pale Criminal," which Freud refers to in "Some
Character-Types Met with in Psychoanalytic Work."[73] He states
that a friend pointed out how, in this section, Nietzsche recognized the "criminal from a sense of guilt," the criminal act "rationalizing" a guilty consciousness. Zarathustra also speaks of unconscious envy.[74] Finally, Zarathustra can be regarded, in part, as an
exploration of the nature of the relationship between a teacher of
new, disturbing ideas and his disciples. (At a later point we will
consider Freud's response to Jung's letter of 1912 in which the latter quoted a passage from Zarathustra that addresses this relationship as it applies, in Jung's view, to Freud and his disciples. We will
also return to some of the ideas of Zarathustra, such as the will to
power and eternal recurrence, as well as ideas expressed in "On the
Pale Criminal.")

Before concluding this chapter, mention will be made of what
may be, in the context of this study, two of the most remarkable

passages from the works preceding *Zarathustra*. In *Daybreak*, Nietzsche brings together the ideas of unconscious wishes and oedipal-related desires as they relate to dreams:

> *Dreams and responsibility.*—You are willing to assume responsibility for everything! Except, that is, for your dreams! What miserable weakness, what lack of consistent courage! Nothing is *more* your own than your dreams! Nothing *more* your own work! Content, form, duration, performer, spectator—in these comedies you are all of this yourself! And it is precisely here that you rebuff and are ashamed of yourselves, and even Oedipus, the wise Oedipus, derived consolation from the thought that we cannot help what we dream! From this I conclude that the great majority of mankind must be conscious of having abominable dreams.[75]

As Rudnytsky points out, this is coming close to suggesting that dreams are the royal road to the unconscious. And in particular,

> Nietzsche alludes to precisely those lines from *Oedipus the King* where Jocasta attempts to reassure Oedipus that "many men before now even in dreams/have lain with their mother"—lines later quoted by Freud in *The Interpretation of Dreams* in support of his contention that "the legend of Oedipus sprang from some primordial dream material" (SE 4:263). In insisting that nothing is "more our own" than our "abominable dreams," Nietzsche comes preternaturally close to Freud.[76]

Nietzsche is stating that nothing reflects who we deeply are more than our dreams, and he specifically refers to the dream and myth pertaining to oedipal wishes. The passage he refers to is the very same passage Freud refers to in *The Interpretation of Dreams*.[77] It is significant that the passage Nietzsche refers to and the wishes in regard to which he urges us to learn to take responsibility refer to the *continuing presence in adulthood* of sexual desires of the son for the mother. Of even greater importance than specific dream content is the fact that while in the play it is the reliability of prophecy that is at issue, that is, whether or not the dream anticipates the future,[78] Nietzsche turns his interpretation to what the dream tells us about our abominable, shameful thoughts and desires for which we are reluctant to take responsibility.

Perhaps of even greater importance is section 1 of *Human, All Too Human*. We have already commented on the discussion of sublimation in this section. However, as Young points out,[79] in this section Nietzsche also heralds a *new methodology*. He contrasts "metaphysical philosophy" with his "historical [later geneological] philosophy." His is a methodology for philosophical inquiry into the origins of human psychology, a methodology to be allied with the natural sciences. This inquiry "can no longer be separated from natural science." And as he will do on other occasions, he offers a call to those who might have the ears to hear: "Will there be many who desire to pursue such researches? Mankind likes to put questions of origins and beginnings out of its mind: must one not be almost inhuman to detect in oneself a contrary inclination?"[80]

# Chapter 4

## THE MID-1880S
## THROUGH THE MID-1890S

*Europe owes the Jews no small thanks for making
people think more logically and for establishing
cleanlier intellectual habits—nobody more so than
the Germans.*

—Nietzsche, *The Gay Science*

Since this study does not focus on the strictly scientific and
medical influences on the development of Freud's thought, I want
to at least briefly indicate at the outset of this chapter that the influence of the theories and medical practices of such figures as
Koch, Breuer, Meynert, Charcot and others may outweigh any immediate and direct influence Nietzsche may have had on Freud
specifically during the late 1880s and early 1890s.

Robert Koch (1843–1910) developed a germ theory of disease,
formulating the conditions to be met in order to be able to confidently assign causal status to a hypothesized cause of a disease.
Freud looked to this theory for his understanding of the etiology of
various forms of psychopathology.[1] Breuer had developed a "talking cure" in his work with Anna O. and her hysterical symptomatology, attempting to reach pathogenic memories. In 1893 Freud
wrote that "Breuer learnt from his first patient that the attempt at
discovering the determining cause of a symptom was at the same
time a therapeutic manoeuvre."[2] Charcot (1825–1893), under

whom Freud studied in Paris in late 1885 and early 1886, worked with patients suffering from neurasthenia and hysteria, utilized hypnosis to reproduce hysterical symptoms and demonstrated the psychogenic nature of certain symptoms. Malcolm Macmillan points out that another concept that influenced Freud was Charcot's idea that the pathogenic idea or memory was generated from sensations produced during the relevant trauma: "For Charcot, a symptom *had* to have the same sensory content as the idea that caused it. Likewise for Freud: the quality to be sought in the causal memory was the sensory content present in the symptom[3] . . . the sensory content of the symptom was based on and reflected the sensations experienced in the trauma."[4] As Macmillan also points out,[5] Meynert developed a theory of mental associations from which causal relations could be inferred. This was an important factor in Freud's attempts to trace connections between symptom and traumatic memory. Freud was deeply involved in searching out the ways in which he could confidently trust the chain of memories and associations that led from a symptom to a causally relevant memory. Macmillan suggests that in his trust in the internal determinants (as opposed to external determinants such as suggestion) of the process by which memories were recovered, Freud drew on Meynert's associationism and the general deterministic view of Charcot.[6] According to Macmillan, by the time he developed the therapeutic technique of free association, "Freud assumed that ideas produced during free association were under the guidance of an unconscious idea connected with the one being focused upon."[7]

We can also note that figures such as Charcot, Janet and Krafft-Ebing, among others, explored the relationship between dreams and other unconscious mental processes, including those pertaining to symptomatology.[8] Janet himself at a later time discussed the work of Maury in 1861 and, ten years earlier, Charma regarding how the passions of human beings find freer expression in dreams. He quotes Charma: "Often enough, that which we do not dare either to do or say when we are awake, will present itself to us in a dream when we are asleep."[9] Janet also points to Alphonse Daudet writing that "the dream is a safety valve."[10]

The central and really obvious point I wish to make here is that Nietzsche, although he constantly wrote about and struggled with notions of sickness and health, did not apply his psychological insights to work with patients suffering from hysteria, anxiety, phobias, obsessions, etc. So far as I have found, he had no special interest in clinical hypnosis, which played an important part in Freud's development (although he was well aware of Bernays' ideas on catharsis). And he did not develop associationist theories connecting a patient's symptoms to pathogenic memories (although it is of interest that he and Paneth did discuss Meynert). He also developed no theory and practice of cure analogous to what was developed by Freud's great teachers and, of course, Freud himself. Such influences (and many others of a related nature) had great impact on Freud, and Nietzsche does not link up directly with them to any great degree. (We can, though, recall Meynert's open acknowledgement of Schopenhauer's influence.) Nietzsche did not conceive of a special interpersonal situation and structure in which a doctor and a patient could more readily observe and understand the unconscious workings of drives, defenses, conscience, etc; a situation created so as to allow such unconscious processes to manifest themselves more clearly and understandably than would otherwise be the case. Whether or not this special setting allows for special access to unconscious processes is another matter.

On the other hand, we can consider that around the same time (1883–1884) Freud was commenting on Koch's germ theory, Paneth was for a three-month period writing a great deal to Freud about Nietzsche. During this period friends and acquaintances around Freud continued to discuss Nietzsche. It is also true that Nietzsche's general psychological observations and concepts—such as those pertaining to the nature of the drives, repression, dreams, expenditures of energy, the consequences, in Freud's words, of drives "failing to find adequate discharge" and of memory, in certain states, being capable of returning to our individual childhood and our primitive human past—are all relevant to Freud's explorations. And Nietzsche's great interest in the operations and functions of memory, forgetting, and repression are evident in his formulations regarding the origins of such conditions as *ressentiment* and bad conscience. Also, recall that Nietzsche wrote specifically of how we "forget," "banish . . . from our minds" aspects of *"our own past"* that contradict the images of ourselves— "our self-conceit"—that we wish to maintain (emphasis added). We create an "image of ourself that shines upon us out of the past to deceive us and flatter our self-conceit—we are engaged continually on this self-deception."[11]

Furthermore, I believe that passages of Nietzsche's that we have considered, and others to be considered, demonstrate that he was a more purely dynamic and depth psychologist along the lines Freud would ultimately develop than any of Freud's great scientific mentors. Although interested in the needs of, the drives of, the body and their influence on thought, feeling and behavior, there is usually not the same kind of equation in Nietzsche of what is unconscious with the cerebral, the physical and the physiological that often appears in the writings of Freud's mentors and Freud himself in the 1880s and early 1890s.[12] For example, Wallace points out that in his 1888 "Preface to Bernheim"[13] Freud was "insufficiently attending to the unconscious factors he would more and more emphasize."[14] Wallace points out that "after 1895, his [Freud's] theorizing became progressively psychological."[15] Nietzsche, while at times writing of both physiolial and psychological processes, is usually quite clear when he is discussing unconscious *mental* operations; for example, an "*interpretation* of the intellect which, to be sure, generally does this work without rising to consciousness."[16]

McGrath suggests that while Freud conceptualized dream formation as motivated by a wish in 1895, "his theory of dreams remained inchoate until [in late 1897 and early 1898] he realized that what he had previously conceptualized narrowly as hysterical censorship had a general application in mental life that could be observed in the censorship of dreams."[17] As we will see, it may be no accident that in the late 1890s, as we find the Freud who in very essential ways remains the thinker and psychologist he was from this point on, we also find the presence of Nietzsche. Freud may have found help from Nietzsche in his "general application." And let us recall that it is Freud himself who on a number of occasions will state that Nietzsche's psychological insights were very close to those of psychoanalysis. We can also note that no less an authority than Ellenberger, who writes at great length on the many early scientific and medical influences on Freud, concludes that Nietzsche stood out among the leaders of the new intellectual orientation of the mid-1880s which had an impact on, among other things, "dynamic psychiatry." Regarding the impact of Nietzsche's thought in the 1890s, Ellenberger compares Nietzsche's influence to that of Darwin's on the previous generation. Ellenberger has no doubt about Nietzsche's influence on Freud.[18] It may be that philosophers such as Schopenhauer, Feuerbach and Nietzsche laid the foundations for dynamic depth psychology to as great a degree as did Freud's great scientific and medical teachers and mentors.

---

After Freud's work in Paris for about six months under Charcot from late 1885 through early 1886, it would not be long before he was making observations and formulations that can be considered the beginnings of psychoanalysis. By 1888 he was working on "Some Points for a Comparative Study of Organic and Hysterical Motor Paralyses."[19] This paper, completed and published in 1893, links the hysterical symptom to affect-laden "subconscious" associations. Certain subconscious associations are not accessible to conscious associations. One student of the period has suggested that "Freud began that paper as a neurologist. He ended it as a psychologist."[20]

Of course by the early 1890s Freud was, on his own and in collaboration with Breuer, deeply immersed in working out conceptualizations which would be elaborated upon and integrated into a more comprehensive psychoanalytic system by the end of the decade. By 1895 Freud had written of abreaction, a complex, displacement, fixation, the principle of constancy, quota of affect, repression, return of the repressed, symbolization, conversion, defense, flight into illness, libido, cathexis, censorship, projection, resistance and transference.[21]

In January of 1889 Nietzsche became permanently insane. Although there does not appear to be information available on the matter, it would be difficult to imagine Freud not taking an interest in this. Whatever his reaction may have been, by 1891 or 1892, the time that Freud entered his truly creative period of psychological insights and formulations, Nietzsche was famous throughout the German-speaking world and beyond. Not only was his influence soon felt in the philosophical and literary fields, but in the areas of political thought and social theory as well.[22] In 1892 the first edition of Nietzsche's collected works was published;[23] in 1894 Lou Andreas-Salomé published her study of Nietzsche; and in 1895 Förster-Nietzsche published the first volume of her biography of Nietzsche.[24]

It would appear that by 1890 or so it would have been almost impossible for any German-speaking intellectual or well-read person to avoid coming into contact with some of Nietzsche's ideas.

Freud may or may not have begun avoiding Nietzsche during this period to preserve his independence of thought, but he could scarcely have avoided at least some exposure to his ideas.

Of course we do not know which of Nietzsche's ideas Freud may have been exposed to in the late 1880s and early 1890s, but one can at least note that there are any number of passages from Nietzsche's later works which would have relevance for the development of psychoanalysis. Two works of particular interest are *Beyond Good and Evil*, (1886) and its sequel *On the Genealogy of Morals* (1887). At this point it can be mentioned that, among other things, *On the Genealogy of Morals* is concerned with how drives, especially aggressive drives, once expressed more directly and then prevented expression and repressed, are turned inward or directed against the self ("the internalization of man") and how this process is part and parcel of the development of "bad conscience." It should also be noted that in *Beyond Good and Evil* Nietzsche refers to himself as a psychologist and describes psychology as the queen of the sciences. A few passages from these two works will convey a sense of Nietzsche's continuing concern with matters pertinent to the development of Freud's thought.

From *Beyond Good and Evil:*

A proper physio-psychology has to contend with unconscious resistance in the heart of the investigator. . .

Psychology shall be recognized again as the queen of the sciences, for whose service and preparation the other sciences exist. For psychology is now again the path to the fundamental problems.[25]

The decisive value of an action lies precisely in what is *unintentional* in it, while everything about it that is intentional, everything about it that can be seen, known, "conscious," still belongs to its surface and skin—which, like every skin, betrays something but *conceals* even more. In short, we believe that the intention is merely a sign and symptom that still requires interpretation.[26]

"I have done that," says my memory. "I cannot have done that," says my pride, and remains inexorable. Eventually—memory yields.[27]

The degree and kind of a man's sexuality reach up into the ultimate pinnacle of his spirit.[28]

It was precisely during the most Christian period of Europe and altogether only under the pressure of Christian value judgments that the sex drive sublimated itself into love (*amour-passion*).[29]

From *On the Genealogy of Morals:*

Forgetting is no mere *vis inertiae* as the superficial imagine; it is rather an active and in the strictest sense positive faculty of repression (Positives Hemmungsvermogen).

Active forgetfulness . . . is like a doorkeeper, a preserver of psychic order. . . . [The opposing force or faculty is memory, which is also not passive "but an active *desire* not to rid oneself, a desire for the continuance of something desired once, a real *memory of the will*."]

This (human) animal which needs to be forgetful. . . . [At times Freud refers to the censor as a "doorkeeper," and in *The Interpretation of Dreams* he writes of the censoring agent as "the guardian of our psychic health."][30]

All instincts that do not discharge themselves outwardly turn inward . . . Hostility, cruelty, joy in persecuting, in attacking, in change, in destruction—all this turned against the possessors of such instincts: that is the origin of the "bad conscience."[31]

This *instinct for freedom* forcibly made latent . . . this instinct for freedom pushed back and repressed, incarcerated within and finally able to discharge and vent itself only on itself: that, and that alone, is what the *bad conscience* is in its beginnings.[32]

At later points we will return to such passages for specific comparison with Freud. We can note here ideas pertaining to the discipline of psychology, how the conscious as a symptom can be interpreted for both its revealing and concealing of what is unconscious, that attempting to preserve one's self-image or ego-ideal ("pride") can lead to repression, and that the spiritual can be understood in terms of sublimated sexuality. We also read of forgetfulness as active repression functioning as a doorkeeper (or censor), the relationship between memory and desire and pain, and that drives deprived of outward expression may be vented upon the self, the self being substituted for the original object, this being the origin of "bad conscience." Nietzsche also writes of the psychologist having to contend with his or her own "unconscious resistance."

It also might prove helpful to present a few passages from these works in which Nietzsche comments on Jews and the Jewish Scriptures. It is possible that such passages would have added to Nietzsche's impact on Freud given the fact that Freud, despite his not being a believing or practicing Jew, had a strong, though complex and ambivalent, sense of Jewish identity and heritage. Nietzsche can justifiably be accused of writing passages critical of Jews as well as passages on race and aggressive domination which later lent themselves to antisemitic propaganda. However, on numerous occasions he spoke out forcefully against antisemitism. Although it was easy for him to overlook Wagner's antisemitism during the period in which he idealized him, when Wagner gained a wider public and his antisemitism became more intense Nietzsche did forcefully condemn him for it.[33] In *The Gay Science* Nietzsche wrote that "Wagner is Schopenhauerian in his hatred of the Jews to whom he is not able to do justice even when it comes to their greatest deed; after all, the Jews are the inventors of Christianity." (It is important to recognize that while Nietzsche frequently attacks those forces that led to the development of Christianity and its destructive impact, there is no simple condemning. Here Nietzsche is genuinely castigating Wagner [and Schopenhauer] and recognizing this greatest deed of the Jews. The consequences may have been a deeply neurotic creature, but a creature who brought into the world something new and full of promise. More generally we can note, in the words of Bernard Williams, Nietzsche's "ever-present sense that his own consciousness would not be possible without the developments that he disliked."][34]

Mandel points out that even in a relatively early work, *Human, All Too Human*, Nietzsche wrote that the ostracized Jew is an essential "ingredient for the breeding of the most strong European race," and that it is the Jews "to whom one owes the noblest human (Christ), the purest philosopher (Spinoza), and the mightiest book."[35] In the same section Nietzsche further praises Judaism: "If Christianity has done everything to orientalize the occident, Judaism has always played an essential part in occidentalizing it again: which in a certain sense means making of Europe's mission and history *a continuation of the Greek*."[36]

Overall, in his mature writings Nietzsche strongly attacked antisemitism, right up until his last lucid moments.[37] Also, it will be recalled that Paneth was quite definite about Nietzsche being above antisemitism. Nietzsche expressed great admiration for Jews and great appreciation and respect for the Jewish Scriptures,[38] often at the expense of the New Testament and of Germans:

> In the Jewish "Old Testament," the book of divine justice, there are human beings, things, and speeches in so grand a style that Greek and Indian literature have nothing to compare with it. With terror and reverence one stands before these tremendous remnants of what man once was . . . To have glued this New Testament, a kind of rococo of taste in every respect, to the Old Testament to make *one* book, as the "Bible," as "the book par excellence"—that is perhaps the greatest audacity and "sin against the spirit" that literary Europe has on its conscience.[39]
>
> "Admit no more new Jews! And especially close the doors to the east (also to Austria)!" thus commands the instinct of a people whose type is still weak and indefinite, so it could easily be blurred or extinguished by a stronger race. The Jews, however, are beyond any doubt the strongest, toughest, and purest race now living in Europe . . . and this bent [towards assimilation] . . . should be noted and *accommodated:* to that end it might be useful and fair to expel the antisemitic screamers from the country.[40] [However, it should be noted that this accommodation is to be accomplished "with all caution, with selection."]
>
> All honor to the Old Testament! I find in it great human beings, a heroic landscape, and something of the very rarest quality in the world, the incomparable naïveté of the *strong heart;* what is more, I find a people. In the New one, on the other hand, I find nothing but petty sectarianism, mere rococo of the soul, mere involutions, nooks, queer things, the air of the conventicle, not to forget an occasional whiff of bucolic mawkishness that belongs to the epoch (*and* to the Roman province) and is not so much Jewish as Hellenistic.[41]

Even when it comes to the prophets, who in Nietzsche's eyes helped pave the way for developments leading to Christianity, they are compared favorably with the Gospel writers. In *The Antichrist*, after quoting from Luke 6:23, in which the prophets are mentioned, Nietzsche writes: "*Impertinent* rabble! They compare themselves with the prophets, no less."[42]

Gilman mentions Nietzsche in commenting on antisemitism and caricatures of Jews in the press of Vienna and Berlin in the 1880s:

> These extraordinary caricatures stressed one central aspect of the physiognomy of the Jewish male, his nose, which stood for the hidden sign of his sexual difference, his circumcised penis. For it was the Jews' sign of sexual difference, their sexual selectiveness as an indicator of their identity, which became, as Nietzsche strikingly observed in *Beyond Good and Evil*, the focus of the Germans' sense of insecurity about their recently created national identity. This fear was represented in the caricatures by the elongated nose. (The traditional folkloric association between the size of the nose and that of the male genitalia was made a pathological sign.)[43]

Also, in the second edition of *The Gay Science*, published in 1887, Nietzsche wrote:

> Europe owes the Jews no small thanks for making people think more logically and for establishing cleanlier intellectual habits—nobody more so than the Germans who are a lamentable *déraisonnable* [unreasonable] race . . . Wherever Jews have won influence they have taught men to make finer distinctions, more rigorous inferences, and to write in a more luminous and cleanly fashion; their task was ever to bring a people "to listen to *raison.*"[44]

Freud, though rejecting religious belief and observance of Jewish ritual, valued what he felt to be an analytical, rationalist kernal of Judaism.[45]

Nietzsche's positive comments about Jews (including his regarding them as among his de-Germanized true readers) and his attack against antisemitism are particularly striking in light of the long line of respected German intellectual figures in whose thought antisemitism played a significant role. It is also clear that

Nietzsche's positive comments about Jews and Judaism were not lost on German-speaking Jews in the 1890s. In fact, by the 1890s Jews were thought by some antisemites to be the mediators of prevalent distorted views on Nietzsche's philosophy.[46]

In *Twilight of the Idols*, which was published in 1889 just as Nietzsche became insane, Nietzsche refers to his work as that of a psychologist.[47] (The original title, which Nietzsche was disuaded from using, was *A Psychologist's Idleness*.) In this work Nietzsche explores morality, science, religion, the psychology of the Dionysian state and the value of integrating instinct and the passions rather than attempting excision or "castration." He is aware of upper displacement and symbolization, referring to the eyes and the teeth in the same passage as he refers to castration.[48] He also writes of the value of creative internal conflict and how one can be grateful to one's internal and external enemies:

> The spiritualization of sensuality is called *love* . . . another triumph is our spiritualization of *hostility*. It consists in a profound appreciation of the value of having enemies . . . A new creation in particular . . . needs enemies more than friends: in opposition does it *feel* itself necessary, in opposition alone does it *become* necessary. . . .
>
> Our attitude to the "internal enemy" is no different: here too we have spiritualized hostility; here too we have come to appreciate its value. The price of fruitfulness is to be rich in internal opposition.[49]

Of course Freud had his own great internal oppositions that he came to utilize so creatively. Also, Freud always needed an enemy, as he himself stated in his interpretation of his "Non Vixit" dream, a dream to which we will return.

In 1895 *The Antichrist* and *Nietzsche Contra Wagner* (both completed in 1888) were first published. Nietzsche refers to himself as a psychologist in both works, referring in the former work to his analysis as "the psychology of conviction, of 'faith.'"[50] He states that "one cannot be a philologist or physician without at the same time being an *anti-Christian*,"[51] that "philology and medicine [are] the two great adversaries of superstition"[52] and that "'Faith' as an imperative is the veto against science."[53] Nietzsche offers a psychological analysis of the powerful and primitive forces at work in the experience and condition of faith and a scathing attack on the Apostle Paul. He contrasts the practice of Jesus with the teachings of Paul:

> On the heels of the "glad tidings" came the *very worst:* those of Paul. In Paul was embodied the opposite type to that of the "bringer of glad tidings": the genius in hatred, in the vision of hatred, in the inexorable logic of hatred . . . nothing remained [of Jesus' life, doctrine, death, example] once this hate-inspired counterfeiter realized what he alone could use . . . he *invented his own history of earliest Christianity* . . . he had no use at all for the life of the Redeemer—he needed the death on the cross *and* a little more . . . His need was for power; in Paul the priest wanted power once again—he could use only concepts, doctrines, symbols with which one tyrannizes masses and forms herds.[54]

Although Freud had an affectionate feeling for Paul, he was an atheist and understood religious experience and belief from a psychological perspective that was related to Nietzsche's understanding (as well as to Feuerbach to whom both Nietzsche and Freud were indebted[55]). We will return to this matter at a later point, but we can note here the particular importance for psychoanalysis (and for understanding Freud) of the idea of inventing a history (including of one's self) to meet particular needs.

Regarding *Nietzsche Contra Wagner* (a compilation, with modifications, of passages from earlier works), in the preface Nietzsche writes that "this is an essay for psychologists." At a later point he writes:

> If there is anything in which I am ahead of all psychologists, it is that my eye is sharper for that most difficult and captious kind of *backward inference* in which the most mistakes are made: the backward inference from the work to the maker, from the deed to the doer, from the ideal to him who *needs* it, from every way of thinking and valuing to the *want* behind it that prompts it.[56]

Nietzsche looks for the latent impulse, wish, desire behind ways of thinking and valuing.

One can only wonder if Freud read these works or sections of them or had certain concepts brought to his attention. There can be little doubt that Freud would have been particularly interested in *The Antichrist*,[57] and we know that later in life he owned it as a single volume in English as well as in the collected works in German.[58] There is no evidence that Freud read it at or around the time of its publication in 1895.

Another point to be made, and a possible factor in Freud's own considerations as to whether or not he might read Nietzsche at this time, is the possibility that Freud met with Lou Andreas-Salomé in the spring of 1895, around the time of publication of *Studies in Hysteria*, perhaps through the literary figure Arthur Schnitzler (whom Freud admired so much and regarded as having intuitively arrived at many psychoanalytic insights). Andreas-Salomé was the object of Nietzsche's passionate feelings in 1882 and would later, in 1912 and after a distinguished literary career, enter the psychoanalytic movement and quickly establish a close relationship with Freud. It has been suggested that her circle of friends crossed with Freud's and Breuer's. It is known that she was in Vienna in the spring of 1895, and it has been reported that a Lucia Morawitz, who knew Andreas-Salomé, distinctly remembered a conversation with her being disrupted at that time due to Andreas-Salomé having to see Freud.[59]

If this 1895 meeting took place, one can wonder at the impact it may have had on Freud given Andreas-Salomé's reputation, her having been the object of Nietzsche's passion, and her having published, in Vienna, her study on Nietzsche the year before. We will return to Andreas-Salomé, but we can note here that her understanding of the overman as overcoming the conflict between instinct or drives and conventional morality and as having become autonomous in his valuing is related to the goals of psychoanalytic therapy. Freud and Andreas-Salomé never refer to such a meeting in their correspondence of later years. If the meeting took place, it would seem very possible that Nietzsche was discussed, given Andreas-Salomé's knowledge of him and Freud's interest in him. Anzieu has suggested that in mid-1895 Freud turned to or returned to Goethe, a figure of identification in his adolescence, "for a creative regression" in the service of moving ahead on his own in his work. Could Freud have also turned to or returned to the "remote and noble figure" of his youth at this time? We may never know the answer. But, as we shall shortly see, there is evidence from Freud's letters to Fliess indicating that shortly after this time Freud was reading and thinking about Nietzsche. And regarding Andreas-Salome's thought at this time, we can note that in 1923, after reading the study on Nietzsche, Anna Freud would write to her: "Was it not written very long before your analytic period? . . . But so much in it has an altogether analytic tone. Did people then already think like this or was it all only your very own perception?" Some people already thought like this.[60]

Consideration might also be given to the links to Nietzsche in the literature Freud read. Grinstein[61] discusses the "ten good books" Freud chose when he and other figures were asked to do so by the publisher Hugo Heller in 1906. In his book Grinstein also discusses additional literature that Freud read from the early 1890s through the first years of the twentieth century. While it will not be undertaken in the present study, it would be of interest to explore the extent to which the authors and the works Freud read were influenced by Nietzsche. (We can also note, regarding the matter of Freud's interest in philosophy, that one of his ten books was Gomperz's *The Greek Thinkers*.[62]) After 1890 it would have been difficult for many literary figures to avoid some influence by Nietzsche. As an example, we can mention one of the ten books chosen by Freud, *The Romance of Leonardo Da Vince* (published in 1901 and for the moment taking us beyond the mid-1890s) by Dmitri Merejkowski (1865–1941). There are scenes in this novel in which the Antichrist is referred to and Leonardo regarded as an Antichrist figure. There is a witches' sabbath, "a sexual orgy glorifying Dionysus and the resurrection of the pagan gods."[63] There is the idea of reconciliation between the Christian and the pagan in the figure of a Dionysus—Christ.[64] (This very possibility was, as we shall see, raised to Freud by Jung not long after Freud read the book.) Nietzsche was so associated with Dionysus and the Antichrist that some sense of his presence would have been unavoidable for Freud. Merejkowski began his trilogy *Christ and Antichrist* in 1893. *Leonardo* is the second volume. Clowes[65] has written an article on how Nietzsche's ideas on history, time and the "higher nature" are integrated in Merejkowski's early historical novels. She writes that "the greatest inspiration of his early years came from writings of Friedrich Nietzsche" and quotes Merejkowski as exclaiming: "'When I read Nietzsche, I thrill from head to toe.'"[66]

Another author of a chosen book was Gottfried Keller whom Nietzsche had praised in *Human, All Too Human*[67] and *The Will to Power*.[68] Nietzsche also spoke admiringly of Keller to Paneth.[69] Nietzsche sent Keller copies of his work, and the two corresponded and met. A biographer of Keller writes:

> Keller did not know what to make of Nietzsche; he could sense that this was a man of extraordinary talent who yet had something queer and offputting about him. Keller and Nietzsche never met in anything more than a superficial sense; they made polite conversation, each sensed that the other had something to give him if they became sufficiently intimate, and yet somehow this never happened.[70]

Grinstein mentions none of these links to Nietzsche; he only indicates that another author of one of Freud's chosen books, Eduard Douwes Dekker, "has been compared to such writers as Nietzsche."[71]

The point to be made here is that we have not really begun to understand how Freud may have been influenced by Nietzsche through other literary figures and their works (as well as through figures from other disciplines).

Returning to matters raised at the beginning of this chapter, attention can also be called to the similarity of certain ideas of Freud, even before the late 1890s, to passages in Nietzsche. In his important early paper of 1894, "The Neuro-Psychoses of Defense," Freud writes, regarding psychic functioning, of "a quota of affect or sum of excitation—which possesses all the characteristics of a quantity . . . which is capable of increase, diminution, displacement and discharge."[72] In an appendix to the article, the editor, Strachey,[73] singles out this one passage for its importance.

Certainly, theories of energy received a great deal of attention during the latter part of the nineteenth century, and Freud and Nietzsche were both influenced by various sources on such concepts. (Ellenberger[74] points out that Alwin Mittasch drew attention to Nietzsche's drawing upon Julius Robert Mayer's principle of conservation and transformation of energy.) But it is worth noting that the language of Freud and Nietzsche on this matter is very similar. In the additional book 5 to the second edition of *The Gay Science*, Nietzsche writes:

> I have learned to distinguish the cause of acting from the cause of acting in a particular way . . . The first kind of cause is a quantum of dammed-up energy that is waiting to be used up somehow . . . while the second kind is . . . for the most part a little accident in which this quantum "discharges" itself in one particular way . . . the tremendous quantum of energy that presses . . . to be used up somehow.[75]

And, as we have seen, Nietzsche was well aware that problems arise when this energy cannot find adequate discharge. While there may or may not be direct influence here, and the contexts of the two passages differ, both Freud and Nietzsche concern themselves with the power of a quota of psychic energy or affect to find avenues for discharge. Also, Nietzsche is distinguishing between the aim (relief through discharge of dammed-up energy) and the particular ways in which the energy may be discharged (which may vary), a kind of conceptualization generally thought to be one of Freud's important and original formulations. Strachey was not the only one to regard such formulations as of great importance. Whatever the influences on Nietzsche, he recognized his formulation as "one of my most essential steps and advances."

Also of interest, in 1894 as he is making his crucial turn to the role of repression in producing symptoms, Freud begins to sound more Nietzschean (again in "The Neuro-Psychosis of Defense") as he writes of his patients having ideas and feelings arousing affects so painful that they are forgotten or repressed. These patients doubt their ability to resolve the incompatibility between such ideas and their ego.[76] For Nietzsche, forgetting is an active faculty of inhibition or repression involved in banishing from our minds aspects of our past that contradict our images of ourselves (as well as maintaining psychic order).

We can also note here Rosset's observation that for Nietzsche the vicious man (and the man of *ressentiment*) is one who suffers from passivity and an incapacity to act:

> The only reaction of which he is capable is powerless to constitute itself as an act and . . . in this powerlessness resides his principal motive for suffering and hatred . . . the hateful person is the one who finds . . . it is impossible to hate (that is, to give to his hatred some expression or form of existence, to

make of his hatred an act). In a quite comparable manner, as early as the *Studies on Hysteria,* of 1895, Freud defines repression as the effect . . . of an *absence of reaction* (or of an "'abreaction'"). It is an effect which adds to the wound the impossibility of being present and responding to it fully.[77]

This passivity and inability to be fully present and act in the face of certain kinds of wounds is a fundamental notion in Nietzsche's psychology and in Freud's psychology and neuro-psychology of the mid-1890s.

The period from the mid-1880s to the mid-1890s is, in the context of this study, unique in that it is the only period of this length in Freud's adult life for which there is virtually no information available pertaining to any specific contacts he may have had with the ideas of Nietzsche. During every other period of Freud's life it is never more than, at most, a few years before Nietzsche's name, ideas or influence turn up once again in one form or another. What can be concluded regarding this particular period is that Nietzsche's writings were so popular in educated circles by 1890 that during the early 1890s Freud, even if he hadn't been reading Nietzsche during the previous few years, would have had some contact with Nietzsche's ideas from friends, acquaintances, newspapers, journals, literature, etc. We do not know which writings or which ideas, in what form or context, or with what degree of accuracy, may have reached Freud and how they may have interacted with the many scientific and medical influences of the period of which we are more certain. We might, however, imagine Freud's response if during this period he came across the following passage from *Beyond Good and Evil:*

To see to it that man henceforth stands before man as even today, hardened in the discipline of science, he stands before the *rest* of nature, with intrepid Oedipus eyes and sealed Odysseus ears,[78] deaf to the siren songs of old metaphysical bird catchers who have been piping at him all too long, "you are more, you are higher, you are of a different origin!"—that may be a strange and insane task, but it is a *task.*[79]

# Chapter 5

## THE LATE 1890s:
## THE PERIOD OF SELF-ANALYSIS AND
## *THE INTERPRETATION OF DREAMS*

*He turns up his nose—he regards himself as something particularly noble.*
—Freud to Fliess, November 1897

*On his way to becoming an "angel" . . . man . . . holds his nose in his own presence.*
—Nietzsche, *Genealogy of Morals*

### THE FREUD-FLIESS CORRESPONDENCE

Freud's father died on October 23, 1896. His attempt to understand his intense emotional reaction was one of the factors that led Freud to his self-analysis and work on *The Interpretation of Dreams*. In his second letter to Wilhelm Fliess after the death of his father, Freud wrote that "in [my] inner self the whole past has been reawakened by this event."[1]

During the 1890s Freud wrote a great deal to his friend Fliess, a nose specialist and surgeon, about his professional and personal concerns. He looked to Fliess as a highly idealized figure and a sympathetic reader and critic for his newly evolving psychoanalytic concepts during a period in which there were few others he felt he could look to for professional support. The correspondence began in 1887, deepened by 1892 and, except for a few letters, ended in 1902. Almost half of the Freud-Fliess correspondence took place from October 1896 through 1900. Among the factors leading to the deterioration of the relationship were Freud's increasing unease with some of Fliess' theories (for example, on the functions and influences of the nose) and Fliess' anger at Freud having picked up certain ideas, such as inherent bisexuality, from him without giving him credit. Also, as interest in and recognition of Freud's work grew, he no longer required the support of Fliess for the continuation of his work. (The analyst Richard Chessick suggests that while Freud needed Fliess to take his steps forward, Nietzsche required the break-up of his idealization of Wagner to move into his most creative work.[2])

There are a number of Freud's letters to Fliess which contain possible allusions to Nietzsche, although his name is mentioned only in a letter of February 1900.[3] Two of these letters strongly suggest some familiarity with Nietzsche during this period. There are also other letters which have some bearing on the question of Nietzsche's influence. Consideration will be given to the relevant passages in the correspondence.

On May 31, 1897, Freud enclosed "Draft N" with his letter to Fliess. According to Grinstein, this time "marked a period of momentous change in his [Freud's] life . . . There were several major achievements during this period. He began his self-analysis."[4] "Draft N" includes a passage entitled, "Definition of 'Holy.'" Freud writes:

> "Holy" is something based on the fact that human beings, for the benefit of the larger community, have sacrificed a portion of their sexual liberty and their liberty to indulge in perversions. The horror of incest (something impious) is based on the fact that, as a result of communal sexual life (even in childhood), the members of a family remain together permanently and become incapable of joining with strangers. Thus incest is antisocial—civilization consists in this progressive renunciation. Contrariwise, the "superman."[5]

Freud's use of the word "superman" or "overman" in and of itself might indicate only a superficial familiarity with a popular term associated with Nietzsche. However, as Holmes[6] has pointed out, Freud is discussing the holy, or saintly, and its relation to repression and the giving up of freedoms of instinctual expression, central concerns of the third essay of *On the Genealogy of Morals,* "What Is the Meaning of Ascetic Ideals?"

Nietzsche writes of the anti-nature of the ascetic ideal, how it relates to a disgust with oneself, its continuing destructive effect upon the health of Europeans, and how it relates to the realm of "subterranean revenge" and *ressentiment.* In this essay and the preceding one, "'Guilt,' 'Bad Conscience,' and the Like," Nietzsche writes of the repression of instincts (though not specifically of impulses towards sexual perversions) and of their being turned inward against the self. In the second essay he writes of the "instinct for freedom forcibly made latent . . . this instinct for freedom pushed back and repressed."[7] In closing the third essay he writes of the ascetic ideal, "this hatred of the human, and even more of the animal, and more still of the material."[8] Zarathustra also speaks of the tyranny of the holy or sacred: "He once loved 'thou shalt' as most sacred: now he must find illusion and caprice even in the most sacred, that freedom from his love may become his prey: the lion is needed for such prey."[9] It would appear that while Freud's formulation as it pertains to sexual perversions and incest certainly does not derive from Nietzsche (although along different lines incest was an important factor in Nietzsche's understanding of *Oedipus*), the relating of the idea of the holy to the sacrifice or repression of instinctual freedom was very possibly influenced by Nietzsche, particularly in light of Freud's reference to the "holy" as well as to the "overman." These issues were also explored in *The Antichrist* which had been published just two years earlier. In addition, in an earlier letter of the same month Freud wrote, perhaps for the first time, of sublimation:

> I have gained a sure inkling of the structure of hysteria. Everything goes back to the reproduction of scenes. Some can be obtained directly, others always by way of fantasies set up in front of them. The fantasies stem from things that have been *heard* but understood *subsequently*, and all their material is of course genuine. They are protective structures, sublimations of the facts, embellishment of them, and at the same time serve for self-relief.[10]

Nietzsche had written of sublimation, and he specifically wrote of the sublimation of sexual drives in the *Genealogy*.[11] Freud's use of the term here differs somewhat from his later and more Nietz-schean usage such as in *Three Essays on the Theory of Sexuality*, but as Kaufmann notes, while "the word is older than either Freud or Nietzsche . . . it was Nietzsche who first gave it the specific con-notation it has today."[12] Kaufmann regards the concept of sublima-tion as one of the most important concepts in Nietzsche's entire philosophy.[13] Furthermore, in the May 31 letter Freud wrote that a "presentiment" tells him, "I shall very soon uncover the source of morality,"[14] the very subject of Nietzsche's *Genealogy*.

Of course it is difficult to determine whether or not Freud may have been recently reading Nietzsche or was consciously or unconsciously drawing on material he had come across some years earlier. It is also possible that Freud had recently or some time ear-lier read only limited segments of the *Genealogy* or other works. At a later time in his life Freud claimed he could not read more than a few passages of Nietzsche due to being overwhelmed by the wealth of ideas.[15] This claim might be supported by the fact that Freud demonstrates only a limited understanding of certain of Nietzsche's concepts. For example, his reference to the "overman" in the above quotation demonstrates a lack of understanding of the overman as a being of the future whose freedom involves creative self-overcoming and sublimation, not simply freely gratified primi-tive instincts. Later in life, in *Group Psychology and the Analysis of the Ego*,[16] Freud demonstrates a similar misunderstanding in his equating the overman with the tyrannical father of the primal horde. Perhaps Freud confused the overman with the "master" whose morality is contrasted with that of "slave" morality in the *Genealogy* and *Beyond Good and Evil*. The conquering master more freely gratifies instinct and affirms himself, his world and his values as good. The conquered slave, unable to express himself freely, creates a negating, resentful, vengeful morality glorifying his own crippled, alienated condition; and he creates a division not between good ("noble") and bad ("contemptible"), but between good ("undangerous") and evil (wicked and powerful—"dangerous-ness").[17] It should be noted though that for Nietzsche, master and slave moralities "at times . . . occur directly alongside each other—even in the same human being, within a *single* soul."[18]

One certainly might wonder about the extent to which Freud read Nietzsche or how carefully he read him given this and other misunderstandings. On the other hand, many of Nietzsche's readers failed to understand various aspects of his thought. Also, we will see that in his essay on Michelangelo's *Moses*, Freud may have demonstrated much greater understanding of the overman. Freud may have held different and conflicting notions of the overman (perhaps even reflecting conflict within).

It would seem, given the language of this May 31, 1897, letter and "Draft N," that Freud probably had at least some familiarity with *On the Genealogy of Morals*. (Another letter, to be discussed below, supports this conclusion.) It is of interest that with Freud very likely being aware of some of Nietzsche's ideas at this time, he wrote to Fliess on May 16 of starting work on his dream book and happily finding that no one knows that dreams are not nonsense.[19] Yet during this period of "momentous change" and "major achievements," including a growing emphasis on the importance of wish fulfillment in symptoms and dreams, Nietzsche would seem to be a presence for Freud; and Nietzsche clearly knew that dreams were not nonsense.

Before moving on to a discussion of the November 14 letter, mention can briefly be made of a possible allusion to Nietzsche in a letter of September 21, 1897. Having in mind his abandonment of the seduction theory (the idea that an actual seduction of the child was the key etiological factor in the development of neurosis), Freud reflects that "in this collapse of everything valuable, the psychological alone has remained untouched. The dream [book] stands entirely secure and my beginnings of the metapsychological work have only grown in my estimation."[20] Jones[21] translates the opening phrase of this passage as "in the collapse of all values" and in a footnote states that it is a paraphrase from Nietzsche. Nietzsche did write of a collapse of all values or, rather, a transvaluation and revaluation of values.[22] Freud does use the term "transvaluation of all psychical values" in *The Interpretation of Dreams*[23] and in *On Dreams*[24] in discussing the transformation that takes place between the material of the latent dream-thoughts and the manifest dream content. In any event, whether a reference to Nietzsche or not, there is nothing else in this letter that has any particular relationship to Nietzsche. It is in the next month, on October 15 (the date of Nietzsche's birth), that Freud announced to Fliess his discovery of universal oedipal impulses.[25]

In the letter of November 14, 1897, Freud states: "I gave birth to a new piece of knowledge. Not entirely new, to tell the truth; it has repeatedly shown itself and withdrawn again."[26] At the end of this passage Freud placed an asterisk and wrote below: "Only tall fellows for Sa Majesté le Roi de Prusse."[27] In an editor's footnote Masson writes: "Freud is referring to the Potsdam guard under Friedrich Wilhelm I, which was recruited wholly from giants."[28] A reference to a "Friederich Wilhelm," a very common name, might have some significance given the content of the letter that follows. Freud writes of the relationship between repression and "the changed part played by sensations of smell: upright walking, nose raised from the ground, at the same time a number of formerly interesting sensations attached to the earth becoming repulsive . . . He turns up his nose=he regards himself as something particularly noble."[29] Later in the letter Freud writes that "in the same manner as we turn away our sense organ (the head and nose) in disgust, the preconscious and the sense of consciousness turn away from the memory. This is *repression*."[30]

Keeping in mind our previous discussion of *On the Genealogy of Morals*, consider the following passage from the second essay:

> On his way to becoming an "angel" . . . man has evolved that queasy stomach and coated tongue through which not only the joy and innocence of the animal but life itself has become repugnant to him—so that he sometimes holds his nose in his own presence and . . . disapprovingly catalogues his own repellent aspects . . . hideous stink, secretion of saliva, urine, and filth.[31] [At a later point we will note Binion's commentary on the influence of this passage on a paper of Andreas-Salomé which Young-Bruehl suggests influenced Freud's paper, "On Transformations of Instinct as Exemplified in Anal Eroticism."[32]]

The context of this passage includes the discussion, a few pages earlier, of "active forgetfulness, which is like a doorkeeper" and the "apparatus of repression."[33] Becoming "noble" or an "angel" for man involves the turning away from, the repressing of, holding one's nose in the presence of, one's "hideous stink"; so, Freud concludes, consciousness turns away from, represses, its hideously stinking memories.

This letter and the May letters suggest the possibility that at some time Freud became familiar with ideas expressed in *On the Genealogy of Morals*. These letters reflect the beginnings of Freud's anthropological explorations,[34] and although Freud was familiar with the writings of a number of anthropologists,[35] he is writing in terms close to Nietzsche of the relationship between the growth of civilization and the suppression of instincts. There is also his early use of the term "sublimation."

There is a passage in a letter of August 31, 1898, which also raises a relevant issue: "I found the substance of my insights [in regard to psychology] stated quite clearly in Lipps, perhaps rather more so than I would like."[36] Freud was reading *Fundamentals of the Life of the Soul*[37] by the German philosopher and psychologist Theodore Lipps (1851–1914). What is particularly interesting in the light of this study is that here as elsewhere Freud acknowledges reading authors who explore ideas similar to his own. For example, in the literary world there is the figure of Arthur Schnitzler (1862–1931) who was already receiving recognition by the late 1890s. Freud was greatly impressed by Schnitzler's psychoanalytic-like insights into mental functioning and human relationships. Freud even referred to Schnitzler as his double. Freud also acknowledged the contributions of certain anthropologists and of authors who demonstrated some understanding of the fact of and importance of childhood sexuality,[38] although he would also stress the solitary nature of his own journey and conquests (as he did in his comparison of himself to Einstein[39]).

It appears that Nietzsche has been particularly singled out for avoidance in the attempt to preserve autonomy of thought and as someone to be seen as having no influence whatsoever upon him. It is of interest that as Freud is discussing his literature review for *The Interpretation of Dreams* in the letter of August 6, 1899, he writes, in the spirit of his May 16, 1897, comment, of "the dark forest of authors (who do not see the trees), hopelessly lost on wrong tracks."[40] Given Nietzsche's popularity and the nature of his psychological and anthropological investigations, one has to wonder about how Freud regarded Nietzsche during this period, particularly since there are a number of important references in Nietzsche's works to dreams. Nietzsche had written on dreams as far back as his first major work, *The Birth of Tragedy*, which Freud very possibly read as a university student. (If he didn't read it, he definitely did hear it being discussed all around him. Also, if he read only the first few pages, he would have read comments on dreams. This last point is also true of *Human, All Too Human*.) Whether or not Freud had any idea as to what he might find in Nietzsche pertaining specifically to dreams, there can be no doubt that he knew he would find material pertaining to the nature of the instincts, repression, conscience, unconscious mental functioning and so on.

It may have been the case that Freud avoided actually reading Nietzsche in the late 1890s or at certain points during the late 1890s. However, he would have had to have had some contact with his ideas given the popularity of Nietzsche's writings, and as has been argued, two of his letters of this period do suggest a familiarity with at least segments of *On the Genealogy of Morals*. It should also be kept in mind that at the 1908 meeting of the Vienna Psychoanalytic Society in which *On the Genealogy of Morals* was discussed, while Freud states that he does not know Nietzsche's work and has not been influenced by him, he does not go so far as to say he hasn't read him at all. What he says, according to the minutes, is that "occasional attempts at reading it were smothered by an excess of interest."[41] As any reader of Nietzsche is aware, while certain of his passages require a reading of extended sections or the entire work in question (and more) for a comprehensive understanding, there are many sections of two or three pages, or even less, that include groundbreaking explorations. It would seem that for Freud to have been overwhelmed by an excess of interest, he would have had to have read enough to allow for such an experience to unfold. This relates to Freud's ongoing claim to have avoided Nietzsche due to how close his ideas were to psychoanalysis. As he wrote later in life: "It was plain that I would find insights in him very similar to psychoanalytic ones."[42] What exactly did Freud know of Nietzsche's work to make such a conclusion this plain? And again we can ask, Why does Freud, while regarding Nietzsche as one of the few persons he considers great, never acknowledge reading any specific work of Nietzsche, not to speak of revealing any thoughts, feelings, or opinions regarding anything he read?

As mentioned earlier, in a letter of February 1, 1900, in a gloomy mood over the reception of *The Interpretation of Dreams*, Freud describes himself to Fliess as "not a thinker . . . but a conquistador."[43] Towards the end of the letter he mentions looking to another conquistador for inspiration at this time: "I have just acquired Nietzsche, in whom I hope to find words for much that remains mute in me, but have not opened him yet. Too lazy for the time being."[44] It is not clear just what work or works Freud had acquired or if it was an edition of the collected works. The Freud library contained later (1920s) editions of *The Antichrist* in English and the collected works but no earlier editions of Nietzsche's works.[45] Let us note that Freud has acquired Nietzsche, has thought of looking to Nietzsche for help. Freud feels that there is much that is mute in him, and he looks to Nietzsche for the very words that are mute in himself. He looks to Nietzsche to provide the words (and perhaps something more) for what will not, at this difficult time, come of itself. We may never know if at this time Freud found words (or, if he did, what they were) that spoke to him and helped him to speak. And we might ask, What kind of special effort would it have been to read Nietzsche and in relation to which Freud felt lazy?

While we do not know what Freud read after acquiring Nietzsche, it might be that his interest in him continued. The next month, in a letter of March 23, 1900, Freud wrote to Fliess again of his disappointment at the reception of his book: "I explain this by telling myself that I am fifteen to twenty years ahead of my time. Then, of course, the usual qualms associated with forming a judgment about oneself set in."[46] He states, "No one can help me in the least with what oppresses me; it is my cross."[47] (As we will see, an identification with Christ may not have been all that alien to Freud.) Later in the letter Freud mentions something else: "Last week we heard a lecture by G. Brandes on reading. The topic was nothing special . . . the man was refreshing . . . Martha, in whom ambition is a very important trait, persuaded me to send a copy of the dream book to his hotel."[48] We know from Freud himself that when we are particularly told that something is nothing special without revealing what that something is, we should take notice. Georg Brandes was a Danish author, a highly regarded literary critic who was also the leading exponent of Nietzsche's work outside of the German-speaking world. Although Freud does not mention the topic of the lecture, there is a good chance that aspects of Nietzsche's work were discussed. In any event, by this time Brandes' name was intimately linked with that of Nietzsche, and as early as 1889 he referred to Nietzsche as "the most interesting writer in German literature at the present time."[49] He had corresponded with

Nietzsche and was writing articles on his work by the late 1880s. He also knew Andreas-Salomé and in 1882 dedicated a book to her.[50] Freud not only attended the lecture, but (mentioning Martha's ambition rather than his own) sent a copy of his dream book to Brandes. Could Freud have hoped that the man who was an exponent of the work of Nietzsche (Nietzsche being regarded by himself and others as ahead of his time) would become an exponent of his own work? Perhaps Freud, with his great concerns about being appreciated, particularly at this time, hoped for appreciation from Nietzsche's interpreter and advocate.

Nietzsche died a few months later, on August 25. Freud would have been aware of commentary in the press, such as the Viennese literary figure Karl Kraus in his magazine *Die Fackel* (The Torch) attacking the popular newspaper *Neu Freie Presse* for belittling Nietzsche's reputation in its obituary. Kraus held Nietzsche in the highest regard.[51] Freud was an appreciative reader of *Die Fackel* until Kraus began attacking psychoanalysis. (We still await research on the possible influence on Freud of newspaper articles, journal articles, book reviews and the like about Nietzsche that he, Freud, may have read throughout his adult life.) Just after Nietzsche's death (a few months after Freud had acquired Nietzsche's work, attended Brandes' lecture and sent him his dream book), Brandes wrote: "During those very years in which he lived on in the night of insanity, his name has acquired a lustre unsurpassed by any contemporary reputation."[52] Brandes' words here are of importance regarding our appreciation of the enormous impact of Nietzsche from 1890 on into the twentieth century.

## NIETZSCHE AND FREUD ON DREAMS

Regarding *The Interpretation of Dreams*, we can call attention to a few links to Nietzsche. As mentioned, Freud refers to Nietzsche's notion of a transvaluation of values, applying it to psychical values, a "'transvaluation of all psychical values,'"[53] as the dream work transforms dream thoughts into manifest content. Freud may have also responded to the notion of a revaluation of values in the sense that "the royal road to a knowledge of the unconscious activities of the mind,"[54] the deepest level of psychic reality, is found here not in the study of normal waking consciousness, but in the study of dreams. As noted, Nietzsche had written as early as *The Birth of Tragedy* that contrary to usual assumptions, dreaming states rather than waking states are more important "in relation to that mysterious ground of our being of which we are the phenomena."[55]

Nietzsche also wrote that "the dream is a relaxation for the brain which has had enough of the strenuous demands in the way of thinking such as are imposed by our culture during the day."[56] Also: "Nights the higher intellect sleeps, the lower steps into consciousness (dream)."[57] In other words, there is a relaxation that would ease suppression, repression or censorship (recall that in the *Genealogy* Nietzsche refers to the "doorkeeper") and allow greater fantasied gratifications that are not so readily allowed during the day under the demands of culture. Freud writes that "in waking life the suppressed material in the mind is prevented from finding expression,"[58] and that censorship "relaxes its activities during the night, allows the suppressed impulses in the Ucs. to find expression."[59] As regards the expressions of or in dreams, Nietzsche states that what "we do not know or feel precisely while awake . . . the dream informs us of without any ambiguity,"[60] and that in dreams "there is nothing unimportant or superfluous."[61] Freud writes that "the most trivial elements of a dream are indispensable to its interpretation."[62]

Nietzsche also wrote of how the dream accounts for or integrates impinging internal and external events:

> In sleep our nervous system is continually agitated by a multiplicity of inner events . . . the dream is the *seeking and positing of the causes* of this excitement of the sensibilities, that is to say the supposed causes . . . Everyone knows from experience how quickly a dreamer entwines with his dream a sound that strongly impinges upon him from without, the ringing of bells or the firing of cannon, for example.[63]

Golumb, citing this passage, points out that "Freud's analyses concur with and confirm Nietzsche's view that the dreamer attempts to create a rational causal framework for external stimuli [and 'inner events'] by incorporating them into the narrative of the dream."[64] Golumb also points out that Freud, like Nietzsche, specifically utilizes the example of the "pealing of bells" in illustrating how a potential interruption was interwoven into the dream content.[65] Freud's concepts of condensation (an element from the dream content representing a number of dream thoughts[66]) and displacement (essential elements of the dream thoughts, charged with intense interest, having their place taken in the dream content by elements of small value in the dream thoughts[67]) may have been, as Golumb[68] suggests, approached by Nietzsche in his comment that the dream "continually confuses one thing with another on the basis of the most fleeting similarities."[69] It should be noted, though, that the context of this particular passage is not the dream work's utilization of these similarities to express a latent dream thought but our failure in dreams to "recognize correctly" and, rather, to "erroneously [suppose] one thing to be the same as another," which is the "ground of the false conclusions of which we are guilty in dreams." However, in this passage Nietzsche does relate dream processes to the mythologies and hallucinations of primitive man, and though he characterizes these processes as "confused and capricious," he writes that "in sleep and dreams we repeat once again the curriculum of earlier mankind."[70] It may be that it was after the first volume of *Human, All Too Human* was written that Nietzsche gained a clearer idea as to our dreams expressing specific personal thoughts, feelings and wishes that "we do not know or feel precisely while awake,"[71] including such "abominable" wishes as sexually desiring our parents.[72] It is one thing to relate the dream to the ground of our being or to more primitive and irrational forces linked (in Nietzsche's view) to the mind of primitive man; it is another thing, though related, to connect dreams to specific and personal unacceptable unconscious thoughts, feelings and wishes.[73]

In regard to Freud's idea of drive-related wish as the instigating force of dreams, let us recall Nietzsche's idea that "our *dreams* . . . *compensate* to some extent for the chance absence of 'nourishment' [or gratification of the drives] during the day . . . These inventions . . . give scope and discharge to our drives."[74]

Regarding the language of dreams, Nietzsche states that "our dreams are . . . chains of symbolic scenes and images in place of the language of poetic narration."[75] Dreams operate not according to more rational secondary process rules but according to the symbolic language that functions like poetic narration. For Freud primary process is characteristic of unconscious processes in the service of "securing free discharge of excitations" whereas the secondary process involves the capacity to inhibit discharge.[76] The disguised compromise formations in dreams are a result of the dream work contending with unconscious, repressed wishes and the repressing or censoring forces. The dream work, operating according to the primary process and utilizing symbolization, displacement, condensation, etc., does its work under conditions in which censorship is relaxed but instinctual (wishful) and repressing forces contend with one another. There is one system constructing "the wish which is expressed by the dream, while the other exercises a censorship upon the dream-wish and, by the use of that censorship, forcibly brings about a distortion of the expression of the wish."[77] The dream portrays a disguised wish fulfillment.

Nietzsche distinguishes between two types of mental processes and is aware, as we have seen, of the conflict between unconscious instinctual impulses or wishes and inhibiting or repressing forces. He even writes that

the human qualities of which we are conscious . . . are subject to altogether different laws of development than are those qualities which we know either badly or not at all and which also conceal themselves . . . [these "invisible" qualities] also follow their own course—probably, a wholly different course; and they probably have lines, subtleties, and sculptures that might give pleasure to a god with a divine microscope.[78] [At later points we will also see that ideas pertaining to Freud's pleasure principle and notions of bound and unbound energy[79] are related to ideas of Nietzsche.]

However, Nietzsche does not write of the manifest content of dreams as compromise formations in the manner of Freud. It would seem that Nietzsche believes the expressions of dreams are in some ways and at some times less disguised and distorted than does Freud. (It would also appear that Nietzsche's ideas are compatible with those of the contemporary dream researcher J. Allen Hobson who writes that "most dreams are neither obscure nor bowdlerized . . . They contain meaningful, undisguised, highly conflictual impulses worthy of note by the dreamer and any interpretative assistant."[80])

We have also seen that Nietzsche refers to exactly the same passage that Freud refers to in *Oedipus Rex* regarding men dreaming of having sex with their mothers. Nietzsche chides us with our willingness "to assume responsibility for everything! Except, that is, for your dreams! What miserable weakness, what lack of consistent courage! Nothing is *more* your own than your dreams! Nothing *more* your own work [*dream work*]! Content, form, duration, performer, spectator—in these comedies you are all of this yourself!"[81] Not only the unconscious wish, but the entire dream work is the "responsibility" of the individual. For Nietzsche the issue is not so much deciphering disguised wishes and defenses against them (although his emphasis on competing mental forces would include this), but taking seriously, as one's own, taking responsibility for, abominable wishes, "abominable dreams" in which wishes not usually in awareness find expression, often quite directly. Of course one may have to learn how to interpret "symbolic scenes and images" which operate according to mental processes analagous to "the language of poetic narration," but this does not *necessarily* imply always interpreting dream images as compromise formations in the manner of Freud with his emphasis on the need to understand censorship and distortion of the latent dream wish. (We can also note, with Grünbaum, that Freud's interpretation of his famous dream of "Irma's Injection"[82] does not greatly rely upon dynamically repressed wishes [not to mention dynamically repressed infantile wishes] as the motivating or instigating forces of the dream. Before he had the dream, Freud was apparently quite conscious of events and his reactions that would prove pertinent to an understanding of the dream. As Grünbaum points out, Freud hadn't dynamically repressed these thoughts and feelings; and this also makes it difficult to see how essential free association could have been for at least *this level* of understanding of the dream.[83])

We can also recall that Nietzsche connected the expressions of dreams (and insanity and outbursts of passion) with a man rediscovering "his own and mankind's prehistory."[84] In these states one's "memory goes sufficiently far back" to such "primal experiences" of the individual and mankind. Our "civilized condition evolves out of a forgetting [repressing] of these primal experiences." In dreams we have access to forgotten "primal experiences" of our own and mankind, the forgetting of which is necessary for the individual and collective evolving of our "civilized condition." For Freud our development into civilized human beings involves (for males) our "detaching our sexual impulses from our mothers and in forgetting our jealousy of our fathers,"[85] primal experiences to which we may gain access in dreams. In a later (1919) edition of *The Interpretation of Dreams,* Freud will add: "We can guess how much to the point is Nietzsche's assertion that in dreams 'some primaeval relic of humanity is at work which we can now scarcely reach any longer by a direct path.'"[86] This is not an exact quotation, and Freud would seem to be referring to either *Human, All Too Human* (1, sec. 13) or *Daybreak* (sec. 312), although in neither passage does Nietzsche write of there being no direct path to "some primaeval relic of humanity." Nietzsche also believed (as did others, including Darwin) that "feelings belonging to the first stages of life are . . . closer to those of earlier times than to those of the present century."[87]

If one were to summarize Nietzsche's theory of dreams, one might state that during sleep internal (bodily) and external stimuli impinge upon the dreamer who interprets them and weaves them into a "text." In important ways this text operates according to different laws than does typical waking consciousness. The reason dreams differ from night to night even though the internal and external stimuli may be similar, is that the "prompter of the reasoning faculty" differs from night to night, and this prompter is "a different *drive* [that] wanted to gratify itself, to be active, to exercise itself, to refresh itself, to discharge itself." Of particular importance is a drive that has been aroused but not allowed discharge while the person was awake during the day. For Nietzsche, "the meaning and value of our *dreams* is precisely to *compensate* to some extent for the chance absence of 'nourishment' during the day."[88] These drives also include "abominable" wishes, such as having sex with one's parent as well as other strong and unacceptable reactions to other people. The dream also takes us back to states of mind characteristic of our individual childhood and the childhood of humankind. Dreams are also a source of the belief in "a second real world" and souls and gods.

However, even when we are awake, our drives are operative, interpreting internal and external stimuli, and "our moral judgments and evaluations too are only images and fantasies based on a physiological process unknown to us . . . all our so-called consciousness is a more or less fantastic commentary on an unknown, perhaps unknowable, but felt text."[89] Even during waking life we interpret internal and external stimuli in terms related to those dri- ves assuming prominence for us. But for Nietzsche, unlike Freud, this realm of the drives and instinctive, repressed unconscious men- tal processes does not operate only according to "laws of develop- ment" and principles that are unrelated to reality and adaptation.

Although Nietzsche never gave dreams anything like the at- tention and analysis given by Freud, he certainly was not one of "the dark forest of authors (who do not see the trees), hopelessly lost on wrong tracks."[90] Yet here, where he is reviewing the litera- ture on dreams, as well as throughout his life, Freud will not, in specific and detailed terms, discuss Nietzsche's ideas as they per- tain to psychoanalysis, just as he will never state exactly when he read or did not read Nietzsche or what he did or did not read. We may never know which of Nietzsche's passages on dreams Freud may have read or heard of or read of as he was working on *The Interpretation of Dreams*. But we can recall that "Draft N" of Freud's May 31, 1897, letter to Fliess includes reference to the overman, contrasting this figure with the saintly or holy which is (as is civilization) connected to instinctual renunciation, particu- larly incest and sexual perversion. Freud also writes that he has a presentiment that he shall "soon uncover the source of moral- ity,"[91] the subject of Nietzsche's *Genealogy*. Earlier in the month he made what may have been his first reference to sublimation,[92] a concept explored and developed by Nietzsche. We have also pointed to possible, perhaps even likely, allusions to Nietzsche in letters of September and November 1897[93] which refer respectively to Nietzsche's notion of a revaluation or transvaluation of all val- ues and Nietzsche's idea of the relationship of our turning our nose away from what disgusts us, our own filth, to our civilized condi- tion, our becoming "angels." Regarding this last point, Freud adds specifically that so too consciousness turns away from memory: "This is *repression*."[94] It is also exactly during this period, with a beginning conceptualization in "Draft N" of May 31 and a more explicit announcement in the letter of October 15[95] that Freud for- mulates the Oedipus complex. Then there is Nietzsche's passage on dreams in which he refers to *Oedipus* and to the exact passage that Freud refers to in *The Interpretation of Dreams*. One author has referred to Nietzsche's ideas as coming "preternaturally close to Freud." (We can note a dictionary definition of preternatural: "1: exceeding what is natural 2: inexplicable by ordinary means."[96]) At a later point we will see that in Freud's remarks in *The Inter-pretation of Dreams* on the distinctiveness of psychoanalysis and his achievements regarding the understanding of the unconscious (his unconscious versus the unconscious of philosophers), Nietz-sche is perhaps made present through his very absence.

These ideas of Nietzsche's on dreams are not merely of inter-est in regard to the ways in which they anticipate Freud. They are very much related to more recent therapeutic approaches to the understanding of dreams. Consider the following passages written by Montagu Ullman, an acknowledged authority in the fields of dream research and dream interpretation or, as he prefers, dream appreciation:

> Wish fulfillment is certainly an aspect of dreams, but in my opinion, is by no means their sole instigator . . . dreaming is a naturally recurring period of partial arousal during sleep, which occurs when our brain is awake enough to give us the opportunity to react to any tension arising out of our recent life experience.[97]
>
> Imagery is a primitive way of apprehending reality . . . we have learned to refine it, use it not to reflect reality directly, but rather the world and our relationship to it metaphori-cally.[98]
>
> We are witnesses to, as well as the participants in, our dreams . . . The dreamer is engaged in fashioning a communi-cation to himself. That the message appears puzzling and strange doesn't negate the fact that it is intended for the dreamer alone.[99]
>
> When we are awake it isn't easy for us to see ourselves with the same honest vision that our dream projects.[100]
>
> We are the witness to, as well as the participants in, our dreams.[101]
>
> Nothing in a dream is trivial.[102]
>
> When read correctly these images tell us who we are in-stead of who we think we are.[103]

Regarding Nietzsche's ideas on dreams, we have just considered the following: Nietzsche values dreaming states over waking states regarding the dream's closeness to the "ground of our being";[104] the dream "informs" us of feelings and thoughts that "we do not know or feel precisely while awake";[105] in dreams "there is nothing unimportant or superfluous";[106] the language of dreams entails "chains of symbolic scenes and images in place of [and akin to] the language of poetic narration";[107] we are responsible for ("nothing *more* your own work") "content, form, duration, performer, spectator—in these comedies you are all of this yourself" (and these comedies include the "abominable");[108] and recent life experiences and tensions, "the absence of 'nourishment' during the day," give rise to these dream inventions which "give scope and discharge to our drives."[109]

Charles Rycroft's book on dreams,[110] which reflects directions in which some analytically oriented therapists have been moving, also presents an approach to understanding and working with dreams that has affinities with Nietzsche (and Ullman), although he states elsewhere that "Hegel and Nietzsche are not in my bones."[111] Consider the following passages:

Dreaming is an imaginative activity and . . . the imagery occurring in dreams is to be understood metaphorically.[112]

The metaphors appearing in dreams tend both to be derived from bodily processes and to refer to them.[113]

In Groddeck's view the It is that by which we are dreamt, it is the agent which sends us messages to which we may or may not listen, which we may or may not understand. It is the impersonal self by which our personal, egotistical self is lived.[114]

I have adopted a position in many ways the opposite of his [Freud's], assuming that imagination is a natural, normal activity of an agent or self, and that dreaming is its sleeping form, while recognizing that conflicts within the imagining self, or between different aspects or parts of the self, will manifest themselves in dreams which can only be understood if one assumes that the dreamer has been in two minds as to whether he wants to understand his dreams—or whether he wants his dream to be understood—and has, therefore, used symbolism to disguise, not reveal, meaning in the way held by Freud to be characteristic of all dreams.[115]

The agent who constructs dreams tends to possess insights into the person's true nature which the recipient, i.e. the person's waking self, is reluctant to acquire.

This hypotheses presupposes that people tend to be, to a greater or lesser extent, out of touch with their whole selves and are, therefore, predisposed to dismiss as meaningless non-sense messages which, if granted meaning, would compel them to alter and widen their conception of themselves.[116]

This active dreamer . . . seems to be part of oneself and yet at the same time more than oneself, to be one's true self and yet impersonal.[117]

I would maintain that while dreaming we may know more than we know while awake and may voice thoughts and wishes that evoke guilt when we awaken.[118]

Much of what Rycroft writes is similar to, implicit in, or at least compatible with what we have seen of Nietzsche on dreams as well as other material which we will consider. Rycroft specifically states that he takes up "a position much nearer Groddeck's [on the nature of the "it" or id] than Freud's."[119] He doesn't mention that Freud was aware of Groddeck's concept of the "it" and understood the term to be derived from Nietzsche. We should note, however, that Nietzsche also writes of even the inference to the "it" as going beyond "the process itself" as a consequence of grammatical habit—that the activity, "thinking," requires an agent.[120]

The self, as in its manifestation in constructing dreams, may be an aspect of our psychic lives that knows things that our waking "I" or ego may not know and may not wish to know, and a relation-ship may be developed between these aspects of our psychic lives in which the latter opens itself creatively to the communications of the former. Zarathustra states: "Behind your thoughts and feelings, my brothers, there stands a mighty ruler, an unknown sage—whose name is self. In your body he dwells; he is your body."[121] However, Nietzsche's self cannot be understood as a replacement for an all-knowing God to whom the "I" or ego appeals for its wisdom, com-mandments, guidance and the like.[122] To open oneself to another as-pect of oneself that is wiser ("an unknown sage") in the sense that new information can be derived from it, does not necessarily entail that this "wiser" component of one's psychic life has God-like knowledge and commandments which if one (one's "I") deciphers and opens to correctly will set one on the straight path. It is true though that when Nietzsche writes of the self as "a mighty ruler and unknown sage" he does open himself to such an interpretation and even to the possibility that this "ruler" is unreachable, unapproachable for the "I." However, as Alan White points out, the context of the passage (Nietzsche/ Zarathustra redeeming the body) and the two sections after "On the Despisers of the Body" make it clear that there are aspects of our psychic selves that interpret the body, that mediate its directives, ideally in ways that do not deny the body but that aid in the body doing "what it would do above all else: to create beyond itself."[123]

Also, the idea of a fully formed, even if unconscious, "mighty ruler" and "unknown sage" as a true self beneath an only apparent surface is at odds with Nietzsche's idea (to which we will return) that there is no one true, stable, enduring self in and of itself to be found once the veil of appearance is removed. And even early in his career Nietzsche wrote sarcastically of "that cleverly discovered well of inspiration, the unconscious."[124] There is, though, a tension in Nietzsche between the notion of bodily based drives pressing for discharge (which can, among other things, be sublimated) and a more organized bodily based self which may be "an unknown sage" and in relation to which the "I" may open to potential communications in the manner discussed by Rycroft. For Freud there is no such conception of self and the dream is not produced with the intention of being understood.[125]

Nietzsche explored the ideas of psychic energy and drives pressing for discharge. His discussions of sublimation typically imply an understanding of drives in just such a sense as does his idea that dreams provide for discharge of drives.[126] However, he did not relegate all that is derived from instinct and the body to this realm. While for Nietzsche there is no stable, enduring true self awaiting discovery and liberation, the body and the self (in the broadest sense of the term, including what is unconscious and may be at work in dreams as Rycroft describes it) may offer up potential communication and direction to the "I" or ego. However, as we will also see, at times Nietzsche describes the "I" or ego as having very little, if any, idea as to how it is being lived by the "it."[127]

Let us also note that Nietzsche commented on self-observation in dreams: "It is a dream, I will dream on."[128] "Even when this dream reality is most intense, we still have glimmering through it, the sensation that it is *mere appearance*: at least this is my experience."[129] A page and a half before he writes of "a transvaluation of all psychical values"[130] in *The Interpretation of Dreams*, Freud writes of "the mental agency which [during the dreaming state] remains awake . . . this self-observing agency . . . may be particularly prominent in philosophical minds."[131]

Finally, with all of the emphasis on metaphor-like activity in dreams by authors such as Ullman and Rycroft, let us note that Nietzsche writes of the place of metaphor in myth, art, and the dream. In an early paper that Nietzsche never published, he writes of myth, art, and the dream being rooted in "that drive to form metaphors, that fundamental desire in man" which operates according to principles other than the "rigidly regular web of concepts" of waking reality. However, even

> the wide awake person is certain that he is awake only because of the rigidly regular web of concepts, and so he sometimes comes to believe that he is dreaming when at times that web of concepts is torn apart by art . . . The waking day of a mythically excited nation . . . is, by the constant action of marvels, indeed more like a dream than like the day of the scientifically sober thinker . . . then at any moment, as in a dream, anything is possible.[132] [Oliver Sacks, commenting on the research of Rodolfo Llinàs on waking and dreaming brain states, suggests that "waking consciousness is dreaming—but dreaming constrained by external reality."[133]]

Nietzsche, like Freud, describes two types of mental processes, one which "binds [man's] life to reason and its concepts in order not to be swept away by the current and to lose himself," the other, pertaining to the worlds of myth, art and the dream, "constantly showing the desire to shape the existing world of the wideawake person to be variegatedly irregular and disinterestedly incoherent, exciting and eternally new, as is the world of dreams." Art may function as a "middle sphere" and "middle faculty" (transitional sphere and faculty?) between a more primitive "metaphor-world" of impressions and the forms of uniform abstract concepts.[134]

# Chapter 6

## "Non Vixit"

*My brilliant friend P., whose whole life had been devoted to science . . . my friend P., who was very greatly my superior.*
—Freud, *The Interpretation of Dreams*

A few days after October 16, 1898, Freud had the following dream:

My friend Fl. [Fliess] had come to Vienna unobtrusively in July. I met him in the street in conversation with my (deceased) friend P., and went with them to some place where they sat opposite each other as though they were at a small table. I sat in front at its narrow end. Fl. spoke about his sister and said that in three quarters of an hour she was dead, and added some such words as "that was the threshold." As P. failed to understand him, Fl. turned to me and asked me how much I had told P. about his affairs. Whereupon, overcome by strange emotions, I tried to explain to Fl. that P. (could not understand anything at all, of course, because he) was not alive. But what I actually said—and I myself noticed the mistake—was, "Non Vixit." I then gave P. a piercing look. Under my gaze he turned pale; his form grew indistinct and his eyes a sickly blue—and finally he melted away. I was highly delighted at this and I now realized that Ernst Fleischl, too, had been no more than an apparition, a "revenant" ["ghost"—literally, "one who returns"]; and it seemed to me quite possible that people of that kind only existed as long as one liked and could be got rid of if someone else wished it[1] (editor's brackets).

Both Grinstein and Anzieu[2] present extended analyses of this dream, and the reader is referred to these excellent accounts for a comprehensive understanding of various possible interpretations of the dream. However, neither of these authors considers early background information on the relationship between Freud and Paneth, particularly as their relationship had a connection to Nietzsche.

From background material and associations presented by Freud and material presented by Grinstein and Anzieu, we learn of some of the facts and issues which would appear to be pertinent to an understanding of the dream.

Fliess had been ill, had had an operation, and was not doing well. Fliess' in-laws had asked Freud not to discuss the former's illness with anyone, and Freud was offended by what he felt was the implication that he might not have done so if not asked. Associations led Freud back to another incident in which confidentiality was an issue and involved another Joseph, which we know was Joseph Breuer.[3] Fliess' wife had recently given birth to a long-awaited child whom the couple named Pauline. Pauline was the name of Fliess' sister who had died in childhood. Pauline was also the name of Freud's niece (a year younger than Freud) with whom he had played along with his nephew John (a year older than Freud). They played together in early childhood in Freiberg before Freud's move first to Leipzig at about (or shortly before) the age of three and then soon afterwards to Vienna. There was some kind of aggressive and/or sexual play the boys perpetrated upon Pauline.[4] (Later in life there was some consideration given in Freud's family to the possibility of Freud and Pauline marrying.[5]) Also, at around the time of the dream, a niece was born to Freud.[6]

A few days before the dream, on October 16, Freud had attended a memorial for the scientist Ernst Fleischl (who figures in an earlier dream of the same evening) in the cloisters of the university. Fleischl was an assistant in Brücke's lab, the position not available to Freud in 1882, this leading to Freud's leaving the lab. Freud had later prescribed, with disastrous consequences, cocaine for Fleischl in an attempt to break a morphine addiction that had arisen in Fleischl's attempt to cope with great pain due to an injury. (Freud had been exploring cocaine's potential as an anesthetic.) While at the memorial, Freud had also seen the Brücke memorial. He thought of Joseph Paneth ("P."), his brilliant friend, whose early death had cut short his scientific career and prevented his attaining the achievements which would have resulted in his having his own memorial. It will be remembered that it was Paneth who replaced Freud in Brücke's lab in 1882 and who eventually, in 1889, did receive the promotion to assistant to Brücke that was not possible earlier for Freud. He died of tuberculosis a year after the promotion. In Freud's earlier, financially difficult years, Paneth had given him money. Freud mentions the ambivalent feelings towards Paneth expressed in the dream; on the one hand affection and admiration, the desire to erect a memorial for him, while at the same time annihilating him with a piercing look, the image Freud describes as the central one of the dream.

Freud mentions the Kaiser Joseph Memorial in the Imperial Palace, the source of the words "Non Vixit." (A number of Josephs, including the biblical one, are implicated in the dream.) The Latin inscription on it was remembered by Freud as reading: "Saluti patriae vixit non diu sed totus"[7] (For the well-being of his country he lived not long but wholly). Freud points to the dream, on the face of it, requiring "Non Vivit" (he is no longer alive) rather than "Non Vixit" (he did not live).

Freud's associations take him to themes of competition, rivalry (including relating his hostile feelings to Paneth to his relationship with his nephew John) and concerns about plagiarism. Grinstein and Anzieu point out that concerns about plagiarism were also expressed a few weeks earlier in the dream of "The Three Fates" and possibly related to Fliess' ideas on bisexuality.[8] We can add that it was around this time that Freud had been finding ideas similar to his own in the work of Theodore Lipps.[9]

Freud emphasizes the theme of his having survived a number of people connected with the dream. They are revenants about whom he had ambivalent feelings and towards whom at times he might wish to direct an annihilating glance to get rid of them easily, with a mere wish, and it be as if they had never existed. He writes of being delighted to survive (although there is also guilt and fear of punishment) and, as he puts it, to be "left in possession of the field."[10] Issues of surviving others are also felt to relate to his having survived his younger brother, Julius, who died at six months of age. Julius was about a year and a half younger than Freud as was Paneth.

In relation to Paneth, Freud mentions that he, Paneth, had expressed to Freud his impatience for promotion in Brücke's lab and that the implication was that death wishes towards those holding the desired positions, Flieschl being one of them, were involved. Anzieu suggests that this comment of Freud's is a disguise for Freud's own wishes.[11] Anzieu also suggests that the person Freud truly wishes to be annihilating in the dream is Fliess, the object of Freud's concerns around plagiarism; Fliess is seriously ill, and if he dies (like Flieschl, Paneth, and Julius), Freud will be happy to have survived him.[12]

Grinstein and Anzieu discuss other pertinent matters, including literary works possibly alluded to, which are helpful in considering various possible interpretations of the dream. Here consideration will be given to matters not explored by either of these authors or Freud himself.

Of central importance is the history of the relationship between Freud and Paneth, including their connection with Nietzsche, a figure Freud highly regarded and about whom he had even more to be concerned than Fliess as regards "who got there first" or who is "left in possession of the field," themes expressed in the dream. When we consider that Freud had read Nietzsche, had a high regard for him, that Nietzsche was so prominent a figure in the late 1890s, and that Freud may have been reading Nietzsche the year before, issues of rivalry and plagiarism could easily include implications concerning Nietzsche. This line of thought also brings us to what reasons Freud may have had for such intense hostility towards Paneth in the dream. Freud states that there is "little basis in reality for my hostility to my friend P."[13] He then goes on to state that Paneth "was very greatly my superior and for that reason was well fitted to appear as a new edition of my early playmate. This hostility must therefore certainly have gone back to my complicated childhood relations to John."[14] Freud describes associations and fantasies that lead to John.[15]

Freud also relates the hostility towards Paneth to "the dream punish(ing) my friend, and not me, for this callous wish"[16] of impatience at desired promotion at Brücke's lab and wanting others out of the way. Freud writes: "As he was guilty of an evil wish . . . I annihilated him."[17] This wish of Paneth's in and of itself would hardly account for such intense hostility, and, as Anzieu mentions, it is Freud's ambitious desires that are relevant here.[18]

Freud also mentions the piercing look of the revered Brücke, particularly the look when angry as he was when he confronted Freud one morning regarding Freud's lateness.[19] Freud states that in the dream he, Freud, is in the position of Brücke in being the one to cast the piercing, annihilating look, and also that the other person being a "Joseph" reflects hostile feelings towards another person with that same name (Joseph Breuer).

However, along with all that Paneth may represent, all the figures that may lay behind him, consider a "basis in reality" for Freud directing such hostile feelings towards him.[20]

Freud had left Brücke's lab when it became clear he wasn't going to get the promotion he desired. Paneth replaced him and eventually did get the promotion, only to die a year later. Keeping in mind that Freud wrote of his years in the lab in the most positive terms,[21] it would seem likely that he felt anger (as well as other feelings) towards both Brücke and Paneth, the former for not finding a way to keep him at the lab, and the latter for replacing him with the revered Brücke and eventually receiving the promotion.

We can also mention another revered figure connected to both Freud and Paneth. Freud had the highest regard for his childhood religious instructor, Samuel Hammerschlag. Paneth had lived with the Hammerschlags after his parents' death and later married their niece, Sophie Schwab. (In January 1884, when Paneth was writing to him of Nietzsche, Freud wrote to Martha of his preference for the Hammerschlag family over the Schwabs.[22] In May of 1884 he wrote to Martha mocking the religious ritual of the wedding of Paneth and Sophie Schwab.[23])

Of course, there is another figure for whom Freud had high regard and with whom Paneth was also able to have a relationship. Paneth would be meeting with Nietzsche a year and a half after he had replaced Freud in Brücke's lab. As Freud is at work on *The Interpretation of Dreams* and as concerns about rivalry, originality and plagiarism occupy his mind, it is reasonable to raise the possibility of aggressive and envious feelings towards Paneth and Nietzsche and concerns about who told what to whom about the other's affairs (ideas), who got there first and who was in possession of the field. Paneth, if he were a revenant and returned (which he did when Freud was at the memorial), would be someone who knew a great deal, perhaps the person who knew most, about Freud's study of and readings in philosophy, including the work of Nietzsche. Recall that during their university years Freud wrote to his friend Silberstein at one point of having only Paneth with whom to share his philosophical ideas.[24] Paneth was intensely involved with Nietzsche's work, and during his meetings with Nietzsche over the three months from December 1883 to March 1884 he had written a great deal about Nietzsche to Freud. Apparently, the letters were among the correspondence and other writings that Freud destroyed in 1885. (One wonders if Freud wrote to Paneth and, if so, whether or not any letters may have survived.) If Paneth returned, what might he know and reveal about what Freud owed to Nietzsche?[25] (As far as I know, it was not until near the end of his life that Freud mentioned Paneth's letters and his meetings with Nietzsche. From published correspondence there is, as far as I know, no indication that Freud wrote to anyone of the Paneth-Nietzsche meetings during the period Paneth was writing to him.)

It certainly appears that Fliess talking about his sister had its most direct links to his new child, his sister who died in childhood, Freud's niece and playmate, and the meaning of all of this in regard to Freud's relationship to Fliess. This would include Freud's feelings regarding Fliess' child. This part of the dream may have no relationship to Nietzsche. However, there is also the fact that, as was well known, Nietzsche was being cared for by his sister with whom he had had a close but complex and ambivalent relationship that included feelings of rage towards her. Or it might not be the sister but Nietzsche who might be dead "in three quarters of an hour," particularly since in the summer of 1898 he had had a stroke and his condition had deteriorated.[26] Nietzsche too might soon be gone. And we can note that Nietzsche was so prominent a figure in the late 1890s that German newspapers were reporting everything they could simply about his being moved from Naumberg to Weimar (1897[27]) and that according to Hayman, his name "was constantly appearing in the papers."[28]

It is also possible that Nietzsche may be linked to Brücke in that he was noted for his expressive, intense eyes which were evident in photographs. (In this regard, perhaps Freud is not only identifying with Brücke, but also with Nietzsche.) In his early teens, students around Nietzsche sometimes found his presence inhibiting, and according to one boy, "He looked at you in a way that made the words stick in your throat."[29] When he taught at Basel, he was described as giving the impression of staring.[30] One person who saw Nietzsche two years before his death commented: "I felt as if I were looking into the eyes of the Sphinx."[31] In his letters, Paneth had commented on Nietzsche's deep-set eyes as well as his vision problems. We might also wonder if Freud had seen the photograph of Nietzsche that Nietzsche had given Paneth. Freud and Paneth certainly met very shortly after Paneth's meeting with Nietzsche.[32] Andreas-Salomé had written that Nietzsche's "eyes truly betrayed him . . . They looked . . . like guardians of treasures and unspoken secrets which no trespassers should glimpse."[33] According to Mandel, Mathilde Trampedach—to whom Nietzsche had proposed marriage years before he had met Andreas-Salomé— "spoke of feeling the probing gaze of Nietzsche's deep eyes."[34]

Perhaps when he began work in earnest on *The Interpretation of Dreams* in February 1898, or even earlier, Freud immersed himself in his work and psychologically distanced himself from certain other material and influences as he pursued efforts towards his monumental scientific work, to be as respectable and respected as a work of science as any contribution from the natural sciences. He may have particularly wished to distance himself from philosophy as he was pursuing science and was desirous of the work being received and accepted as such. Nietzsche might have been one of the early influences that Freud would have wanted to leave behind. Freud may have repressed a good deal of what he knew of Nietzsche (or repressed that some things he knew derived from Nietzsche), such repression perhaps not being as difficult as it might seem when one considers the enormous range of knowledge and influences that Freud absorbed as well as the goals he was pursuing. Also, during this time Nietzsche's depth psychology and anthropological explorations were not the major areas of Nietzsche's work under discussion. Although by 1900 Nietzsche was regarded, among other things, as a psychologist, one should not have the impression that there was already a widespread appreciation and discussion of the relevant psychological concepts constantly surrounding Freud. In fact, we are probably able to read Nietzsche on psychology as we do in great part because of the work of Freud.

On the other hand, Nietzsche was, among other things, a self-defined psychologist, and it was just in 1895 that his last work, *Nietzsche Contra Wagner* was issued publicly with the subtitle, *Out of the Files of a Psychologist.*[35] In the preface he states "This is an essay for psychologists."[36] In a section of the work with the title "The Psychologist Speaks Up," he writes of the true psychologist as "a born and inevitable psychologist and unriddler of souls."[37]

As mentioned earlier, Nietzsche's *Antichrist* was also published in 1895. In addition to the possibility of Freud's sympathetic response to the work given his own psychological approach to (and rejection of) religious belief, it has been suggested that Freud had a particular fascination with the figure of the Christian Antichrist,[38] a figure with which Nietzsche was identified. We have also mentioned the possible meeting with Andreas-Salomé in 1895, a year after the publication of her study of Nietzsche. (A work of Andreas-Salomé was published in 1898 and found its way into Freud's library.[39]) In 1895 and 1897 volumes one and two of Elisabeth Förster-Nietzsche's biography of her brother were published.

We also have to consider that Freud's philosophical and speculative inclinations were never far beneath the surface for very long. Also, in addition to the allusions to Nietzsche in the letters to Fliess and the possible allusions in the "Non Vixit" dream, in one letter to Fliess in 1896 and another in 1897, Freud refers to being, with his move from medicine to psychology, on the verge of attaining his goal of philosophical knowledge.[40] There also can be little doubt that Freud was familiar with at least some of Nietzsche's psychological and anthropological explorations, which made their way into letters to Fliess in 1897.

We can also note that in certain dreams of 1897 and 1898, including those in the summer of 1898, Freud returned to his university years and his "German student's club," including discussion there "on the relation of philosophy to the natural sciences" and to such figures as Viktor Adler.[41] Although, as suggested by McGrath,[42] the most important context of such memories may be of a political nature and the relationship of these political concerns to Freud's work, this was also a return to a period in his life during which Nietzsche had a great impact on those around Freud, including Adler. And we can recall that in his article on Freud's exposure to philosophy and philosophical discussions in the 1870s and 1880s, Godde writes of Paneth as the person who was the mediator of

Nietzsche for Freud.[43] One might suggest, therefore, that a reasonably comprehensive understanding of "Non Vixit" requires consideration of Paneth's connection to Nietzsche and the implications of
that connection for his relationship with Freud, a relationship that
had links to Nietzsche from its beginnings and for years afterwards.

In his analysis of "Non Vixit," William Beatty Warner writes
that "Freud's analysis of the 'Non Vixit' dream lays the ground-
work for interpreting Freud as the founder of psychoanalysis," and
that "Freud ends up claiming to be the (one and only) father of psychoanalysis." Warner points out that although in the dream and associations Freud is concerned with "who got there before the
other" and who "remained in possession of the field," in fact he
did not get there first in regard to the incident under discussion, although through strength and force he "remained in possession of
the field."[44] Including material on Paneth and Nietzsche helps to
fill in and complete such an analysis.

At times Freud certainly viewed himself as a solitary con-
queror, virtually uninfluenced by previous thinkers[45] as regards his
major achievements. At certain points in his life he also acknowledged that ideas he thought were original with him in fact had at
earlier points been introduced to him by others and then forgotten.[46]

When Freud is at the memorial for Fleischl he thinks of
Paneth and his brilliant career cut short. There is sadness but also
guilt and anger. He (unconsciously) thinks of aspects of his rival-
ries with Paneth, including Paneth having had the opportunity to
get to know Nietzsche over a three-month period. Fliess/Nietzsche
is a figure in relation to whom Freud is rivalrous and concerned
about plagiarism (although he might also want this father figure's
approval and love). Freud and Paneth know that Freud was aware
of Nietzsche's work, had read him, and that Paneth had written to
Freud about him. At the beginning of the dream it is Paneth and
Fliess, with Nietzsche as possibly one figure behind Fliess (and
Brücke another), who are together in conversation. We might consider that there are a number of possibilities regarding who has
told what to whom regarding another's affairs. Might it be better if
Paneth just had not lived ("Non Vixit") than if he were simply not
alive ("Non Vivit")? When it is Fliess who asks Freud how much
he, Freud, had told Paneth about his affairs, there is for the moment a reversal of positions. Fliess/Nietzsche and Paneth had been

together in conversation when Freud met them, as Paneth and Nietzsche *had* actually spent many hours together in friendly conversation, but now it is Freud, not Paneth, to whom Fliess/Nietzsche had been confiding about his affairs. Freud gives to Paneth his annihilating look, which he would also like to direct to Fliess/Nietzsche. He gives this annihilating look, which delights him, after saying that Paneth cannot understand anything of Fliess' (Nietzsche's) affairs (ideas) because not only is he not alive, but "Non Vixit," he did not live. Paneth knows nothing, can know nothing, since he is not alive, in fact did not live, though Freud in his rage still annihilates him with his piercing look. While on one level Freud will now have Fliess/Nietzsche to himself, on another level perhaps now Freud's ambitious desires will be satisfied and he will be seen as the one who got there first and the one who will be "left in possession of the field."[47]

To understand who Paneth is for Freud in the context of this dream, with its concerns about Freud's achievements, his priority and plagiarism, one should consider the history of Freud's relationship to Paneth. This history includes Nietzsche spending time "in conversation with my (deceased) friend P.," and the question being raised not about "how much I had told P. about his affairs," but how much P. had told Freud about Nietzsche's "affairs." Even fifty years after the event, Freud would recall that Paneth wrote a great deal to him about Nietzsche as he also recalled what a remote and noble figure Nietzsche was for him.

# PART II

# 1900–1939

# Chapter 7

## MEETINGS OF THE
## VIENNA PSYCHOANALYTIC SOCIETY

*Nietzsche has come so close to our views that we
can ask only, "Where has he not come close?"*
—Paul Federn, 1908

By the time of the April 1, 1908, meeting of the Vienna
Psychoanalytic Society, during which the third part of *On the
Genealogy of Morals* was discussed, Freud spoke of "the similarities
which many people have pointed out" between his work and that of
Nietzsche.[1] It would appear then that for some time before this
meeting Freud had already heard and/or read of such comparisons.
Nietzsche's recognition was such that by 1906, thirty-six thousand
copies of *Beyond Good and Evil* were in print.[2] The prominent
philosopher and social theorist Georg Simmel (1858–1918) had just
published a book on Schopenhauer and Nietzsche in 1907.[3]
    The early prominent followers and colleagues of Freud in-
cluded men who were familiar with Nietzsche. Rank, Jung and
Jones were all familiar with Nietzsche before they met Freud.
Although Nietzsche did not figure significantly in Alfred Adler's
thinking before the 1908 meeting, subsequently Adler was very
impressed by Nietzsche's work, particularly his emphasis on the

will to power and the manifold expressions of aggression. Adler was already familiar with Schopenhauer and "once tried to establish a direct line from Schopenhauer through Marx and Mach, to Freud."[4] At this meeting Adler stated his opinion that "Nietzsche is closest to our way of thinking."[5] He continued:

> In Nietzsche's work, one finds almost on every page observations reminiscent of those we make in therapy, when the patient has come rather a long way and is capable of analyzing the undercurrents in his mind. Thus it was given to him to discover in all the manifold expressions of culture just that primal drive which has undergone a transformation in civilization, and which is then, in the mind of the philosopher, condensed as the ascetic ideal.[6]

In his introductory comments at the meeting, Eduard Hitschmann mentioned Elisabeth Förster-Nietzsche's account of her brother's boyhood and that "already as a boy of thirteen he posed the principal questions—the origin and development of morality— which later dominated his life."[7] It would appear that at least some members were familiar with Förster-Nietzsche's biography. The biography is mentioned again at the second meeting at which Nietzsche was discussed in October 1908. It was in 1904 that the second part of the second volume was published which contained Paneth's letters to his fiancé regarding his meetings with Nietzsche. No mention is made at the society meetings of Paneth having written a great deal to Freud about Nietzsche during the same three-month period. It may be that Freud wished to avoid being linked to Nietzsche through Paneth.

Before the discussion, the contents of the first two essays were briefly reviewed by Hitschmann who then read aloud sections five through nine of the third essay. The members of the group were impressed by Nietzsche's observations. In addition to Adler's comments, Paul Federn exclaimed that "Nietzsche has come so close to our views that we can ask only, 'Where has he not come close?'"[8] Otto Rank pointed out that "he explored not the external world, as did other philosophers, but himself."[9]

Freud states that he "does not know Nietzsche's work; occasional attempts at reading it were smothered by an excess of interest. In spite of the similarities which many people have pointed out, he can give the assurance that Nietzsche's ideas have had no influence whatsoever on his own work."[10] Yet Freud also states, in response to Federn's comment noted above, that "Nietzsche failed to recognize infantilism as well as the mechanism of displacement."[11] Nietzsche did not explore infantilism (the role of early childhood in development) to any significant degree, though displacement was obvious to him as a mechanism involved in drive discharge.[12] The question to be raised here, though, is how Freud could form such an opinion without reading Nietzsche. He certainly could not reasonably make such a statement on the basis of only one work, and he does not indicate that he is referring only to this one work. Freud does acknowledge making attempts to read Nietzsche, and he did read enough to be "smothered by an excess of interest." Also, Freud did read and hear discussed at least some of Nietzsche's early writings while at the University of Vienna. Although that was more than thirty years earlier, it should be remembered that these works were being passionately discussed over a period of years by fellow students and friends for whom Freud had great admiration and respect. Consideration has also been given to other links to Nietzsche, such as the link through Paneth.

After declaring he has no knowledge of Nietzsche's work and that Nietzsche has had no influence on his own work, Freud goes on to "demonstrate how complex, and at times peculiar, the origin of new ideas can be."[13] He mentions that as regards his idea of the sexual etiology of the neuroses, "three great physicians, Breuer, Charcot, and Chrobak, had expressed this idea in his presence. Yet he recalled this fact only later when, faced with the (general) repudiation of this concept, he attempted to justify himself."[14] It appears that Freud is inadvertently indicating the possibility that he could have absorbed some of Nietzsche's ideas and then forgot or repressed them. It has also been suggested by E. James Lieberman that perhaps Freud is unable or unwilling to acknowledge the influence of Nietzsche and defensively attempts to demonstrate that he is in fact able to acknowledge influence. However, Lieberman points out that the influences he refers to are only passing comments made in the course of informal conversation to the effect that "hysteria is a problem . . . of the boudoir (Breuer); of the genitals (Charcot); curable by repeated doses of a normal penis (Chrobak . . .)."[15] These passing comments are hardly comparable to Freud's exposure to

Nietzsche's ideas, however limited, and the relevance of these ideas to psychoanalysis.

The minutes of this meeting are contained in only a few pages. There are a few general comments on the *Genealogy* pertaining to Nietzsche's concerns with the origins of morality and culturally sublimated expressions of drives as well as Federn's comment that Nietzsche "was the first to discover the significance of abreaction, of repression, of flight into illness, of the instincts— the normal sexual ones as well as the sadistic instincts."[16] There are also some comments speculating on Nietzsche's personality and relevant psychodynamics.

The second essay of the *Genealogy*, "'Guilt,' 'Bad conscience' and the Like," explores, among other things, how at a critical juncture in the development of civilization and morality, drives that had been more freely expressed were constrained and turned inward. This led to the "internalization of man," the development of the "bad conscience" and the "entire inner world, [which] originally thin as if it were stretched between two membranes, expanded and extended itself, acquired depth, breadth, and height."[17] The third essay, "What is the Meaning of Ascetic Ideals?" under discussion at the meeting explores how bad conscience or guilt is appropriated by the ascetic priest in the service of comforting, and thus ensuring the obedience of, the vulnerable "herd." The ascetic priest, exercising his own will to power (such as by imposing his interpretations on the minds of others), provides meaning and justification for what would otherwise be meaningless suffering. He provides comfort of sorts with a realm of existence that is divine, holy, pure and true. He counsels that to enter this realm one must accept one's own guilt, one's sinful nature, as the cause of one's suffering. In order to find relief one must subdue sinful drives. Nietzsche objects not to the subduing of drives, a process which can be a part of creative sublimation, but to the ascetic priest's counsel having the effect of weakening and enfeebling the individual, reducing the value of life, the feeling of life, will and desire while fostering *ressentiment* or subterranean desires for revenge.

While the will to power may have had certain cosmological and mythic dimensions for Nietzsche, the concept is also rooted in psychology. Nietzsche attempted to demonstrate that there is an overriding expansive, growth-directed, aggressive, appropriating, mastering drive that can be satisfied through behaviors, beliefs and values not typically associated with such a drive. For example, this drive may be directed inward towards the self and may be sublimated in various forms.

The ascetic ideal which the priest imposes upon the herd involves a valuing of self-denial and a devaluing of this earthly world and existence. The highest truth one can attain is linked to another world or realm, a world superior to this earthly realm. There is a denial of basic human instincts in the service of devaluing essential aspects of our human nature as well as denigration of the empirical world. The priest seeks power not only over himself and others, but over life itself through its devaluation. The priest satisfies his will to power in part by imposing his values and beliefs on others. He is also performing the useful function of providing meaning for suffering (an interpretation of the "depression" which results when drives are not permitted discharge) so that at least something can be willed, there can be some goal, and so, in a certain sense, life is affirmed and goes on.[18] However, for Nietzsche, although the sufferer may be comforted, the "cause" of suffering, "the real sickness,"[19] is not dealt with. Nietzsche makes the distinction between comforting or alleviating symptoms and addressing the underlying disorder.

As Nietzsche puts it, *"the ascetic ideal springs from the protective instinct of a degenerating life* which tries by all means to sustain itself and to fight for its existence; it indicates a partial physiological obstruction and exhaustion against which the deepest instincts of life, which have remained intact, continually struggle with new expedients and devices."[20] (When Nietzsche writes of depression occurring as a consequence of frustration of the drives being expressed more directly outward upon the world, he comes close to Freud's first theory of anxiety in which libido that is inadequately discharged is transformed into anxiety. What Nietzsche sometimes characterizes as "physiological"—depression, obstruction, exhaustion—Freud will later discover to be, at least in some cases, of psychological origin. However, Nietzsche may have had a relatively inclusive notion of the physiological which at times may have encompassed the psychological, as when he writes of the unconscious resistance that the investigator has to contend with in "a proper physio-psychology." It may be that Nietzsche, as well as Freud, was influenced by a prevalent view of psychology as a neurophysiology of the mental.[21])

The priest helps to relieve or avoid the depression caused by the helplessness and hopelessness of those unable to express their will to power more directly. For the herd, turning aggression against the self in the context of the ascetic ideal, rather than leading to depression, actually relieves or helps to avoid depression related to helplessness and hopelessness. For Nietzsche,

> every sufferer instinctively seeks a cause for his suffering, more exactly an agent, still more specifically a *guilty* agent who is susceptible to suffering—in short, some living thing upon which he can, on some pretext or other, vent his affects, actually or in effigy: for the venting of his affects represents the greatest attempt on the part of the suffering to win relief . . . This . . . constitutes the actual physiological cause of *ressentiment*, vengefulness, and the like: a desire to *deaden pain by means of affects.*[22]

While Nietzsche is aware of a course in which the individual avoids looking into himself and finds an enemy on which to vent his affects, the ascetic priest also helps the suffering individual to seek the cause of his suffering "in himself, in some *guilt*, in a piece of the past, he must understand his suffering as a *punishment.*"[23] The resulting "orgy of feeling" (which would include self-pity) is the "most effective means of deadening dull, paralyzing, protracted pain."[24] Aggressive drives are also satisfied for the priest and the herd in the fantasies and beliefs pertaining to the fate of unbelievers and others who oppress them. Nietzsche refers to Aquinas' words: "'The blessed in the kingdom of heaven will see the punishment of the damned *in order that their bliss be more delightful for them.*'"[25] (Nietzsche's quote is not exact.) There is also the more earthbound project of infecting nobler types with bad conscience.

Nietzsche goes on to discuss how philosophers themselves have utilized the ascetic priest as a model, with the ascetic ideal providing a form through which to think, when they posit timeless, changeless, perfect realms of being in relation to which absolute truth is attained and is valued absolutely, animal nature is transcended for pure spirit and death avoided. Nietzsche regards much of modern scholarship and science (in the broadest sense of the word as pertaining to various disciplines of contemporary scholarship) as *"the latest and noblest form"* of the ascetic ideal.

(The ascetic priest's form of the ascetic ideal is not characterized as noble, perhaps, as White suggests, due to its slave morality and condemnation of sensuality.[26]) Nietzsche writes of philosophers that "they all pose as if they had discovered and reached their real opinions through the self-development of a cold, pure, divinely unconcerned dialectic."[27]

According to Nietzsche, the faith in truth, in the absolute value of truth, in this metaphysical value, stands or falls with the ascetic ideal. Such faith, with its "unconscious imperative," involves "the desire to keep something hidden from oneself: Science as a means of self-narcosis: *do you have experience of that?*"[28] (Of course this does not mean that science *must* function as self-narcosis.) The "rigid and unconditional" faith in truth commits one to "that venerable philosopher's abstinence . . . that *desire* to halt before the factual, the *factum brutum* . . . that general renunciation of all interpretation."[29] Among the things thus kept hidden is that what we regard as knowledge involves interpretation—

> forcing, adjusting, abbreviating, omitting, padding, inventing, falsifying, and whatever else is of the *essence* of interpreting . . . a philosophy, a "faith," must always be there first of all, so that science can acquire from it a direction, a meaning, a limit, a method, a *right* to exist . . . From the moment faith in the God of the ascetic ideal is denied, *a new problem arises:* that of the *value* of truth [not the *possibility* of truth] . . . the value of truth must for once be experimentally *called into question.*[30]

As Martin Warner puts it, "Not only is there no God, but not even truth is 'divine' in the sense of being 'unconditioned.'"[31]

Maudemarie Clark points out that "by providing a goal, the ascetic ideal gave life meaning and saved the will, but it did so in a way that deprived life of intrinsic value, that accorded it value only as a means to its own negation."[32] Now the will to truth requires an ideal other than the ascetic ideal, if for no other reason, as Clark points out, than one cannot very well embrace a life-devaluing ideal if one believes that "one's motive was to get a sense of power necessary for feeling better about life."[33]

For Nietzsche the aggressive (though also possibly playful) imposition of order and meaning (which is, of course, not arbitrary and not out of contact with the real world), this expression of the will to power, is inherent in interpretation (is of its "essence") which is always active, from a particular point of view and, to varying degrees and in varying ways, serving unconscious motivations. The will to truth is always in the service of other, often unconscious, motivations (which does not entail that something we may reasonably regard as the truth cannot be reached).

This state of affairs regarding interpretation and imposition of meaning is not something that can be transcended. What can be done, and is an aspect of intellectual conscience, is to develop the capacity to step back from one's own perspective (though while arriving at that perspective it may be unavoidable at times to feel that one's perspective provides "the truth" in itself), examine one's assumptions and examine things creatively out of as many affects and from as many relevant perspectives as possible. This would include an openness to or entry into the inner world of (or shared reality with) another person, although the openness or entry would, unavoidably, be from a particular perspective.

Nietzsche also states that without grounding in the ascetic ideal, the absolute valuing of truth, that is, the valuing of truth being given highest priority over other possible values for life, is brought into question. In other words, there may be values other than truth that may be of equal or greater value for ideas and life.

One would imagine that there was much for the members of the society to discuss relating to the relationship between the repression of instincts and the development of the inner world, guilt and bad conscience as these relate to individual and cultural development (areas Freud will soon explore in *Totem and Taboo* and other social-anthropological works) as well as Nietzsche's explorations on the nature of interpretation.

Regarding interpretation and the nature of the analytic relationship, there are prominent contemporary analysts such as Irwin Hoffman who refer to their position as perspectivist (or constructivist), although without mentioning Nietzsche. Hoffman writes that such a position "fosters [an] appreciation on the analyst's part that whatever he or she is doing in keeping with preestablished principles . . . may have other unconscious meanings (for example, maintaining a position of power)."[34] Also, that "what they [analysts] know about their own participation retrospectively and prospectively, is always selective and always suspect."[35] Another analyst, Donell B. Stern, drawing on the work of Hans-Georg Gadamer (who was significantly influenced by Nietzsche), has written: "In bringing one possibility into the light, experience is organized in such a way that other possibilities are 'darkened.'"[36] Nietzsche didn't merely anticipate such ideas in some vague way. He explored and elaborated upon such ideas (though not, of course, in terms specific to the therapeutic relationship) at length and in depth, including in the *Genealogy*.

We might even consider that there are aspects of Freud's self-creation and creation of psychoanalysis that can be viewed in terms of the ascetic ideal. In many ways the ascetic ideal does not apply to Freud since he attempted to find a legitimate place for, not a denial of, the body. Also, his concern was with this earthly life, not its devaluation in relation to some transcendent realm. However, in the following, the aescetic ideal, in however "noble" a form, may be somewhat applicable to Freud: in his desire at times "to halt before the *factum brutum* . . . that general renunciation of interpretation," or as Nietzsche terms it, "that venerable philosopher's abstinence";[37] in his conviction at times that he brings forth "nothing but observed facts"; or that "the choice of a point of view" or "presumptions" can be avoided by science;[38] in his positing of an unknown, directly unknowable but true realm to which psychoanalysis has special access; in the rules of the analytic relationship which stress analyst neutrality and minimal gratification for the patient as the stance from which one has access to this truth; in his attitude towards the psychoanalytic relationship and process (the concept of countertransference notwithstanding) in which he "systematically pursued theoretically based lines of interpretation with his patients while not taking account of himself as a participant in an interaction";[39] and in his creation of himself as a relatively uninfluenced and solitary conquistador who discovered (as scientist, as father, as son for the father as opposed to what had been intuitively anticipated by the artist-philosopher-mother) the truth about the functioning of the mind. (Not that Nietzsche doesn't have his own complex relationship to the ascetic ideal.)

Among the many passages in the essay which have direct relevance for psychoanalytic developmental theory and the place of sexuality, one might note in particular the following passage which was included in the sections read aloud at the beginning of the meeting:

The sweetness and plenitude peculiar to the aesthetic state might be derived precisely from the ingredient of "sensuality" (just as the "idealism" of adolescent girls derives from this source)—so that sensuality is not overcome by the appearance of the aesthetic condition, as Schopenhauer believed, but only transfigured and no longer enters consciousness as sexual excitement.[40] [Julian Young points out that for Nietzsche art beautifies, perfects and idealizes as does sexual love.[41]]

Nietzsche links the realm of sexuality and sensuality to both the aesthetic state or condition generally and to the idealism (specifically in girls) characteristic of the period of adolescence. The sexual-sensual realm remains (it "is not overcome"), exerting its influence, but no longer enters consciousness as sexual excitement. The sexual-sensual elements are, in other words, sublimated. No mention of this passage was made at the meeting. Very shortly before this meeting Freud wrote in "'Civilized' Sexual Morality and Modern Nervous Illness" that the sexual instinct's "capacity to exchange its originally sexual aim for another one, which is no longer sexual but which is psychically related to the first aim, is called the capacity for *sublimation*."[42] Kaufmann points out that for Nietzsche, though he writes of sublimated sexuality, more typically the fundamental energy and objective that remain the same, the essence present throughout sublimated transformations, pertain to the will to power.[43] On the other hand, the most fundamental drives seem to involve "the mysteries of sexuality . . . the eternal joy of creating."[44] The feeling of increase of power may be experienced most intensely and completely in the eternal joy of creating. The will to power entails not only a "willing to be stronger" but a "willing to grow" and a willing to create beyond oneself.[45]

For Nietzsche, what in its origins is will to power, remains will to power in its sublimations. For psychoanalysis, what in its origins is sexual in nature may on one level be "canceled," be nowhere in evidence, yet the sexual energy and objective somehow remain.[46] As Kaufmann puts it, for Nietzsche (who in Kaufmann's view is a dialectical monist, in contrast to Freudian dualism regarding the drives), "when reason overcomes . . . the impulses, we cannot speak of a marriage of two diverse principles [since reason itself is a manifestation of will to power] but only the self-overcoming of the will to power. This one and only basic force [there certainly may be other forces that are important but not as basic] has first manifested itself as impulse and then overcomes its own previous manifestation."[47] However, essay 3, section 8 of the *Genealogy*, quoted above, is clearly in line with psychoanalytic notions of sublimation.

Returning to "'Civilized' Sexual Morality and Modern Nervous Illness," on the page preceding the comment on sublimation, Freud writes that "civilization is built upon the suppression of instincts" and that each individual surrenders some part "of the aggressive or vindictive inclinations in his personality."[48] The next year, at a meeting of the Vienna Psychoanalytic Society in March 1909, Freud states that from the psychological point of view the "entire development of humanity" could be characterized in terms of "an enlargement of the consciousness of mankind (analogous to the coming into consciousness of instincts and forces hitherto operating unconsciously) . . . [and] repression that progresses over the centuries . . . more and more of our instincts become subject to repression, for which there are beautiful illustrations, particularly in poetic productions."[49] Nietzsche had written that with repression of instincts and their turn inward, "the entire inner world, originally as thin as if it were stretched between two membranes, expanded and extended itself, acquired depth, breadth, and height, in the same measure as outward discharge was *inhibited*."[50] He also had written of "'bad conscience' . . . [as] the womb of all ideal and imaginative phenomena . . . an abundance of strange new beauty and affirmation and perhaps beauty itself."[51]

We can also note that Freud had, three years earlier in the *Three Essays on the Theory of Sexuality*, written of the sublimation of sexual instincts and of the relationship of such sublimation to artistic appreciation and creation.[52] And there is the possibility that in 1905 Freud had already had Nietzsche brought to his attention at a society meeting. (This was before the society's official status as the Vienna Psychoanalytic Society and the taking of minutes. The group was reformed under its new name in April 1908.) In an introduction to *Beyond the Pleasure Principle*, the analyst Gregory Zilboorg states: "It is a matter of record that Hitschman, one of the earliest adherents of Freud, read a paper in Freud's house as early as 1905 (Freud being present, of course) on the very subject of Nietzsche's ideas as compared with some of Freud's theories."[53] While Zilboorg could conceivably be referring to one of the 1908 meetings, he is quite specific about the date and that a paper was presented in which Freud and Nietzsche were compared. (Later, in 1915, at the time he is exploring the nature of sadomasochistic relationships in "Instincts and Their Vicissitudes,"[54] Freud will add to the *Three Essays* the idea that masochism "is nothing more than an extension of sadism turned round upon the subject's own self, which thus, to begin with, takes the place of the sexual object."[55] This is directly related to Nietzsche's discussions in the *Genealogy*.)

Another work of 1905, *Jokes and their Relation to the Unconscious,*[56] if not directly influenced by Nietzsche, is in line with Nietzsche's thinking in its theme of latent aggression and the various ways aggression is expressed in jokes. As Nietzsche put it: "Laughter means: being malicious but with a good conscience."[57] A number of times Freud mentions Lipps who in 1898 had written a book on the comic and humor. Freud states that "Lipps . . . has attempted, as an amplification to Kant's statement that the comic is 'an expectation that has turned to nothing,' to derive comic pleasure quite generally from expectation."[58] Consider the following passage from *Human, All Too Human* in which the matter of expectation turning to nothing has a particular kind of importance for and relevance to the comic:

*Origin of the comic.*—
If one considers that man was for many hundreds of thousands of years an animal in the highest degree accessible to fear and that everything sudden and unexpected bade him prepare to fight and perhaps to die; that even later on, indeed, in social relationships all security depended on the expected and traditional in opinion and action; then one cannot be surprised if whenever something sudden and unexpected in word and deed happens without occasioning danger or injury man becomes wanton, passes over into the opposite of fear: the anxious, crouching creature springs up, greatly expands—man laughs. This transition from momentary anxiety to short-lived exuberance is called the *comic.*[59] [At a later point we will note this passage in relation to a passage from Freud's 1927 paper "Humour."[60]]

At the next society meeting mention was made of the publication of Nietzsche's letters to his sister, Elisabeth, again an indication of an interest in the life as well as the work of Nietzsche by these early analysts.[61] Otto Rank read from the letters and spoke of Elisabeth's envy of Lou Andreas-Salomé. April 1908 was also the time of the first psychoanalytic congress which took place in Salzberg, so that this gathering of analysts (as well as the reforming of the society) took place at a time when much discussion was taking place about Nietzsche's life and work.

The other meeting devoted to Nietzsche was held on October 28, 1908, and the work under discussion was *Ecce Homo*, an intellectual autobiographical work written at the very end of Nietzsche's productive life in late 1888 but not published until 1908.

In the opening comments, Förster-Nietzsche's biography, and particularly the second volume (in which Paneth's letters appear), is again mentioned. Mention is made of Nietzsche presenting Dionysus in opposition to Christ. The last words of the work are, "Have I been understood?—*Dionysus versus the Crucified.*"[62] We can also take note of Nietzsche's fantasy that he was descended from Polish nobility. Freud had his own fantasies pertaining to family romance themes (descendents from Cologne), and such matters, as we will see, may have a bearing on *Moses and Monotheism.*[63]

During the discussion mention is again made of Nietzsche anticipating a great deal that appears in Freud's teachings, "for instance, the significance of forgetting, of the ability to forget."[64] Freud speaks of the mastery of form, that the work is "fully valid and to be taken seriously,"[65] not to be written off as a product of impending insanity. He also states that "there is no evidence whatsoever of a neurotic illness"[66] and that the "degree of introspection achieved by Nietzsche had never been achieved by anyone, nor is it likely ever to be reached again."[67] This is remarkable praise coming from Freud, particularly in light of his own self-analysis. Also, since this work refers to and comments on earlier works, could Freud make such a comment without some knowledge of these works?

Freud goes on to again state that "he has never been able to study Nietzsche, partly because of the resemblance of Nietzsche's intuitive insights to our laborious investigations, and partly because of the wealth of ideas, which has always prevented Freud from getting beyond the first half page whenever he has tried to read him."[68] Freud started to read Nietzsche on a number of occasions, read enough to be smothered by the wealth of ideas and his own excess of interest, and read enough (and perhaps heard enough and read about Nietzsche enough) to be aware of the resemblance of Nietzsche's "intuitive insights" to the "laborious investigations" of psychoanalysis.

It should also be kept in mind, as Golumb[69] has pointed out, that Nietzsche's name and ideas would come up from time to time at meetings, lectures, and in analytic journal articles over the next few years and beyond. What follows is some of what Golumb reports, indicating the involvement of early analysts with Nietzsche.

At a November 1908 meeting, Wittels quotes Nietzsche. At a March 1909 meeting, Rank discusses Nietzsche's moral theory. At meetings in January, April and November 1910, Tausk, Oppenheim, and Hitschmann refer to Nietzsche. At a meeting in January 1911, there is a reading from *Daybreak* on dreams. In February 1912 Victor Tausk gives a lecture, "Nietzsche as Psychoanalyst," to the Medical Society of Vienna (and it was reported in the *Zentralblatt*, the analytic movement's official journal, edited by Freud). (Tausk, who had a complex, highly emotional relationship with Freud and passionate feelings for Andreas-Salomé, committed suicide in 1919. Freud's relationship to Tausk and his suicide have been the subject of some heated debate.) In March 1912 Nietzsche is mentioned at a society meeting and also in December 1912 in a lecture by Winterstein that was published in *Imago*.[70] We can also mention that in 1908 Nietzsche was brought up by Freud's patient, the "Rat Man," who quoted Nietzsche to Freud: "'I did this,' says my Memory. 'I cannot have done this,' says my Pride and remains inexorable. In the end—Memory yields." Freud responded to the quote enthusiastically.[71]

As had been the case over thirty years earlier when he was a university student, Freud was, from shortly after the turn of the century, surrounded by persons, and now in particular analysts, who were reading, writing about and discussing Nietzsche.

*Ecce Homo* also probably impressed Freud in its attempt to create an intellectual life history of the genius, the hero. Pletsch has written of the "autobiographical life . . . a life plan, a project that the prospective genius uses to organize his life."[72] He writes that "Nietzsche made the problems of the autobiographical life of the genius—ordinarily a functionally unconscious dimension of the thought of a genius—into a conscious issue of his thought and writing . . . Nietzsche addressed himself directly to the ideology of the genius, ultimately calling it into question."[73] Pletsch discusses how self-conscious notions around myths of the heroic journey are applicable to Freud in his ideas of himself and creation of himself as scientific hero.[74] Pletsch does not deal with the relationship of Freud's autobiographical life to Nietzsche's.

We might wonder about the reaction of Freud and other analysts to these words near the conclusion of *Ecce Homo:*

> Who among philosophers was a *psychologist* at all before me, not rather the opposite, a "higher swindler" and "idealist"? There was no psychology at all before me.—To be the first here [What would Freud have thought and felt here? "Non Vixit"?] may be a curse; it is at any rate a destiny: *for one is also the first to despise.—Nausea* at man is my danger.[75] [The joke, the comic, humor and laughter may be, for Freud and Nietzsche, creative responses to this nausea and suffering.[76]]

Nietzsche also writes that to be capable of loving one must resist the "Circe of humanity, morality . . . that gruesome nonsense that love is supposed to be something 'unegoistic.'—One has to sit firmly upon *oneself,* one must stand bravely on one's own two legs, otherwise one is simply *incapable* of loving." Nietzsche states that this is what women look for in a man and then adds: "Perhaps I am the first psychologist of the eternally feminine."[77] Nietzsche had also referred to the "Eternal-Feminine," a phrase from Goethe, in *Beyond Good and Evil.*[78]

One may ask if Freud would have a special feeling for this passage. In his dream "Dissecting My Own Pelvis," which probably occurred in May 1899 as he was completing *The Interpretation of Dreams,*[79] Freud refers to the dissecting of himself in the dream as reflecting his journey of self-dissection, self-analysis. The occasion of the dream involved an acquaintance asking Freud to recommend and lend her a book to read. He offered her Haggard's *She.* He explained to the acquaintance that it was "a *strange* book, but full of hidden meaning . . . the eternal feminine."[80] In the book two men, one a mentor, go in search of She, woman, the eternal-feminine, truth.[81] In the dream content and associations Freud is concerned, regarding his journey, with the "tired feeling in my legs," with the thought, "'How much longer will my legs carry me?'"[82]

For Freud, here was another thinker, perhaps a secret guide or mentor, "the first psychologist of the eternally feminine," who writes that to win over woman, the eternally feminine, truth, "one must stand bravely on one's own two legs."

# Chapter 8

## JUNG, ANDREAS-SALOMÉ AND
## TOTEM AND TABOO

*In later years I have denied myself the very great pleasure of reading the works of Nietzsche . . . I had therefore to be prepared—I am so, gladly—to forgo all claims to priority in the many instances in which laborious psychoanalytic investigation can merely confirm the truths which the philosopher recognized by intuition.*
—Freud, *History of the Psycho-Analytic Movement*

Over the next few years, after the 1908 meetings, Nietzsche would often emerge in one form or another in Freud's life and work. In this regard we will first consider Freud's relationships with Jung and Andreas-Salomé and then his first major social-anthropological work, *Totem and Taboo*, published in 1912 and 1913.[1]

In 1909 Freud wrote to Jung: "If I am Moses, then you are Joshua and will take possession of the promised land of psychiatry."[2] These words reflect Freud's strong feelings for and identification with the figure of Moses as well as his great hopes for Jung. Freud was concerned that psychoanalysis would be viewed as a Jewish discipline and as such have increased difficulties being more widely accepted. It was hoped that by the gentile Jung assuming a position of leadership, some of this kind of resistance could be overcome. In August 1908, a time between the two society meetings on Nietzsche, Freud wrote to Jung of his hopes that he would "continue and complete my work by applying to psychoses what I have begun with neuroses." Freud specifically mentioned "your strong and independent character . . . your Germanic blood which enables you to command the sympathies of the public more readily than I."[3] A few years later, as their relationship came to an end, Freud would make repeated visits to Michelangelo's *Moses* in part for inspiration in dealing with his reactions to the split with Jung as well as dealing with his concerns for the continued development of the psychoanalytic movement and his leadership position within it.

Jung had studied Nietzsche as a young man, had attended the university (Basel) at which Nietzsche had earlier taught, and likely had a strong identification with Nietzsche. The beginnings of the Freud-Jung relationship involved Jung sending his book *The Psychology of Dementia Praecox*[4] to Freud. In the correspondence that ensued there was particular discussion of a dream which Jung presented in the book as a friend's but which he quickly revealed to Freud was his own. In an examination of this dream, Lehman[5] concludes that the dream and Jung's associations reflect the prologue of *Zarathustra*, particularly relating to the figure of the tightrope walker (who falls to his death) and to issues of losing control over precarious mental equilibrium. In the dream a horse is being hoisted by a cable, the cable breaks and the horse crashes to the ground. (Perhaps relevant, Nietzsche's insanity was supposed to have exploded with full force when he saw a horse being beaten in the street. He is said to have flung his arms around the horse in an attempt to protect it. Whether Freud or Jung was aware of this fact is not discussed by Lehman.) Whether or not Freud on some level picked up on the dream's possible connection to Nietzsche is not known, but he gave no expression to any such ideas. However, there is also the possibility that Freud knew of or soon became aware of the fact that Jung had carefully studied *Zarathustra*, had discovered an example of cryptomnesia on Nietzsche's part and had published it in 1905, the same year as the dream. Also, Jung mentions that to check on biographical details he had been in correspondence with Elisabeth Förster-Nietzsche.[6] It is possible that this relationship, of such great importance to both men, may have had its beginnings with Nietzsche present. (We can also note that a person who had a substantial impact on both men and their relationship, Sabina Spielrein, would later, as an associate of Freud, show the influence of Nietzsche in her work.[7]) There is no question about Nietzsche's presence a few years later.

Freud might have wondered about and even been a bit alarmed about a quasi-Nietzschean comment of Jung's in a letter to him in 1910. Jung wrote of the possibility of psychoanalysis revivifying "among intellectuals a feeling for symbol and myth, ever so gently to transform Christ back into the soothsaying god of the vine, which he was."[8] It will be recalled that at the October 1908 meeting of the Vienna Psychoanalytic Society, Nietzsche's closing words in *Ecce Homo*, placing Dionysus in opposition to Christ, were discussed.[9] Now here is Jung not placing Dionysus and Christ in opposition but finding Dionysus in Christ and suggesting that psychoanalysis should help promote such a recognition as well as a positive feeling for the value of symbol and myth more generally. Freud did not respond strongly, but merely indicated that he had no intention of psychoanalysis being a religion and that religious needs should be sublimated.[10]

In March 1912, when the relationship between Freud and Jung had already become quite strained, Nietzsche directly emerged in the form of a quotation from *Zarathustra* in a letter from Jung to Freud. Jung felt that Freud was discouraging his followers' attempts at explorations which moved in directions other than Freud's own. He expressed his own thoughts and feelings regarding a creative relationship between a teacher and a disciple, stating that he was a true follower of Freud's, with the following words of Zarathustra:

> One repays a teacher badly if one remains only a pupil.
> And why, then, should you not pluck at my laurels?
> You respect me; but how if one day your respect should tumble?
> Take care that a falling statue does not strike you dead!
>     You had not yet sought yourselves when you found me.
> Thus do all believers—.
> Now I bid you lose me and find yourselves;
> and only when you have all denied me will I return to you.[11]

Freud responded that he was in full agreement with the quotation. But while consciously intending to write that a third party would ask "when" he had ever tried to tyrannize Jung intellectually,[12] he slipped and wrote that "a third party . . . would ask me *why* I had tried to tyrannize you intellectually" (emphasis added). With this slip it would appear that Freud unconsciously acknowledged at least an ambivalent response to Jung and to Nietzsche's words spoken by Zarathustra. Freud frequently had Nietzsche brought to his attention regarding anticipation of psychoanalytic concepts, and now in 1912 the man he hoped would be his intellectual son, his Joshua, was quoting Nietzsche to him regarding proper teacher-disciple relationships.

As Golumb[13] points out, not only Jung, but Rank and others utilized Nietzsche in their attempts to liberate themselves from Freud. In 1926, as their split was approaching, Rank's birthday present for Freud's seventieth birthday was an expensive edition of Nietzsche's complete works, a gift with multiple intentions and meanings including, it would seem, calling Freud's attention to his relationship to Nietzsche. According to Golumb, Rank, who for many years was one of Freud's closest associates, would later contrast what he saw as Nietzsche's more affirmative psychology with Freud's more Schopenhauerian pessimism, and he even regarded Freud as more of a moralist and philosopher and less a psychologist than Nietzsche.[14]

———

In January 1912, only two months before Jung's quote to Freud, Freud and Jung had written to one another regarding Lou Andreas-Salomé.[15] Andreas-Salomé had developed an interest in psychoanalysis and attended the Weimar Congress in the fall of 1911. It was during this congress that Ernest Jones and Hanns Sachs called on Elisabeth Förster-Nietzsche and discussed with her the similarity of some of Freud's ideas and those of her brother.[16] Also, in 1911 Andreas-Salomé had a reprint of her book on Nietzsche published in Vienna.[17] At the congress she met Freud and requested to study psychoanalysis with him.[18] While Freud and Jung do not appear to take Andreas-Salomé very seriously, she must have had some impact in Weimar as Jung refers to her as "Frau Lou Andreas-Salomé, of Weimar fame."[19] Interestingly, she wanted to send Jung a paper on the topic of sublimation, a topic explored by Nietzsche. Freud would soon hear of a very favorable impression of her from a most respected source. In April 1912 Karl Abraham wrote of her: "I have come to know her very well and must admit that I have never before met with such deep and subtle understanding of analysis. She will visit Vienna this winter and would like to attend your meetings."[20] Freud was impressed, and on the basis of this recommendation Andreas-Salomé would be welcomed to the Vienna Society meetings a few months later. She would be at the 1913 Munich congress to console Freud on the last occasion that he and Jung would see one another. It may be that in some respects she replaced Jung. Freud certainly looked to her as a judge of the conflict among his followers.[21]

In October 1912 Andreas-Salomé came to Vienna and for six months attended the meetings of the Vienna Psychoanalytic Society. Freud quickly developed an unusually close relationship with her and spent a good deal of time with her. Only a few weeks after Andreas-Salomé began attending the meetings, she missed a meeting and Freud wrote to her: "I have adopted the bad habit of always directing my lecture to a definite member of the audience, and yesterday I fixed my gaze as if spellbound at the place which had been kept for you."[22] During this period Andreas-Salomé "would always leave a note at the hotel so I could be located in case Freud had time free. I would come to him as quickly as possible, no matter where I was."[23]

Although Andreas-Salomé had her quiet disagreements with Freud and wrote perceptively on his work and of his difficulties regarding the acceptance of the independence of followers,[24] she remained loyal and devoted until her death in 1937. Among her last words to him were: "If only . . . I might look into your face but ten minutes—into the father-face over my life."[25] Freud was probably closer to her for a longer period of time than to any other female colleague.[26] On April 3, 1931, Freud wrote to her, reprimanding her for not informing him of the occasion of her seventieth birthday; he wrote, "how greatly I esteem and love you."[27] Andreas-Salomé had been one of the analysts to eventually be given a special ring by Freud, this ritual having been earlier restricted to Freud's secret committee.[28] Appignanesi and Forrester point out that Freud had referred to her as his "Sunday Child," the name he had given his favorite daughter, Sophie.[29] And as Freud would refer to Nietzsche as a remote and noble figure of his youth, according to Abram Kardiner he regarded Andreas-Salomé as having "an intrinsic superiority . . . an inborn nobility."[30] Her picture remains in Freud's consulting room in the Freud Museum in Hampstead.

Andreas-Salomé was five years younger than Freud, the same age as his wife. She became a kind of surrogate intellectual wife to

Freud, specifically regarding her role with Anna Freud. In 1921 Freud invited her for an extended visit to his home "to occupy Anna, for whom I mainly invited her."[31] She would become Anna Freud's teacher, a kind of training analyst as well as confidant. Freud and Andreas-Salomé would refer to her as their shared "Daughter-Anna."[32] Estelle Roith, drawing on the research of Binion,[33] points out that when Freud looked to Andreas-Salomé to help wean Anna from an oedipal fixation on him, Andreas-Salomé wasn't so readily inclined to comply, suggesting, perhaps only somewhat in jest, that Anna's incestuous set-up was more blissful than any normal alternatives. (The relevant passages are not included in the collected letters edited by Pfeiffer.) In 1923 Andreas-Salomé wrote to Freud, thanking him for financial help. She wrote of "all the feelings which I can only indicate when we are together," and regarding Freud and Anna on their trip in Rome, she wrote of herself as "the unseen companion who always wishes to be near you." Regarding her life overall, she continued: "Recently I tried to think what things would have been like if I had grown old without ever having met you. I would have been thoroughly disgusted at this old woman, while as things are I am utterly contented with the life that I have, as long as it may last." Appignanesi and Forrester conclude that "the analytic parenting of Anna brought the two of them so close that, in later years, Freud said that Lou stood next in line of intimacy to his daughter."[34]

The reason this material is of importance for this study is, of course, that Andreas-Salomé was intimately associated with Nietzsche. Not only was she very familiar with his work, having written her study of him, but she was the object of his passionate feelings. Nietzsche would not have the close relationship with her that he longed for in 1882, but now Freud in effect displaces the intellectual father figure and has the intimate (although, as with Nietzsche, unconsummated as far as we know) relationship with her. In addition, it is worth noting that Nietzsche had thought of Andreas-Salomé as possibly the person who would understand his work and carry it on. Now Andreas-Salomé is the disciple not of Nietzsche, but of Freud. And while Andreas-Salomé in some ways does carry on Nietzsche's work, Freud does so on a grand scale. Andreas-Salomé is both wife and daughter. She may also be sibling as both she and Freud are Nietzsche's children. She is also a sexually aggressive woman, a free spirit, who has had a number of prominent men become very attracted to and involved with her. Although Freud never commented on the Nietzsche–Freud–Andreas-Salomé triangle, it would seem likely that regarding the interplay of emotional and intellectual forces, the relationship with Andreas-Salomé would have intensified Freud's complex relationship to Nietzsche. (As far as the Freud–Andreas-Salomé correspondence is concerned, there is almost no discussion of Nietzsche.)

Freud was beginning to give thought to *Totem and Taboo* in mid-1911. Andreas-Salomé entered the analytic scene in the fall of that year with her presence at the Weimar Congress. She had a reprint of her book on Nietzsche published in Vienna that year. As mentioned, another connection to Nietzsche for Freud was the visit Jones and Sachs made to Elisabeth Förster-Nietzsche to discuss the similarity of her brother's ideas and those of psychoanalysis.

It was also in 1911 in the Shreber study that Freud referred to the section "Before Sunrise" in *Zarathustra* and wrote of his patient's, and what he speculated was Nietzsche's, longing to rediscover a lost father in nature. (As mentioned, Freud looked towards idealized father and/or older brother figures for support and inspiration. This was in part a result of childhood experiences in relation to his own father that undermined idealization, as when his father told him that some years earlier he did not retaliate when a gentile mocked him and knocked off his hat.) At the 1911 congress, in a postscript to the Shreber study,[35] Freud told a tale of the eagle and the sun in which the eagle forced its young to look at the sun (symbol of the father) without blinking. This tale illustrated a theme of the son having to confront the father, and it could have had implications for Freud's relationship to Jung as well as Nietzsche. Towards the end of the postscript Freud stated that "Jung has excellent grounds for his assertion that the mythopoeic forces of mankind are not extinct,"[36] and he closes the postscript with the following words:

> "In dreams and neuroses," so our thesis has run, "we come once more upon the child and the peculiarities which characterize his modes of thought and his emotional life." "And we come upon the savage too," we may now add, "upon the primitive man, as he stands revealed to us in the light of the researches of archaeology and ethnology."[37]

Compare this with the following words from *Human, All Too Human* and *Daybreak:*

> In the dream this piece of primeval humanity continues to exercise itself . . . the dream takes us back again to remote stages of human culture and provides us with a means of understanding them better.[38]
>
> In the fantasising of dreams and insanity, a man rediscovers his own and mankind's prehistory. [Perhaps it is of some significance that Shreber's memoirs were recommended to Freud by Jung and that Shreber himself was influenced by Nietzsche.][39]

As we have noted, the first volume of *Human, All Too Human* had been published in 1878, the last year that Freud was a member of the Leseverein. We have also seen that there was a reading on dreams from *Daybreak* at a society meeting in January 1911. Freud refers to these ideas of Nietzsche in a 1919 addition to *The Interpretation of Dreams.*[40] Of course we do not know when Freud first read or learned of such passages in Nietzsche.

As Freud's relationship with Jung was beginning to strain and move towards the breaking point of 1913, Andreas-Salomé entered the psychoanalytic scene. When the break did come, Andreas-Salomé was there to console Freud in correspondence and in person at the Fourth International Psychoanalytic Congress in Munich in September 1913, at which Jung was present. She would write: "I have never felt so close to Freud as here; not only on account of this break with his 'son' Jung."[41]

According to Livingstone, during her earlier stay in Vienna, Andreas-Salomé and Freud discussed ideas that were going into the fourth (and most original and controversial) part of *Totem and Taboo.*[42] Regarding the extent to which Freud may have felt comfortable sharing ideas with Andreas-Salomé, we can consider the high praise from Abraham and our knowledge of how quickly Freud and Andreas-Salomé developed a very close relationship. One can also consider her long-standing psychological orientation. Apparently, she believed that however much she learned from Freud and psychoanalysis, in some important ways psychoanalysis had confirmed what she already knew.[43] As Livingstone points out, it was her relationship with Nietzsche (and Paul Rée, the other member of their threesome) in 1882 that was "the beginning of her lifelong concern with psychology, and her understanding of all ideas in psychological terms, a concern which eventually led her to Freud and psychoanalysis."[44] In September 1913 she made the following entry in her journal, a criticism which would have been one of Nietzsche's criticisms of Freud: "I cannot escape the idea that the tendency to death and rest—which Freud attributes to every living being as its essential being, inborn, and from which it is reluctant to be disturbed—is itself a rather neurotic estimation of life."[45] Here are Nietzsche's words:

> That the world is not striving toward a stable condition is the only thing that has been proved.[46]
>
> Every ethic with a negative definition of happiness, every metaphysics and physics that knows some *finale*, some final state of some sort . . . permits the question whether it was not sickness that inspired the philosopher.[47]

Even after she no longer had contact with Nietzsche, Andreas-Salomé would write that in her circle "Nietzsche . . . stood, like a hidden shadow, an invisible figure, in our midst."[48] Later she induced her husband to change his first name to Friedrich.[49]

———————

Shortly after this time and after the final break with Jung, Freud visited, as he had previously, Michelangelo's *Moses* in Rome a number of times (Freud completed his essay on the work in December 1913). Freud saw in the work a figure differing from the biblical Moses. Freud felt that the positioning of the figure indicated that rather than being about to hurl the tablets of the ten commandments at the unfaithful herd, Michelangelo's Moses had restrained himself, controlled his passions for the sake of a greater cause. (Since Michelangelo's Moses has horns [reflecting a mistranslation in the Bible which should have referred to rays of light rather than horns], this Moses might not be the angry Moses who descends from the mountain the first time to find his followers worshipping the golden calf. The horns [rays of light] are present only upon Moses' second descent from the mountain.) Freud had a strong feeling for and identification with the figure of Moses. Here his concerns about and attempts to creatively deal with the break with Jung and his own continued leadership of the psychoanalytic movement, his concern that some might repudiate him for what he felt were the easy answers and illusions of Jung, are reflected in his finding in Moses control, restraint, moderation and thoughtfulness in the face of his anger at finding his people dancing around the Golden Calf: "The giant frame with its tremendous physical power becomes only a concrete expression of the highest mental achievement that is possible in a man, that of struggling successfully against an inward passion for the sake of a cause to which he has devoted himself."[50]

Trosman comments that Freud was expressing his belief that the creative man of action as well as the creative artist struggles with the problem of taming instincts and transforming them through sublimation. Trosman also points out, however, that Freud also related to Michelangelo's *Moses* as a child to a stern father figure whose look of angry scorn evoked feelings of his own faults and shortcomings.[51] (Perhaps it is stretching things a bit to raise the possibility of oedipal guilt in relation to Nietzsche and Andreas-Salomé, the latter never having felt so close to Freud.) However, given the differing ways in which Freud related to and identified with Moses (which would also include the more expressly angry biblical Moses), it might be of some significance that Freud approvingly ("I see nothing to object to") quotes one important commentator, Thode, who describes Michelangelo as having portrayed "the nature of a superman" or overman ("Übermenschen"). Later in the essay Freud describes the figure as superhuman or "more than human" ("Übermenschliches"). The resonance with Nietzsche's term is strong.[52] Adding to the possible significance of Freud's use of this term is the fact that at the 1913 congress Jung's last lecture within the Freudian psychoanalytic movement included discussion of the concepts of the Apollonian and Dionysian as presented in the *Birth of Tragedy*.[53] And we have seen that for Freud, Jung and Nietzsche were already linked.

We can also mention that a characterization of Michelangelo's *Moses* as one of the supermen or overmen demonstrates a much more accurate understanding of the term than Freud's characterization of the father-tyrant of the primal horde as an overman in 1921 in *Group Psychology and the Analysis of the Ego*.[54]

Michelangelo portrays an overcoming that is "the highest mental achievement that is possible in a man." On one level, Freud's *Moses*, the towering figure with whom he identifies, may be Nietzsche's overman, or perhaps even Zarathustra-Nietzsche. (There is also the fact that *Zarathustra* contains allusions to Moses, references to old and new tablets, and a scene in which Zarathustra jumps into the middle of a group of guests that he believes has forsaken the more difficult path for an easier and more primitive one.[55])

We can also consider that in 1914, the year of publication of the essay on Michelangelo's *Moses*, Freud also completed *History of the Psycho-Analytic Movement* in which he wrote:

> In later years I have denied myself the very great pleasure of reading the works of Nietzsche, with the deliberate object of not being hampered in working out the impressions received in psychoanalysis by any sort of anticipatory ideas. I had therefore to be prepared—I am so, gladly—to forgo all claims to priority in the many instances in which laborious psychoanalytic investigation can merely confirm the truths which the philosopher recognized by intuition.[56]

It is difficult to understand what Freud could mean by not reading Nietzsche in his later years as well as to determine if this is acknowledgment of having read Nietzsche in earlier years. Freud never tells us exactly what he read of Nietzsche and never tells us exactly which years were those during which he avoided Nietzsche. We do know, of course, that a few years earlier, in 1908, Freud had read and discussed Nietzsche, including a work of direct relevance to his own anthropological explorations as well as to ideas pertaining to the relationship between repression of instincts and the development of the inner world and conscience. We have also seen that lectures, articles, and discussions on Nietzsche continued around Freud. It does seem though that here Freud demonstrates a readiness to "forgo all claims to priority" regarding the psychological observations of Nietzsche and others that the science of psychoanalysis has confirmed.

None of this may be of much significance if it cannot also be demonstrated that Nietzsche's influence finds its way into Freud's work in a substantial way at this time. Additional isolated quotes or allusions, such as the possible allusion in 1913 to Nietzsche's concept of eternal recurrence in "The Theme of the Three Caskets,"[57] will certainly not do, although it is of interest that the term is used at this time.

———

It is in this light that we can recall Wallace's comment that "Nietzsche . . . anticipated, one can almost certainly say influenced, a chain of ideas central to *Totem and Taboo*."[58] Wallace makes this statement without alluding to most of the relevant material presented in the present study. The influences Wallace has in mind pertain to Nietzsche's ideas regarding the relationships among dreams, unconscious dynamics, creativity, insanity and the prehistory of humankind as such ideas are expressed in early works such as *Human, All Too Human*. Wallace points out that as early as *Human, All Too Human* Nietzsche connected dreams, the behavior of present-day primitives, prehistoric man and the creative process of poets and artists. Wallace states that the only missing link in relation to Freud is the child.[59] However, he doesn't point out that Nietzsche writes of outbursts of passion, dreams and insanity being related specifically to a person's *own* history as well as mankind's prehistory.[60] Wallace also mentions ideas similar to Freud's in Nietzsche's conceptualization of sorcery as an attempt to coerce a deity and religion as an effort to influence a deity by supplication and prayer as well as his understanding of the importance of projection in religious belief.[61] Wallace does not refer to any of Nietzsche's late works written after *Zarathustra*. (Jones, on the other hand, quotes from the *Genealogy*, mentions the 1908 society meeting at which it was discussed and comments on the similarity between Nietzsche's "bad conscience" and Freud's superego as well as the affinity between the *Genealogy* and *Totem and Taboo*.[62])

We can also note, as Wallace suggests, that anthropological influences and Freud's anthropological thinking were not peripheral to his other theoretical and clinical writings, but an important "influence on the formation of some of Freud's most important presuppositions and concepts—including projection, the omnipotence of thoughts, neurosis as atavism, the Oedipus complex, the role of phylogeny in human psychology, and the psychic unity of mankind."[63]

In *Totem and Taboo*, completed in the spring of 1913, Freud is concerned with the origin of totemism—the worship of and periodic ceremonial sacrifice of a clan's special identifying animal—and its relation to the origin of exogamy—the horror of incest and rule of marriage outside of one's clan. Freud speculated, drawing on Darwin and other authors,[64] that the beginnings of human society were constituted by a primal horde, a tyrannical father ruling a group of sons and having the women of the horde to himself. At some point the brothers rebelled at such brutal control (which included castration on occasion) and forced suppression of instinctual expression, and they killed and devoured their father. However, they soon recognized that continued rivalry over the women of the group would jeopardize cohesiveness necessary for safety, security and survival. Also, since their feelings for the father were ambivalent, after the deed was accomplished, feelings of affection and remorse emerged. Due to these two factors, the brothers wound up depriving themselves of the women of the group. They revoked their deed by not killing the totem (created as a substitute for the father) except under special ceremoniously prescribed circumstances, this reflecting the ambivalence of their relationship to and identification with the primal father. (Ever since its publication, many have commented on the possible relationship of this work to Freud's wishes, fears and fantasies regarding his psychoanalytic sons.)

Freud also speculates that the origins of totemism were related to conditions of the Oedipus complex, that is, the two prohibitions of totemism, not to kill the totem or have sexual relations with a woman of the same group, coincide with the two primal wishes of children (in this instance, the boy) to kill the father and sexually possess the mother. (It is in this work that Freud forcefully reintroduces the term "Oedipus complex" after having first used it in 1910.[65]) Freud goes on to suggest that unconscious memory and guilt over the original deed have been culturally transmitted (along with genetic transmission of certain psychological underpinnings and the *possibility* of the transmission of memory traces) and form the basis or foundation upon which is built present-day neurosis.[66] Freud will rework these themes through the remainder of his life, at times more or less emphasizing his belief in the actual occurrence of the primal parricide and its phylogenetic transmission versus what might be regarded as a more allegorical reading.[67] At the end of his life, in *Moses and Monotheism,* which Wallace describes as largely a redressing of the primal father motif,[68] Freud again states that the masses retain past experiences in unconscious memory traces, and by this time his belief in phylogenetic inheritance of unconscious memories is definite.

In 1930, a few years before writing *Moses and Monotheism*, Freud had reworked some of the relevant themes in *Civilization and Its Discontents*. He extended his discussion of the origins of civilization as being linked intimately with guilt and the maintenance and progress of civilization as being connected with the setting up of an agency within the psyche, the superego. The superego watches over potentially unruly and disruptive instincts, utilizing guilt and a need for punishment in the ego so that aggression is repressed and directed inward. In all of this, social cohesion, morality and civilization are seen as arising from and being maintained by repression of instincts, guilt, the desire for repentance, even the need for punishment as well as the ambivalent identification with a leader who is in the position of the projected ego-ideal. All of this follows an actual (or allegorically read) primal parricide, with the possibility that such a traumatic event, that is this "original relation to the father," leaves behind a "heritage of emotion" to be found in "customs, ceremonies and dogmas."[69] The totem is a father substitute, and it is also the primal father that is ultimately behind God (and Moses) and the development of religion. There is the expression of aggression as well as obedient renunciation and identification with and internalization of the father's power.

We can also mention that in this work Freud addresses issues pertaining to the origin of Greek tragedy and the relationship of the god Dionysus to the Greek chorus, matters explored in a different vein by Nietzsche in *The Birth of Tragedy*. (In 1930, Arnold Zweig, considering writing an essay on Freud and Nietzsche, will write to Freud: "Nietzsche . . . tried to explain the birth of tragedy; you have done it in *Totem and Taboo*."[70]) Freud does not mention Nietzsche's famous book on this subject.

For Freud (who devotes only a few paragraphs to the matter), the hero of tragedy had to suffer because of his "tragic guilt," which related to "rebellion against some divine or human authority." But underlying this, the hero had to suffer because he was in fact

the primal father, the Hero of the great primaeval tragedy . . . and the tragic guilt was the guilt which he had to take on himself in order to relieve the Chorus from theirs . . . in the remote reality it had actually been the members of the Chorus who caused the hero's suffering; now . . . it was the hero himself who was responsible for his own suffering. The crime which was thrown on to his shoulders, presumptuousness and rebelliousness against a great authority, was precisely the crime for which the members of the Chorus, the company of brothers, were responsible. Thus the Tragic Hero became, though it might be against his will, the redeemer of the Chorus.[71]

In a variation on this theme, Freud later writes in *Moses and Monotheism* of "the true basis for the 'tragic guilt' of the hero of drama . . . the hero and chorus in Greek drama represented the same rebellious hero and company of brothers."[72]

For Nietzsche the chorus in its relation to Dionysian religious rites exists prior to the hero and stage characters. The chorus has its links with the Dionysian realm (the realm of music, singing) out of which emerge the actors with their individual identities: "In the origin of tragedy only the chorus, in the orchestra, is real, while the world of the stage, the persons and events on it, were visible only as living images, as the shining forms of the Apollonian phantasy of the chorus."[73] As for the theme of earliest Greek tragedy: "Greek tragedy in its earliest form had for its sole theme the sufferings of Dionysus"; "until Euripides . . . all the celebrated figures of the Greek stage . . . are mere masks of this original hero, Dionysus."[74] As regards the fate of the hero: "We are forced to look into the terrors of individual existence—yet . . . [w]e are really for a brief moment primordial being itself, feeling its raging desire for existence and joy in existence; the struggle, the pain, the destruction of phenomena, now appear necessary to us, in view of the excess of countless forms of existence which force and push one another into life."[75] Although we view and respond to the "terrors of individual existence" and the destruction of individual existence, we are also participating joyfully in "primordial being itself." It will be recalled, however, that Nietzsche writes of the *illusion,* "the metaphysical comfort that beneath the whirl of phenomena, eternal life flows on indestructibly."[76] While there may be a problem here regarding truth and illusion, in the passage just quoted, there is no positing of a comforting illusory belief in indestructible, eternal life as the realm of joy beneath the painful whirl of phenomena. The "joy in existence," in feeling the raging desire for existence of primordial being, includes the *appearance* to us of the necessity for life of struggle, pain and destruction. This *feeling* of raging desire for and joy in existence is not the same as the comforting *belief* that eternal life flows on indestructibly beneath the whirl of phenomena.

Regarding the chorus and spectators, Sallis writes:

> The primal dramatic phenomenon thus consists in being outside oneself, exceeding the limits of one's individuality . . . Even though the chorus is the primary site of this phenomenon, it also occurs on the side of the spectators—indeed to such an extent as to efface the very opposition between the spectators and the chorus whose resounding songs could not but draw those spectators into the very ecstasy they celebrate.[77]

Lenson points to positive consequences in the fall of the hero: "Oedipus finds a greater power than Kingship; in *Hamlet*, Fortinbras ('strong-arm man') marches in to restore order to a world gone out of balance. Dionysus, cyclic god that he is, is a figure for this compensation."[78] From a Freudian perspective, on the other hand, a play like *Oedipus Rex* "serves as a collective, publicly constituted fantasy that corresponds to the unconscious incestuous and rivalrous fantasies harbored by each member of the audience as repressed residues of childhood."[79]

As Lawrence Hatab points out, in the Nietzschean analysis the hero's dilemma and suffering cannot be traced back to personality characteristics or particular psychosocial circumstances. The circumstances of the characters reflect "a richly specified enactment of a deep, underlying religious meaning—the immersion of humans in a sacred, coercive fatality."[80] For Nietzsche there is no one actual critical event and its aftermath, such as the primal parricide, that is reenacted. Just as for Nietzsche there is no primal act and its aftermath that is reenacted in tragedy (unless we regard the emergence into individuated form as such a primal act), so too when Nietzsche discusses the origins of "bad conscience," while he suggests the kinds of circumstances under which "bad conscience," morality, religion and civilization developed, he does not suggest a single act such as the primal parricide in which these developments specifically originated and were then specifically transmitted down through generations.

In the *Genealogy* Nietzsche writes of the origins of morality and of the origins and maintenance of civilization as inextricably linked with the suppression and then repression of instincts, the direction of these instincts turned inward, the "internalization of man," with particular emphasis on internalized guilt, including its use for power and control by the likes of the ascetic priest. In addition, for Nietzsche one of the ways "bad conscience" develops on the historical plane is by the "masters" or "blond beasts of prey" violently expelling freedom and imposing form upon the "slaves" with the result that the *"instinct for freedom* [is] forcibly made latent—this instinct for freedom pushed back and repressed, incarcerated within and finally able to discharge and vent itself only on itself: that, and that alone, is what the *bad conscience* is in its beginnings." In this same passage Nietzsche even goes so far as to state that this initial "disaster . . . precluded all struggle and even all *ressentiment.*"[81]

As Anderson[82] points out, both Freud and Nietzsche reject the notion of gradual or contractual change and account for the origin of civilization by violent events. Both also regard the consequences of such origins as the creation of an inherently neurotic creature, and both emphasize the necessary price paid for civilization and its achievements, as well as what may emerge from this state of being: "The existence on earth of an animal soul turned against itself, taking sides against itself, was something so new, profound, unheard of, enigmatic, contradictory, *and pregnant with a future* that the aspect of the earth was essentially altered."[83] The bad conscience, illness that it is, is nonetheless "the womb of all ideal and imaginative phenomena [and has also] brought to light an abundance of strange new beauty and affirmation, and perhaps beauty itself."[84] Even the ascetic priest, "this *life-inimical* species . . . must indeed be in the *interest of life itself.*"[85] It is very important to keep such comments in mind when suggestions are made to the effect that Nietzsche glorifies the blond beasts of prey, the masters, and ruthless, primitive expression of the will to power. Nietzsche, even as he seems to decry the slave revolt in morality inherited from the Jews, also states that "human history would be altogether too stupid a thing without the spirit that the impotent have introduced into it."[86] Nietzsche is concerned with the relationship of our "animal" nature to our genealogy of ascetic suppression and devaluation of this (so to speak) nature, and our potential transformations of the resulting condition in light of the death of God.[87]

Mention can also be made of the fact that Nietzsche's language in the *Genealogy* is at times very close to the central ideas of *Totem and Taboo*. Consider the following passage:

> This man of the bad conscience . . . apprehends in "God" the ultimate antithesis of his own ineluctable animal instincts: he reinterprets these animal instincts themselves as a form of guilt before God (as hostility, rebellion, insurrection against the "Lord," the "father," the primal ancestor and origin of the world).[88]

Freud takes this "guilt before God" as reflective of the actual deed perpetrated upon the primal father.

Regarding the origin of gods Nietzsche writes:

> The ancestors of the *most powerful* tribes are bound eventually to grow to monstrous dimensions through the imagination of growing fear and to recede into the darkness of the divinely uncanny and unimaginable: in the end the ancestor must necessarily be transfigured into a *god*. Perhaps this is even the origin of gods.[89]

Of course Nietzsche is not discussing totemism or the significance of a prehistoric primal parricide, but he is discussing the individual's guilt over his own instincts which are viewed as hostility, rebellion and insurrection towards the Lord, the father, "the primal ancestor." He sees the origins of gods in powerful, feared ancestors, although for certain "noble tribes" there is also piety and gratefulness, a paying back of "their ancestors . . . with interest all the qualities that had become palpable in themselves, the *noble* qualities."[90]

However, we can add that there is in fact a well-known and most crucial parricide in Nietzsche as well as in Freud. *Zarathustra* is famous for its announcement of the death of God, this death being presented as of central significance for humankind. God is presented at one point as dying of pity at mankind's state and at another point is presented as having been murdered by "The

Ugliest Man."[91] But there is also one of Nietzsche's most well-known passages from another book, the parable of the madman in *The Gay Science:* "'Whither is God?'" he cried; "'I will tell you. *We have killed him*—you and I. All of us are his murderers.'"[92] *We have murdered the Father.* For Nietzsche this symbolic parracide marks a critical juncture in the course of civilization, and its full consequences and implications must be, with great difficulty, fully absorbed and integrated in the service of creative growth and affirmation of life. For Freud the primal parracide, an actual parracide, is placed at the other critical juncture, the origin of civilization and, ultimately, the birth of God, although it is endlessly repeated.

# Chapter 9

## "On Narcissism" and "Instincts and Their Vicissitudes"

*It is only themselves that such women love . . . another person's narcissism has a great attraction . . . as does the charm of certain animals . . . such as cats and the large beasts of prey.*
—Freud, "On Narcissism"

*What inspires respect for women . . . is : . . . the genuine, cunning suppleness of a beast of prey . . . the naïveté of her egoism . . . this dangerous and beautiful cat "woman."*
—Nietzsche, *Beyond Good and Evil*

If Nietzsche's presence and influence can be detected in an anthropological work such as *Totem and Taboo*, can the same be said for non anthropological work during this period? Of course many of Nietzsche's psychological concepts, such as unconscious guilt, unconscious envy, unconscious resistance, the turning of drives against the self, sublimation and so many more, have direct bearing on all of depth psychology, not merely its more strictly anthropological explorations. But can we discern such influence or affinity in Freud's work of the period other than in the area of anthropology or as regards broad and general psychodynamic principles?

We might discern Nietzsche's influence in an important paper of this period, the 1914 paper "On Narcissism: An Introduction."[1] In this paper, Freud explores, among other things, the ramifications of his finding of an original libidinal cathexis of the ego, from which some is later given off to objects, but which fundamentally persists and is related to the object-cathexes much as the body of an amoeba is related to the pseudopodia which it puts out.

The development of the ego consists in a departure from the primary narcissism and results in a vigorous attempt to recover that state. This departure is brought about by means of the displacement of libido on to an ego-ideal imposed from without; and satisfaction is brought about from fulfilling this ideal.

At the same time the ego has sent out the libidinal object-cathexes. It becomes impoverished in favour of these cathexes, just as it does in favour of the ego-ideal, and it enriches itself once more from its satisfactions in respect of the object, just as it does by fulfilling its ideal.[2]

Freud considers the implications of these findings for his dual instinct theory which divides instincts into the duality of ego instincts and libidinal instincts. Freud questions this division, but does not definitively abandon it, which he will do in *Beyond the Pleasure Principle.*

As indicated, one of Freud's important points is that the ego makes vigorous attempts to recover its state of primary narcissism. This is related to important themes running through Nietzsche's writings. Nietzsche is aware of how we relate to others on the basis of projections of idealized images of ourselves, and he is consistently looking for the ways in which we are loving ourselves and aggrandizing ourselves in activities which would seem to be reflective of contrary motivations. We can recall his words regarding mother and child:

A mother gives to her child that of which she deprives herself . . . Is it not clear that in [such] instances man loves *something of himself* . . . more than *something else of himself* . . . The *inclination for something* (wish, impulse, desire) is present in all [such] instances; to give in to it, with all the consequences, is in any event not "unegoistic."[3]

Here is Freud on parental love: "Parental love, which is so moving and at bottom so childish, is nothing but the parents' narcissism born again, which, transformed into object-love, unmistakenly reveals its former nature."⁴ Marcia Cavell points out that Freud posits ego libido, object libido and two kinds of object choice, narcissistic (modeled on a primary narcissistic choice of oneself) and anaclitic (genuine object-choice modeled on the child's attachment to the mother). For those who love according to the anaclitic type, the ego libido "becomes self-love at another level; love for the ideal self one would like to be, or perhaps phantasizes one is."⁵ Nietzsche writes that "the sexes deceive themselves about each other—because at bottom they honor and love only themselves (or their own ideal, to put it more pleasantly)."⁶ (See also "Deception in love," *Human*, 1, sec. 57, quoted below.)

On the other hand, as Jean Graybeal points out, Zarathustra says: "One loves from the heart only one's own child and one's work; and where there is great love of oneself, then it is a sign of pregnancy."⁷ This provides a different twist on the notion of narcissism or self-enjoyment, reversing the order of priorities with true love of oneself being the sign or symptom of something greater— pregnancy of one kind or another. Regarding the child, Graybeal points out that for Nietzsche "every child is an opportunity to step further along the tightrope toward the Übermensch, and every human being moving in that direction must discover or give birth to a child within. Thus to make the child one's end, as Zarathustra says women do, may be praiseworthy or wise."⁸ Among the tensions, some might say contradictions, in Nietzsche is that between primal motivations towards self-enjoyment, that can be described as narcissistic in nature, and primal motivations towards pregnancy, towards creating beyond one's self, towards surpassing one's self.

One may wonder if Andreas-Salomé's presence can be recognized in the essay when Freud writes of a type of woman who is beautiful and self-sufficient:

> Strictly speaking, it is only themselves that such women love . . . Nor does their need lie in the direction of loving, but of being loved . . . The importance of this type of woman for the erotic life of man-kind is to be rated very high . . . it seems very evident that another person's narcissism has a great attraction for those who have renounced part of their own narcissism and are in search of object-love. The charm of a child lies to a great extent in his narcissism, his self-contentment

and inaccessibility, just as does the charm of certain animals which seem not to concern themselves about us, such as cats and the large beasts of prey . . . It is as if we envied them for maintaining a blissful state of mind—an unassailable libidinal position which we ourselves have since abandoned.[9]

Besides the facts of Andreas-Salomé being known as a "femme fatale" or "femme savante"[10] and known for her wearing of furs, it may be that there is some link to Nietzsche here. Sarah Kofman, in discussing Nietzsche's ideas on women and the feminine mentions that the "tiger and the panther, all felines and animals of Dionysus, are related to women, the most feline and natural animal of all. She is beautiful, graceful, and fierce."[11] In a footnote Kofman adds: "Freud [in "On Narcissism"], probably by the intermediary of Lou Salomé, seems to have drawn upon this conception of the woman-panther."[12] In *Beyond Good and Evil*, Nietzsche writes:

What inspires respect for woman and often enough even fear, is her *nature*, which is more "natural" than man's, the genuine, cunning suppleness of a beast of prey, the tiger's claw under the glove, the naïveté of her egoism, her uneducability and inner wildness, the incomprehensibility, scope, and movement of her desires and virtues . . . this dangerous and beautiful cat "woman."[13]

As Kofman also points out in her book on Freud's writings on women, Freud's view of woman here is not one of an inborn deficiency and primal envy of the penis; rather, here it is man who envies this woman for her unassailable narcissism and self-sufficiency (or what he views as such), a "blissful" position he has "renounced" and for which he longs.[14]

Perhaps there is another point at which Nietzsche's presence can be felt. In responding to a criticism of libido theory from Jung, Freud mentions that Jung believes that "introversion" of libido would lead not necessarily to loss of reality (to demential praecox, as Freud believed was the case) but "the psychology of an ascetic anchorite."[15] Here is Freud's criticism of Jung:

How little this inept analogy can help us to decide the question may be learnt from the consideration that an anchorite who "tries to eradicate every trace of sexual interest" (but only in the popular sense of the word "sexual") does not even necessarily display any pathogenic allocation of the libido. He may have diverted his sexual interest from human beings entirely, and yet may have sublimated it into a heightened interest in the divine.[16]

Both Jung and Freud were well aware of Nietzsche's analyses of the ascetic ideal and the ascetic priest (who differs in some ways from the more secluded anchorite) and of his conception of sublimation, including sublimated sexuality and will to power. Nietzsche writes both of attempts at extirpation of the drives and of how, for example, "in Paul the priest wanted power" and used concepts and symbols to tyrannize; power is sought over oneself as well as over others. It can be recalled that at one of the 1908 meetings, a passage was read aloud which although not using the word "sublimation" clearly described sublimated sexuality, particularly in the aesthetic experience and in the idealism of the adolescent girl.[17] Nietzsche also specifically wrote of the "men and women of sublimated sexuality [who] have made their find in Christianity."[18] Freud points out that the anchorite is not one who has necessarily withdrawn his libido into himself, but rather may have found a sublimated expression of libido, thus avoiding the most severe pathology (loosening the contact with reality) that would result from such an introversion of libido.

There is also the more general notion in Freud's paper to the effect that the working over of stimuli in the mind "helps remarkably towards an internal draining away of excitations which are incapable of direct discharge outwards."[19] (This working over of stimuli should be distinguished from a mere withdrawl of libido back into the self.) This has a clear affinity with Nietzsche's idea that drives not allowed outward expression turn inward, and, what is more important, that this turning inward such as in the development of consciousness and conscience, even "bad conscience," has a temporary therapeutic function in that relief is brought to what would otherwise be experienced as an utterly and profoundly hopeless and helpless experience or condition of having no outlet for discharge of "excitations."

Later in the essay Freud states that "the activity of the mind which has taken over the function of conscience has also placed itself in the service of internal research [or introspection], which furnishes philosophy with the material for its intellectual operations."[20] He goes on to write of "self-observation" in dream formation and that it is not invariable: "Probably the reason why I overlooked it is because it does not play any great part in my own dreams; in persons who are gifted philosophically and accustomed to introspection it may become very evident."[21]

We have seen that in *The Birth of Tragedy* Nietzsche wrote of self-observation in dreams[22] and that in *The Interpretation of Dreams* Freud made a comment that in philosophical minds the self-observing agency may be prominent.[23] Here Freud is linking that functioning in the mind which pertains to conscience with introspection and self-observation. He once again places philosophy in the realm of introspection and contrasts this with his own nature. It should also be recalled that in the *Genealogy* Nietzsche linked the development of conscience with the widening of the depth and breadth of the entire internal world.[24]

In 1915 Freud wrote another important and well-known essay, "Instincts and Their Vicissitudes."[25] In the same year he issued a third edition of the *Three Essays on the Theory of Sexuality*. In both works Freud discusses aspects of sadomasochistic relationships. In the third edition of the *Three Essays*, Freud writes of masochism as "an extension of sadism turned round upon the subject's own self, which thus, to begin with, takes the place of the sexual object."[26] In "Instincts and Their Vicissitudes" Freud discusses how sadist and masochist can experience and derive gratification from the position of the other through identification,[27] so that, for example, drives initially directed outward may be turned inward, but in addition the initial position and its impulses may be simultaneously experienced and gratification achieved through identification.

Terry Eagleton suggests that "Freud like Nietzsche deconstructs at a stroke the whole problematic . . . of the encounter between self-identical subject and stable object . . . [For Freud] subject and object, as for Nietzsche, are a passing product."[28] Henry Staten writes of Nietzsche demonstrating that

> the relation between self and other has to be rethought as a dialectic in which the self finds its reflection in the other and the other is then reflected back into the self.

This is the same dialectic rediscovered by Freud in the metapsychology of 1915 and later. Pain that is experienced as pleasure; the pervasiveness of narcissism; and aggressivity in the dialectic of identifications by which the self is constituted: Freud's articulation of these themes is strikingly parallel to Nietzsche's, but it is more explicit and systematic.[29]

A few pages later Staten adds the following:

Both Freud and Nietzsche are engaged in a redefinition of the root of subjectivity, a redefinition that replaces the moral problematic of selfishness with the economic problematic of what Freud would call narcissism . . . [Freud and Nietzsche elaborate upon] the whole field of libidinal economy: the transit of libido through other selves, aggression, infliction and reception of pain, and something very much like death (the total evacuation of the entire quantum of excitation with which the organism is charged).[30]

Nietzsche suggests that in our concern for the other, in our sacrifice for the other, we are concerned with ourselves, one part of ourselves represented by the other. That for which we sacrifice ourselves is unconsciously related to as another part of ourselves. In relating to the other we are in fact also relating to a part of ourselves and we are concerned with our own pleasure and pain and our own expression of will to power. In one analysis of pity, Nietzsche states that "we are, to be sure, not consciously thinking of ourself but are doing so strongly unconsciously."[31] He goes on to suggest that it is primarily our own pleasure and pain that we are concerned about and that the feelings and reactions that ensue are multidetermined: "We never do anything of this kind out of *one* motive."[32] He goes on to describe a number of unconscious motives that may be involved in reactions of pity.

Nietzsche is aware of our divided natures and that we respond to others in part on the basis of projecting and identifying with aspects of ourselves in them. In a section from *Human, All Too Human* from which we have quoted above, Nietzsche writes:

*Morality as the self-division of man.*—A soldier wishes he could fall on the battlefield for his victorious fatherland . . . A mother gives to her child that of which she deprives herself . . . are these all unegoistic states? . . . Is it not clear that in all these instances man loves *something of himself*, an idea, a desire, an offspring, more than *something else of himself*, that he thus *divides* his nature and sacrifices one part of it to the other? . . . The *inclination for something* (wish, impulse, desire) is present in all the above-mentioned instances; to give in to it, with all the consequences, is in any event not "unegoistic." —In morality man treats himself not as *individuum* but as *dividuum*.[33]

In another section from this work he writes:

*Deception in love.*—We forget a great deal of our own past and deliberately banish it from our minds . . . we want the image of ourself that shines upon us out of the past to deceive us and flatter our self-conceit—we are engaged continually on this self-deception.—And do you think, you who speak so much of "self-forgetfulness in love", of "the merging of the ego in the other person", and laud it so highly, do you think this is anything essentially different? We shatter the mirror, impose ourself upon someone we admire, and then enjoy our ego's new image, even though we may call it by that other person's name.[34]

In *Daybreak* Nietzsche describes man, in the person of the ascetic, as "split asunder into a sufferer and a spectator," enduring and enjoying within (as a consequence of his drive for "distinction," his will to power) that which the barbarian imposes on others. And in concluding this section, as Staten[35] points out, Nietzsche asks if the basic disposition of the ascetic and of the pitying god who creates suffering mankind can be held simultaneously, and that one would do "hurt to others in order thereby to hurt *oneself*, in order then to triumph over oneself and one's pity and to revel in an extremity of power!"[36] Nietzsche appears to be suggesting that in hurting the other I may, through identification, be attempting to hurt one part of myself, so that whatever my triumph over the other, I may be as concerned with one part of myself triumphing over that part of myself I identify with in the other as well as thereby overcoming pity and in consequence "revel in an extremity of power." (Or in a variation of such dynamics, as Michel Hulin has put it, the individual may be "tempted to play both roles at once, contriving to torture himself in order to enjoy all the more his own capacity for overcoming suffering."[37])

We should also keep in mind that in addition to Nietzsche writing specifically of the sublimation of the sexual drive, the will to power and its vicissitudes are described at times in ways related to sexual as well as aggressive drives, particularly in the form of appropriation and incorporation. As Staten[38] points out, this notion of the primitive will to power is similar to Freud's idea in *Group Psychology and the Analysis of the Ego* according to which, "identification [is] the earliest expression of an emotional tie with another person . . . It behaves like a derivation of the first *oral* phase of the organization of the libido, in which the object that we long for and prize is assimilated by eating."[39] It would appear that Nietzsche goes a step further than Freud in one of his notes when he writes: "'Nourishment'—is only derivative; the original phenomenon is: to desire to incorporate everything."[40] Staten also concludes that "if Freudian libido contains a strong element of aggression and destructiveness, Nietzschean will to power never takes place without a pleasurable excitation that there is no reason not to call erotic."[41]

We can also note that in a May 11, 1913, entry in her journal, Andreas-Salomé writes of the "enigma of cruelty: that it is only imposed on the beloved object and increases in proportion to the love . . . Cruel people being always masochists also, the whole thing is inseparable from bisexuality . . . The first time I ever discussed this theme was with Nietzsche."[42] One can only wonder here as elsewhere about the extent to which Nietzsche's ideas or something approximating them may have reached Freud through Andreas-Salomé.

# Chapter 10

## THE PALE CRIMINAL

*The pre-existence of the feeling of guilt, and the utilization of a deed in order to rationalize this feeling, glimmer before us in Zarathustra's sayings "On the Pale Criminal."*
—Freud, "Some Character-Types Met with in Psycho-Analytic Work"

In 1916, in his paper "Some Character-Types Met with in Psycho-Analytic Work,"[1] Freud mentions Nietzsche. The title of the third and last section of this paper is "Criminality from a Sense of Guilt." Freud discusses a particular type of criminal, one who was

> suffering from an oppressive feeling of guilt, of which he did not know the origin, and after he had committed a misdeed this oppression was mitigated. His sense of guilt was at least attached to something.
>   Paradoxical as it may sound, I must maintain that the sense of guilt was present before the misdeed, that it did not arise from it, but conversely—the misdeed, arose from the sense of guilt.[2]

Freud closes this section and the paper by informing us that a friend has recently called his attention to the fact that the "criminal from a sense of guilt" was recognized by Nietzsche: "The pre-existence of the feeling of guilt, and the utilization of a deed in order to rationalize this feeling, glimmer before us in Zarathustra's sayings 'On the Pale Criminal.' Let us leave it to future research to decide how many criminals are to be reckoned among these 'pale' ones."[3] Freud grasps Nietzsche's understanding of an "obscure" sense of guilt which propels the individual towards transgressing action which will rationalize and relieve this feeling. Only three pages or so earlier in *Zarathustra* Freud could also have read Nietzsche discussing unconscious envy.[4] Unconscious guilt and envy are explicitly discussed and/or implied throughout Nietzsche's writings. It is also possible that at some time Freud read these passages which appear early in the first part of *Zarathustra*. One might ask if Freud's writing of Nietzsche's words as he does— they "glimmer before us"—does not, in its language, convey a sense of familiarity with this work or at least that he read this section after his friend called his attention to it. (It will be recalled that Freud also demonstrated his familiarity with the section "Before Sunrise.")

In the section "On the Pale Criminal"[5] Nietzsche describes a "madness *after* the deed" (the crime) and "yet another madness . . . that comes *before* the deed." The madness after the deed, a deed which we understand as a murder, pertains to the criminal, who "was equal to his deed when he did it," not being able to "bear its image after it was done." This image "made this pale man pale." He could only see himself, define himself, find his essence "as the doer of one deed." The madness before the deed pertains to the pale criminal rationalizing his desire for blood, "the bliss of the knife," with a robbery. "He did not want to be ashamed of his madness." Actually, the transgression of the robbery is prompted by the guilt and shameful madness over the desire for blood, the intention to allow himself to thirst "after the bliss of the knife." The thirst after the bliss of the knife itself is not necessarily a transgression prompted by guilt. The secondary crime is an act, a transgression, involving rationalizing the primary wishes, intentions, and deed, and dealing with the guilt over them.

However, the "murderous lust" is not a manifestation of some primary and irreducible instinctual desire. The pale criminal has "suffered and coveted." He is a "heap of diseases," a turmoil of conflicting forces, "wild snakes," seeking prey in the world. What this "poor body . . . suffered and coveted[,] this poor soul interpreted for itself: it interpreted it as murderous lust and greed for the bliss of the knife." The murderous lust, while not specifically prompted by guilt, is prompted by the soul's interpretation, is in fact the soul's interpretation, of the body's suffering, covetousness, and the turmoil of conflict that cannot be mastered, the "ball of wild snakes, which rarely enjoy rest from each other: so they go forth singly and seek [their] prey." Conflict not being mastered or integrated, any single element among the conflicting forces, any single wild snake, may go forth and seek its prey. The act is a result of, or is in itself, an interpretation of this sorry state of a heap of diseases, a ball of wild snakes.

Zarathustra states that "thought is one thing, the deed is another, and the image of the deed still another: the wheel of causality does not roll between them." So during the deed the criminal is equal to it. Regarding the thought or wish or intention, it arises out of the interpretation of his suffering, but there is also shame leading to a second act as a defense against recognition of the primacy of the original desire. After the deed the image of it is unbearable because he can see his essence only as the doer of this one deed. He could have dealt with his suffering or his shame or his self-image in relation to the deed in any number of ways.

One of the points Nietzsche is making in this section can be clarified with his own words from *The Will to Power:* "The 'bite' of conscience: a sign that the character is no match for the deed."[6] Also, from *Twilight of the Idols:* "Not to perpetrate cowardice against one's own acts! Not to leave them in the lurch afterwards! The bite of conscience is indecent."[7]

Nietzsche is not counseling us to go out and murder and then not to succumb to the bite of conscience, not to leave our act in the lurch. We must keep in mind that the very thirst for the bliss of the knife is an interpretation by a heap of diseases, a ball of snakes. Rather, one working towards becoming a more integrated human being should be working towards developing the character to accept one's desires and one's acts as one's own and not, out of guilt or shame, repudiate them, leave them in the lurch, through other desires and acts the functions of which are primarily to repress or defend against the original desires and intentions. For Nietzsche a basic satisfaction with oneself would accompany the development of such capacities. The pale criminal on the other hand, with his madness before and after the deed, has contempt for himself. His eyes say "my ego is to me the great contempt of man."

This judgment of himself, his self-contempt, prompts Zarathustra to conclude: "There is no redemption for one who suffers so of himself, except a quick death." He counsels the judges of the pale criminal not to deprive him of his self-judgment: "That he judged himself, that was his highest moment." Their killing of him is to be a deed of pity and not revenge. As they kill they are to "be sure that you yourselves justify life!" That there are judges (in part superego manifestations) and an impending execution in this section may lead one to add the factor of anticipated punishment to the madness of the pale criminal. He has condemned himself, and one may wonder if Zarathustra's counsel to the judges of providing "a quick death" might not also be the wish of so tormented and self-condemning a soul. Zarathustra sees that the judges "do not want to kill . . . until the animal has nodded." But he tells them that with his self-contempt "the pale criminal has nodded," the pale criminal has said "yes" not to life but to death. In this context one might consider that the "interpretation" of suffering that led to the thirst for the bliss of the knife might also be leading to the nod to punishment and death. The pale criminal, it would seem, may have already given his nod before the deed. This takes us not only into the realm of Freud's criminal from a sense of guilt but also into the realms of depression, masochism and the provocation of punishment.

In his paper "Mourning and Melancholia" (1917, first draft 1915), Freud emphasizes the part played by a criticizing conscience and self-criticism or "dissatisfaction with the ego on moral grounds" as by far "the most outstanding feature" of depression.[8] Freud also states that the unconscious loss that is the major factor in the onset of depression concerns an object choice that had been effected on a narcissistic basis. In mourning too, if it is pathological, the loss may involve an ambivalent relationship effected to too great a degree on a narcissistic basis. For Freud, object love, which cannot be given up (though the object is given up), takes refuge in narcissistic identification.[9] The threatened libidinal cathexis at last abandons the object, only however to "draw back to the place in the ego from which it had proceeded. So by taking flight into the ego love escaped extinction."[10] After this regression there may appear in consciousness "a conflict between one part of the ego and the critical agency."[11] The self-torments are a means of taking revenge on the internalized original objects which are related to ambivalently. Freud would likely ask us to consider that there is an ambivalently related-to object to whom the sadism of the pale criminal's self-torments is directed. Freud writes that "the ego debases itself and rages against itself."[12] The pale criminal states: "My ego is to me the great contempt of man." And we can note here Ellenberger's observation:

> Nietzsche taught that no one will complain or accuse himself without a secret desire for vengeance, thus "Every complaint (Klagen) is accusation (Anklagen)." The same idea with the same play on words is to be found in Freud's celebrated paper Mourning and Melancholia: "Their 'complaints' are actually 'plaints' in the older sense of the word."[13]

We may also ask if the pale criminal's readiness to nod to death relates to Freud's discussion in his 1924 paper "The Economic Problem in Masochism" in which he states that "masochism creates a temptation to perform sinful acts which must then be expiated by the reproaches of the sadistic conscience . . . or by chastisement"[14] from parental substitutes. Freud writes that a good part of the individual's conscience "may have vanished into his masochism."[15] Are not the condemning judges, to whom the pale criminal nods with his self-contempt, the parental substitutes or internalized parental figures bringing anticipated, even sought for, chastisement?

The next paragraph in the paper relates directly to Nietzsche's *Genealogy*. Freud writes that the

> turning back of sadism against the self regularly occurs where a *cultural suppression of the instincts* holds back a large part of the subject's destructive instinctual components from being exercised in life . . . the destructiveness which returns from the outer world is . . . taken up by the super-ego . . . The sadism of the super-ego and the masochism of the ego supplement each other . . . [regarding] the origin of the ethical sense . . . the first instinctual renunciation is enforced by external powers, and it is only this which creates the ethical sense, which expresses itself in conscience and demands a further renunciation of instinct.[16]

As we have seen, these ideas are very close to Nietzsche's ideas in the *Genealogy* (cultural suppression of instincts, drives turned inward upon the self, the creation of "bad conscience") as well as in "On the Pale Criminal." We will see that Freud was almost certainly again reading the *Genealogy* at about this time.

# Chapter 11

## *BEYOND THE PLEASURE PRINCIPLE*

> True *life as the over-all continuation of life through*
> *procreation, through the mysteries of sexuality . . .*
> *the eternal joy of creating.*
> —Nietzsche, *Twilight of the Idols*

In 1917, in a letter to Ferenczi, Freud refers to the "eternal re-currence of the same," which he places in quotation marks, indi-cating the obvious reference to Nietzsche.[1] In 1919 in his essay "The Uncanny," Freud refers to the "constant recurrence of the same thing"[2] (without quotation marks) and describes the experi-ence of the uncanny as related to the hidden recurrence of the same from one's past. In *Beyond the Pleasure Principle*, published in 1920 (first draft completed in 1919 at about the time of writing of "The Uncanny"), Freud puts a similar phrase, "the perpetual re-currence of the same thing," in quotation marks.[3] As already noted, it was also in 1919 that Freud added the following words to *The Interpretation of Dreams*: "We can guess how much to the point is Nietzsche's assertion that in dreams 'some primaeval relic of humanity is at work which we can now scarcely reach any longer by a direct path.'"[4]

In a 1920 footnote to the *Three Essays on the Theory of Sex-uality* Freud mentions and briefly summarizes Andreas-Salomé's (1916) paper "'Anal' and 'Sexual.'" He points out that Andreas-Salomé has shown how the history of the first prohibition which a child comes across—the prohibition against getting pleasure from anal activity and its products—has a decisive effect on his whole development. This must be the first occasion on which . . . he carries out the first "repression" of his possibilities for pleasure. From that time on, what is "anal" remains the symbol of everything that is to be repudiated and excluded from life.[5]

Binion comments that

Lou's notion that culture begins with man's disgust at his own excretion was a pretty pendant to Nietzsche's that culture ends with man's holding his nose before his whole person. More, it was Nietzsche's thesis that man acquired a moral conscience as well as a soul through turning the wrath meant for his masters inward, self-debasingly—and Lou's that original hate brought a conscience or virtual "clean self" as well as an ego or self or soul [the separating of the clean self from the "hideous stink . . . urine and filth" (Nietzsche) of the body]. The perfect motto for her genealogy of conscience was in fact her favorite dictum of Nietzsche's: that moral valuation is a "sign language of the affects." And speaking of genealogies: Nietzsche's phylogenetic sequence of "master" affirming the world and himself, "slave" alienated from both through a rancorous negation, and "overman" reconciled with both was the original for Lou's ontogenetic sequence of Narcissus, post-Narcissus, and transindividuated Narcissus.[6]

While Binion might be regarded by some as particularly hostile towards Andreas-Salomé (her work is increasingly being valued in its own right), there is little doubt as to Nietzsche's great influence upon her. This is also acknowledged by another biographer, Angela Livingstone.[7] Among other things, we have noted Andreas-Salomé's 1913 comment that she first discussed certain issues relating to sadomasochism (and perhaps bisexuality) with Nietzsche (and we can note that the encounter between them on this matter was an emotionally intense one[8]). We have also noted that in Andreas-Salomé's circle Nietzsche "stood, like a hidden shadow, an invisible figure, in our midst."[9]

In 1919 Freud wrote to Andreas-Salomé that he was reading Schopenhauer and "all kinds of things relevant" to his work on the notion of the death instinct as it would be elaborated upon in *Beyond the Pleasure Principle*.[10] As Freud is entering into his study of the destructive instincts—the death instinct and its manifestations outward as aggression as well as its secondary turn back inward upon the self—one might wonder if Nietzsche, who had explored the vicissitudes of aggression and was famous for his concept of will to power, was among the "all kinds of things" Freud was reading. At least it is clear that Freud had the "recurrence of the same" on his mind during this period. And while Freud's pessimism and emphasis on pleasure as a state to be reached through release of or discharge of and decrease of tension have strong affinities with Schopenhauer, there is the somewhat different "pleasure" of Eros.

Also, as Gay[11] points out, Freud himself was puzzled as to why it took so long for him to recognize an aggressive drive, though of course he had paid attention to aggression in earlier work. In 1909 in the "Little Hans" case Freud had written: "I cannot bring myself to assume the existence of a special aggressive instinct alongside of the familiar instincts of self preservation and of sex and on an equal footing with them."[12] Aggressiveness appeared as an aspect of the self-preservative instincts (and libidinal instincts) which were soon to become subsumed under the libido. The editor's introduction to *Civilization and Its Discontents* points out that a footnote to the above-quoted passage from "Little Hans" was added in 1923 indicating that "I have myself been obliged to assert the existence of an aggressive instinct, but it is different from Adler's. I prefer to call it the 'destructive' or 'death instinct.'" The editor's note in *Civilization and Its Discontents* suggests that Adler's concept had "been more in the nature of an instinct of self-assertiveness."[13]

Gay mentions Adler's emphasis on aggression, Jung's claim that libido aims at death no less than at life,[14] and that Freud's difficult relationships with these two men were likely factors obstructing Freud's acceptance of a destructive drive. Gay does not point out that Nietzsche had explored the nature, manifestations, and sublimations of aggression, positing the will to power as the primary drive of the organism, nor that both men were admirers of and were influenced by Nietzsche. One might even wonder if

Freud's focus on sexuality in his earlier years and his insistence on the sexually related etiology of the neuroses had anything to do with Nietzsche having already focused on the vicissitudes of aggression to such a substantial degree. Later in his life, Jung wrote:

> I saw Freud's Psychology as, so to speak, an adroit move on the part of intellectual history, compensating for Nietzsche's deification of the power principle. The problem had obviously to be rephrased not as "Freud versus Adler" but "Freud versus Nietzsche." It was therefore, I thought, more than a domestic quarrel in the domain of psychopathology.[15]

In *Beyond the Pleasure Principle* Freud questions the primacy and universality of the pleasure principle as a regulating force in mental life. In various phenomena, both symptomatic (for example, traumatic neurosis) and in the transference, Freud sees attempts at repetition (which he had noted earlier but here regards as instinctive), at return to an earlier state, that cannot, he feels, be explained by the pleasure principle. Ultimately Freud sees the repetition compulsion (the desire to return to an earlier state) and the constancy principle (the drive to reduce tension to a low and constant level) as subsumed under the death instinct, the inherent drive of the organism to return to an inorganic state from which it emerged (although returning to repeat and returning to reach an inorganic state would appear to be quite different principles). The death instinct is opposed by Eros ("the preserver of life," the striving for immortality, the life instincts) which seeks to "hold together portions of living substance."[16] Freud is here outlining his new dual-instinct theory, that of life versus death instincts, in the wake of his findings that "the original opposition between the ego-instincts and the sexual instincts proved to be inadequate. A portion of the ego-instincts was seen to be libidinal; sexual instincts— probably alongside others—operated in the ego."[17] At one point Freud even writes that "the ego is the true and original reservoir of libido."[18] Freud's new dual-instinct theory attempts to take account of the "libidinal character of the self-preservation instincts" so that "the opposition [is] not between ego-instincts and sexual instincts but between life instincts and death instincts."[19] Eros appears as a "life instinct" and the "sexual instincts" constitute "the part of Eros which is directed toward objects."[20] He explains the (long-known) "sadistic component in the sexual instinct"[21] as emerging when the death instinct, "under the influence of narcissistic libido, has been forced away from the ego and has consequently only emerged in relation to the object[.] It now enters the service of the sexual function . . . the sadism which has been forced out of the ego has pointed the way for the libidinal components of the sexual instinct, and . . . these follow after it to the object."[22]

One point to be made is that Nietzsche's concept of the will to power was also an attempt to go beyond the pleasure principle (and *Beyond* good and evil), a principle of which, as we have seen, Nietzsche was well aware. For Nietzsche the primary drive is towards expansion, mastery, growth, appropriation and domination in all its primitive and more sublimated manifestations. Pleasure is a by-product of the experience of the feeling of increase of power. Kaufmann's interpretation on this matter is as follows:

> If happiness is defined as the state of being man desires; if joy is defined as the conscious aspect of this state; and if pleasure is defined as a sensation marked by the absence of pain and discomfort; then Nietzsche's position can be summarized quite briefly: happiness is the fusion of power and joy—and joy contains not only ingredients of pleasure but also a component of pain . . . Ultimate happiness consists in the inextricable fusion of power and joy.[23]

Pain is an essential ingredient here since it is not a state attained at the end of suffering but the process of overcoming itself (as of obstacles and suffering) that is the central factor in the experience of increase of power and joy.[24]

A few years after publication of *Beyond the Pleasure Principle*, in his essay "The Economic Problem of Masochism," Freud will specifically utilize the terms "will to power" and "instinct for mastery": "The libido has the task of making the destroying instinct innocuous, and it fulfills the task by diverting that instinct to a great extent outwards . . . The instinct is then called the destructive instinct, the instinct for mastery, or the will to power."[25] So the death instinct may be diverted outward as will to power and mastery, and it may enter the service of the sexual function, pointing the way to the object for the libidinal components of the sexual instinct.

In *Beyond the Pleasure Principle,* too, Freud writes of "an instinct for mastery"[26] regarding the repetitive behaviors of the *fort—da* ("gone"—"there!") game. Freud describes the child throwing a reel attached to a string over the edge of a curtained cot so that it could not be seen *(fort)* and then pulling the reel by the string and hailing its reappearance with a joyful *"da."* Freud writes of such behaviors as children's attempts to "make themselves master of the situation."[27] The underlying situation over which the child is achieving mastery is that of the mother's departure and return, the child now being in an active rather than passive position and even able to express aggression and revenge of sorts as well as independence in being able to throw and retrieve the reel at will. The child compensates for the instinctual renunciation of "allowing his mother to go away without protesting" with this game, this symbolic activity, a development which is "the child's great cultural achievement." (Ultimately, the component instincts of self-preservation, self-assertion and mastery are in the service of preventing external interference with the organism's return to inorganic existence on "its own path . . . in its own fashion.")[28]

In his closing comments Freud writes of another kind or level of mastery, the binding of instinctual impulses that is a preparatory act. Although this binding and the replacement of primary process with the secondary process operate before and without necessary regard for "the development of unpleasure, . . . the transformation occurs on *behalf* of the pleasure principle; the binding is a preparatory act which introduces and assures the dominance of the pleasure principle . . . The binding . . . [is] designed to prepare the excitement for its final elimination in the pleasure of discharge."[29]

In these closing comments Freud also writes that it is a "universal characteristic of instincts" to seek "to restore an earlier state" and that "the most universal endeavor of all living substance" is to "return to the quiescence of the inorganic world." And the pleasure principle "is a tendency operating in the service of a function whose business it is to free the mental apparatus entirely from excitations or to keep the amount of excitation in it constant or to keep it as low as possible." It is no wonder that Freud winds up writing that "the pleasure principle seems actually to serve the death instincts."[30]

Regarding the binding of excitations, in the sense of energy restrained from immediate discharge, we can note Nietzsche's emphasis (although in a different context) of the importance of not reacting at once to a stimulus, the problem in a "physiological inability *not* to react."[31] This important capacity is the opposite of Dionysian frenzy in which "the whole affective system is excited and enhanced; so that it discharges all its means of expression at once."[32] (We can also note that in Nietzsche's later writings Dionysus comes to represent not only the capacity to enter into this subterranean realm of experience but to face, endure, and creatively utilize the most harsh, painful truths, to say "Yes" to life even in its harshest aspects, to suspend primary concern with self-preservation and to overflow the self in the "eternal joy of creating," in affirming this life. We can also remind ourselves that the ultimate danger situation for Freud of being unable to master or bind excitations and being flooded and overwhelmed by them, is related to Nietzsche's idea that with no opportunity to directly discharge drives outward, drives will be directed inward upon the self. Such discharge upon the self prevents the emergence of what would otherwise be a profoundly painful, hopeless, depressed condition, whereas for Freud it would be overwhelming flooding of unbound excitations and anxiety. To avoid such flooding, drives require discharge or binding.[33])

It is significant that at the end of his life Freud specifically writes that the aim of Eros is "to establish ever greater unities to preserve them thus—in short, to bind together,"[34] while the aim of the destructive instinct is "to undo connections and so to destroy things . . . its final aim is to lead what is living into an inorganic state . . . the death instinct fits in with the formula . . . that instincts tend towards a return to an earlier state. In the case of Eros (or the love instinct) we cannot apply this formula."[35] In this same section Freud defines libido as "the total available energy of Eros." It would appear that the "pleasure" of Eros would in some sense have to be distinguished from that implicit in the constancy principle. In *Beyond the Pleasure Principle* Freud writes that "the dominating tendency in mental life . . . is the effort to reduce, to keep constant or remove tension due to stimuli," but also that "union with the living substance of a different individual increases those tensions." He also finds that "we cannot ascribe to sexual instincts the characteristic of a compulsion to repeat."[36] He does write of the pleasurable release of tensions produced by the life instincts,[37] but this does not account for the activity of Eros. A few years later Freud will write that pleasure and unpleasure "cannot be referred to an increase or decrease of a quantity [of tension] . . . It appears that they depend on . . . some characteristic . . . which we can only describe as a qualitative one."[38] The individual cannot be seen as fundamentally seeking pleasure only through decrease in the quantity of drive-related tension.

The will to power, though related to Freud's explorations of aggression and destruction, does not contain or imply a death instinct. However, there is a notion of death of sorts involved in the sense of the individual's creative, expansive growth involving a willingness to die to the self in its current form, that is, one's expansion may break the boundaries of the self as currently constituted and experienced. Zarathustra states that "your self . . . what it would do above all else: to create beyond itself."[39] Also, as already mentioned, the will to power, though including the destructive, aggressive instincts, also has affinities with the realm of Eros. Kaufmann suggests that the will to power has aspects or manifestations which can be described as "a creative Eros," and, quoting from Plato's *Symposium*, "the love of generation and of birth in beauty."[40] And consider the following passage from *Twilight of the Idols: "True* life as the over-all continuation of life through procreation, through the mysteries of sexuality . . . the eternal joy of creating, that the will to life may eternally affirm itself . . ."[41] Nietzsche might agree with Camille Paglia when she writes that "sexuality, even at its most perverse, is implicitly religious. Sex is the ritual link between man and nature."[42] (Paglia also suggests that "what is partial and reductive in most Freudian interpretations of art is that they focus on sex without realizing that . . . [e]verything sexual or unsexual in art carries world-view and nature theory with it."[43]) It may be that the ultimate form or ground of will to power is the inexhaustible procreative power of the "eternally creative primordial mother."[44]

Freud ultimately separates Eros and the death instinct as two separate instinctual forces although regarding "these two instincts [as] struggling with each other from the very first."[45] For Nietzsche the Dionysian realm includes both life and death, pain and pleasure, creation and destruction, love and hate, inextricably intertwined. The god Dionysus ruled over sexual energy and was associated with the figure of Eros,[46] but Dionysus was also specifically identified with the realm of the dead and its god, Hades. The presocratic

philosopher Heraclitus, whom Nietzsche greatly admired, specifically identified Hades with Dionysus: "If it were not Dionysus for
whom they march in procession and chant the hymn to the phal-
lus (aidoia), their action would be most shameless (anaidestata).
But Hades (Aidés) and Dionysus are the same, him for whom they
rave and celebrate Lenaia."[47] This passage refers to Dionysian religious ritual, and as Charles Kahn points out, it expresses the equiv-
alence or interchangeability of life and death. An observer of the
rituals would recognize Dionysus as Hades, the identity of Dionysus with Hades. (Also, what would otherwise be "shameless" is
not shameless in the context of the ritual and celebration.) Kahn
points to another level of meaning related to another passage in
Heraclitus to the effect that

> sexual activity [is] a waste of the psyche, an expense of life-
> force liquefied as semen, just as drunkenness is a partial death
> and darkening of the soul by liquefaction . . . The "death" of
> psyche by the "birth" of fluid in ejaculation coincides in the
> long run with the birth of the son that will supplant his father.
> Thus the desires of men "to live . . . and to leave children be-
> hind" is really a desire for their own death and replacement.[48]

Life and death, immortality and mortality, are inextricably linked.
    Dionysus is the god of the vine, a god associated with fertil-
ity, spring rituals, the unleashing of ecstatic but terrifying instinctual forces, and with death and birth, death and rebirth, as with
burial of the seed so that it may generate new life.[49] The Dionysian
realm of experience is associated with individuated life surpassing
its experience of boundaries, experiencing oneness with others (at
least other revelers) and nature. The Dionysian uniting or merging
of persons has at least some affinity with Freud's Eros, and Freud's
idea of life as making its "detours" on the way back to death is anticipated in Nietzsche's related idea of the "eternal phenomenon"
of "the insatiable will always find[ing] a way to detain its creatures
in life and compel them to live on."[50] Sallis suggests that tragedy
provides a crossing from the Dionysian back to the everyday, "a
crossing like that made by Eros, back from Hades, identified by
Heraclitus with Dionysus."[51]
    The Dionysian is also associated with the realm of the femi-
nine in that, among other things, the original worshippers of

Dionysus were women, maenads (from which is derived "mania"). Nietzsche's emphasis on the importance of Dionysus may even be seen in part as an overturning of western masculine-dominated ideology.[52] Also, Freud indicated in his essay on *Leonardo* that gods associated with Dionysus were depicted as androgynous figures.[53]

For Freud all organic life is ultimately and inherently driven to the destruction of its individuated boundaries as it returns to, is driven back towards, that preindividuated realm of non being from which it emerged. For Freud this preindividuated realm is the realm of death. Eli Sagan[54] points out that it was Karen Horney who asked: "Does the man feel, side by side with his desire to conquer, a secret longing for extinction in the act of reunion with the woman (mother)? Is it perhaps this longing which underlies the 'death instinct'"?[55]

Freud does of course discuss other experiences in which individuated boundaries are transcended, such as in his discussion of the "oceanic" feeling and the experience of being in love in *Civilization and Its Discontents*. The oceanic feeling, "a sensation of 'eternity,' a feeling as of something limitless, unbounded,"[56] particularly as a source of "religious energy," as well as the experience of being in love in which "the boundary between ego and object threatens to melt away,"[57] are reactivated remnants of the earliest stages of development in which the "ego includes everything" and in which the "ego-feeling . . . corresponded to a more intimate bond between the ego and the world about it."[58] Freud distinguishes such states from the "narrower and more sharply demarcated ego-feeling of maturity."[59] Freud does not see in any such transcending of boundaries any terrible but ecstatic truth and reality as could be characteristic of the Dionysian insight in which individuated boundary-defined forms are seen as necessary temporary forms above but infused with the turmoil of Dionysian destruction and creation. Rather, Freud sees such feelings, at least specifically the oceanic ones, as "a first attempt at a religious consolation, as though it were another way of disclaiming the danger which the ego recognizes as threatening it from the external world."[60] Freud also states: " I cannot discover this 'oceanic' feeling in myself."[61]

Although both men are atheists, they differ in their sensibilities as to the truth or reality to be found in certain experiences of transcending individuated boundaries. One wonders if this is a factor in Freud's statement in his essay on Michelangelo's *Moses* that he found it difficult to give himself up to the experience of works of art, particularly music, without first being able to explain to himself why he would be so moved: "Some rationalistic, or perhaps analytic, turn of mind in me rebels against being moved by a thing without knowing why I am thus affected and what it is that affects me." Whenever he cannot do this, "as for instance with music, I am almost incapable of obtaining any pleasure."[62] In 1929 Freud coupled music with mysticism when he wrote to Romain Rolland: "Mysticism is as closed to me as music."[63] While such statements may be exaggerations given that Freud did attend the opera and had some appreciation of music,[64] they may reflect a certain sensibility regarding the loss of boundaries which is so common in the experience of listening to music. For Nietzsche music is the artistic expression most closely reflecting the realm of the Dionysian, that realm of terrifying abyss as well as rapture and ecstasy. It would seem that for Freud the transcending of individuated boundaries reflects reactivation of infantile longings and states or the return to the preindividuated realm of non being.

This is one of the areas in which the kind of heroism envisaged by the two thinkers diverges to some degree, both valuing the maintenance of autonomy and boundaries (which for both thinkers is a form of integrity and a resistance against intoxicated self-deception), but Nietzsche also valuing what is experienced and revealed in certain experiences in which boundaries are transcended (such as in the potentially revelatory experience for the spectators of Greek tragedy). There is no doubt that Nietzsche would agree with Freud regarding the defensive nature (as well as the gratification involved) in some boundary-transcendent experiences which involve a turning away from life and towards quiescence and death (which, of course, Freud posits as a primal instinct), which some variants of the oceanic experience and the experience of being in love may involve.[65] However, he also finds realities beyond the "narrower and more sharply demarcated ego-feeling of maturity." (Let us be clear that while Nietzsche writes of creative Dionysian rapture, ecstasy and frenzy [Rausch], he is no advocate of indiscriminate blotting out or altering of ego and consciousness through intoxicants: it is those who are ordinarily "wretched and miserable . . . [who] regard these [intoxicated] moments as their real 'self' . . . Intoxication counts as . . . their actual ego: they see in everything else the opponent and obstruction of intoxication."[66] Nietzsche regarded the compulsive seeking out of intoxicating stimulation as an indication of an individual's and a culture's deterioration.)

---

There is also the matter of Freud's discussion of repetitive phenomena and Nietzsche's concept of eternal recurrence. At times Nietzsche presented the idea of the eternal recurrence of the same as a scientific discovery, that given a finite number of ways in which the elements of the universe could be organized and an infinite amount of time, ultimately exact replications of configurations would have to take place. However, Nietzsche, as are most Nietzsche scholars, is also interested in the personal psychological ramifications of the affirmation or rejection of this idea. That is, what would it say about the state of psychological health of a person ("how well disposed would you have to become to yourself and to life") if he or she would accept that no one part of life, such as the most pleasurable or satisfying, could be willed for repetition without willing all aspects of life for repetition. What would it indicate about the health of a person if he or she were able to will wholeheartedly (to "crave") that all of his or her life be repeated endlessly (things get a bit more complicated if one is to will that all life be repeated endlessly)? Also, how would one go about living one's life if one accepted and integrated such an affirmation: "What, if some day or night a demon were to steal after you into your loneliest loneliness and say to you: 'This life as you now live it and have lived it, you will have to live once more and innumerable times more.'"[67] For Nietzsche, saying "Yes, I will that my life in all its details be repeated endlessly" is indicative of the highest affirmation of life. Note that he writes not only of one's relationship to the past, but of "this life as you now live it."

We might say that the Freudian repetition compulsion involves an unwillingness or inability to give up distorted and conflicting views of the past. Lichtenstein points out that the "tendency inherent in the repetition compulsion is directed toward fixation within the flow of time, toward duration—indeed, we must dare say it: toward eternity . . . it takes on the quality of a defiance against acceptance of the changes imposed by time."[68] This can be seen as an attempt to negate time and with it life (as one attempts to avoid death). It involves a vengeance against time and life. For Nietzsche the excruciating fact that we are powerless in relation to the past in the sense that time will not run backwards[69] leads him to the ultimate test of whether one can say "yes" to the eternal recurrence of the same. What Butler writes of how one might describe the compulsively repeated pleasures Freud writes of in *Beyond the Pleasure Principle* might be said of our relation to time as presented by Nietzsche:

> For the individual who suffers this repeated and frustrated effect of pleasure, it is not only the object of the past that cannot be recovered, nor the relation that cannot be restored or reconstructed, but it is time itself that resists the human will and proves itself unyielding. Between pleasure and satisfaction, a prohibition or negation of pleasure is enacted which necessitates the endless repetition and proliferation of thwarted pleasures. The repetition is a vain effort to stay, or indeed, to reverse time; such repetition reveals a rancor against the present which feeds upon itself.[70]

Zarathustra states:

> What is it that puts even the liberator himself in fetters? "It was"—that is the name of the will's gnashing of teeth and most secret melancholy. Powerless against what has been done, he is an angry spectator of all that is past. The will cannot will backwards; and that he cannot break time and time's covetousness, that is the will's loneliest melancholy. . . .
>
> *The spirit of revenge,* my friends, has so far been the subject of man's best reflection; and where there was suffering, one always wanted punishment too.
>
> For "punishment" is what revenge calls itself; with a hypocritical lie it creates a good conscience for itself.
>
> Because there is suffering in those who will, inasmuch as they cannot will backwards, willing itself and all life were supposed to be—a punishment. . . .
>
> But has the will yet spoken thus? . . . Has he unlearned the spirit of revenge and all gnashing of teeth?[71]

Nietzsche presents this dilemma in terms related to Freud's discussion and strikingly similar to the discussions of Lichtenstein and Butler. His response involves offering us the idea, the possibility, of saying "yes" to the test of eternal recurrence, the possibility of saying "thus shall I will it" to one's life as lived as an indication and reflection of unlearning the spirit of revenge against time and life itself.[72] (There will, of course, inevitably be aggression and revenge, but they can, to the extent possible, be utilized against what condemns life rather than against life. Regarding morality, although he also attacks traditional ideas of morality more generally, Nietzsche condemns those moralities that condemn life, "the morality that would unself man." And we can note that his highest affirmation includes "a yes-saying . . . even to guilt."[73]) Also, perhaps there is a mutually reinforcing relationship between the growing capacity to say "Yes, thus shall I will it" and the growing capacity of the self to do what it would do above all else, that is, to create beyond itself.

In addition, and quite relevant to psychoanalytically oriented therapy, the context of my future-directed decisions and actions involves a replacing of my past into a different context, a different interpretation, so that in a very real sense the past can, after all, be transformed.[74] Clearly, my past is no longer the past it was for me once I say "yes" to the test of the demon. Regarding the "fables" (the "madness") which ask, "Where is redemption from the flux of things and from the punishment called existence" (with implications for the matter of the metaphysical comfort of section 18 of *The Birth of Tragedy*), Zarathustra states: "I led you away from these fables when I taught you, 'The will is a creator.' All 'it was' is a fragment, a riddle, a dreadful accident—until the creative will says to it, 'But thus I willed it.' Until the creative will says to it, 'But thus I will it; thus shall I will it.'"[75]

Alexander Nehamas sees saying "yes" to eternal recurrence as related to Nietzsche's idea of becoming who one is. It is a saying "yes" to what one is and has become: "It is to identify oneself with all of one's actions, to see that everything one does (what one becomes) is what one is. In the ideal case it is also to fit all this into a coherent whole and to want to be everything that one is: it is to give style to one's character; to be, we might say, becoming."[76] For Julian Young one cannot accomplish the Nietzschean redemption without knowing and choosing who one is: "To decide that some past event was a benefit presupposes and commits me to certain views as to who I am, what my dominant desires and goals are now."[77] Maudemarie Clark points out that affirming eternal recurrence involves an affirmation of life, of the intrinsic value of life in opposition to the ascetic ideal's devaluation of the intrinsic value of life. Regarding this new ideal, Clark writes that "Nietzshe's ideal is to love the whole process enough that one is willing to relive eternally even those parts of it that one does not and cannot love."[78] From a different perspective, Magnus, Stewart and Mileur suggest that the "reason for wishing most fervently the repetition of each unaltered moment" is that one

> would prefer to be—wants eternally to be—the very person she already is . . . Nietzsche's thought of eternal recurrence suggests that the most radical of all desires is to want unconditionally to be the very person one already is . . . imagine having just the same attitude toward the catalogued moments of your greatest anguish [as you might have toward the most entirely satisfactory experience] . . . (j)ust that is what Nietzsche's eternal recurrence requires of each and every moment wanted for its own sake.[79]

Stephen Byrum has suggested that the response to the challenge of eternal recurrence brings together the will to power and play, particularly some things to be found in child's play: "Here will to power 'embraces' the eternal recurrence of the same in play, and by playing instead of despairing, the 'embrace' is a positive action, a 'Yes-saying' affirmation of existence."[80] Zarathustra states that "the child is innocence and forgetting, a new beginning, a game, a self-propelled wheel, a first movement, a sacred 'Yes.' For the game of creation, my brothers, a sacred 'Yes' is needed." (Perhaps it is in part in this sense that Nietzsche writes elsewhere that "infancy and childhood have their ends in themselves, they are not *stages*.")[81] For Byrum, the child's play, the child's sacred "yes," includes Dionysian-like creation and destruction; the "innocence" and "forgetting" of the child pertain to the ever new destructions and creations, the "recurrent succession of 'new beginnings.'"[82] We should also note that in this section Zarathustra states that these capacities are the very capacities necessary for the important task of creating new values. And as we soon move to a discussion of Nietzsche on truth, it is important to keep in mind Clark's suggestion that "the major role of play in Nietzsche [is] not a substitute for truth, as post-modernists sometimes seem to think, but an activity that supports truthfulness in . . . [a] non-ascetic reincarnation."[83]

One can raise the question as to the possible affinities of Nietzsche's conception of play with play in the therapeutic process. George Moran writes that "play material helps the child to discharge instinctual trends in bringing things together (constructive activities) and dispersing them and breaking them apart (destructive activities)."[84] However, while a number of psychoanalytically oriented therapists, particularly since Winnicott, have been conceptualizing interaction in the therapy relationship as a form of play and characterizing psychoanalysis as a "highly specialized form of playing in the service of communication with oneself and others,"[85] the type of play envisioned is of a more tame and orderly kind—with caution regarding potential instinctive and bodily disruption—than Nietzsche has in mind.[86] Writing on what Winnicott regards as the nonorgiastic aspects of transitional phenomena and play, Loewald states that "one might ask whether the culmination in celebration—the 'manic' element . . . might not be a form of climactic phenomena."[87] Of course Freud wrote that analysis can curb "the patient's compulsion to repeat . . . and [turn it] into a motive for remembering . . . We admit it into the transferrence as to a playground."[88] Creative play may help to limit uncreative repetition.

The above-mentioned commentators on eternal recurrence differ in emphasis but agree on the importance of the concept as it pertains, for Nietzsche, to psychological transformation. It instantiates an alternative to the ascetic ideal. Also, it should not be lost on the psychoanalytically oriented that for "it was" to be redeemed, the creative will must learn to say not only "But thus I will it; thus shall I will it," but also, and perhaps first, "But thus I willed it."

# Chapter 12

## 1921–1931: AN OVERVIEW

*The self says to the ego, "Feel pain here!" Then the*
*ego suffers and thinks how it might suffer no more—*
*and that is why it is* made *to think.*

*The self says to the ego "Feel pleasure here!" Then*
*the ego is pleased and thinks how it might often be*
*pleased again—and that is why it is* made *to think.*
                                   —Nietzsche, *Zarathustra,*
                              "On the Despisers of the Body"

Moving on chronologically, we can remind ourselves that in 1921, in *Group Psychology and the Analysis of the Ego,* Freud equates the father of the primal horde with the "superman,"[1] an equation, as discussed, that is inaccurate and at variance with Freud's characterization of Michelangelo's *Moses.* We have also noted Freud's positing of identification behaving like an incorporative derivative of the oral stage, as "the earliest expression of an emotional tie with another person," and Nietzsche describing even behind incorporative nourishment an "original phenomenon . . . [the] desire to incorporate everything." (Freud would add: to incorporate everything good and eject everything bad.) And we have noted how both thinkers have an important place for fantasy about fulfilled ideals as a factor in binding members of a group to a leader.

In 1922 an essay of Franz Brentano's was published in which Nietzsche, the author of *The Antichrist,* and the founder of Christianity were juxtaposed.[2] As noted, when he was a student Freud held Brentano in high regard. He and Paneth took a number of philosophy courses with Brentano and visited with him at his home.

In 1923, in *The Ego and the Id*, Freud mentions Georg Groddeck's idea that the ego is "lived" by unknown and uncontrollable forces which he terms "das Es," "the it," later, in English, "the id." In a footnote Freud states that "Groddeck himself no doubt followed the example of Nietzsche, who habitually used this grammatical term for whatever in our nature is impersonal and, so to speak, subject to natural law."[3] One point to raise is how Freud would know of a term Nietzsche used "habitually" and what that term entailed if not by reading Nietzsche or reading of him. One might also wonder if there is any significance in the fact that in this major work heralding Freud's structural theory (the organizing of mental functioning along lines of id, ego, and superego), he utilizes a term associated with Nietzsche for the deepest layer of psychic reality. In a sense it might seem strange (though perhaps just reflecting one side of his ambivalence) that for his "laborious" science Freud would choose a term associated with someone regarded by many as a kind of prophet. As Wittels wrote in his book on Freud, "Nietzsche . . . is revered in Germany as a god."[4] Of course Freud had strong identifications with certain prophets.

We can also mention that Freud's use of "das Ich," "the I" (later to become in translation "the ego") also followed Nietzsche's usage, although such usage did not originate with Nietzsche. Nietzsche also used the Latin term "ego."[5] Regarding "das Über-Ich," "the Over-I" (later to become "the superego" in translation), we can recall Jones' words regarding the striking similarity between Freud's concept and Nietzsche's idea of the "bad conscience" as developed in the *Genealogy*. We can also mention that there is an important place in this work for conscience and guilt, particularly unconscious guilt, an area explored by Nietzsche and previously commented upon by Freud (then only as an "obscure" sense) in regard to "On the Pale Criminal."

In this work Freud also makes the point that the ego is first a bodily ego, the ego ultimately being derived from bodily sensations. For Freud the formation of the "I" is intimately linked with one's experience of one's body and image (and fantasies) of one's body. Nietzsche does not make the same point, but regarding the fundamental ground of our self as pertaining to the body, Nietzsche has Zarathustra state:

"Body am I, and soul"—thus speaks the child. And why should one not speak like children?

But the awakened and knowing say: body am I entirely, and nothing else; and soul is only a word for something about the body.[6] [Compare this view with Plato who, in the words of Gregory Vlastos, "regards the soul's conjunction with the body as a doom calling for a life-long discipline whose aim is to detach soul from body . . . sexual bliss . . . 'nails' the soul to the body and distorts its sense of what is real." Nietzsche rejects this dualism.[7]]

Nietzsche, as we have seen, also has a place for a largely unconscious bodily based "self" which encompasses the ego. This self is something more or other than mere drives pressing for discharge since Nietzsche (Zarathustra) writes of the self as "an unknown sage," as goal directed, and as the prompter of the ego's concepts. This notion of self is not comparable to anything in Freud and would be rejected by Freud. However, Zarathustra goes on to make statements that are closer to Freud's viewpoint. In the following passage Zarathustra comments on how the ego is made to think so that it can procure pleasure and avoid suffering:

Behind your thoughts and feelings, my brother, there stands a mighty ruler, an unknown sage—whose name is self. In your body he dwells; he is your body.

There is more reason in your body than in your best wisdom. And who knows why your body needs precisely your best wisdom?

Your self laughs at your ego and at its bold leaps. "What are these leaps and flights of thought to me?" it says to itself. "A detour to my end. I am the leading strings of the ego and the prompter of its concepts." [The ego finds the detour for the satisfaction of the body or bodily based self.]

The self says to the ego, "Feel pain here!" Then the ego suffers and thinks how it might suffer no more—and that is why it is *made* to think.

The self says to the ego, "Feel pleasure here!" Then the ego is pleased and thinks how it might often be pleased again—and that is why it is *made* to think.[8]

Nietzsche, like Freud, posits the primacy of the body even to the extent that it is bodily states such as pleasure and pain and reactions to these states by the ego (to feel pleasure and avoid pain) that are instrumental in the creation and development of thought processes (cf. SE 5:598–99). But Nietzsche also recognizes that the commonly held "proposition" that "pleasure and displeasure are [simple] opposites" is one of our "naive blunders."[9]

However, though both write of the ego as "thinking" it wills when it is "will" that leads it, Nietzsche still finds a certain wisdom in the body, such as when it rebels with symptoms in the face of psychological maltreatment.[10] Although blind drives pressing for discharge cannot be thought of as possessing intelligence or wisdom, certain bodily states or reactions may be thought of, if only metaphorically, as in a certain sense possessing a kind of wisdom or offering a communication of sorts. The unconscious self, the encompassing self in which the ego is embedded, is, as we have seen, an idea compatible with certain therapeutic approaches, including those that regard dreams as an expression of and offering from the self to the "I" or ego that is prepared to view such expressions as potential communications. Even a contemporary analyst like Robert Langs can write of a "deep unconscious response, so filled with its own intelligence, " and that "the unconscious system . . . is capable of working through an emotional issue."[11] Some would argue that for Freud, although he acknowledges that rational and complex thought is possible without consciousness, only that aspect of what is unconscious that is preconscious, that is, the system Pcs. as opposed to the Ucs. (which is the realm of drive derivatives, primary process, and the dynamically repressed), can possess what one author refers to as "strategicality," while other authors allow for multiple agents and homuncular explanations.[12] However, in his own and different way, Freud is not content to leave the sexual instincts as only drives pressing for discharge. There is the purposefulness of "Eros, whose purpose is to combine single human individuals, and after that families then races, peoples and nations, into one great unity, the unity of mankind."[13]

There is one particular passage in *The Ego and the Id* that, although using different imagery, bears striking resemblance to a passage in Nietzsche. Freud is writing of the well-known analogy of horse and rider in which, for Freud, the ego is like a man on horseback, who has to hold in check the superior strength of the horse; with this difference, that the rider tries to do so with his own strength while the ego uses borrowed forces [from the id] . . . Often a rider, if he is not to be parted from his horse, is obliged to guide it where it wants to go; so in the same way the ego is in the habit of transforming the id's will into action as if it were its own.[14]

There is no bodily wisdom here or in Nietzsche's words to follow. The ego is often clearly operating in the service of the id even though it is acting as if its will were its own. In the following passage Nietzsche goes even further than Freud:

. . . the tremendous quantum of energy that presses, as I have said, to be used up somehow . . . People are accustomed to consider the goal (purposes, vocations, etc.) as the *driving force*, in keeping with a very ancient error; but it is merely the *directing force*—one has mistaken the helmsman for the steam. And not even always the helmsman, the directing force.

Is the "goal," the "purpose" not often enough a beautifying pretext, a self-deception of vanity after the event that does not want to acknowledge that the ship is *following* the current into which it has entered accidentally? that it "wills" to go that way *because it—must?* that is has a direction, to be sure, but—no helmsman at all?[15]

Similar points are being made although the imagery differs, with Nietzsche utilizing a helmsman directing a ship running on steam and responding to the current in contrast to Freud's rider and horse. Freud suggests that often the will of the ego is actually a transformed will of the id, that the ego guides the id where it wants to go. Nietzsche suggests that often the ego-related goals and purposes we think are driving forces are in fact merely directing or guiding forces. One has mistaken the id for the ego. However, might it not also be possible that while there *is* direction, there may be no ego operative at all pertaining to that direction, that the person follows the "current" into which he or she "has entered accidentally," and with no directing ego or helmsman at all, "wills to go that way *because it—must?*" Nietzsche raises questions regarding even the guiding functions of the ego as described here by Freud. Also, while Freud's horse may have a clear idea of where it wants to go, Nietzsche's steam can only provide the driving force. It is the current, perhaps with some place for the helmsman, that provides the directing or guiding force.

Regarding 1923, let us also recall that Anna Freud was writing to Andreas-Salomé regarding how she found a psychoanalytic way of thinking in her study of Nietzsche. It is very likely that she would have discussed this book with her father.

Moving chronologically to 1924, we have commented on Freud's use of the term "will to power" in "The Economic Problem of Masochism" and the possible affinity of this essay with "On the Pale Criminal." And let us note regarding masochism, that for Nietzsche the ascetic priest finds relief for suffering through his identity as a sinner: "Life again became *very* interesting . . . he had obviously won, *his* kingdom had come: one no longer protested *against* pain, one *thirsted* for pain; '*more* pain! *more* pain!'"[16] We can also remind ourselves of Freud's important statement that "pleasure and unpleasure, therefore, cannot be referred to an increase or decrease of a quantity (which we describe as 'tension due to stimulus') . . . It appears that they depend on . . . some characteristic . . . which we can only describe as a qualitative one."[17] The Nirvana principle, or tendency to extinguish excitations or maintain them at as low a level as possible, expresses not the tendency of the pleasure principle but the tendency of the death instincts. The pleasure principle *here* represents the claims of "the life instinct, the libido, which has thus, alongside of the death instinct, seized upon a share in the regulation of the processes of life."[18]

Also in 1924, Freud and Wittels were corresponding regarding the 1924 English-language edition of Wittels' book on Freud and possible revisions for a second edition. As Golumb[19] points out, Wittels had compared Nietzsche and Freud in his book and in particular mentioned the *Genealogy*. Freud, on vacation, wrote to Wittels: "I cannot compare the English edition with the German, for I didn't bring the latter with me (and the same applies to the Nietzsche)."[20] Freud has the work in question and apparently intends to read it and discuss matters with Wittels. It appears that he may have the English edition of Wittels' work with him.

Golumb writes that in the 1924 edition of Wittels' work, Wittels "claims that Freud took Nietzsche's *Genealogy of Morals*, which deals with philogenetic patterns, and gave it an ontogenetic basis in his investigations of individual development of the child."[21] In other words, what Nietzsche wrote of the repression of instincts, the turning of the drives upon the self, the formation of morality, bad conscience, sublimation, etc., as they pertain to the origins of civilization, Freud applied to the development of the individual. We should also note that Freud had read the first (1923) German biography and recommended emendations to Wittels.[22] The next year, in the English translation (with emendations of the German text), Wittels wrote about Freud insisting that he knew little of Nietzsche and had to renounce the study of Nietzsche in order not to be hampered in his explorations by preconceptions:

> This was rather a strange thing to say. Nietzsche's writings are to-day part of the common heritage of culture. We meet his ideas at every turn—in the street, in the tea-shop, in conversations between analysts and their patients. Freud may refuse to make direct acquaintance with Nietzsche's thoughts, but he will still have these thoughts in his mind, and they will appear there in a garbled form. There are no water-tight doors by which he will be able to exclude the current of Nietzschean ideas. Indeed, Freud has changed his mind, and now takes Nietzsche as well as Schopenhauer with him on his travels.[23]

There is nothing quite like this passage in the revised and expanded 1931 American edition of Wittels' biography of Freud.

In 1924, in *An Autobiographical Study* Freud writes:

> Even when I have moved away from observation, I have carefully avoided any contact with philosophy proper . . . The large extent to which psycho-analysis coincides with the philosophy of Schopenhauer—not only did he assert the dominance of the emotions and the supreme importance of sexuality but he was even aware of the mechanism of repression—is not to be traced to my acquaintance with his teaching. I read Schopenhauer very late in my life. Nietzsche, another philosopher whose guesses and intuitions often agree in the most astonishing way with the laborious findings of psychoanalysis, was for a long time avoided by me on that very ac-

count; I was less concerned with the question of priority than with keeping my mind unembarrassed.[24]

In light of Wittels' words, this passage would seem to indicate that the period of avoiding Nietzsche (though of course Nietzsche was not avoided) is now over, that "Freud has changed his mind." But Nietzsche's ideas are once again categorized into the realm of "guesses and intuition" to be contrasted with the "laborious" scientific realm of psychoanalysis. Again, Freud does not say during which period he avoided Nietzsche, not to mention what he did read and when he read it. And we know that Freud certainly was concerned about questions of priority[25] and that he acknowledged reading other material in which his ideas were anticipated, such as Lipps' philosophy and Schnitzler's plays. Furthermore, for the remainder of his life Freud does not comment on specific ideas of Nietzsche and their relationship to psychoanalysis (though perhaps we will learn more from correspondence yet to be published).

In 1926 after he left Vienna and the relationship with Freud had reached the breaking point, Otto Rank sent an elegantly bound edition of Nietzsche's works to Freud for his seventieth birthday.[26] Rank, who in his youth had been deeply immersed in Nietzsche's writings, was apparently in part conveying a message about Freud's relationship to Nietzsche as well as commenting on their own teacher-disciple relationship. (As Zarathustra received a staff from his disciples, on his seventieth birthday Freud received canes from two of his disciples.[27])

In 1927 the pastor and psychoanalyst Oskar Pfister responded to Freud's attack on religion (which emphasized infantile need that has not been outgrown) in *The Future of an Illusion* with the following words: "Your substitute for religion is basically the idea of the eighteenth-century Enlightenment in proud modern guise. I must confess that, with all my pleasure in the advance of science and technique, I do not believe in the adequacy and sufficiency of that solution of the problem of life . . . Nietzsche summed up your position in the words:

The reader will have realised my purport; namely that there is always a metaphysical belief on which our belief in science rests—that we observers of today, atheists and anti-metaphysicians as we are, still draw our fire from the blaze lit by a belief thousands of years old, the Christian belief, which was also that of Plato, that God is truth and that the truth is divine . . . But supposing that this grew less and less believable and nothing divine was left, save error, blindness, lies?"[28]

With this quote from *The Gay Science* (sec. 344), Pfister is bringing to Freud's attention that underlying his own quest, his "fire," may be the blaze of the ascetic ideal in the form of truth being divine, in the absolute valuing of truth. And he raises the question, What if this belief, ultimately derived from the very beliefs criticized in Freud's book, grew less and less believable and no absolute valuing of truth, nothing sacred or divine in truth remained? What then? We have then questions pertaining to the value of truth and to what other ideal might serve as a foundation for the will to truth. Also of importance, Pfister is declaring to Freud that Nietzsche had, forty years earlier, "summed up your position."

In *The Future of an Illusion* Freud writes of the believer seeking protection from God, the powerful father figure, and of the father complex being related to man's helplessness and need for protection.[29] Consider Nietzsche's words in *Daybreak:*

> By devoting yourselves with enthusiasm and making a sacrifice of yourselves you enjoy the ecstatic thought of henceforth being at one with the powerful being, whether a god or a man, to whom you dedicate yourselves: you revel in the feeling of his power, to which your very sacrifice is an additional witness. The truth of the matter is that you only *seem* to sacrifice yourselves: in reality you transform yourselves in thought into gods and enjoy yourselves as such.[30]

In his paper on Nietzsche's debt to the anthropologist Lubbock, Thatcher writes: "In a remarkable anticipation of the theory Freud advanced in *The Future of an Illusion* (1927), Nietzsche proposed a rationale of the will-to-power based on its opposite, the powerlessness of primitive man to cope with the unpredictable power of hostile forces, real or imaginary:

> In the inner psychic economy of the primitive man, fear of evil predominates. What is evil? Three things: chance, the uncertain, the sudden. How does primitive man fight against evil?—He conceives it as reason, as power, even as a person.

In this way he establishes the possibility of entering into a kind of treaty with it and in general to exercise influence over it in advance—to forestall it."[31]

It was also in 1927 that Freud wrote his paper, "Humour." Freud writes that the listener expects that the other

> will produce the signs of an affect—that he will get angry, complain, express pain, be frightened or horrified or perhaps even in despair; and the onlooker or listener is prepared to follow his lead and to call up the same emotional impulses in himself. But this emotional expectancy is disappointed; the other person expresses no affect but makes a jest . . . the essence of humour is that one spares oneself the affects to which the situation would naturally give rise and dismisses the possibility . . . with a jest . . . The grandeur in it clearly lies in the triumph of narcissism, the victorious assertion of the ego's invulnerability.[32]

In a passage on the origin of the comic, from which we have already quoted in relation to Kant and Lipps, Nietzsche touches on factors very close to those raised by Freud:

*Origin of the comic:*

> If one considers that man was for many hundreds of thousands of years an animal in the highest degree accessible to fear and that everything sudden and unexpected bade him prepare to fight and perhaps to die; that even later on, indeed, in social relationships all security depended on the expected and traditional in opinion and action; then one cannot be surprised if whenever something sudden and unexpected in word and deed happens without occasioning danger or injury man becomes wanton, passes over into the opposite of fear: the anxious, crouching creature springs up, greatly expands—man laughs. This transition from momentary anxiety to short-lived exuberance is called the *comic*.[33]

In 1929, the year before publication of *Civilization and Its Discontents*, Thomas Mann wrote: "He [Freud] was not acquainted with Nietzsche in whose work everywhere appear lightning-like gleams of insight anticipatory of Freud's later views."[34] Mann sees anticipation of Freud "everywhere" in Nietzsche's work but remains under the assumption that Freud was not acquainted with Nietzsche, an assumption that Freud evidently did not correct. One can only wonder about Freud's reaction to these words from his great admirer, a man he also greatly admired and who was greatly influenced by Nietzsche.

Also in 1929, an American, Charles E. Maylan, wrote a book on Freud and psychoanalysis, *Freud's Tragic Complex: An Analysis of Psychoanalysis*.[35] According to Yerushalmi,[36] Maylan wrote that the flaws of psychoanalysis lay in Freud's neurotic relationship to his father and his Jewish character. The book expresses antisemitic sentiments. Jung apparently expressed some approval of Maylan, and so did Stefan Zweig. Freud had corresponded with Zweig, and he expressed his anger to him. In the late sumer of 1930 Freud made a slip of the pen in a letter to Arnold Zweig and in analyzing it concluded that it was due to "the other Zweig . . . [having] given me great cause for annoyance."[37] According to Yerushalmi, Maylan also suggested that psychoanalysis (which he did regard as Freud's very important discovery) should be integrated with Nietzsche's thought to achieve proper philosophical depth. According to Michael Molnar, Maylan attempted to demonstrate that Freud's development of psychoanalysis was a product of his desire for revenge against life (or *ressentiment*).[38] Freud did look through the book and thought little of it, regarding the author as a "malicious fool, arian fanatic" who had already been rejected from an analytic training institute.[39]

Lorin Anderson[40] has pointed to the striking similarities between parts of *Civilization and Its Discontents* and Nietzsche's ideas, particularly as expressed in the *Genealogy*. Following are a few pertinent passages from chapter 7 of Freud's work:

> What happens in him [the individual] to render his desire for aggression innocuous? . . . His aggressiveness is introjected, internalized . . . directed towards his own ego . . . "conscience," is ready to put into action against the ego the same harsh aggressiveness that the ego would have liked to satisfy upon other extraneous individuals.[41]
>
> The super-ego torments the sinful ego . . . and is on the watch for opportunities of getting it punished . . . it is pre-

cisely those people who have carried saintliness furthest who reproach themselves with the worst sinfulness.[42]

Thus we know of two origins of the sense of guilt: one arising from fear of an authority, and the other, later on, arising from fear of the super-ego. The first insists upon a renunciation of instinctual satisfactions; the second, as well as doing this, presses for punishment, since the continuance of the forbidden wishes cannot be concealed from the super-ego.[43]

Every renunciation of instinct now becomes a dynamic source of conscience and every fresh renunciation increases the latter's severity and intolerance.[44]

Our discussions on the sense of guilt . . . corresponds faithfully to my intention to represent the sense of guilt as the most important problem in the development of civilization.[45]

We can also note that at the end of this work Freud states that he can offer no consolation and that "I have not the courage to rise up before my fellow man as a prophet."[46]

Since it should be clear at this point that Nietzsche's ideas pertaining to the origin and maintenance of "bad conscience" have a striking affinity to these passages in Freud, I will quote only briefly from Nietzsche:

All instincts that do not discharge themselves outwardly *turn inward*—this is what I call the *internalization* of man . . . all those instincts of wild, free, prowling man turned backward *against man himself* . . . a declaration of war against the old instincts . . . an animal soul turned against itself, taking sides against itself.[47]

This *instinct for freedom* forcibly made latent . . . pushed back and repressed, incarcerated within and finally able to discharge and vent itself only on itself: that, and that alone, is what the *bad conscience* is in its beginnings.[48]

For Nietzsche the origins and maintenance of guilt are inextricably linked with the origins and development of civilization:

I regard the bad conscience as the serious illness that man was bound to contract under the stress of the most fundamental change he ever experienced—that change which occurred when he found himself finally enclosed within the walls of society and of peace . . . suddenly all their instincts were disvalued and "suspended" . . . at the same time the old instincts had not suddenly ceased to make their usual demands! . . . they had to seek new and, as it were, subterranean gratifications . . . The entire inner world, originally as thin as if it were stretched between two membranes, expanded and extended itself . . . in the same measure as outward discharge was *inhibited* . . . thus began the gravest and uncanniest illness . . . man's suffering *of man, of himself*—the result of a forcible sundering from his animal past, as it were a leap and plunge into new surroundings and conditions of existence . . . the existence on earth of an animal soul turned against itself, taking sides against itself, was something so new, profound, unheard of, enigmatic contradictory, *and pregnant with a future* that the aspect of the earth was essentially altered.[49]

Nietzsche addresses this matter in much of his work. And we have mentioned Nietzsche's discussion of the priest's utilization and maintenance of bad conscience with the masses of people as well as the concept of the criminal from a sense of guilt. Freud was aware of such ideas in Nietzsche. In addition to the likelihood of Freud having some familiarity with these ideas in the late 1890s and his reading and discussing the *Genealogy* in 1908, we have seen that in all likelihood he was also comparing his own work to the *Genealogy* in 1924. It is no wonder that Jones commented on the "truly remarkable correspondence between Freud's conception of the super-ego and Nietzsche's exposition of the origin of the 'bad conscience.'"[50] More recently, Nehamas has stated that in the relevant passages of the *Genealogy* Nietzsche "anticipates not only Freud's pessimistic conclusions in *Civilization and Its Discontents* but also the very reasoning that led Freud to them."[51] (*Civilization and Its Discontents* is a much more pessimistic work than *The Future of an Illusion* which demonstrates greater confidence in the power of reason, science, and the progress of civilization.[52] One should also note differences in the pessimism of the two thinkers.) Richard Simon points out that Freud's "discussion in *Civilization and Its Discontents* of civilization, religion, suffering, guilt and their interrelationships closely parallels Friedrich Nietzsche's discussion of these same four concepts in *The Genealogy of Morals* (1887), most particularly in Part III, 'What Is the Meaning of Ascetic Ideals?'"[53] (This was the part read and discussed at the April 1908 Vienna Psychoanalytic Society meeting.) And Marcia Cavell, a philosopher with the highest regard for Freud, comments on Nietzsche's influence on Freud: "Nowhere is Freud's debt to Nietzsche more apparent than in his views about valuing, particularly as Freud states them in *Civilization and Its Discontents.*"[54]

Gellner makes a particularly important point regarding the superego:

> The essence of Freudianism is that the super-ego is seen as of this world, tainted by the same ailments, and above all with the same self-deception and irrationality as anything else. This is a crucial part of the Nietzschean heritage.
>
> Nietzsche . . . saw that the super-ego was not to be taken at face value, that it represented, in a viciously twisted and devious and cunning way, the very same interests as did all other psychic forces, and that it had no genuine claim to the special position which it arrogated to itself.[55]

And Nietzsche was very much aware of the role of aggressive drives in the formation of conscience, a crucial idea for Freud: "the psychology of the *conscience* . . . is the instinct of cruelty that turns back after it can no longer discharge itself externally. Cruelty is here exposed for the first time as one of the most ancient and basic substrata of culture that simply cannot be imagined away."[56] With all of these similarities, it is striking that Freud states it "was a discovery first made by psycho-analytic research" that while the "ego appears to us as something autonomous and unitary, . . . on the contrary the ego is continued inwards, without any sharp delimitation, into an unconscious mental entity which we designate as the id and for which it serves as a kind of facade."[57] That the ego is not something unitary or autonomously marked off from the id and that the ego serves as a facade for the id (or the realm of drives and their derivatives) was not a discovery first made by psychoanalysis.

Loewald comments on the affinity between Nietzsche and Freud on the matter of internalization and instincts turned upon the self when not discharged outwardly. He refers to the well-known

passages from the *Genealogy*[58] and states that in such passages
Nietzsche conceives of instincts

> not . . . as internal stimuli impinging on a psychic apparatus,
> but as psychic forces that when turned inward and deployed
> in the interior of the psychic force-field, bring about the for-
> mation of a soul, of a "psychic apparatus." In psychoanalytic
> terms, what Nietzsche describes is the transformation of li-
> bidinal and aggressive cathexis into narcissistic and mas-
> ochistic cathexis.[59]

One might say that for Nietzsche "the interior of the psychic
force-field" is, before the turning of instincts inward, "thin as if it
were stretched between two membranes."[60] The inner world, including but not necessarily restricted to what might be termed the
psychic apparatus, "expanded . . . in the same measure as outward
discharge was *inhibited.*"[61] This inner world, this soul, and this
bad conscience are "pregnant with a future." While the "bad conscience is an illness" it is an "illness as pregnancy."[62] This shift in
viewpoint from the negative to the positive, Loewald relates to
Hartman's idea of "change of function," for example, a means of
defense becoming a goal in itself or internalized struggle coming to
be valued in itself.[63]

In 1931 an American edition of Wittels' book on Freud was
published in which Nietzsche's name and ideas appeared at various
points. Wittels wrote that "time and again comparison has been
made between Freud and Nietzsche, Schopenhauer, even Plato,"
and that "Nietzsche . . . is revered in Germany as a god."[64]

Also in 1931, Freud wrote in a letter that he rejected the
study of Nietzsche because "it was plain I would find insights in
him very similar to psychoanalytic ones."[65] Yet just a few years
earlier, in *The Future of an Illusion,* Freud wrote:

> I have said nothing [pertaining to a critique of religion] which
> other and better men have not said before me in a much more
> complete, forcible and impressive manner. Their names are
> well known, and I shall not cite them, for I should not like to
> give an impression that I am seeking to rank myself as one of
> them. All I have done—and this is the only thing that is new

in my exposition—is to add some psychological foundation to the criticisms of my great predecessors.[66]

Nietzsche would very likely be one of the great predecessors that Freud evidently was familiar with and among those with whom he would like to be associated and ranked, yet will not name.

# Chapter 13

## WOMAN, TRUTH AND
## PERSPECTIVISM

> . . . *the others are seeking* cures *for themselves—
> they are* not *seeking truth . . . these others take so
> little real pleasure in science, and make of the
> coldness, dryness and inhumanity of science a re-
> proach to it: it is the sick passing judgment on the
> games of the healthy.*
>
> —Nietzsche, *Daybreak*

> *That it does not matter whether a thing is true, but
> only what effect it produces—absolute lack of in-
> tellectual integrety.*
>
> —Nietzsche, *The Will to Power*

In 1933, in the *New Introductory Lectures on Psycho-
Analysis,*[1] Freud again mentions the derivation of the term "Das
Es," "the it," later "the id," from Nietzsche. Also, Freud once again
asks,

> Why have we ourselves needed such a long time before we de-
> cided to recognize an aggressive instinct? . . . We should proba-
> bly have met with little resistance if we had wanted to ascribe
> an instinct with such an aim to animals. But to include it in
> the human constitution appears sacrilegious . . . we have ar-
> gued in favour of a special aggressive and destructive instinct .
> . . on the basis of general considerations to which we were led
> by examining the phenomena of sadism and masochism.[2]

Of course Nietzsche recognized the aggressive instincts and will to power in various forms and manifestations, including sublimated forms, the drives turned inward upon the self, and as an instinct for mastery, all of which are prominent in Freud's writings.

We can also note in this work Freud's description of the power and importance of rational thinking and scientific laws. Freud writes that a Weltanschauung erected upon science includes "submission to the truth and rejection of illusions."[3] He writes, quoting Goethe, of "Reason and Science, the highest strength possessed by man," and of "the bright world governed by relentless laws which has been constructed for us by science."[4] But he also writes that "from the very beginning when life takes us under its strict discipline, a resistance stirs within us against the relentlessness and monotony of the laws of thought and against the demands of reality-testing. Reason becomes the enemy which withholds from us so many possibilities of pleasure."[5]

However "bright" the world of science is and however much reason and science represent "the highest strength possessed by man," this world, these laws, these faculties, require from us "submission" to a withholding enemy that imposes "strict discipline" with "relentlessness and monotony." However much this language pertains to a description of universal problems in human development, one may wonder if it does not reflect Freud's own experience of the call of reason as a relentless, monotonous, disciplining force to which he must reluctantly (laboriously?) submit.

We can contrast these descriptions with Freud's remarks on occultism. He writes of various conjectures of occultism: "Of these conjectures no doubt the most probable is that there is a real core of yet unrecognized facts in occultism round which cheating and phantasy have spun a veil which it is hard to pierce."[6] Later he writes that "taking them [cases he is considering and has accumulated] as a whole, there remains a strong balance of probability in favour of thought-transference as a fact."[7] Freud the heroic rationalist is indicating that there is "a real core of yet unrecognized facts in occultism," particularly pertaining to thought transference. And he makes two other interesting and related statements. First, in considering that the tradition and sacred books of all peoples include descriptions of "miraculous" events and superhuman powers, Freud states that "it will be hard for us to avoid a suspicion that the interest in occultism is in fact a religious one."[8]

Towards the end of this chapter he writes: "It may be that I too have a secret inclination towards the miraculous which thus goes half way to meet the creation of occult facts."[9]

It may be that Freud was a heroic (masculine oriented) rationalist with a secret inclination towards (and fear of) the miraculous and the religious (and the feminine). This inclination contrasts with Freud's belief that it is "simply a fact that the truth cannot be tolerant, that it admits of no compromises or limitations, that research regards every sphere of human activity as belonging to it and that it must be relentlessly critical if any other power tries to take over any part of it."[10] "Our best hope for the future is that the intellect—the scientific spirit, reason—may in the process of time establish a dictatorship in the mental life of man."[11] (Freud also states that it is "the nature of reason . . . to give man's emotional impulses . . . the position they deserve."[12]) Nietzsche, while highly valuing reason, science and intellectual conscience, does not think in such absolute terms or rule out alternate forms of disclosure. He also calls into question the absolute value of truth.

## WOMAN AS TRUTH

These lectures also include a chapter on femininity, and here is one area in which some in the psychoanalytic community are quite willing to argue for a definite influence of Nietzsche upon Freud, a destructive one.[13] As is well known, both thinkers are regarded as having made numerous misogynist statements and to have devalued and denigrated women.

In the *New Introductory Lectures*,[14] Freud writes of the primacy of the girl's penis envy, "the fact that women must be regarded as having little sense of justice is no doubt related to the predominance of envy,"[15] the lack of strength and independence (not just harshness) of a woman's superego due to absence of castration anxiety as it is experienced and dealt with by the boy and her hatred of her mother. He also writes of women's inherent narcissism and passivity, their need to be loved being stronger than their need to love, that a mother's "unlimited" satisfaction comes only in her relation to a son, that "with the change to femininity the clitoris should wholly or in part hand over its sensitivity, and at the same time its importance, to the vagina,"[16] and that the "suppression of women's aggressiveness" is not only imposed socially but "is prescribed for them constitutionally . . . favour[ing] the development of powerful masochistic impulses."[17]

Also, regarding the idea of the "oceanic" feeling as pertaining to the infant at the breast, Marianna Torgovnick suggests that we have here a conjoining of the primitive, the infantile, and the female.[18] Such states are to be superseded. Where females compare favorably to males they are more masculine than feminine.[19] Although at times Freud places his emphasis on the dimensions of activity and passivity in both men and women and also stresses the bisexuality of men as well as women, it is ultimately the realm of the "masculine" qualities that is superior. (The superiority of the masculine realm and qualities is also evident for Freud on the historical level as regards the development of civilization, a point to which we will return when we discuss *Moses and Monotheism*.) Also, it is one thing to present these ideas as worthy of exploration and, as Freud does, to caution that they are "certainly incomplete and fragmentary."[20] But it is something else to present them as central to female sexuality and thus to female development overall and as unbiased, reasonably secure findings of science, as bringing forth "nothing but observed facts almost without speculative additions."[21]

Nietzsche writes: "Woman has much reason for shame . . . and so far all this was at bottom best repressed and kept under control by *fear* of man"; "the woman who 'unlearns fear' surrenders her most womanly instincts"; "women themselves always still have in the background of all personal vanity an impersonal contempt—for 'woman.'"[22] These statements are not at all atypical.

On the other hand, Nietzsche begins his well-known sections on women in *Beyond Good and Evil* (secs. 231–39) immediately after the section (230) in which he calls for us to be "hardened in the discipline of science," standing before ourselves "with intrepid Oedipus eyes." He states that what he offers emerges from something "very deep down" and "unteachable" in himself, and "how very much these are after all only—*my* truths." He also confesses: "Let us men confess it: we honor and love precisely *this* art [of "the lie"] and *this* instinct [concern with "appearance and beauty"] in woman."[23] To some degree Nietzsche here offers his ideas on woman as an opportunity for us to know him "very deep down" on this "unteachable" level, and to learn from him perhaps some things about woman (the essence and the image or representation) and women but also some things about himself, including his own limitations. But he also acknowledges and then, at the conclusion of this part, asks: "Fear and pity: with these feelings man has so far confronted woman . . . And this should be the end?"[24] Clearly, Nietzsche would like to see men move beyond such fear and pity, for their own sakes as well as for that of women.

Both thinkers are often regarded as having been to a significant extent locked into a point of view reflective of their masculine position in which the masculine is equated with reason and culture and the feminine is equated with the irrational, the unconscious, nature and the sexual. According to George Makari, the feminine may be envied, desired and degraded, and it may be regarded as a source, reflection or symbol of a romanticized notion of natural truth.[25] Woman is also the "other," the not-male who is the recipient of the projections of what is unconscious and unacceptable in the male. She may have added burdens placed upon her as God and truth, in their traditional forms, may have disappeared. And there may be for Freud the projection onto woman of the repressed image of the primitive yet castrated eastern European Jewish male from which Freud may have wanted to distance himself.[26]

Carolyn Heilbrun describes Freud as having created a certain type of "masculine grammar of the psyche."[27] Perhaps there is some truth to this, and perhaps Freud is here influenced to some degree by Nietzsche. However, there are serious problems in equating the two thinkers on such matters or in arguing that Nietzsche's actual ideas on related matters had a substantial influence on Freud. While Makari's paper makes a number of interesting points on Freud's views of women and provides some relevant material on Schopenhauer and Nietzsche (as well as pointing out Schopenhauer's likely significant influence on Freud, which Freud denied), it offers such a limited presentation of Nietzsche's ideas as to make it an extremely narrow view of Nietzsche's thoughts on woman and truth. The reason this is of particular importance is that discussions of Nietzsche do not appear all that often in psychoanalytic journals, and this paper was published in a prominent psychoanalytic journal. Readers of this paper who are not very familiar with Nietzsche or recent writings on his views of woman and truth can only come away with a very limited view of his ideas on truth and woman. Nietzsche is often regarded as renouncing any hope for attaining truth and objectivity as well as being hostile towards science. While one can certainly find irrationalist and subjectivist (as well as misogynist) strains in Nietzsche's thought, we will see that this is a very limited and even inaccurate characterization of his mature thought.

Jean Graybeal, in her book *Language and 'the Feminine' in Nietzsche and Heidegger*, analyzes numerous passages in Nietzsche which appear to be, and may in fact be, justifiably considered misogynist, such as the old woman telling Zarathustra, "You are going to women? Don't forget the whip!"[28] or "Everything about woman is a riddle, and everything about woman has *one* solution: it is called pregnancy."[29] Graybeal points out that one has to appreciate Nietzsche's revised symbolic universe to understand such statements. For example, we should understand that pregnancy is "Nietzsche's image for creation, for fertility, for the possibility of the new."[30] As regards the whip, Graybeal suggests that the old woman has mocked Zarathustra and is in effect indicating that as long as he thinks and talks the way he does about women, "he had better arm himself . . . for they will not let his notions stand . . . he will be powerless in their domain."[31] Graybeal suggests that, "the great feminine figures reappear throughout the book, to undermine and unsettle any pretense Zarathustra makes of coming up with a program, a plan, a new symbolic structure which would only issue again in nihilism."[32]

As regards Nietzsche's criticism of emancipated or "defeminized" women, he is at least in part concerned that men are corrupting women "to imitate all the stupidities with which 'man' in Europe, European 'manliness,' is sick."[33] As Hatab suggests, on some levels Nietzsche considered the feminine and the Dionysian to be closely linked if not synonymous, and he feared the loss of the "Dionysian connection."[34] At least to a certain extent and in certain contexts, "Nietzsche seems to be saying that the repudiation of feminine traits in favor of masculine traits is an exchange of strength for weakness."[35] (We can note here that the god Dionysus' revelation, while directed to men and women, is given first to women.[36] Also of some interest, it has been pointed out by Louise Bruit Zaidman that Dionysian maenads "transgress the requirements of the two activities that defined the Greek woman: weaving and motherhood."[37]) Of course, this should not blind us to the more oppressive side of Nietzsche's concerns about, perhaps fears of, educated, emancipated women. But it does appear that Nietzsche might, in the words of Robert Ackerman, support a type of feminism that argues for "a divergent, genuinely feminine set of insights that would be essential for the correction or improvement of a society otherwise headed toward male scientistic control."[38] (For Nietzsche it is clear that women *could* be educated in such ways as to create, in most spheres of life, equality between men and women: "In the three or four civilized countries of Europe women can through a few centuries of education be made into anything, even into men: not in the sexual sense, to be sure, but in every other sense."[39] It is just this, given his views on the men of contemporary Europe, that Nietzsche greatly fears.)

It is also noteworthy that Nietzsche writes of a sage who tells a youth that "'it is men . . . that corrupt women; and all the failings of women should be atoned by and improved in men. For it is man who creates for himself the image of woman, and woman forms herself according to this image.'"[40] While this statement does not refer to the oppression and violence involved in man's creating the image of woman according to which woman forms herself or consider women as capable of rejecting man's image of her, it is a call for men to accept guilt, atone and create a less corrupt image of woman which will affect themselves and women. Nietzsche asks that "the failings of women should be . . . improved in men." And Freud will prove to be of great help in this task in writings in which he is sensitive to the social and developmental factors that have an impact on women and the ways in which woman is created and maintained in the male psyche.[41] Of course, the fact that Nietzsche and Freud can write sensitively and perceptively on "woman" (and women) does not obliterate the misogynist sentiments. Also, as Gilman suggests, one might find Nietzsche's ideas on truth and woman or his ideas on women's response to their creation by a phallic world as still trapped in extreme polarities rather than reflecting fruitful oppositions.[42]

However, if we are to understand the notion of woman-truth, we should also appreciate the more positive side of Nietzsche's views on woman and on truth. In doing so I believe we also find that these are areas in which Nietzsche and Freud differ in significant ways and that any influence of Netzsche on Freud is quite limited.

Makari points out that in *The Gay Science* Nietzsche equates truth with a Greek demon, Baubo. (This is a figure of which Freud too was aware.[43]) He suggests that Nietzsche's misogynistic tone is reflected in his use of such a vulgar demon that represents the female genitals.[44] What Makari fails to note, and what is essential, is that whatever else Baubo may be associated with, she is a figure in a myth involving the goddess Demeter who is mournfully searching for her daughter Persephone. Through a spontaneous act of erotic, baudy and comical behavior Baubo breaks through to Demeter and frees her for more effective action so that she can find her daughter. Also involved in the story is the god Iacchus who is intimately linked in Greek mythology to Dionysus.[45] It is evident that Baubo performs a highly laudable act, an act that implicitly involves the figure of Dionysus and that utilizes a particular means, the comical (rather than rational analysis) in the service of breaking Demeter's bondage to depressive mourning, thus freeing her for action. What is revealed here, the truth here, is laughable and freeing.[46] (We can also note that for Zarathustra, laughter [along with dancing, singing and playing] is a sign of the divine.) This is quite consistent with Nietzsche's idea that through affirmative laughter one may triumph over "the spirit of gravity."

There is also the matter of Nietzsche's equation of woman with appearance, with surfaces, as the veiled figure desired and whose veil is necessary for the desire to be aroused. She makes man believe she is "deep."[47] There is no one true, stable, fixed reality in and of itself behind the veil. Woman is compared to the artist who prefers appearance to reality, but "appearance means reality repeated *once again*, as selection, redoubling, correction."[48] As Sarah Kofman, a more radical interpreter of Nietzsche on truth, discusses it:

> To respect female modesty is thus to be able to hold oneself to appearance, to interrogate oneself indefinitely on the infinite riddles of nature/Sphinx, without seeking—perhaps it is only prudence—to "unveil" truth.
> The attitude of metaphysicians is ambivalent. They wish to see and strip away all veils, but they also fear to see.[49]

Regarding the figure of Baubo:

> Baubo can appear as a female double of Dionysus.
> The figure of Baubo indicates that a simple logic could

never understand that life is neither depth nor surface, that behind the veil there is another veil, behind a layer of paint, another layer. It signifies also that appearance should cause us neither pessimism nor skepticism, but rather the affirming laugh of a living being who knows that despite death, life can come back indefinitely and that "the individual is nothing and the species all."[50]

Mary Ann Doane draws on Derrida's discussion of Nietzsche's views of woman-truth and finds an affirming woman in addition to a denigrated and denigrating woman in Nietzsche:

> According to Derrida, Nietzsche recognized the fragile structure of truth in its relation to the veil and both refuse to perform the gesture of either veiling or unveiling.[51]
>
> He locates three types of proposition about the woman in Nietzsche's text. In the first, the woman is a figure of falsehood, against which the man measures his own phallogocentric truth. Here, she is castrated. In the second proposition, she is the figure of truth but plays with it at a distance through a guile and naivete that nevertheless ratify truth. Here, she is castrating. In the first two types of proposition in Nietzsche's text, the woman is "censured, debased and despised." Only the third type of proposition is conceived outside the bind of castration. Here, the woman is an "affirmative power, a dissimulatress, an artist, a dionysiac." Derrida succinctly outlines the desire of Nietzsche: "He was, he dreaded this castrated woman. He was, he dreaded this castrating woman. He was, he loved this affirmative woman."[52]

Even more radical interpreters of Nietzsche's views on woman as truth, such as Kofman and Derrida, find, along with what may be denigrating, an affirmative woman as truth in Nietzsche. (Carol Diethe, a scholar who is highly critical of Nietzsche's views on women, who sees such views as inextricably linked to a gender-based will to power that is "the archetypal phallic symbol" and sees Nietzsche as accepting the view that by definition male sexuality is active and female sexuality passive [though she points to Nietzsche's characterization of woman as a sexual predator, even if in the service of pregnancy], also acknowledges some praiseworthy aspects of Nietzsche's positive attitudes towards female sexuality [and believes that some of Nietzsche's fears of educated, liberated women result from his fear that such instincts will be damaged by what is regarded as emancipation]. Diethe also acknowledges that Nietzsche should, to a certain extent, be respected for his positive views on childbearing.[53] We might also keep in mind that many early-twentieth-century feminists found inspiration in Nietzsche.)

Nietzsche certainly experiments with the idea of woman as a symbol of truth, and this can be seen as an aspect of Nietzsche's struggle with notions of surface-depth, appearance-reality as they pertain to the notion of truth. According to Makari, for Nietzsche the true world as female is incomprehensible, nameable but un-knowable, and knowledge is illusion that is irrational, with this humiliation at the hands of woman-truth, instead of leading to ac-cepting the irrational in all of us, leading to hatred of woman-truth, of woman.[54] Makari does mention that "consciousness with its rational struggles is equated with the illusion of male philoso-phers" who do not know how to approach truth-woman, and he contrasts in Nietzsche the duality of male illusion and female truth. But he declares that what is true is unknowable, "nature's mysterious, irrational forces as symbolized by the woman."[55] (It should also be noted that even when the world as flux and becom-ing is associated with woman, it is not necessarily in a manner that denigrates and devalues. Flux and becoming are associated with the processes of the "eternally creative primordial mother."[56]) Makari believes that this maneuver allows Nietzsche to write of truth and dismiss the illusions of all other male philosophers while preserving his own male subjectivist philosophy. This follows from Makari's notion that Nietzsche was seeking a way out of dilemmas posed by perspectivism understood as including the notion that the idea of truth is an illusion.

Some authors do argue that for Nietzsche the world is (truly) one of flux and change, that the (real) world is one of "imperma-nent illusion and changing appearance" and that "woman is the untruth of truth." However, it is more accurate to view Nietzsche's late work as arguing that the senses do not lie insofar as they show "becoming, passing away, and change"[57] and as ques-tioning the notion of enduring, stable self-identical objects and subjects, while arguing for a kind of objectivity. Also, as Schacht has pointed out, the world of becoming and flux is for Nietzsche the "absence of an inherent, immutable order" that exists in and of itself. And he points out that "not everything about the world changes even though everything in it does."[58] At certain points Nietzsche does regard our concepts as falsifications of chaotic raw sensations, but even when he states that the antithesis of "the adapted world which we feel to be real" is "the formless unformulable world of the chaos of sensation . . . a kind [of world] 'unknowable' for us," he emphasizes that this "unknowable" world is "*another kind* of phenomenal world"; it "is not the 'true world.'"[59]

Regarding the idea that Nietzsche was attempting to escape dilemmas of his perspectivism (for Makari, the problem of self-reference and the problem of the need to postulate some true world in relation to which Nietzsche can write of lies), first, it can be noted that Nietzsche's perspectivism is quite complex, as indicated by recent studies such as those of Schacht, Nehamas, Warner and Clark.[60] To prove his point Makari would have to offer a much more detailed discussion of Nietzsche's perspectivism. (Also, he does not indicate that in fact many analysts are moving exactly in the direction of some kind of perspectivism.[61]) Secondly, Nietzsche did not consistently hold to the idea that truth is illusion. He certainly did not believe that there was a realm of "the things-in-themselves" for which "woman" was the metaphor, or use "woman" as "a metaphor for the chaotic and unknowable true world that lay beyond perception."[62] The real world is flux and change for Nietzsche, but in his later works there is no "unknowable true world." Also, the split between a surface, apparent world and an unknowable but true world of the things-in-themselves was, as is well known, a view Nietzsche rejected. For one thing, as Mary Warnock points out, Nietzsche was attempting to get across the point that there is only one world, not two. She also suggests that for Nietzsche, if there is anything we contribute to the world, it is the idea of a "thing," and in Nietzsche's words, "the psychological origin of the belief in *things* forbids us to speak of 'things-in-themselves.'" (And Schacht points out that in regard to the distinction between "appearance" and "reality," what Nietzsche repudiates is the distinction between and separation of a *merely* apparent world and a world of "true being.")[63]

It can also be noted, following Dannhauser,[64] that in the famous passage from the preface to *Beyond Good and Evil*, Nietzsche does not assert that truth *is* a woman. He writes, "*Supposing* truth is a woman—what then?" (emphasis added). He also does not claim that truth is unwinnable, but that it has not been won. "She has not allowed herself to be won" by the "awkward" and "improper" methods that have been utilized to approach truth. Nietzsche's perspectivism is an approach to truth that he believes is more productive, more proper, less awkward. Nietzsche was not looking for a conception of woman-truth to escape a dilemma of his perspectivism. His perspectivism was a working out of the type of truth and objectivity he believed to be possible. (We can also note that for Nietzsche perspectivism may be connected to the idea of saying "Yes" to life and loving one's fate [*amor fati*]. Joseph Valente, in his paper on Nietzsche and Joyce, points out that for both writers saying "Yes" to life [and for Nietzsche saying "Yes" to eternal recurrence as presented by the demon], loving one's fate [*amor fati*], involves living without static, universal forms and saying "Yes" to the absence of absolute meaning or value, to reanimating "the play of appearance, of style which they associated with the ancient Greek artificers, Homer and Daedalus . . . For Nietzsche and Joyce, the road to *amor fati* led through the epistemological pass of perspectivism."[65] Both had "the aim of . . . developing our interpretive capacities" and of enabling us to "dwell amid the indeterminacy of . . . [our] own creative-destructive activity."[66])

Regarding what Makari terms Nietzsche's "subjectivist philosophy," one of Nietzsche's replies might be that he wishes to convey the importance of the point of view that "'knowledge-in-itself' is as impermissible a concept as 'thing-in-itself.'"[67] Or, as he writes in another context: "Let us be on guard against the dangerous old conceptual fiction that posited a 'pure, will-less, painless, timeless knowing subject.'"[68] And he might add: "No longer the humble expression, 'everything is *merely* subjective,' but 'it is also [not *only*] *our* work!—Let us be proud of it!'"[69] And he might agree with a contemporary thinker such as Rorty when he writes that "there is no such thing as the way the thing is in itself, under no description, apart from any use to which human beings might want to put it."[70] Or with Kolakowski who states: "Man does not possess a ground outside himself on which he could both stand and know that he is standing there."[71] Or with Yovel who suggests: "Even the most universally alleged form cannot be applied outside a definite context, determined by previous life-forms and interpretations . . . By being open to . . . mutable interpretations, the world is no less real or immanent; it only escapes encapsulation by 'eternal' forms, essences, and the like."[72]

None of this entails that the idea of truth is inherently an illusion. The fact that the world is viewed from a perspective does not negate the existence of the world or relegate it to a true (in and of itself) but unknowable realm. It does raise the possibility that our idea of the reality to which truths are to correspond may not be perspective-free.

Even in an early, more "subjectivist" work, "On Truth and Lying in an Extra-Moral Sense" (1873), Nietzsche writes of terrible "truths" against which scientific truth defends.[73] In a later note, also reflective of a more extreme position, Nietzsche does conclude the passage with the words, "there is no 'truth.'" However, he places the word "truth" in quotation marks. And while he states that the world with which we are concerned is "not a fact but a fable," he indicates that this world with which we are concerned is not a fable unrelated to truth but is an "approximation on the basis of a meager sum of observations." This leaves open the possibility of further productive observations and more accurate approximations. He also writes of the opening up of "new perspectives" and "new horizons," of "the overcoming of narrower interpretations."[74] In a note of 1888 in which Nietzsche declares that "the concept 'truth' is nonsensical," he clearly explains that this is the case in regard to application to an "'in-itself'" and allows that the "domain of 'true-false' applies . . . to relations."[75] And of course when Nietzsche offers his analyses and interpretations, he evidently believes he has opened up new perspectives and horizons and that he has overcome certain narrower interpretations. He evidently believes that in addition to providing a life-affirming interpretation, he has provided one that in some important ways is closer to the truth than others.

Karl Popper, who is considered by some to be one of the twentieth century's greatest philosophers of science and far removed from Nietzschean modes of thought, has written the following:

> Although I do not think that we can ever describe . . . an ultimate essence of the world . . . we may seek to probe deeper and deeper into . . . properties of the world that are more and more essential, or of greater and greater depth. I believe that this word "deeper" defies any attempt at exhaustive logical analysis, but that it is nevertheless a guide to our intuitions.[76]

Martin Warner approvingly quotes Warnock as stating: "This might well be taken as a statement of Nietzsche's belief."[77] (Warnock also relates Nietzsche's more pragmatist inclinations, similar to philosophers such as Pierce, to his conception of truth in science.)

Regarding Nietzsche's attitude towards truth and science, we can note that at the end of his productive life, in *The Antichrist*, he writes that "'faith' means not *wanting* to know what is true." He regards the imperative of faith as "the veto against science," and he offers "philology and medicine [as] the two great adversaries of superstition." In *Ecce Homo* he writes of "knowledge, saying Yes to reality" and of "truth enter[ing] into a fight with the lies of millennia."[78] Nietzsche also greatly values the intellectual cleanliness of rigorous logical thinking and writes admiringly of the Jewish contribution to logical thinking: "They have taught men to make finer distinctions, more rigorous inferences."[79] And as Stephen Jay Gould has put it, "all science is intelligent inference."[80]

Even in the *Genealogy*, in which Nietzsche comments on perspectivism and is critical of the scientists and scholars of his day, he is critical not in principle, but because, for example, "their voices obviously do *not* come from the depths, the abyss of the scientific conscience does *not* speak through them—for today the scientific conscience is an abyss—the word 'science' in the mouths of such trumpeters is simply an indecency, an abuse, and a piece of impudence."[81] This is no repudiation of science and scholarship; it is a call to scientists to develop the scientific conscience and enable the abyss of that conscience to speak "from the depths" through them, as they search for truth. (Let us note that for Nietzsche, intellectual or scientific conscience includes the "abyss" of such a conscience. Clearly, "bad conscience" is not the only kind of conscience for Nietzsche. In addition to intellectual conscience there is "healthy morality . . . dominated by an instinct of life"[82] and the "call" of conscience to "be your self!,"[83] later to be, "Become who you are." And there is conscience as the sovereign individual's awareness of freedom and the "privilege of *responsibility*," as the sovereign individual's right, through knowledge of his strength, to make and keep promises.[84])

Nietzsche advises *not* that we guard against the snares of reason or spirituality or knowledge, but of "'*pure* reason,' '*absolute* spirituality,' 'knowledge *in itself*': these always demand that we should think of an eye turned in no particular direction, in which the active and interpretive forces, through which alone seeing becomes seeing *something*, are supposed to be lacking" (first three emphases added). Such a possibility involves "the dangerous old conceptual fiction that posited a 'pure, will-less, painless, timeless knowing subject.'"[85]

As for Nietzsche's commitment to the struggle for truth and intellectual conscience:

> At every step one has to wrestle for truth; one has had to surrender for it almost everything to which the heart, to which our love, our trust in life, cling otherwise. That requires greatness of soul: the service of truth is the hardest service . . . that one makes of every Yes and No a matter of conscience.[86]

And again we can consider that Nietzsche clearly thought he had uncovered some truths regarding the areas into which he had inquired, whether it be the origins of bad conscience or the psychological motivations of the Apostle Paul. Truth is not illusory but it does unavoidably entail perspectival appearance. For Nietzsche, the apparent world is not cut off from a world of absolute truth.[87] While Nietzsche is quite willing, as in his psychological explorations, to draw distinctions between "deeper" realities in relation to "surface" appearances, he also argues that on a fundamental level one cannot draw a distinction between a merely apparent world and a perspective-free true factual world. The "deeper" realities he discovered cannot be regarded as facts-in-themselves or anything else of the kind that would be free of embeddedness in human schemes, practices, theories, and interpretations, of perspectival seeing and knowing.

Although Nietzsche calls into question the absolute value of truth, values the illusions (the truthful illusions) of art that are a stimulant to life, values masks, veils and even the creative lie, he also answers the call of truth. Truth calls to us, tempts us to unveil her. If we have integrity we will say "Yes" to the hardest service, surrendering much that we hold dear, including our wishes "*not* to see . . . [what] . . . one does see."[88] When the unveiling takes place we come upon not truth (or woman) in-itself but an appearance which is reality by way of a particular perspective. One might regard this situation as, among other possibilities, an opportunity for the creative play of our interpretive capacities, for the creating and destroying of play, for a creative sublimation of the will to power. But none of this obviates our capacity to sometimes reach what can be reasonably regarded as truth. What it does involve, in the words of Linda Alcoff, is that for Nietzsche "neither a noumenal realm nor an historical synthesis exists to provide an absolute criterion of adjudication for competing truth claims," and "perhaps most importantly, Nietzsche introduces the notion that truth is a kind of human practice." Alcoff also suggests that "perspectives are to be judged not on their relation to the absolute but on the basis of their effects in a specific area." For Alcoff this entails "local, pragmatic" truths even though Nietzsche does posit trans-historical truth claims such as his claim regarding the will to power.[89] Nietzsche *is* concerned with what corresponds to or fits the facts, but such facts are not established without a human contribution, without interpretation. Of course for those for whom the term "fact" should entail a "halt before the factum brutum," there may be an objection to the use of such terms as "fact," "reality," etc., in such a context.

When Nietzsche writes of seeing things as they are, one meaning of this is to be able to see them with "more eyes, different eyes."[90] The greater the number of relevant affects and perspectives we can take into account the more complete may be our interpretation:

> the ability to control one's Pro and Con and to dispose of them, so that one knows how to employ a *variety* of perspectives and affective interpretations in the service of knowledge . . . There is *only* a perspective seeing, *only* a perspective "knowing"; and the *more* affects we allow to speak about one thing, the *more* eyes, different eyes, we can use to observe one thing, the more complete will our "concept" of this thing, our "objectivity," be. But to eliminate the will altogether, to suspend each and every affect, supposing we were capable of this—what would that mean but to *castrate* the intellect?[91]

The "will" may lead to selecting, padding, falsifying, etc., but that is not all it leads to or allows for. Its presence is the inescapable condition for the formulation of an interpretation. To imagine eliminating it is to imagine eliminating a source of the intellect's pleasure, potency, energy and capacity to generate life. But Nietzsche is quite explicit about working in "the service of truth" and developing, in the sense he believes this is possible, more complete, more objective concepts. In addition, Nietzschean perspectivism might even be viewed as a more "feminine" orientation to knowledge, truth and reality which exists in relationship with the more "masculine" realm of a disembodied ascetic ideal and the one complete, perspective-free, and true account.

These issues also relate to Nietzsche's undermining of the notion of a subject's individual, stable and enduring identity. The individual consists of drives and perspectives in conflict, any one ruling or organizing drive and perspective able to be replaced. This is somewhat related to psychoanalytic notions of the predominance at any time of a given self-representation and the shifting nature of such representations. Nietzsche also anticipates Lacan who writes of the agency of the ego being situated "in a fictional direction."[92] In his study of Lacan, Ragland-Sullivan writes of Lacan's idea of "conscious knowledge which flees from 'truth' in the name of rationality, wisdom and convention. In this theory Lacan is close to Nietzsche."[93] Ragland-Sullivan begins his book by stating that Lacan is "the most innovative and far ranging thinker in Europe since Friedrich Nietzsche and Sigmund Freud."[94] Rudnytsky mentions "The Child and the Mirror" in part 2 of *Zarathustra*. Zarathustra dreams of looking into a mirror carried by a child. The child tells Zarathustra to look at himself, but Zarathustra sees "a devil's grimace and scornful laughter." Rudnytsky suggests that this incident "conforms to Lacan's theory of the 'mirror stage' in the formation of the ego, which holds that the ego is from its inception constituted by a sense of self-alienation epitomized by a child's beholding of its own reflection in a mirror."[95] In his discussion of the mirror stage, Stephen Frosh writes that the child's perception of himself in the mirror that is the gaze of the other leads to a fiction, "the fiction that s/he is whole and has a clearly ascertainable identity."[96]

Nietzsche writes: "The evidence of the body reveals a tremendous multiplicity." Also: "Suppose all unity were unity only as an organization? But the 'thing' in which we believe was only invented as a foundation for the various attributes."[97] Similarly: "'The subject' is the fiction that many similar states in us are the effect of one substratum."[98] Warnock points out that for Nietzsche there is no "I" "which thinks as a separate entity from the relations which persons have to the world in general. Nietzsche denies that one can suppose any inner *thing* apart from its expression in relationships."[99] Unity can be attained to a degree, and such unity is highly valued by Nietzsche. But there is no perfect unity through self-creation nor one fixed true self, conscious or unconscious, waiting to be uncovered. (As there is also in analysis no true fixed memory in and of itself to uncover or latent dream content in and of itself to uncover.[100]) And the structure of any ruling unity may at the same time be open to creative self-conflict and possible transformation. If we are to "become who we are" we will open ourselves to "unremitting *transformation*—: you must, within a short space of time, pass through and throughout many individuals. The means is *unremitting struggle*."[101] If we allow ourselves to have access to, and develop and utilize, more affects and more eyes, different eyes, we may be on the way to passing through and throughout many individuals. Such possibility may be both potentially enriching and dangerous.

---

Moving further into the discussion on truth and reality as it relates to Freud, we can note that Freud's approach to truth is basically realist. According to Robert Holt, "Freud assumed as a matter of course that perception is a simple matter of coming into contact with reality."[102] (Such an approach to truth would be one factor in Freud's being able to state that his lecture "brings forth nothing but observed facts." He also believed he had the scientific instruments with which to approach truth and self-knowledge enough to control for countertransference in its broadest sense. Each of these matters is highly problematic.) According to Gellner, Freud's position is more specifically a "conditional realism"—that the mind fails to know objects it is concerned with "because it chooses (unconsciously) to deceive itself . . . But once the veil is off, knowledge becomes unproblematical."[103] Gellner asks, "Is there an unambiguous reality out there, in the Unconscious or anywhere else, which can be automatically seized by anyone, provided only one has mastered and neutralized one's inner self-deceptions?"[104] He suggests that there are no pure minds encountering "naked" objects,[105] and he emphasizes the role of theoretical assumptions and how they square with the relevant facts, many of which are simply unavailable at any given time.[106]

Freud was much more sophisticated on these matters, such as the interplay of theory and observation,[107] than Gellner allows. Also, realists infer to the unobservable. While writing on knowledge in "The Unconscious" and indicating that the correction of internal perception "will turn out not to offer such great difficulties as the correction of external perception—that internal objects are less unknowable than the external world,"[108] at the end of his life Freud writes (as well as writing in similar terms in *The Interpretation of Dreams*[109]) that "reality will always remain 'unknowable' . . . in psycho-analysis . . . we infer a number of processes which are in themselves unknowable."[110] However, Freud did sometimes write as if he were in possession of the Truth and as if the concept of and evidence for truth were not problematic. He also sometimes wrote as if he believed that psychoanalysis had unique access to this "unknowable" realm. There is of course much debate on the relationship between what we refer to as theory and observation, and distinctions can be made between more and less theoretical levels of observation,[111] but *at times* Freud seemed to believe that observation could be thoroughly separated from theory in his realms of inquiry. We have commented on his words to the effect that his chapter on femininity "brings forth nothing but observed facts." He also wrote in "On Narcissism" that "the foundation of science, upon which everything rests . . . is observation alone."[112] And in a letter to Theodore Reik he wrote that "scientific research . . . must be without presumptions. In every other kind of thinking the choice of a point of view cannot be avoided."[113]

Freud also contrasted "scientific work" with intuition and introspection in a way that is untenable: "Scientific work is the only road which can lead us to a knowledge of reality outside ourselves. It is once again merely an illusion to expect anything from intuition and introspection; they can give us nothing but particulars about our own mental life."[114]

We can recall that Nietzsche, although considered a great thinker and as having anticipated psychoanalytic concepts, was relegated by Freud to the realm of guesses, intuitions and introspection. But of course ideas that are ultimately validated scientifically may emerge in any number of ways. It has been suggested, for example, that certain religious concepts may have predisposed Newton to certain discoveries. As Anthony O'Hear puts it: "Scientific rationality is constituted not by the provenance of ideas, but by their criticism and testing. In science, it does not matter where ideas come from, so long as they are then tested in an open spirit."[115] (As it may be that the analytic setting can be a fertile "provenance of ideas" while being quite limited insofar as "criticism and testing" can be carried out "in an open spirit.") Or in Stephen Jay Gould's words: "Objectivity lies in the flexibility to reject a cherished theory when an anticipated observation cannot be affirmed, and a perception of contrary meaning . . . delights us instead."[116]

Freud also makes too facile a distinction between the "illusions" of religious believers and the possible illusions of persons like himself. He states in *The Future of an Illusion:*

> My illusions are not, like religious ones, incapable of correction. They have not the character of a delusion. . . . You have to defend the religious illusion with all your might. If it becomes discredited . . . then your world collapses . . . From that bondage I am, we are, free. Since we are prepared to renounce a good part of our infantile wishes, we can bear it if a few of our expectations turn out to be illusions.[117]

There is, of course, a valid distinction drawn here, but it is also not quite as clear-cut as Freud implies. There are many who believe that there has been "experience" or evidence for some time that should lead to the discrediting of certain psychoanalytic concepts and claims but that it very well may be that it is in part a defense against a world that would collapse (in Freud's terms, being unable to renounce "infantile wishes") that leads to the maintenance of what, to others, appear to be illusions. Also, consider that Freud writes here not that he can bear it if fundamental principles of psychoanalysis turn out to be illusions, but that "we can bear it if a *few of our expectations* turn out to be illusions" (emphasis added). One wonders if he too would have despaired if some of his central beliefs were discredited (by someone other than himself) and if this could have played a part in his dismissive attitude towards extra-clinical tests on psychoanalysis. And such secular illusions are not necessarily any less destructive (or creative) than religiously based illusions.

Also, while Freud, like Nietzsche, regards ideas that are comforting and consoling as, pertaining to their truth, inherently suspicious,[118] one can ask if there could be any idea more comforting to men threatened by women and the feminine than the notion that bedrock for women is to be found in penis envy. Any concerns about the threat of envious women pales beside the bolstering of man's superior position, superior organ, superior intellect, superior conscience, sense of justice, etc. Also, as Nietzsche and Freud have taught us, almost any belief can be, in part, utilized for comfort. (The physicist Paul Davies, in a review of a book by the physicist Steven Weinberg, writes of Weinberg that "he continues to defend . . . dismal reductionism robustly . . . Although many of his readers will be repelled, Mr. Weinberg himself seems to find inspiration in the austere beauty of a universe reduced to stark formulas."[119]) Furthermore, there is no particular reason why we might not discover important truths that are in fact comforting. For example, the research of Weiss and Sampson suggests that correct interpretations by the analyst may reduce rather than increase anxiety.[120] Of course Nietzsche and Freud do alert us to our attachments to beliefs and to our pain in letting go of them as we pursue truth, but in general, comfort or lack of comfort are no sure criteria by which we are led to truth.

It may be that while in certain ways Freud was philosophically sophisticated, he did not attempt, to the degree that Nietzsche did, to draw out the implications of his model of man for his own ideas. In his study of the understanding of aggression in Nietzsche and Freud, Drew Nash points out that "Nietzsche makes constant reference to his method."[121] Nash believes that "there is not nearly the awareness of the problem of method in Freud's thought, or a similar consideration of the necessity to break down and examine the premises that are assumed by a theoretical system," while Steven Ellman concludes that Freud "must have felt he was partially immune to the influences that psychoanalytic theory describes."[122]

Drawing on Passmore's survey of recent philosophy, we can consider that for the most part there is no getting beyond one theory or another, that some prominent philosophers argue that alternative scientific theories which are not inter-translatable may be equally sound,[123] that "the data at a scientist's disposal always permit of more than one explanation," that "it is, of course, by no means clear what constitutes a well-formed theory, or how theories are to be evaluated," and that there are respected philosophers who argue for the inherent impossibility of "giving the One True Picture of the world."[124] These issues continue to be debated and are relevant to Nietzsche's explorations (as well as having implications for psychoanalytic theory and practice). As the philosopher Anthony Flew has commented, "Nietzsche touches upon epistemological questions that are very much alive at present."[125]

## Perspectivism and Contemporary Psychoanalysis

Debates on such matters and on the nature of interpretation in psychoanalytic therapy as carried out by Grunbaum, Spence, Wallace[126] and others might be enriched by an engagement with Nietzsche. He explored issues directly linked to these discussions, and it sometimes seems as if his work might have informed a discussion, although he is given, in the context of psychoanalytic debates, little attention in the United States.

When Spence writes that Freud "tended to treat his metaphor as if it were a confirmed piece of reality,"[127] that the metaphor of evenly suspended attention "perpetuates the myth that the analyst is only hearing what is 'there' and is in no sense participating in the construction of meaning,"[128] that the "idea of multiple interpretations is surprisingly absent in Freud . . . Once we assume that meanings are multiple, it hardly follows that the one we discover will be the most significant,"[129] he is raising issues explored by Nietzsche (as well as, of course, by other philosophers he does mention). And he refers to European hermeneutic approaches to interpretation which in some ways draw on Nietzsche.

Spence also quotes Hayden White, whose view of the modern historian has some affinity with Nietzsche. According to White the modern historian is "one who, like the modern artist and scientist, seeks to exploit a certain perspective on the world that does not pretend to exhaust descriptions or analysis of all the data in the entire phenomenal field but rather offers itself as *one way among many* of disclosing certain aspects of the field."[130] He also quotes Richard Bernstein on "Cartesian anxiety," the fear that there may be nothing fixed and nothing securely known. Bernstein has some affinity with Nietzschean perspectivism and becoming when he writes that from the objectivist's point of view either there is some support for our being, a fixed foundation for our knowledge, or we cannot escape the forces of darkness that envelop us with madness, with intellectual and moral chaos . . . At the heart of the objectivist's vision, and what makes sense of his or her passion, is the belief that there are or must be some fixed, permanent constraints to which we can appeal and which are secure and stable.[131]

In this regard we can note Flew's comment that "Nietzsche is probably the greatest psychological critic of what Schopenhauer called 'Man's need for Metaphysics.'"[132] Of course, as the objectivist may be seen as defending against terror in the face of the absence of stable foundations, some might view the perspectivist as defending against terror in the face of the possibility that there *is* a stable foundation ("Truth," God) from which one is cut off. If there is no God or Truth, one is protected against being cut off from him (or her) or it.

Rudnytsky suggests that when Rank wrote that "in the psychical sphere there are no facts, but only interpretations of them," he was returning to Nietzsche and, in this return, was anticipating the hermeneutic approach to interpretation advocated by Spence. However, Rudnytsky fails to note that Nietzsche has in mind that there are no facts *in and of themselves* to be described apart from our interests, concerns, and descriptions. Nietzsche writes: "Facts is precisely what there is not, only interpretations. We cannot establish any fact *'in itself'"* (emphasis added). What counts as fact is, at least for many important purposes, not simply given, but depends in part on perspective and interpretation. And we should note that in *Beyond Good and Evil*, in his discussion of identity, Nietzsche objects to the idea that there are immediate certainties such as "I think" or "that the subject 'I' is the condition of the predicate 'think,'" and as clearly as possible states of such a view "that it is a falsification of the facts of the case." Certainly there are "facts," "facts of the case," and "falsification of the facts of the case" for Nietzsche.[133]

We can also note here that Mahoney, in his book *Human Change Processes*, presents a number of recent developments in psychology and psychotherapy that share a good deal with Nietzsche, although Nietzsche is not mentioned. For example, in his chapter on constructivism Mahoney writes of the view that "perceptions and all manner of other cognitive activities often reflect more about their owner than they do about the events in the physical world that may have occasioned them."[134] Mahoney also writes that the perspective of the observer is neither passive nor detached.[135] At a later point he writes: "Contrary to the claims of modern rationalism—including the rationalist cognitive therapies—thought does not dictate either feeling or action."[136] He writes of the mistaken model which "assumes that rational, intellectual functions came to rule over the visceral 'animal' from which they emerged."[137] He writes of Western philosophy and science as having traditionally glorified order and denigrated disorder and of the newer "'science of becoming' (as contrasted with the earlier preoccupation with fixed states of being)."[138] Mahoney also mentions the hermeneutic tradition and Hans-Georg Gadamer whose views on truth and method, such as his idea that active interpretation is primary to all understanding, are "remarkably parallel to those expounded by the psychological 'constructivists.'"[139] These ideas are related to Nietzsche's psychology and his explorations on truth and interpretation. In particular, Gadamer was influenced by Nietzsche in his (Gadamer's) ideas pertaining to looking at an object as it relates to one's own concerns and that interpretation is active or productive rather than reproductive. As Alan Megill points out, Nietzsche was the first great exponent of this point of view.[140]

Nietzsche's influence on Gadamer extended beyond the realm of understanding and interpretation. Regarding the nature of and relationship between art and play, Gadamer wrote:

> We looked for the anthropological foundations of art in the phenomenon of play as an excess. For it is constitutive of our humanity that our instincts are underdetermined and we therefore have to conceive of ourselves as free and live with the dangers that this freedom implies. This unique characteristic determines all human existence in the most profound fashion. And here I am following the insights of philosophical anthropology developed by Scheler, Plessner, and Gehlen under Nietzsche's inspiration.[141]
>
> Play and seriousness, the exuberance and superabundance of life, on the one hand, and the tense power of vital energy on the other, are profoundly interwoven. They interact

with one another, and those who have looked deeply into human nature have recognized that our capacity for play is an expression of the highest seriousness. For we read in Nietzsche, "Mature manhood: that means to have found again the seriousness one had as a child—in play" [B.G.E., sec. 94]. Nietzsche also knew the reverse of this as well, and celebrated the creative power of life—and of art—in the divine ease of play.[142]

We have seen that for Nietzsche creative play as a response to and stance towards life and the challenge of eternal recurrence is a sacred "Yes," a great affirmation of existence.

Regarding implications for the nature of the therapeutic process and relationship, Nietzsche's views explicitly or implicitly anticipate recent views of the therapeutic relationship; for example, views which maintain that "almost any behavior of the analyst, including restraint or silence, immediately influences the patient's responses."[143] While there may be, generally, reasons to advocate for restraint in the relationship (such as keeping the focus on the client's concerns and avoidance of destructively implicating the client in the therapist's own personal concerns), from Nietzsche's perspective, one would not necesarily expect to be any more privy to truth whether one did or did not practice systematic frustration of the client's or patient's wishes. As Milton Viederman (along with many others) has pointed out: "There are no pure observers as there are no perfectly abstinent physicians." Also, our "interventions alert the patient to areas of our particular interest and concern," and "gratified wishes are subject to analysis as are ungratified ones."[144] (Some might attempt to save an abstaining position for the analyst with the claim that "a wish can be felt and acknowledged as a wish only if it is not gratified."[145])

Regarding the client's description of self and childhood, perhaps Nietzsche would, *to some extent*, also agree with Rorty who writes:

The choice of a vocabulary in which to describe either one's childhood or one's character cannot be made by inspecting some collection of neutral facts . . . It is to give up the urge to purification[146] . . . the enlightened, liberated self—the self that has finally succeeded in shaping itself—[can be viewed] as a self that has given up the need "to see things steadily and see them whole," to penetrate beyond shifting appearances to a constant reality. Maturity will, according to this view, consist rather in an ability to seek out new redescriptions of one's own past . . . to find new self-descriptions whose adoption will enable one to alter one's behavior.[147] [Nietzsche *is concerned* with the truth of interpretations as well as their usefulness, their ability to alter one's behavior. And finding "new self-descriptions" does not convey the arduousness of the struggles Nietzsche has in mind.]

There is no reason why empirical research cannot be of help in determining what kinds of "self-descriptions" or narratives (as well as, of course, many other aspects of the therapeutic process) may be effective for different kinds of persons with different kinds of difficulties in different kinds of situations. From a Nietzschean perspective, while it is obvious and desirable that the therapist will influence the patient's or client's self-descriptions and narratives, and the converse as well, a high value will be placed, however much it is a joint creation of a shared reality, on encouraging the individual to fashion a self-understanding, self-description or narrative that is to a significant extent his or her own creation. That one has been creative in this way (and hopefully can thus go on creating) will be a very different experience than having the therapist's narratives simply replacing the original narrative brought to therapy by the client or patient. Perhaps one desirable outcome of therapy can be thought of as the individual's increased capacity for playful creative application of a perspectivist approach to his or her life experience and history, though this approach, as any other, would be understood in part as related to the sublimation of drives as an aspect of the pursuit of truth. This does not entail that one abandons the search for truth and the facts of one's life. It entails that one searches with the understanding that what one finds was not uncovered like an archeological find.

Nietzsche would, one might imagine, have no objection to a therapy which helped a person understand his or her wishes "*not* to see . . . [what] one does see" and as one sees it and which helped one to see things as they are. But seeing things as they are would entail seeing them "out of a hundred eyes, out of *many* persons." And while self-overcoming, integration and unification would be a goal, as would be discharging one's potential capacities "in works and actions,"[148] becoming who we are would also mean an openness to and struggle for any given temporary unity in a process of unremitting transformation. This would entail the reconciliation of certain kinds of conflict but also the creative utilization of and joy in conflict (including that between "masculine" and "feminine" forces), the creative play of conflict, thus a valuing of internal and external "enemies." (And we should note that creative, genuine play, including as it is applicable to the analytic relationship, includes the capacity to play spontaneously, without self-conscious awareness.[149])

In the premier issue of a new journal, in a symposium on reality and the analytic relationship, Nietzsche is not mentioned, but a perspectivist or constructivist (or constructionist) approach to reality in the analytic relationship is presented as a new and viable paradigm for psychoanalysis. In the introduction, the editor Stephen A. Mitchell, in whose book *Relational Concepts in Psychoanalysis*[150] Nietzsche is mentioned a few times, writes that

> Psychoanalytic models seem . . . clearly to be particular perspectives, personal (although sometimes shared) visions . . . We need to learn to regard differences in theoretical perspectives not as unfortunate deviations from one accurate understanding, but as fortunate expressions of the countless ways in which human experience can be organized.[151]

In the same issue, Irwin Hoffman states: "Although not amorphous, unformulated experience is understood to be intrinsically ambiguous and open to a range of compelling interpretations and explications."[152] The paradigm change he is advocating involves the idea of a wedding of

> the analyst's personal involvement . . . [and] a constructivist or perspectivist epistemological position . . . the personal participation of the analyst in the process is considered to have a continuous effect on what he or she understands about himself or herself and about the patient in the interaction . . . the analyst's understanding is always a function of his or her perspective at the moment.[153]

Perspectivist epistemology is put forth here although no mention is made of Nietzsche's well-known perspectivist approach to interpretation.

One question here pertains to the implications of perspectivism for its own position. Hoffman, for example, writes as if he is convinced that his perspective on reality in the analytic relationship is more accurate, closer to the truth, than others he mentions. There appears to be the problem here of whether or not a perspectivist epistemological approach is self-refuting. If one believes that a theory about reality in the therapy relationship may be true while the interpretive constructions of the therapist are regarded as typically reflecting more "personal involvement" and as perspectival in a sense in which the theory is not, then this case has to be argued. If one doesn't regard one's theory as largely true, then one has to offer other grounds for its acceptance. Along with most of us, Hoffman does believe that interpretations and theories can include a recognition of facets of reality, that interpretations and theories may correspond to "facts," and that there are criteria for choosing one point of view over another. But we are left with the question as to whether or not Hoffman's (or Nietzsche's) theory is selective and suspect, as Hoffman states of what analysts can know about their participation. Is the type of explanation applied by Hoffman to the analytic situation equally applicable to theories (including his own) of the analytic situation?

It could conceivably be argued that certain kinds of interpretations in relation to certain kinds of phenomena or data cannot typically be regarded as true with as great confidence as an interpretation of such interpretations. Nehamas writes of Rorty's view that "perspectivist theories should be construed so as to apply only to first-order, 'real' theories about the world and not to theories about such things, like perspectivism itself."[154] Schacht suggests that when various relevant perspectives and affective interpretations "are played off against each other, one ceases to be locked into any one of them; and so it becomes possible to achieve a meta-level perspective [and a different epistemic status] from which vantage point various lower-order interpretations may be superseded in favor of others less narrow and distorting than they."[155] Or we might consider the approach of Nehamas who asks, in effect, that perspectivism be tried out: "Perhaps not all views are interpretations. But we shall know this to be true only when one is actually produced."[156] He argues that to refute perspectivism "we must develop a view that does not depend on antecedent commitments and that does not promote a particular kind of person and a particular kind of life—a view that applies equally to everyone at all times and in all contexts."[157] Nehamas also concludes that for any interpretation "an alternative *could*, in principle, always be devised."[158] We also may simply want to consider that in applying Nietzsche's (or Hoffman's) perspectivism we may discover that we achieve illuminating and worthwhile results.

Clark, commenting on Nehamas' view of perspectivism, writes that "the interpretive character of P [the thesis that every view is an interpretation] shows only the *possibility* that some views are not interpretations, and therefore the possibility that P is false. But this cannot show that P *is* false." She also makes the simple but important point that our interpretations are not of the form of "reality is only x."[159] More recently Nehamas has written that

> to call any view, including perspectivism, an interpretation is to say that it can be wrong, which is true of all views . . . Perspectivism does not deny that particular views can be true . . . it attributes to specific approaches truth in relation to facts specified internally by those approaches themselves. But it refuses to envisage a single independent set of facts, to be accounted for by all theories . . . The existence of many purposes and needs relative to which the values of theories is established—another crucial element of perspectivism—is sometimes thought to imply a rampant relativism . . . This is correct only in that Nietzsche denies the existence of a single set of standards determining epistemic value once and for all. But he holds that specific views can be compared with and evaluated in relation to one another.[160]

Clark argues that in his last works and mature perspectivism, Nietzsche does not deny truth; that while he rejects the existence of metaphysical truth—correspondence to the thing-in-itself—he does not reject truth itself.[161] She cites passages from the *Genealogy* to support her argument. But in the *Genealogy*, Nietzsche also writes, and Clark does not deal with this passage, of interpretation as "forcing, adjusting, abbreviating, omitting, padding, inventing, falsifying, and whatever else is of the *essence* of interpreting."[162] However, if the essence of interpretation includes (but obviously is not restricted to) unconscious adjusting, padding, falsifying, etc., this can only arise in relation to something that one can pad, falsify, etc. What this may entail is that for Nietzsche, at least in certain areas of inquiry, we can never be certain of the ways in which we select, pad, and falsify in our interpretations. This leaves us with the serious problem of finding appropriate criteria or ways to differentiate between what is true and what is padded, falsified, etc. Although I may have the unconscious intention or inclination to pad and falsify, I cannot very well know at which points and to what extent this intention or inclination has resulted in a distorted understanding of the phenomena in question until after I subject the relevant beliefs and propositions to the appropriate kinds of examinations or tests. Of course the position from which the beliefs or propositions are examined may be open to similar examination. There is here no final account or resting place. Rational acceptability is not absolute.

As noted, it is also obvious that Nietzsche carries out various interpretive projects as if he believed he was arriving at more accurate accounts as compared to previous attempts. It is clear that he does not believe he is creating only creative and therapeutic fictions. It would appear that whatever Nietzsche may or may not be indicating about a definition of truth or the nature of truth or the *essence of truth*, he evidently believes that he is (through appropriate evidence and reasoning) *justified in ascribing truth* to certain of his beliefs, statements or propositions.[163] It would seem to follow that his own interpretations are to be seen as having been arrived at through, among other factors, inevitable attempts at forcing, padding, falsifying, etc., but as nonetheless having also arrived at certain truths. This is not just a matter of separating the origins of a belief from the question of whether or not it is true; that is, a belief may have an all-too-human origin and, of course, be true. For Nietzsche, interpretations pertinent to the acceptance and maintenance of beliefs would also be characterized by padding, forcing, etc. And every interpretation of an interpretation would be carried out from a perspective with (from another perspective) inherent possibilities and limitations. However, if there are often, or even always, varying degrees and kinds of attempts at concealing or even falsifying in the formulating of an interpretation, we can recall that one's wishes "*not* to see" entail what "one does see."

Nietzsche holds that there is an extra-mental world to which we are related and with which we have some kind of fit. For him, even as knowledge develops in the service of self-preservation and power, to be effective, a conception of reality will tend to grasp (but only) a certain amount of, or aspect of, reality. And however much Nietzsche may at times see (the truth of) artistic creation and dissimulation (out of a chaos) as paradigmatic for science (which will not recognize itself as such), in arriving at this position Nietzsche assumes the truth of scientifically based beliefs as foundation for many of his arguments; including those regarding the origin, development and nature of perception, consciousness and self-consciousness and what this entails for our knowledge of and falsification of the external and inner world. In fact, to some extent the form-providing, affirmative, this-world healing of art is a response to the terrifying, nausea-inducing truths revealed by science which by itself has no treatment for the underlying cause of the nausea. (Although Nietzsche also writes of the horrifying existential truths against which science can attempt a [falsifying] defense.) But while there is a real world to which we are related, there is no sensible way to speak of a nature or constitution or eternal essence of the world in and of itself apart from description and perspective. Also, states of affairs to which our interpretations are to fit are established within human perspectives and reflect (but not only) our interests, concerns, needs for calculability, etc. Within such relations (and also perhaps as meta-commentary on the grounds of our knowing) Nietzsche is quite willing to write of the truth, the constitution of reality, and facts of the case. There is no cessation of will to power or the possibility of absolute truth. To expect a pure desire for a pure truth is to expect an impossible desire for an illusory ideal.

However, Nietzsche's praise of science, the intellectual conscience and working in the service of  truth indicate his belief that something in the way of truth can be attained. As a psychologist and philosopher Nietzsche helped reveal ways in which we falsify, and there is every reason to believe that he would, up to a point, be supportive of projects that continue such work. In addition, he indicates in *Beyond Good and Evil* that there are those "scientific scholars" in whom "a drive for knowledge may work on vigorously *without* any essential participation from all the other drives," although this may involve less personally vital areas of inquiry. (The scientific scholar is contrasted with the philosopher for whom "conversely, there is nothing whatever that is impersonal."[164]) And in a neglected passage in *The Antichrist*, Nietzsche even goes so far as to write that

> philology is . . . the art . . . of reading facts without falsifying them by interpretation, without losing caution, patience, delicacy, in the desire to understand . . . The manner in which a theologian, in Berlin as in Rome, interprets a "verse of Scripture" or an event . . . is always so audacious that a philologist can only tear his hair.[165]

Here it would seem that with "caution, patience, delicacy" one may not be as likely to pad and falsify, that one may be able to read "facts without falsifying them by interpretation." (And recall the suggestion by this psychologist of the will to power that to absorb an experience one must "not be an observer of it while in the midst of it," but "give oneself up to the experience and close one's eyes.") However, this does not entail, in the words of Thomas Kuhn, that there is "some neutral, culture-independent [or perspective-independent], set of categories within which the population—whether of objects or of actions—can be described."[166] Nietzsche is quite willing to acknowledge the perspectival and interpretive nature of his work as well as to work in "the service of truth."

It would also appear that Nietzsche accepts that there are more and less theoretical levels of observation and that there may often be observational common ground between perspectives. Clark writes that from a Nietzschean perspective the objective person does not "transcend the perspectival character of knowledge, but only assumes for the moment a different perspective, one that does not take a stand on the points at issue between her usual perspective and a competing one."[167] However, Nietzsche also appears to believe that for certain types and certain levels of inquiry and where it may pertain to vital matters, often common neutral ground for comparison between perspectives cannot be found, that perspectives may be incommensurable. He is also concerned with the therapeutic value of a theory, belief, or interpretation; that is, the extent to which it creatively affirms this world, this life, and helps the individual to do the same. Truth is not the only, nor must it necessarily be the most important, property that should be characteristic of our beliefs.

Regarding therapy, while empirical research and other sources may help us agree upon observations and explanations that can for most purposes be unproblematically regarded as true and which as common ground will affect our theory and practice, there does not appear to be any information on the horizon that would resolve the matter of competing and contradictory perspectives. While there may be descriptions or explanations of aspects of experience that may be consensually agreed upon to a degree that allow us to speak of "facts" and "truth" in relatively unproblematic ways, for many areas of experience there is no consensual agreement, no agreement upon requirements that should be met and nothing that can be appealed to that can settle a particular issue or case. There has been a wealth of information, including the findings of empirical research (on therapy process and outcome as well as child growth and development), that proponents of one perspective or orientation have brought to others with no reduction in the number of orientations or the passion with which they are held and defended. Some may have thought that research over the past twenty years on infant and early childhood development would have drastically altered traditional psychoanalytic theories of development and therapy. However, many still remain unconvinced, and of those who believe drastic change is required, conclusions drawn differ according to perspective.[168] There is not even agreement on the extent to which many particular childhood experiences are etiologically significant in regard to the development of particular problems or the extent to which particular childhood experiences should be addressed in order that therapy be effective.[169] But this may not be simply a matter of incommensurable perspectives; there very well may be (or can be) compelling evidence that supports one perspective over another in regard to certain assumptions.

While in certain areas of scientific inquiry, observations relevant to assessing a theory may be relatively unproblematic, in other areas of inquiry, such as those pertaining to the nature of unconscious motivation in the psychoanalytic sense, finding common ground for relatively neutral comparisons of orientations or perspectives may be particularly difficult. For many areas that are vital to depth psychology it has seemed very difficult, in the words of O'Hear, to "establish a level of observation regarded by all parties to a paradigm dispute as neutral between their respective paradigms [so that] comparisons could be effected through assessing the ability of each paradigm to deal with the data agreed by all to be the data to be explained."[170] Arriving at such agreed-upon "neutral" levels of observation and utilizing empirical research on outcomes and process in therapy should be a very high priority if psychoanalysis is to be scientifically credible. This is not to dismiss narrative knowing or ignore the value of a productive clash of ideas. Nor is it to deny that some of the different viewpoints may reflect different areas of interest while not being contradictory to one another. It is to say, however, that these different views may contradict one another on central issues and that in any event there is an obligation to provide appropriate evidence in support of the theoretical and therapeutic claims.

Grünbaum calls on psychoanalysis to recognize itself as a discipline that is and should be based on the attempt to discover causal linkages between experiences and symptoms, though it has as of yet, to Grünbaum, provided little solid basis for support of many of its important formulations generally or in case presentation. (Others argue that his criteria for establishing causal linkages are overly stringent and inappropriate for psychoanalysis.[171]) For example, he writes that "after a veritable cornucopia of brilliantly articulated meaning connections [or thematic kinship or affinity] in Freud's case history of the Rat Man, a validated etiology of the patient's obsessions remains deeply obscure to this very day—similarly for the Wolf Man."[172]

One may ask why Grünbaum thinks that psychoanalysis as a therapy *should* be so concerned with its interpretations establishing validated causal linkages. How certain are we that interpretations utilizing material in relation to which it is agreed that there has been demonstration of causal linkages, that there is causal relevance, are more effective than interpretations of other kinds? For example, utilizing metaphors in ways that help clients open to new areas of experiencing, or attending very carefully to the implicit or preconscious moment-to-moment experiencing of the client,[173] or introducing novelty that confounds the client's maladaptive expectations may turn out to be more conducive to therapeutic change than interpretations offering rational understanding of causal linkages. (Of course there might then be some question about the use of the term "psychoanalytic" to define the therapy.)

In a recent paper Grünbaum states that "analysts have come to appreciate that a grasp of meaning connections may well fail to be therapeutic."[174] However, he uses the word "may" and provides no compelling reason, empirical research for example, for the reader to accept this statement as correct. Also, meaning connections may be presented and worked with in many different ways, and it may be that some such ways are therapeutically effective. (Empirical research can help us here; one can bring to bear a scienfitic approach to understanding and evaluating the impact of various kinds of meaning connections.) Grünbaum himself has stated: "For the purpose of effecting a change in the agent's odd behavior, it may be quite irrelevant whether the therapist's reading of the instigating unconscious motive is mythic."[175] I recall him saying something similar at a conference in New York City in 1988; his objection was to terming unvalidated narratives "narrative *truths*,"[176] not to the possibility of their being therapeutic. Shouldn't this possibility lead us, among other things, to the effort to determine whether or not, in regard to positive outcome of therapy, accuracy of typical analytic interpretations is among the most important determining factors. (And whether or not things might be any different when it comes to accuracy of basic reflective empathic responsiveness, which may certainly border on, or in fact be, interpretation with very limited leaps of inference.) It is also possible that certain psychoanalytically oriented "narratives" happen to be, under certain conditions, associated with positive therapeutic outcome even when we later determine that such narratives appear unlikely to have touched upon what has been etiologically relevant. It could be, however, that a conviction of truth during treatment is a critical factor in regard to therapy process and outcome.

In a different vein, Ellman suggests that

> the past as an actuality is not the main issue; rather, the dynamic meanings of the past are the important issue in any interpretative effort . . . reconstructions are not mainly concerned with facts, but, as Blum states, with "patterns and interrelationships" . . . The important aspect of an interpretation is the way it integrates patterns and relationships, and, to paraphrase Freud, how the analysis is deepened by the intervention.[177]

This comment by a respected analyst may actually discount "facts" and "the past as an actuality" to a degree that is not characteristic of Nietzsche's mature perspectivism. (And there remains

the matter of the truth value of "patterns and relationships.")
Neitzsche would not despair of uncovering facts, the past as an actuality and causal linkages; but the knowledge achieved would be
understood as a perspectival knowing and not as pertaining to
some fixed entity which was waiting to be uncovered in just this
way. One would imagine that for Nietzsche, uncovering facts and
the past as an actuality (and saying "Yes" to that actuality) would
in fact be one potential ingredient in therapeutic change. Recall
that Nietzsche's view of Dionysian health emphasizes one's capacity to bear painful truths. We have also seen that from the period of
his early writings on history, Nietzsche was concerned with the
capacity to "incorporate into oneself what is past and foreign."[178]
And the historian Gertrude Himmelfarb asks, "Supposing History
Is a Woman—What Then?" Himmelfarb concludes that

> for Nietzsche the past has a real and independent existence . . .
> Nietzsche's muse turns out to be unexpectedly modest, sensi-
> ble, even domesticated . . . If the historian can learn to dis-
> pense with absolute truth, to pursue not 'woman in herself'
> but a real woman, not the chimera of the 'Eternal Objective'
> but the reality of something only partially knowable, he can
> love the past and live happily with her.[179]

Although of course the disciplines of history and psychoanalysis
diverge at numerous points, this passage may well be applicable to
both.

Carlo Strenger offers an epistemology for psychoanalysis, a
pluralist view, that has certain affinities with Nietzschean perspectivism:

> I propose to view the conceptual frameworks to be found in
> present-day clinical psychology . . . as different perspectives
> on man.[180]
> There is no neutral substratum which all theories deal
> with.[181]
> There will always be incommensurable ways of conceiv-
> ing aspects of reality.[182]
> The conceptual frames of these schools [of psychother-
> apy] are often incommensurable.[183]

However, I believe that at times Strenger is too quick to assume that competing perspectives are simply incommensurable (rather than commensurable but with incompatibilities) without addressing their truth or falsity, or their contradictory claims:

> Perspectives are not true or false, but they can be more or less useful or more or less encompassing.[184]
>
> There is no sense to be attached to a claim that any of these descriptive frameworks is "truer" than the others. At most, one could talk about degrees of usefulness given a context of action and interest.[185]

But in any area of inquiry, certain perspectives or frames (as well as the emergent interpretations) may be (and have been) truer than others as well as more useful; and certain perspectives may tend to generate more truthful interpretations than others.

At times Strenger also seems to believe that since all therapists, given their conceptual frameworks, inevitably exert a suggestive influence on patients, the issue of suggestibility is not of great concern:

> The suggestion charge in its most general form rests on a naive picture of the relation between theory, practice, and the world. The theory *always* guides the practice . . . and thus determines what kind of data will be obtained.[186]
>
> The analyst's interventions guide and influence the patient's associations. But we have seen that the very idea that this might not be the case is incoherent: every approach to patients selects and organizes the material.[187]

While these statements are in line with Nietzschean perspectivism, they do not dispose of the problem of suggestibility. One can operate within a given framework and test not only on neutral common ground but within and upon that framework. And of course when we move to the domain of the therapist's suggestion to the patient of particular content as opposed to more accurate understanding of what a patient is experiencing or attempting to convey, research can be conducted, again both from within a given framework and from agreed-upon neutral common ground, to help us determine the extent to which the therapist is suggesting content rather than demonstrating a more accurate understanding of what a patient is attempting to convey. It may be that it is not always incommensurable perspectives that stand in the way.

From a Nietzschean perspective one might also want to ask how the therapist can possibly encourage and respond helpfully to the kind of careful attunement to and critical reflection on the nuances of behavior, thought and feeling in the client or patient that run counter to the therapist's investments but that the person might need to bring to the therapy if she is to find and help create a therapeutic relationship and process suited to who she most "deeply" is? How can the therapist be of help here when she is in part involved in maintaining and enhancing personal power, economic power and the power of the school of thought with which she is affiliated? Among other things, this would seem to require of the therapist that along with her organized body of assumptions, theories and practices (informed by empirical research), she develop a capacity for destruction and creation (unremitting struggle, unremitting transformation) of her therapeutic self, seeing and feeling things out of different affects, different eyes.

Finally, it may be that while we can sometimes reach the truth about various matters, we act and practice in a state of partial ignorance and untruth regarding exactly what we are doing and what is going on at any given time. Perhaps Nehamas' words are apposite here:

> Nietzsche's apparently extreme view that untruth is a condition of life ultimately refers to our ignorance of the exact ways in which our views, at every time, are simplifications of the world and are dependent on particular values; it calls to our attention the fact that we may have to remain ignorant of these simplifications and values if we are to engage in a practice for some time.[188]

An unwillingness to accept untruth, and even deception and illusion, is an unwillingness to accept life. Such an attitude can coexist with a belief in the attainability of "deeper" or "truer" understanding, a valuing of truth and science, and the utilization of empirical research[189] to help us determine the influence of various factors, bearing painful truths among them, on therapeutic process and outcome.

# Chapter 14

## NIETZSCHE, LIPPS AND THE UNCONSCIOUS OF PHILOSOPHERS

*What part is there left to be played in our scheme by consciousness?*
—Freud, *The Interpretation of Dreams*

For what purpose *then any consciousness at all?*
—Nietzsche, *The Gay Science*

In 1936, in an address honoring Freud on his eightieth birthday, Thomas Mann described Freud as "an independent spirit, 'a man and knight, grim and stern of visage' as Nietzsche had said of Schopenhauer."[1] What Nietzsche said about his own mentor, the words he used, are now being applied to Freud by Mann. Schopenhauer, Nietzsche and Freud (and perhaps Mann himself) are linked in the contexts of mentorship and intellectual heroism.

In 1937 Nietzsche is mentioned in Freud's obituary for Andreas-Salomé.[2] Jones also mentions that Freud had admired her greatly, had been very fond of her, "curiously enough without a trace of sexual attraction" (Freud's words), and that "Freud described her as the only real bond between Nietzsche and himself."[3]

Also in 1937, in "Analysis Terminable and Interminable," regarding his notions of the life and death instincts Freud writes: "Not long ago I came upon this theory of mine in the writings of one of the great thinkers of Ancient Greece . . . I can never be certain, in view of the wide extent of my readings in early years, whether what I took for a new creation, might not be an effect of cryptomnesia."[4] Among the readings of his youth, Nietzsche would have been included. And it is in this very same passage that Freud writes of the internalization or turning inward of aggression and that in man's development from a primitive to a civilized state "his internal conflicts would certainly be the proper equivalent for the external struggles that have then ceased."[5] At other points he discusses masochism, the need for suffering, and a propensity for inner conflict. Reviewing these passages, Loewald comments that in discussing inner conflict as a result of internalization or the turning inward of aggression "Freud proposes to understand inner conflict in terms of a thesis that Nietzsche, in his *Genealogy of Morals* (1887), entertained 50 years before Freud wrote 'Analysis Terminable and Interminable.'"[6]

We can also note words of Freud that resonate with Nietzschean creation and destruction:

It is not a question of an antithesis between an optimistic and a pessimistic theory of life. Only by the concurrent or mutually opposing action of the two primal instincts—Eros and the death instinct—never by one or the other alone, can we explain the rich multiplicity of the phenomena of life.[7]

Nietzsche does not write of a death instinct in the manner of Freud but does emphasize the inextricable intertwining of the forces of life and death, creation and destruction.

It will be recalled that in 1898 Freud wrote to Fliess of the philosopher and psychologist Theodor Lipps having written in areas uncomfortably close to the ones he himself was exploring. Nietzsche's writing on related matters was not mentioned. Towards the end of Freud's life, in the 1938 paper "Some Elementary Lessons in Psycho-Analysis," he mentions Lipps as the

German philosopher [who] asserted with the greatest explicitness that the psychical is in itself unconscious and that the unconscious is the truly psychical. The concept of the unconscious . . . Philosophy and literature have often toyed with it, but science could find no use for it. Psycho-analysis has seized upon the concept, has taken it seriously and has given it a fresh content. By its researches it has led to a knowledge of characteristics of the unconscious psychical which have hitherto been unsuspected, and it has discovered some of the laws which govern it.[8]

At this point in his life Freud acknowledges that a German philosopher anticipated (although only "toyed with") certain psychoanalytic findings pertaining to the unconscious, but, as in 1898, Nietzsche is not mentioned.

However, long before this time, in *The Interpretation of Dreams* Freud had made clear his feeling that Lipps' concept of the unconscious differed from his own. Citing Lipps, Freud states:

The physician and the philosopher can only come together if they both recognize that the term "unconscious psychical processes" is "the appropriate and justified expression of a solidly established fact." The physician can only shrug his shoulders when he is assured that "consciousness is an indispensable characteristic of what is psychical," and perhaps, if he still feels enough respect for the utterances of philosophers, he may presume that they have not been dealing with the same thing or working at the same science . . . He thus learns that the conscious effect is only a remote psychical result of the unconscious process and that the latter has not become conscious as such; and moreover that the latter was present and operative even without betraying its existence in any way to consciousness . . . In Lipps' words, the unconscious must be assumed to be the general basis of psychical life . . . the unconscious is the true psychical reality; *in its innermost nature it is as much unknown to us* [this sounds like a "True" but unknowable world] *as the reality of the external world, and it is as incompletely presented by the data of consciousness as is the external world by the communications of our sense organs* . . . [However it] is not without intention that I speak of "our" unconscious. For what I thus describe is not the same as the unconscious of the philosophers or even the unconscious of Lipps. By them the term is used merely to indicate a contrast with the conscious . . . that apart from conscious there are also unconscious psychical processes. Lipps carries things further with his assertion that the whole of what is psychical exists unconsciously and that a part of it also exists consciously . . . The new discovery that we have been taught by the analysis of psychopathological structures and of the first member of that class—the dream—lies in the fact that the unconscious (that is, the psychical) is found as a function of two separate systems and that this is the case in normal as well as in pathological life. Thus there are two kinds of unconscious, which have not yet been distinguished by psychologists. Both of them are unconscious in the sense used by psychology; but in our sense one of them, which we term the Ucs., is also *inadmissible to consciousness*, while we term the other the Pcs. because its excitations—after observing certain rules, it is true, and perhaps only after passing a fresh censorship, though nonetheless without regard to the Ucs.—are able to reach consciousness.[9]

Other than the specific distinction between the systems Ucs. and Pcs., every major point of Freud's, both along with and beyond Lipps, had been explicitly discussed by Nietzsche. Nietzsche was certainly aware of the distinction between unconscious processes that were and were not "inadmissible to consciousness." It is true that he doesn't always specifically make the distinction, though he is clearly aware of it. In *Daybreak* he writes that

in the feeling of pity—I mean in that which is usually and misleadingly called pity—we are, to be sure not consciously thinking of ourself but are doing so *very strongly unconsciously:* as when, if our foot slips—an act of which we are not immediately conscious—we perform the most purposive counter-motions and in doing so plainly employ our whole reasoning faculty. An accident which happens to another offends us: it would make us aware of our impotence, and perhaps of our cowardice, if we did not go to assist him.[10]

Nietzsche goes on to discuss a number of unconscious thoughts, feelings and motivations that are involved in the feeling of pity. Such unconscious motivations are clearly repressed (inadmissible to consciousness), although the analogy of the foot slipping points to what is unconscious but would be admissible to consciousness. In this example Nietzsche does not make the specific distinction, but he writes of both kinds of unconscious processes. As we have seen, his work is filled with explorations of our emotional states that are commonly regarded as selfless and highly moral but which he demonstrates are involved in our self-enjoyment and self-gratification, our disguised expressions of sexuality and will to power, while unconsciously denying that this is so and assuaging conscience. We can also recall that from an early age Nietzsche was interested in "the diverse operations of the conscious and the instinctive."[11] We have seen how he regards conscious and unconscious processes as "subject to altogether different laws of development." And in a note from 1870 or 1871, he also wrote, though in a different sense than Freud, that "all growth in our knowledge arises out of the making conscious of the unconscious."[12] We have also considered passages in which Nietzsche writes of the unconscious conflicts of instincts and motives (for example, *Gay Science*, secs. 333, 360) as well as how in our attempt to preserve our self-image we unconsciously distort the memory of our personal history so as to have it support the desired self-image (for example *Human*, 2, pt. 1, sec. 37).

Nietzsche's discussions of unconscious motivation, conflicting unconscious motivations and the like should be very clear from all of the passages quoted and discussed in this study, passages that run the span of Nietzsche's entire productive life. Also, there are Freud's brief statements that Nietzsche's insights were very close to those of psychoanalysis, evidently indicating that Nietzsche's unconscious was not the unconscious of the philosophers or of Lipps. Nietzsche's psychological analyses of the Apostle Paul, however convincing one may think them, are depth psychological analyses in which conflicting unconscious needs, fears and desires are connected to Paul's conversion and his approach to the founding of organized Christianity.[13] (Contempoarary scholars tend towards a more favorable view of Paul.[14]) Such analyses by Nietzsche are psychoanalytic in nature, although he does not focus on early childhood determinants of belief and behavior.

Even Freud's words about philosophers not recognizing the significance of the unconscious are close to being echoes of Nietzsche who writes:

We could think, feel, will, and remember . . . yet none of all this would have to "enter our consciousness" (as one says metaphorically). The whole of life would be possible without, as it were, seeing itself in a mirror. Even now, for that matter, by far the greatest portion of our life actually takes place without the mirror effect; and this is true even of our thinking, feeling, and willing life, however offensive this may sound to older philosophers.[15]

There is further affinity between Freud and Nietzsche regarding their attempts, after assigning such great importance to the unconscious, of assigning functions to consciousness. As Freud states:

Those philosophers who have become aware that rational and highly complex thought-structures are possible without consciousness playing any part in them have found difficulty in assigning any function to consciousness; it has seemed to them that it can be no more than a superfluous reflected picture ["seeing itself in a mirror"?] of the completed psychical process. We, on the other hand, are rescued from this embarrassment by the analogy between our Cs. system and the perceptual systems.[16]

What part is there left to be played in our scheme by consciousness, which was once so omnipotent and hid all else from our view? *Only that of a sense-organ for the perception of psychical qualities.*[17]

Nietzsche had grappled with the same question:

*For what purpose,* then any consciousness at all when it is in the main *superfluous?* . . . my answer . . . *consciousness has developed only under the pressure of the need for communication* . . . Consciousness is really only a net of communication between human beings; it is only as such that it had to develop . . . That our actions, thoughts, feelings, and movements enter our own consciousness—at least a part of them— that is the result of a "must" that for a terribly long time lorded it over man. As the most endangered animal, he *needed* help and protection . . . first of all, he needed to "know" himself what distressed him, he needed to "know" how he felt, he needed to "know" what he thought . . . Man, like every living being, thinks continually without knowing

it; the thinking that rises to *consciousness* is only the small-
est part of all this . . . only this conscious thinking *takes the
form of words, which is to say signs of communication,* and
this fact uncovers the origin of consciousness . . . the development of language and the development of consciousness (*not
of reason but merely of the way reason enters consciousness*)
go hand in hand . . . The emergence of our sense impressions
into our own consciousness, the ability to fix them and, as it
were, exhibit them externally, increased proportionately with
the need to communicate them to *others* by means of signs.
The human being inventing signs is at the same time the
human being who becomes ever more keenly conscious of
himself. It was only as a social animal that man acquired self-
consciousness—which he is still in the process of doing, more
and more.[18]

Although some may feel that Freud may have a greater degree
of faith or different kind of faith in reason and consciousness (at least
in some of his writings) than does Nietzsche, Freud writes in very
Nietzschean manner that "it is the much-abused privilege of conscious activity, wherever it plays a part, to conceal every other activity from our eyes."[19] And while Nietzsche connects "the thinking
that rises to consciousness" (and "the way reason enters consciousness") with words, with language, Freud recognizes "that the essential feature of a preconscious idea was the fact of its being connected
with the residues of verbal presentations."[20] At another point:

The Pcs. system needed to have qualities of its own which
could attract consciousness; and it seems highly probable that
it obtained them by linking the preconscious processes with
the mnemic system of indications of speech, a system not
without quality. By means of the qualities of that system,
consciousness, which had hitherto been a sense organ for perceptions alone, also became a sense organ for a portion of our
thought-processes. Now, therefore, there are, as it were, *two*
sensory surfaces, one directed towards perception and the
other towards the preconscious thought-processes.[21]

Although there are important differences in these accounts (with
Nietzsche, for example, emphasizing the social animal's need to

communicate), we see that Nietzsche, like Freud, is concerned with "the emergence of our sense impressions into our own consciousness," and that he also describes a perception of preconscious thought processes or "psychical qualities"[22] (as well as what amounts to the emergence of self-consciousness and, ultimately, identity) when he writes that to obtain the help and protection needed, this "most endangered animal" first of all "needed to 'know' himself . . . 'know' how he felt . . . 'know' what he thought."[23] (Schacht suggests that for Nietzsche the calculable, regular conduct and identity of socialized man that follows a consciousness of social origins is a straightjacket which may to an extent be transcended by those on the way towards sovereign individuality and self-becoming. Also, this social origin of consciousness leads Nietzsche to share with Freud a belief in the limitations of introspection for individual self-knowledge: "Given the best will in the world to understand ourselves as individually as possible, 'to know ourselves,' each of us will always succeed in becoming conscious only of what is not individual but 'average.'"[24])

Nietzsche, like Freud, attempts to account for the function of consciousness in light of the new understanding of unconscious mental functioning. Nietzsche distinguishes between himself and "older philosophers" who do not appreciate the significance of unconscious mental functioning, while Freud distinguishes between the unconscious of philosophers and the unconscious of psychoanalysis. What is missing is the acknowledgement of Nietzsche as philosopher and psychologist whose ideas on unconscious mental functioning have very strong affinities with psychoanalysis, as Freud himself will mention on a number of other occasions. Neither here nor in his letters to Fliess in which he mentions Lipps, nor in his late paper in which Lipps (the "German philosopher") is acknowledged again, is Nietzsche mentioned when it comes to acknowledging in a specific and detailed manner an important forerunner of psychoanalysis. Although Freud will state on a number of occasions that Nietzsche's insights are close to psychoanalysis, very rarely will he state any details regarding the similarities. He mentions a friend calling his attention to the notion of the criminal from a sense of guilt, a patient calling his attention to the pride-memory aphorism, Nietzsche's idea that in dreams we enter the realm of the psyche of primitive man, etc. There is never any detailed statement on just what Nietzsche anticipated pertinent to psychoanalysis. This is so even after (according to Wittels) Freud has been taking Nietzsche with him on vacation.

We should also note that it was not only others, such as Wittels, who spoke of Nietzsche's pervasive influence. Freud himself, in a letter to Arnold Zweig on May 11, 1934, wrote that Nietzsche is "someone so near to us in time and whose influence is still . . . active,"[25] or alternatively, "a person of our time with such a living influence."[26] At about the time Freud wrote these words to Zweig, he began work on a book which on one level may have been an acknowledgement of Nietzsche's presence in regard to the development of ideas leading to the creation of psychoanalysis.

# Chapter 15

## *Moses and Monotheism*

> *Now after many years I have come close to him*
> *again, because in you I recognized the man who*
> *carried out all that Nietzsche first dreamt of.*
> —Arnold Zweig to Freud, April, 1934

*Moses and Monotheism* offers an intriguing arena within which to consider Freud's relationship to Nietzsche. Among other factors, commentators have pointed to Freud's relationship to his father and to Jung, the intensification of antisemitism and his ambivalent Jewish identity, his feeling for German culture and the German language (while at the same time never feeling fully assimilated) and his position as founder of a new movement as personal factors relevant to his speculations in this work.[1] Further light may be shed on this work and Freud himself through linking it to Freud's relationship to Nietzsche as an intellectual father figure. However, I wish to make it clear at the outset of this chapter that I do not regard this work as primarily or most importantly a commentary on Freud's relationship to Nietzsche. Rather, I will attempt to demonstrate that Freud's relationship to Nietzsche is one of the important factors that should be given consideration in any attempt to comprehensively understand this work. It is important to keep in mind that it is not only the structure of the story that is pertinent, but also, at a few important points, Freud's language in characterizing Moses and Akhenaten.

Although Freud eventually dropped the idea, he originally conceived this work, at least the first two parts of it, as a historical novel, perhaps due, as Yerushalmi suggests, to the "extreme paucity of reliable historical facts."[2] The first two parts were published in the journal *Imago* in April and August 1937. Part three was not published until the entire book was published in 1939.

Drawing on certain sources,[3] Freud suggests that the name "Moses" is of Egyptian origin and that the Moses myth is a distortion of an earlier one in which Moses was an Egyptian noble rescued by a Jew. In Freud's account, monotheistic worship was introduced, in the form of worship of the sun god, Aten, by an Egyptian pharaoh, Amenophis IV, known as Akhenaten. Freud suggests that among this pharaoh's adherents was a nobleman named Tuthmosis, a name later shortened to Moses. After Akhenaten's death, the former polytheistic religion was restored. Moses attempted to preserve monotheism and chose the Hebrews on whom to impose the monotheist belief as well as an emphasis on the ethical values of truth and justice and the prohibition of creating statues of the god. Drawing on other sources,[4] Freud suggests that the Hebrews found Moses' doctrines difficult to bear and murdered him (there is no discussion of his being devoured as was the case with the father of the primal horde). These Hebrews abandoned the religion, but the religion did not completely disappear. Rather, the power of the beliefs and the connection to the murder of Moses were kept alive through oral communication for two or three generations and remained latent in the masses through unconscious memory traces (although Freud also states that tradition continued to work in the background).

After two or three generations, the Hebrews eventually met up with another related group, which had never been in Egypt, whose leader, a Midianite, was also named Moses (Freud acknowledges elsewhere that there was no compelling evidence for this assumption of a second Moses[5]). They met in the city of Kadesh, between Palestine and the west coast of Arabia. These Hebrews were introduced to another form of monotheism which involved the worship of a volcano god, Yahweh. Circumcision, which was practiced in Egypt, was retained as a condition of the union of the two groups. Over time the two Moses figures converged, and Yahweh, the volcano god, more and more took on the qualities of the god taught by the original Moses. (It was centuries later that the monotheism of the original Egyptian Moses more fully re-emerged with the writings of the prophets who tapped into the latent unconscious memory traces of the people.) As Harold Blum puts it: "In time, the two leaders designated as Moses, as well as the god of righteousness and the volcano god, were merged as the one god represented by Moses."[6] Freud states it in the following way in a letter to Andreas-Salomé:

> The religion of Moses had not been extinguished. A dim memory of it and its founder had remained. Tradition fused the god of Moses with Jahve, ascribed to him the deliverance from Egypt and identified Moses with priests of Jahve from Midian, who had introduced the worship of this latter god into Israel.
> In reality Moses had never heard the name of Jahve . . . Jahve had to pay dearly for having thus usurped the god of Moses. The older god was always at his back, and in the course of six to eight centuries Jahve had been changed into the likeness of the god of Moses. As a half-extinguished tradition the religion of Moses had finally triumphed. This process is typical of the way a religion is created and was only the repetition of an earlier process. Religions owe their compulsive power to the *return of the repressed;* they are reawakened memories of very ancient, forgotten, highly emotional episodes of human history. I have already said this in *Totem and Taboo;* I express it now in the formula: the strength of religion lies not in its *material,* but in its *historical* truth.[7]

During the latency period the power of the murder (the experience of the murder and consequent guilt overlaying the genetically transmitted unconscious memory reflecting the aftermath of the primal parricide) worked towards a return of the repressed and a kind of "deferred obedience" to the teachings of Moses. In this work, the murdered primal father was elevated from totem animal to deity,[8] with the one (father) god behind the one great father, Moses. (It may have been comforting for Freud to contemplate that if his new tablets were too difficult for most to bear and were threatened with destruction [such as by the Nazi terror], there was the possibility of re-emergence, resurrection and ultimate triumph.)

Ritchie Robertson has suggested that "one could perhaps say that *Moses and Monotheism* is Freud's most Nietzschean book."[9] (We might even recall the precarious balance of the tightrope walker of *Zarathustra* when in prefatory note 2 to part 3 Freud writes: "To my critical sense this book . . . appears like a dancer balancing on the tip of one toe."[10] It is of interest here that Graham Parkes suggests that a good translation of Nietzsche's word, "seiltanzer," would be not tightrope walker but "rope-dancer."[11]) Freud usually held to his belief in the truth to be found via rational, scientific methods and in this work also suggested that the new monotheistic religion was a progressive step towards rationality. It corresponded to reality in being founded upon a re-enactment of the actual primal parricide and in stressing truth and justice. Also, the prohibition of image making encouraged abstract thought just as the shift to the realm of masculine-rational (father) thought over feminine-unconscious (mother) forces, as exemplified in the *Oresteia* of Aeschylus, was another critical progressive shift.[12] (Freud doesn't mention that the darker, more primitive, irrational, and feminine forces, the Erinyes, are given their due and referred to as older and wiser. Nor does he mention, as Richard Sewall points out, that Athena's decision in the case of Orestes is based on personal grounds rather than the merits of the case.[13] One would imagine that Freud would approve of Bernhard Zimmermann's comment that "their [the Erinyes'] former function is not to be abolished completely, but neutralized, so to speak, in a new legal order."[14]) Here is Freud's reasoning on this last point:

> This turning from the mother to the father points in addition to a victory of intellectuality over sensuality—that is, an advance in civilization, since maternity is proved by the evidence of the senses while paternity is a hypothesis, based on an inference and a premise. Taking sides in this way with a thought-process in preference to a sense perception has proved to be a momentous step. [In the words of Paul Davies: "Most people see reality in the material objects that surround them. Physicists see reality in abstract laws and the associated mathematical machinery."][15]

Similarly, regarding the prohibition against making an image of God:

If this prohibition were accepted, it must have a profound effect. For it meant that a sensory perception was given second place to what may be called an abstract idea—a triumph of intellectuality over sensuality or, strictly speaking, an instinctual renunciation, with all its necessary psychological consequences.[16]

From a different perspective Nietzsche writes:

Monotheism . . . this rigid consequence of the doctrine of one normal human type—the faith in one normal god beside whom there are only pseudo-gods— . . . threatened us with premature stagnation . . . in polytheism the free-spiriting and many-spiriting of man attained its first preliminary form— the strength to create for ourselves our own new eyes—and ever again new eyes.[17]

However, Freud does pick up on a related theme: "along with the belief in a single god religious intolerance was inevitably born, which had previously been alien to the ancient world."[18] (Gellner writes that "an exclusive, jealous, distant and orderly unique deity may generate a . . . precedent for the rationalist conception of Nature and knowledge, and it may well be the precondition of its emergence."[19] Regarding the relationship between image and word, Paglia comments: "Freud, as a Jew, may have been biased in favor of the word . . . Freudian theory overstates the linguistic character of the unconscious and slights the gorgeously cinematic pictorialism of the dream life."[20] Rycroft suggests that since Freud's formative years were pre-Einstein, pre-Picasso and cubism, pre-Joyce, etc., "it was natural for him to assume a much closer relationship between the verbal, the rational and the realistic on the one hand, and the non-verbal, the irrational and the imaginary or imaginative on the other hand, than any thinker can today."[21] Regarding the turning away from the mother, Paglia points out that "male adulthood begins with the breaking of female chains. But Dionysus reverses loyalties. He remains the son of his mother, wearing her clothes and loitering with bands of women."[22] Nietzsche raises questions regarding the assumed primacy or superiority of and relationship between masculine and feminine, word and image, monotheism and polytheism.)

As Robertson indicates, in a certain sense, *Moses and Monotheism* demonstrates Freud's own doubts about the power of reason in his arguing that the doctrine of Moses is transmitted not by rational means at all but by emotional, psychological, and phylogenetic means. And it points to the necessity of Moses being a somewhat tyrannical leader given the inevitable inclinations of his chosen people to seek a less arduous path. He imposes, forces his religion upon the people he chooses and thus creates the Jews. And later it is due to the murder, reverberating with unconscious memory of the earlier primal murder (and the consequent guilt, repression, latency, and re-emergence of the repressed) that the doctrine takes hold. It is only in this way that the beliefs and practices emerge and are maintained with a power that will enable them to survive. Robertson points to Nietzsche's *Genealogy* and comments on Nietzsche's discussion of the imposition of memory by violence. Nietzsche's "mnemotechnics" entails that "'if something is to stay in the memory it must be burned in: only that which never ceases to *hurt* stays in the memory'—this is a main cause of the oldest (unhappily also the most enduring) psychology on earth."[23] We can note that Moses' giving form to the Jewish people included the slaughter that took place when Moses returned from the mountain to find that the masses had abandoned his arduous path. For Nietzsche, any bringing forth of a belief system that leaders want to be accepted as the one true account involves violent creation and imposition of form and the exclusion of alternatives. For Freud, the group from Egypt in its earlier stages "had no scruples about shaping its narratives according to the needs and purposes of the moment as though it had not yet recognized the concept of falsification."[24]

Regarding imposing a point of view or a belief, consider also Freud's own words in discussing the revisions which have falsified biblical texts in the service of the "secret aims" of those organizing the material (although there are also other inclinations to "preserve everything as it was, no matter whether it was consistent or contradicted itself"): "In its implications the distortion of a text resembles a murder: the difficulty is not in perpetrating the deed, but in getting rid of its traces."[25] One may wonder about what Freud might have thought regarding how rational the means might be by which psychoanalysis might take hold and triumph, even if it too proved to be a progressive step towards heightened and enlightened rationality. It is what returns from the repressed that "exercises an incomparably powerful influence on people in the mass, and raises an irresistible claim to truth against which logical objection remains powerless."[26]

Another aspect of this work links it to Nietzsche. Of course Freud was interested in repetitive phenomena and, as indicated, mentioned Nietzsche's "eternal recurrence of the same" a number of times. Wallace, drawing on the work of Reiff,[27] points out that Freud had two different philosophies of history, one being progressive, unilinear and unidirectional, but the other being a cyclical return of the same. While there is a primal event (the Freudian kairos, the parricide), the history that follows is repetition, "the eternal return of the repressed."[28] Yerushalmi, in his book *Freud's Moses*, writes that in this psychoanalysis of history Freud "presented us with a vision of Eternal Return more seductive, because so much more subtle, than that of Friedrich Nietzsche."[29]

---

*Moses and Monotheism* was written towards the end of Freud's life. Nietzsche was a living presence for him throughout his adult life, and now towards the end of his life and just before beginning work on *Moses and Monotheism* Nietzsche emerges again in a particularly forceful way.

In December 1930, a few years before Freud began work on *Moses and Monotheism* and shortly after Freud wrote *Civilization and Its Discontents*, the literary figure Arnold Zweig (who had been corresponding with Freud for a few years) wrote to Freud of his idea to write an essay comparing Freud and Nietzsche. It should be recalled that a year earlier Freud had come across Charles Maylan's book on Freud and psychoanalysis in which it was suggested that psychoanalysis be integrated with the thought of Nietzsche. Zweig on the other hand wrote of how Freud succeeded where Nietzsche failed. He planned to show that Freud had "achieved everything that Nietzsche intuitively [that word again!] felt to be his task, without his being really able to achieve it with his poetic idealism and brilliant inspirations."[30] He even mentions that Nietzsche tried to explain the birth of tragedy, but that it is Freud who has done so in *Totem and Taboo*.[31] Zweig writes that if Freud would now "make a study of the real 'will to power' . . . the cycle of the Freud-Nietzsche relationship would be complete."[32] In

Zweig's eyes, Freud's relationship to Nietzsche is substantial enough for him to write of "the cycle of the Freud-Nietzsche relationship" and that in effect, the son has accomplished what the father could not.

Freud replied that Zweig should certainly write the essay but, "I don't need to read it. You could write it when I am no longer here and you are haunted by the memory of me."[33] Who is being haunted here? Also, what is Freud attempting to convey when he states that his memory will haunt Zweig?

In August 1932 Zweig mentions that he is "almost falling into the 'Freud and Nietzsche' essay which I have started and laid aside once again,"[34] there being no response from Freud (as far as the edited collected letters demonstrate). In November 1932 Freud sends Zweig a copy of a book of letters (which he had a hand in editing) of his wife's uncle, the famous classical scholar, Jacob Bernays. As a classical scholar Bernays had been well aware of Nietzsche and *The Birth of Tragedy*. In his next letter Zweig states that he is having the book read to him (his vision was impaired) and mentions that the introduction contains much new information on Nietzsche's teacher of classical philology, Friedrich Ritschl.

In April 1934, about four months before Freud's completion of the first draft of *Moses and Monotheism*,[35] Zweig writes about his first draft of a plan for a novel about Nietzsche's madness.[36] It is of interest, given Freud's concerns with latency and return of the repressed, that Zweig writes of having for some time "turned away bitterly from this idol of my youth . . . Now after many years I have come close to him again, because *in you I recognized the man who carried out all that Nietzsche first dreamt of*"[37] (emphasis added). The implication of the identification is evident here, that in Freud, Zweig recognizes Nietzsche (his youthful idol). Zweig has come close to Nietzsche through Freud in whom he recognizes Nietzsche. Freud completes what Nietzsche first attempted, dreamt of, and only began to carry out; the prophet who dreamed and the disciple who would become the prophet and bring the dream to fruition. Freud might even have read words of Nietzsche that would uncannily (although perhaps imperfectly) fit in with this scenario:

I am still waiting for a philosophical *physician* in the exceptional sense of that word—one who has to pursue the problem of the total health of a people, time, race or of humanity—to muster the courage to push my suspicion to its limits and to risk the proposition: what was at stake in all philosophizing hitherto was not at all "truth" but something else—let us say, health, future, growth, power, life.[38]

In the same section Nietzsche writes that "if he ['a psychologist'] should himself become ill, he will bring all of his scientific curiosity into his illness."

Of course Freud the psychologist had his powerful identification with the prophet Moses. Nietzsche is regarded as a prophet and psychologist, as is Zarathustra. Also, Zarathustra, like Moses, jumps angrily into the middle of a group of the "higher men" that he believes is guilty of "idolatry" and of worshipping the old god who lives again.[39] Zarathustra also speaks of being "surrounded by broken old tablets and new tablets half covered with writing."[40] Freud was presenting the world with new tablets.

We have also seen statements of Nietzsche, such as the following one, which would have meant a great deal to Freud, tapping into his feelings and conflicts around his Jewish identity:

"Admit no more new Jews: And especially close the doors to the east (also to Austria)!" thus commands the instinct of a people whose type is still weak and indefinite, so it could easily be blurred or extinguished by a stronger race. The Jews, however, are beyond any doubt the strongest, toughest, and purest race now living in Europe . . . the Jews, if they wanted it—or if they were forced into it, which seems to be what the antisemites want—*could* even now have preponderance, indeed quite literally mastery over Europe, that is certain; that they are *not* working and planning for that is equally certain.

Meanwhile they want and wish rather . . . to be absorbed and assimilated . . . (which may even express an attenuation of the Jewish instincts) . . . it might be useful and fair to expel the antisemitic screamers from the country.[41]

Whether or not he was aware of such specific passages, Freud would have been aware of Nietzsche's attacks on antisemitism (not that this passage may not reflect ambivalence). In fact, as we will shortly see, Zweig himself would bring this to Freud's attention.

All of this lends itself to considering the extent to which Freud may have in fact seen himself on some level as a chosen disciple or prophet who would complete the father's task but also displace him and impose himself and his teachings on his chosen people—his psychoanalytic disciples and those to whom they would spread the good news as well as to "the new Jewry" whose spirit will not remain a stranger to "unprejudiced science."[42] For Freud, in this work "a hero is someone who has had the courage to rebel against his father and has in the end victoriously overcome him."[43] But of course Moses does not rebel against or overcome Akhenaten (such rebellion having been the case in Akhenaten's relationship with his father). Having understood the new ideas and having made them his own, Moses, who is forceful and energetic in contradistinction to the brooding or meditative king, succeeds where the king failed (although Moses too meets with temporary failure). Through the return of the repressed both Moses and Akhenaten triumph. Moses also elevates a chosen people. Although this aristocrat descends to "put himself at the head of a crowd of immigrant foreigners at a backward level of civilization," this relatively small group of "Neo-Egyptians," will, due to their experience with Moses, come to exert a decisive impact on the ultimate form and achievements of the religion.[44] (For Zarathustra, on the other hand, "out of you, who have chosen yourselves, there shall grow a chosen people—and out of them, the overman." An overman emerges from "a chosen people" that has grown out of those who have chosen themselves.[45])

In the April 1934 letter referred to above, Zweig asks if Freud or "Frau Lou" would be interested in helping him with his Nietzsche novel. Freud replies that "no greeting on my 78th birthday has preoccupied me more closely than yours. I would like best to go on thinking about my reply for another week, but what would you be thinking of me by that time."[46] He writes that he is enclosing "the crazy announcement of a book by a probably imperfectly cured psychotic, who claims to have penetrated the mystery of Friedrich Nietzsche."[47] He then continues, regarding Lou: "Our friend Lou is over 70 years old and . . . not in the best of health . . . She must be one of the few people alive who know anything intimate about him. And she is not given to telling it . . . She never wanted to tell me about him."[48]

In a letter of the next day Freud writes that while facts may be disregarded or modified in the service of poetic license regarding figures for whom essential information is unavailable or when the figure is sufficiently remote and removed from common knowledge, "where reality is firmly established and has become common property, the writer should respect it,"[49] even though it's "true, the poets usually fail to keep these rules."[50] He goes on to write that

> when it is a question of someone so near to us in time and whose influence is still as active as Friedrich Nietzsche's, a description of his character and his destiny should aim at the same result as a portrait does—that is to say, however the conception may be elaborated the main stress should fall on the resemblance . . . You must know whether there is enough material available to make such a portrait . . . in the case of Friedrich Nietzsche we are confronted with something else, beyond what is usual. It is the case history of a sick man, and this is much more difficult to guess or reconstruct. I mean, there are psychical processes in a certain sequence but not always psychical motivations generating them, and in the unravelling of these one could go very much astray.[51]

Freud then moves on to more personal factors, acknowledging, "I do not know whether these are my real arguments against your plan. Perhaps the relationship you establish between Nietzsche and me also plays a part in my reasons. In my youth he was a remote and noble figure to me. A friend of mine, Dr. Paneth, had got to know him in the Engadine and had written a lot to me about him."[52]

As Freud considers personal motives for his being "against your plan," he thinks of Zweig's comparisons of himself and Nietzsche; this comparison, which might lead to any number of places, leads Freud to his youth, to a period in which Nietzsche was a remote and noble figure to him and to the time in late 1883 and early 1884 when Paneth was writing "a lot" to Freud about his meetings with Nietzsche. As Paneth wrote of Nietzsche fifty years ago, Zweig writes of him now. (Freud will also experience a return of sorts when his correspondence to Fliess is discovered at the end of 1936.)

Shortly after this, in May 1934, Freud writes to Andreas-Salomé about Zweig's project: "He knows that you would be an invaluable mentor; but would you want to? As a matter of fact I have counselled him to give up the whole idea."[53] Freud receives the desired response from Andreas-Salomé: "It is absolutely out of the question that I should participate in this in any way. I cannot consider such a thing and the mere thought of it fills me with dismay. Please tell this to your correspondent in the strongest and most final terms—moreover, how right you are to dissuade him altogether from his Nietzsche plan!"[54]

Exactly why Andreas-Salomé responded in such strong terms is unclear. One could speculate on her own complex feelings for both men and what might be stirred up in her by Zweig's project, but why she would so strongly object to a biographical novel of this kind is not addressed.

In July 1934 Zweig writes that "the Nietzsche plan is very gradually taking shape."[55] Regarding the Nietzsche archives and the tampering with letters and other material by Nietzsche's sister, Zweig writes:

> You have an intimate knowledge of the letters and of the contributions which we owe to Frau Forster on this subject . . . Naturally I shall no longer venture to approach Frau Lou, though I would gladly have details from her of a quite external nature: voice, clothes, accent, etc. . . . The central point in my plan is actually the possibility it offers of discharging an anti-German affect more fiercely and totally than would be conceivable in any other way. Nietzsche's notorious contempt for German antisemitism makes him absolutely vital as the hero of this novel.[56] [It is quite possible that Paneth too wrote and spoke of Nietzsche's contempt for antisemitism.]

Zweig has the very clear impression that Freud has intimate knowledge of Nietzsche's letters. The basis for this conviction is unclear. He doesn't give up entirely on Frau Lou either, still hoping for some help. What is most important, his novel is to offer the possibility "of discharging an anti-German affect *more fiercely and totally than would be conceivable in any other way*" because of "Nietzsche's notorious contempt for German antisemitism" (emphasis added). This is a fundamental way in which Nietzsche is regarded as a "hero." Similarly, Freud's Moses novel will in part have to do with the place of and reasons for antisemitism. As he would write to Zweig two months later: "Faced with the new persecution, one asks oneself again how the Jews have come to be what they are and why they have attracted this undying hatred."[57] We should also consider that Zweig is writing to Freud about his Nietzsche novel, his novel about a prophet, from the "Holy Land," from Haifa, where he had recently emigrated. To the extent that Freud's *Moses* has some of its origins in his response to Hitler coming to power in 1933 and the intensification of antisemitism as these factors pertain to his Jewish identity, Zweig's description of Nietzsche's contempt for German antisemitism and Zweig's plan to portray Nietzsche as a hero would have resonated with Freud's current concerns.

In August, Zweig writes: "Meanwhile Nietzsche must slowly go on simmering. Every word you say on this topic is worth its weight in gold to me."[58] (One can only wonder if anything may have been left out of the published correspondence or if there is other material which would have clarified the matter of just why Zweig had such assumptions about Freud's relationship to and knowledge of Nietzsche.) He goes on to describe how Nietzsche's ideas have been distorted but adds that "there remains his personality, the wonderfully pure essence of his being, his courtesy of heart, his gentleness of manner, his quiet radiance, the halcyon Nietzsche, not a Dionysus but a human being."[59]

With all of this correspondence on Nietzsche, Freud writes in September 1934: "You think you understand why I have not written to you for so long, but in fact you do not. Perhaps you suspect—and not quite without reason—that I did not want to disturb you any more with my continued objections to your Nietzsche project. But the real reason was different."[60] So Freud has not responded for a number of weeks (perhaps about six weeks judging from the published correspondence), and while Zweig might be thinking it has to do with Nietzsche, "and not quite without reason," Freud assures him it is something else; he has been doing something else while Zweig awaits replies on Nietzsche. What has he been doing during this period over which Nietzsche haunts and hovers? "I have written something myself and this, contrary to my original intention, took up so much of my time that everything else was neglected . . . I gave my work the title: *The Man Moses, a historical novel* (with more justification than your Nietzsche novel)."[61]

So rather than continue to answer Zweig on Nietzsche, Freud (who did have interest in his *Moses* hypotheses before this time)

writes his own biographical or historical novel ("with more justification" than Zweig's Nietzsche novel), this on the figure of Moses.
Rather than continue the correspondence on Nietzsche, Freud does-
n't answer directly but instead announces his own historical novel
about a prophet, a founder of a new way for mankind. Was there
even some understanding by both men of what was transpiring?
After Freud's announcement, Zweig virtually ceases to bring up
Nietzsche to Freud in any serious way (at least according to the
available published letters). (However, in 1936 he does present a
paper on the occasion of Freud's eightieth birthday in which he
praises Freud's Apollonian achievements over Nietzsche's Dionysian attempts. He writes of Freud as "the greatest psychologist
since Nietzsche" ["dem größten Psychologen seit Nietzsche"]
whose beginning attempts were fulfilled by Freud. It is also of interest here that regarding predecessors and priority, and returning to
the past, Freud returns, apparently unconsciously, to the year 1912
[Jung, Andreas-Salomé and *Totem and Taboo*] and Karl Abraham's
article which links Moses and monotheism with the figure of
Akhenaten. Although Freud was well aware of the article and had
referred to it in 1923, he does not mention it in his study. Here was
one who, in this particular area, had come before him but goes unacknowledged. Here are other memories likely stirred up by, or at
least occurring in the context of, the correspondence with Zweig.[62])

Although Freud states in this September letter that the starting point of his work has to do with the new persecution of Jews,
was his book also a response to what was transpiring between him
and Zweig (and Andreas-Salomé) and to his lifelong relationship
with the figure of Nietzsche? Might there be a link between the
figures of Nietzsche and Moses or Nietzsche and Akhenaten as
Freud saw them?

Nietzsche was regularly brought to Freud's attention as someone who anticipated his thought in some fundamental respects, as,
in effect, someone who came before him, as someone who stood behind him. Is it not possible that Zweig's words tapped into some
sense in Freud that however much he was a *Moses* figure in his own
right, that in certain ways he was the Joshua to Nietzsche-Moses, or
since Joshua wouldn't really fit Freud (although it had fit Jung who
in this period of the mid- to late 1930s was conducting ongoing
seminars on *Zarathustra*[63]) that he was the second Moses (his own
creation) to the original Nietzsche-Moses? Although the original

Moses triumphs, the two Moses figures are merged. It is true that it is the first Moses who is the more rational figure with the second Moses being more primitive and irrational,[64] but it is also true that Freud created this second Moses. We should also note that Moses was in part a double for Freud.[65] Was this not the case with Nietzsche with whom he was regularly being compared, about whom it was so frequently said that he had anticipated Freud, had come before Freud? And ultimately the two Moses figures are merged as the religion of the original Moses gradually increases its power and influence. (Or, from within a Christian perspective, one might consider Freud as Paul building an organized edifice on the foundation of Nietzsche-Christ [and for Freud, behind the crucified Christ stands the murdered Moses], or Freud as Jesus to Nietzsche–John the Baptist announcing his coming. We have seen how Nietzsche called for the coming of the philosopher-physician.)

Could the *Moses* book in part be a product of "deferred obedience?" Could Freud have felt guilt towards the end of his life (and in the context of the correspondence with Zweig) about his failing to acknowledge Nietzsche's influence on some of the central concepts of psychoanalysis? Could Freud be unconsciously atoning to his intellectual father figure and making reparation? Could his depriving the Jews of their prophet in this book be, in part, a way of saying, You thought it was a Jew of humble origins from the east who brought you the new tablets, but there was one who came before him, a non Jew who was a noble aristocrat. Freud's Moses is not Jewish and is of the nobility. (Freud would have known from reading *Ecce Homo* that Nietzsche fancied himself a descendent of Polish nobility. Freud too had his family romance fantasy of noble German descent from Cologne.[66] Could Nietzsche fit in with this fantasy?) Although Nietzsche was critical of Jews in some instances, there were many ways in which the Jews could have been seen as a kind of chosen people for him or at least as among those "de Germanized" Germans who could and would read him, as we have seen in his many positive comments. (Whatever one may conclude about Nietzsche's attitudes towards Jews and Judaism, it is clear that Zweig conveys to Freud his strong feelings in regard to Nietzsche as a critic and opponent of antisemitism.) And there is Nietzsche's call for the philosopher-physician. Freud could even have felt himself to be the leader of a group particularly favored or "chosen" by Nietzsche.

Let us recall that twenty years earlier, when in addition to his identification with Moses, Freud is looking up as guilty son to father represented by Michelangelo's *Moses,* he approvingly quotes Thode who describes the figure as a "superman" ("Übermenschen"), and he refers to Michelangelo's figure as superhuman or "more than human" ("Übermenschliches"). Yerushalmi, who explores the nature of Freud's relationship with his father as it has bearing on Freud's relationship to the figure of Moses, asks: "Who can Michelangelo's Moses be if not his [Freud's] father Jakob?"[67] Yes, but Nietzsche is among the most important intellectual (and unacknowledged) father figures for Freud. And Freud's characterization of Nietzsche as remote and noble would fit with what Holt describes on the one hand as Freud's father being somewhat of a "distant" (though warm) figure and on the other hand Freud's early idealized father figures being heroic (though specifically military) leaders.[68] (Freud points out that these leaders and heroes sometimes ended their heroic careers in failure and defeat, which may have resonated for Freud with Nietzsche's final collapse. And recall Zweig writing of Nietzsche in heroic terms.)

However, there are problems with identifying Freud with the second Moses, such as this Moses being characterized as meek. There is also Freud's undoubted identification with the figure of the original Moses. In addition to a level of interpretation that considers Nietzsche implicated in the figure of Moses, one can also raise the question that to the extent Freud himself identifies with Moses, is there still a place for Nietzsche's presence, perhaps a more plausible one than what has just been suggested?

In his identification with Moses, Freud is a founder of a new language, discourse, belief, practice, etc., in such a way as to create or at least attempt to create a system, a coherent theory and practice. A question to ask regarding this identification would be, Who then is Akhenaten for Freud? It was Akhenaten after all who was the figure behind Moses, who, even if Moses was Jewish, was unquestionably not Jewish but an Egyptian noble, a pharaoh. Is it not possible that on the level of Freud's identification with Moses as the founder, systematizer and organizer of the new faith of the Hebrews that Nietzsche might be a figure behind Moses, that is, an original source of some of the foundational beliefs that are transmitted to Moses-Freud who then founds and leads an organized movement and is ultimately successful with it (as Zweig had stated that Freud succeeded where Nietzsche failed)? Akhenaten is glowingly written of as resisting "every temptation to magical thought, and he rejected the illusion, so dear to the Egyptians in particular, of a life after death."[69] And as he discusses what we would characterize as traits of a great human being (which turn out to be traits of the father), Freud is quite clear that "the father too was once a child. The great religious idea for which the man Moses stood was, on our view, not his own property: he had taken it over from King Akhenaten . . . he, whose greatness as the founder of a religion is unequivocally established."[70] Freud certainly identified with Moses, and the idea for which Moses-Freud stood "was, on our view, not his own property," but the property of the "founder" who came before him.

There are two great figures, two founders, but one who became father was a child of (and took over, made his own and utilized the property of) the one who came before him. In Christianity "the old God the Father fell behind Christ; Christ, the Son, took his place."[71] There is atonement and reconciliation here, but "the other side of the emotional relation showed itself in the fact that the son who had taken atonement on himself, became a god himself beside the father and, actually, in place of the father."[72] However, with Akhenaten and Moses, while the latter in a sense displaces the former, Moses fulfills Akhenaten's unrealized dream. And while Moses ultimately becomes the towering figure, Freud wants to make certain that Akhenaten also gets the acknowledgment due him. Freud states a number of times that Moses gave the Jews the Egyptian Aton religion. It is not just the two Moses figures that are merged, and it is not merely the religion of the original Moses that triumphs. It is the great Akhenaten, his thought, that ultimately triumphs, even though without the murder of Moses, its reverberations with the primal parracide, and the eventual return of the repressed, such a triumph might have been impossible.

---

One might also consider here the importance to both Nietzsche and Freud of the figure of Paul. Freud might have some identification with Christ behind the figure of Moses. As he writes in this work, "Christ . . . was the resurrected Moses."[73] But Freud also had strong and positive feelings for Paul as the great innovator and organizer without whom Christianity might have vanished. In 1920 Freud had referred to Paul: "I have always had a special sympathy for St. Paul as a genuinely Jewish character. Is he not the only one who stands completely in the light of history?"[74] At the conclusion of *Moses and Monotheism* Freud writes of

> the hostility . . . which had once driven the sons into killing their admired and dreaded father. There was no place in the framework of the religion of Moses for a direct expression of the murderous hatred of the father. All that could come to light was a mighty reaction against it—a sense of guilt on account of that hostility, a bad conscience for having sinned against God and for not ceasing to sin. This sense of guilt . . . kept awake by the Prophets . . . had yet another superficial motivation, which neatly disguised its true origin. Things were going badly for the people . . . it was not easy to maintain the illusion, loved above all else, of being God's chosen people. If they wished to avoid renouncing that happiness, a sense of guilt on account of their own sinfulness offered a welcome means of exculpating God: they deserved no better than to be punished by him since they had not obeyed his commandments . . . in a fresh rapture of moral asceticism they imposed more and more new instinctual renunciations on themselves and in that way reached—in doctrine and precept, at least—ethical heights which had remained inaccessible to other peoples of antiquity . . . These ethical ideas cannot, however, disavow their origin from the sense of guilt felt on account of a suppressed hostility to God.[75]
>
> It is then Paul to whom the monumental perception dawns: "The reason we are so unhappy is that we have killed God the father . . . we are freed from all guilt since one of us has sacrificed his life to absolve us. . . ." In this formula the killing of God was of course not mentioned, but a crime that had to be atoned by the sacrifice of a victim could only have been a murder. And the intermediate step between the delusion and the historical truth was provided by the assurance that the victim of the sacrifice had been God's son . . . Original sin and redemption by the sacrifice of a victim became the foundation stones of the new religion founded by Paul.[76]

While Christianity was appealing to the lower classes, the masses, at a time of malaise and was regressive in some respects (mysticism and polytheism given freer rein, "re-establishment of the great mother-goddess"[77]), there was real historical truth and progress in Paul's revelation and teachings, this being the strength that overcame all obstacles. (It is here in Paul's revelation and teachings that is found the "truth . . . which . . . overcame all obstacles.") Thus, "the supremacy of the father of the primal horde was re-established and . . . the emotions relating to him could be repeated."[78]

In the next to last paragraph in the book Freud states:

A special enquiry would be called for to discover why it has been impossible for the Jews to join in this forward step which was implied, in spite of all its distortions, by the admission of having murdered God. In a certain sense they have in that way taken a tragic load of guilt on themselves; they have been made to pay heavy penance for it.[79]

Not only are the Jewish people deprived of Moses as one of their own, but the great insight, the great revelation of profound historical truth, is brought by a Jew whose teachings led in a direction unacceptable to the vast majority of Jews and towards the foundation of Christianity. ("Paul, who carried Judaism on, also destroyed it."[80]) And Jews have taken "a tragic load of guilt on themselves" because they have not taken "this forward step." This then is one answer to the question, "why they have attracted this undying hatred."

Freud's writing in these passages is, in some ways, reminiscent of Nietzsche. His discussion of the sense of guilt, of bad conscience, of how the prophets kept this alive, of the "fresh rapture of moral asceticism" with which new instinctual renunciations were imposed (and such renunciations relate to the development of the special character of the Jewish people) are reminiscent of Nietzsche's discussions of bad conscience and asceticism and of Paul himself. And for Freud it is Paul who founds the new religion, the foundation for which is "original sin and redemption by the sacrifice of a victim." Freud suggests that a superficial guilt disguises a deeper, "truer" guilt until Paul comes along and also that earlier the Jews were able to maintain their beliefs and stifle their doubts about God in a time of misfortune (with a potential sense of abandonment) by increasing their own sense of guilt.

For Nietzsche bad conscience offers relief not from a deeper, truer guilt or fears of abandonment but from the hopelessness, helplessness, depression, etc., that would exist in the face of the inability to direct one's instincts, one's will to power, one's freedom, outward into and upon the world. But also recall the passage in which Nietzsche suggests that "this man of the bad conscience . . . apprehends in 'God' the ultimate antithesis of his own ineluctable animal instincts: he reinterprets these instincts themselves as a form of guilt before God (as hostility, rebellion, insurrection against the 'Lord,' the 'father,' the primal ancestor and origin of the world)."[81] For Nietzsche this bad conscience is not rooted or grounded in a primal rebellious and hostile deed; rather, it is grounded in a splitting off of the ineluctable animal instincts as guilt before or sin against the father upon whom is projected the antithesis of such instincts. This can occur when more spontaneous instinctual expression is blocked and the self is substituted for the object of instinctual gratification, particularly aggression. As the aggression is turned against the self as the object upon which to discharge this drive, this bad self can be potentially freed and made good by participating in the power of, the being of, God who is the idealized antithesis of such instincts. (When God acts aggressively, it is with the believer's good conscience.) And Freud follows Nietzsche when he states that "the believer has a share in the greatness of his god."[82] He also follows Nietzsche and others who emphasize the spiritual or psychological sickness that accompanies the achievements of civilization with its foundations in repression and guilt. And for both thinkers, guilt, however painful, can provide relief from something more painful, whether a greater guilt or depression.

As regards Paul, Nietzsche too regarded him as a monumental figure who had "the idea of ideas, the key of keys, the light of lights."[83] In all likelihood Freud would have been aware of some of Nietzsche's ideas on Paul as they appear in *The Antichrist*, an individual English-language volume published in 1928 being in his library.[84] And for Nietzsche too it is the idea that with Christ's death "all guilt has been taken away, guilt as such has been destroyed"[85] that is central. However, for Nietzsche this relates not to the murder of the primal father but to Paul's murder of him in his manifestation as "the law or torah." That is, Paul had discovered in himself that he himself—fiery, sensual, melancholy, malevolent in hatred as he was—*could* not fulfil the law ... his extravagant lust for power was constantly combating and on the watch for transgressors and goad. Is it really "carnality" which again and again makes him a transgressor? And not rather, as he later suspected, behind it the law itself, which *must* continually prove itself unfulfillable and with irresistible magic lures on to transgression? But at that time he did not yet possess this way out of his difficulty ... The law was the cross to which he felt himself nailed: how he hated it! ... how he sought for a means of destroying it ... at last the liberating idea came to him ... together with a vision ... Paul heard the words: "Why persecutest thou *me?*" ... his *mind* suddenly became clear: "it is *unreasonable*," he says to himself, "to persecute precisely this Christ! For here is the way out, here is perfect revenge, here and nowhere else do I have and hold the *destroyer of the law!*" ... Hitherto that shameful *death* had counted with him as the principal argument against the "Messiahdom" ... but what if it were *necessary* for the *abolition* of the law! ... from now on he is the teacher of the *destruction of the law!* To die to evil—that means also to die to the law; to exist in the flesh—that means also to become with him the destroyer of the law; to have died with him—that means also to have died to the law! ... God could never have resolved on the death of Christ if a fulfillment of the law had been in any way possible without this death ... now the law is dead, now the carnality in which it dwelt is dead—or at least dying constantly away, as though decaying. Yet but a brief time within this decay!—that is the Christian's lot, before, become one with Christ, he arises with Christ ... With that the intoxication of Paul is at its height ... and the intractable lust for power reveals itself as an anticipatory revelling in *divine* glories.— This is the *first Christian,* the inventor of Christianness! Before him there were only a few Jewish sectarians.[86] [In writing of the law in the form of Freud's superego, Eagleton writes that "the law ... like the Mosaic code in the judgement of St. Paul will merely illuminate how far short of it we have fallen."[87]]

Nietzsche here offers a psychological account of what may have led Paul to his "idea of ideas." And as regards Paul's impact from Nietzsche's point of view, he offers, as Salaquarda puts it, a new source for the feeling of power for the masses through "the concept of a redeemer in the world to come who chooses the *weak* and removes them from the observation of *the* law."[88] We can also note that while antisemitism has often included the criticism that Jews remained stubbornly and legalistically fixated on the law rather than embracing Christian love, Nietzsche argues that Paul embraces Christ (and power and intoxication) due to his own personal failure to live with the law, his own hatred of the law, his own creative psychopathology. (Some contemporary views of conversion follow Nietzsche in suggesting that "the convert's preconversion feelings of unworthiness, self-doubt, and self-depreciation are released or overcome by the conversion process. Psychologically, conversion becomes the solution to unbearable guilt and sin."[89])

Paul is a "great man" in Nietzsche's eyes, and there may even be an identification with him as Nietzsche refers to both Paul's idea and his own eternal recurrence with the phrase "idea of ideas."(The equivalent in Freud, "the key of keys, the light of lights" [or in Freud's words of 1927, "the thread that leads a man out of the labyrinth"], would be the shift in 1897 from the seduction theory to the place of infantile sexual fantasy and its ramifications.)[90] Nietzsche considers Paul as a type of ascetic priest who, in the words of Salaquarda, is strong enough "to channel the 'will to nothingness' of the *decadents* for a time into another direction."[91] But he also had a hatred of Paul, a hatred of what he felt was Paul's life-negating attitude towards the things of this earth, particularly his attitude towards the "flesh." (Or should one say Paul was not life affirming in a manner Nietzsche would regard as creative and more affirmative than his provisional life-affirming approach to channel the will to nothingness? Recall that for Nietzsche even the ascetic priest, "this *life-inimical* species—it must indeed be in the *interest of life itself* that such a self-contradictory type does not die out."[92])

Towards the end of his life, at the end of his *Moses* book, Freud turns to Paul as the figure who brought a new level of historical truth to mankind. Towards the end of his productive life Nietzsche turned to Paul as a figure instrumental in finding a solution for the problem of the will to nothingness, a solution that was "illness as pregnancy." Bad conscience, illness that it is, can still be seen as "the womb of all ideal and imaginative phenomena."[93] It is also worth noting that Paul, Nietzsche and Freud are joined in their great emphasis on the place and functions of, as well as a therapeutic response to, guilt.

---

In the event that the thrust of these suggestions on Nietzsche's presence in *Moses and Monotheism* sounds implausible, I will pull together a few relevant points which may lead the reader to find greater plausibility in the suggestions offered.

Freud was greatly concerned with priority and with his standing as a groundbreaking, heroic figure who demonstrated in a unique way that the ego, rational man, was not master in its own house. His was to be the third great humiliation to mankind, after Copernicus and Darwin. Freud's explorations took him to views of human development, psychopathology and the complex functions of and relationships between different aspects or components of the mental world that moved in directions other than and in important ways beyond those Nietzsche had explored. However, Nietzsche did first explore ways in which we are motivated by repressed unconscious forces with, so to speak, their own agendas, which are often in contradiction to and in conflict with our more usual conscious notions of what we are up to and what we are about. Freud's demonstration of the existence of, nature of and development of the personal-like psychic forces engaged in conflict within us[94] goes beyond anything in Nietzsche. And of course Freud's emphasis on the continuing impact of specific repressed childhood conflicts receives almost no attention from Nietzsche. So while Nietzsche is aware of children's primitive desires,[95] there is no discussion, for example, of how the complications around oedipal desires continue to have an impact on the wishes, fears, goals, behaviors, etc., of the adult. (Although he is aware of the continuing sexual feelings of the child for the parent.[96]) But as we have seen, the foundations (and more) are present in Nietzsche.

Freud was aware of Nietzsche having anticipated him and said so as did many of those around him. Also, in his youth he regarded Nietzsche as a "remote and noble" figure. At that time his highly regarded friends and acquaintances were immersed in Nietzsche's early writings. Freud read at least some of these writings. A bit later on his close friend Paneth would be meeting with Nietzsche over a three-month period and writing a great deal to Freud about Nietzsche. Upon his return to Vienna, Paneth would have spoken with Freud of his impressions of Nietzsche. There are also the links to Nietzsche evident in the correspondence with Fliess. Nietzsche's impact on the intellectual world of the 1890s has been compared to Darwin's influence on the previous generation.

As we have seen, in 1908 Freud read and discussed sections of the *Genealogy* and *Ecce Homo*. Freud spoke of Nietzsche as having attained a degree of introspection never before reached and not likely to be reached again. We have seen that some of Freud's early followers, such as Rank and Jung, had been immersed in Nietzsche's writings before they met Freud. During a period in which Nietzsche was being regularly discussed and written about by analysts, including Jung at the 1913 congress, Freud wrote his essay on Michelangelo's *Moses*, writing of Moses' overcoming his aggressive impulses for a higher course, referring to the figure as representing the highest mental achievement and as "Übermenschliches." Here Nietzsche may be linked with Michelangelo's Moses. Moses may certainly be, as many have noted, linked to Freud's father, but he is here very possibly linked to the father figure of Nietzsche. There are at this time also the possible oedipal issues involved in Freud's relationship to Andreas-Salomé.

Throughout his life Freud regularly had Nietzsche brought to his attention as having anticipated him. Freud in turn denied any influence whatsoever while acknowledging intuitive insights close to his own. He also had read enough to be affected by the "wealth of ideas," even to have felt "smothered by an excess of interest." Nietzsche's name and ideas appear in Freud's work through the years, and in choosing a name for the deepest layer of psychic reality he turns not to a respected scientist but to the author of *Zarathustra*, a prophet like himself as well as a philosopher and psychologist like himself. And according to Wittels, in the mid-1920s Freud was taking Nietzsche with him on his travels. At one point it appears that he was comparing his ideas with those of Nietzsche's *Genealogy*. Freud also felt he knew Nietzsche well enough to comment on the typical use of the "it" in his writings, that Nietzsche did not deal with displacement and infantilism, and that Nietzsche's self-knowledge was unsurpassed. He also knew Nietzsche well enough to regard him as one among a handful of persons he considered to be truly great.

Towards the end of his life, *Moses and Monotheism* emerges in the context (among, of course, other profoundly important contexts, such as Hitler's coming to power in 1933) of his correspondence with Arnold Zweig and Zweig's deep involvement with Nietzsche, including Nietzsche's stance against antisemitism. Zweig writes of Nietzsche as a heroic figure, of the Freud-Nietzsche cycle and of Freud succeeding where Nietzsche failed. Whatever the many other factors may have been which contributed to Freud's account in *Moses and Monotheism*, the issues around creating a new way of seeing mankind and the world, of being a founder, with another figure behind the founder, and with the founder not being of the Jewish people but of a foreign aristocracy ("remote and noble") all resonate with issues Freud had been grappling with in his past and, it is suggested, currently in the context of his correspondence with Zweig.

Along with everything else going on in this work, there is an expression of and perhaps an attempt to resolve Freud's ambivalence regarding his relationship to Nietzsche, perhaps also an attempt to come to terms with his own guilt around his lack of complete honesty regarding the nature of his relationship to Nietzsche. There is also the matter of his attempting to resolve the conflict between his identity as a modern German European and his identity as an eastern European Jew, which included the history and heritage of Judaism. On one level, Freud as a Jew would be taking the key insight of his noble, foreign predecessor (and the cultural heritage of Germany and the West) but impressing upon it his own indelible imprint so that it is transformed into the new tablets which become the foundation for how a civilization comes to understand itself. The father is acknowledged, although on certain levels he is surpassed. And as Freud believed that in one way Christianity was a great progressive step in its symbolic acknowledgement of the murder of the primal father, one may wonder what he thought of Nietzsche's proposal, the step Nietzsche took in announcing that we must come to terms not only with the death of God, but also with the fact that *"We have killed him—you and I. All of us are his murderers."*[97]

At the very least, one is obligated to take account of the

correspondence between Zweig and Freud on Nietzsche, a correspondence which raised important, complex issues for Freud and
aroused strong feelings in him. It may be that if Freud is the Moses
of psychoanalysis and the Moses for psychoanalysts (and many
others), perhaps the psychoanalytic community can appreciate that
Moses remained a towering figure for Freud even if the foundations
of his thought derived from one who came before him. Although
those who regard Freud-Moses as their own unique and sustaining
heroic figure may not so easily relinquish the position reserved
solely for him, in this book Freud is quite clear, as in effect is
Zweig in his letters, that there are two founding figures, two primal fathers, one doing his work shortly after the demise of his predecessor.

# Chapter 16

## CONCLUSION

*An instinct of self-preservation . . . gains its most unambiguous expression as an instinct of self-defense, not to see many things, not to hear many things, not to permit many things to come close.*

—Nietzsche, *Ecce Homo*

*Man takes a real delight in oppressing himself with excessive claims and afterwards idolizing the tyrannically demanding something in his soul. In every ascetic morality man worships a part of himself as God and for that he needs to diabolize the other part.*

—Nietzsche, *Human, All Too Human*

*All subduing and becoming master involves a fresh interpretation, an adaptation through which any previous "meaning" and "purpose" are necessarily obscured or even obliterated.*

—Nietzsche, *Genealogy of Morals*

*In Vienna . . . I have been discovered.*

—Nietzsche, *Ecce Homo*

At the outset of this study we saw that Anzieu and Gellner[1] were among those who pointed to a number of concepts explored by Nietzsche which anticipated basic psychoanalytic concepts developed by Freud. It is now increasingly acknowledged, and can readily be seen in reading Nietzsche and studies of his work, that such ideas were given serious, extended discussion by Nietzsche and can in no way be characterized as flashes of intuitive insight to be contrasted against the laborious, more esteemed scientific investigations of Freud. As regards the scientific status of their ideas, the ideas of Nietzsche and Freud, where desirable and possible, can be submitted to scientific investigation. That Freud elaborated his ideas in the context of his work with patients tells us little in and of itself about the scientific credibility of his ideas; in fact it tells us little in and of itself about the sources of Freud's ideas. (John Kerr is not being entirely outrageous when he writes that "it is now quite clear where Freud actually got his ideas—from his library principally."[2]) Freud regarded himself as a scientific conquistador. His contrast of his laborious but scientific investigations to Nietzsche's mere flashes of intuitive insight allowed him to consider that his heroic efforts were in a certain sense without precedent, without anyone who came before him, and that his endeavor was a truly scientific one to be distanced from the intuitions of artists and philosophers. There is certainly some truth to this, but Freud did incorporate a good deal of Nietzsche's ideas into the creation of psychoanalysis.

Gellner points out some of the additions Freud made to the "NM" ("Nietzschean Minimum"):

Freud added specificity . . . a reasonably specific recipe for personal salvation and therapy . . . an organization . . . an ostensibly scientific terminology . . . and an insertion of these ideas into the context of medicine.[3]

Gellner also emphasizes how disturbing a thinker Nietzsche was, and that "the Will to Power is a far, far more disturbing, more corrosive idea for humanist optimism than is the domination of the human psyche by sexuality."[4]

While one may argue with any number of points made by Gellner, or for that matter with the points made by Anzieu and others referred to in this study regarding the extent to which Nietzsche anticipated Freud, there is, as mentioned, a growing recognition that in very important respects Nietzsche anticipated Freud. This recognition spans a number of disciplines. While Anzieu is an analyst and Gellner an anthropologist and philosopher, in the book *Freud and the Humanities*, Peregrine Horden writes: "The more we learn, say, about the impact of Schopen-hauer or Nietzsche on our century the more we find which we might otherwise have thought purely Freudian. Freud's indebted-ness to nineteenth-century German philosophy is only now be-coming apparent."[5] And Erich Heller writes of Nietzsche as the "prompter" of psychoanalysis.[6]

In addition to growing consensus on Nietzsche having antici-pated Freud, there can be no doubt that Nietzsche was a strong presence in Freud's life. We have seen that from the time of his youth through his last years Freud was regularly having Nietzsche brought to his attention, including direct comparisons of their ideas. We have seen that towards the end of his life, as Freud was being honored by both Zweig and Mann on his eightieth birthday, Nietzsche was there for the occasion. Even as Freud was being honored, Nietzsche's presence haunted him.

It still might be argued by some that while Nietzsche did in fact anticipate important psychoanalytic concepts and was a prominent presence in Freud's life, Freud worked out his own ideas, particularly his most original ideas, to a great degree inde-pendent of Nietzsche's influence. This appears to be the view of Trosman, who writes:

> Some forms of influence may be most effective while one is in the midst of creative work rather than serving as an impe-tus to the beginning phases. It is unlikely that Nietzsche's ideas were best incorporated while Freud felt himself swayed by impressions derived from the clinical context; earlier expo-sure to the weight of Nietzsche's authority might have cur-tailed rather than fostered Freud's observational powers.[7]

There are problems with this point of view. First, it doesn't address the indications of direct contact with Nietzsche's ideas from Freud's university years through the late 1890s. Second, it ig-nores the extent to which the figure of Nietzsche may have been a very live emotional presence for Freud during this period. Third, it assumes that Freud, to the extent he was influenced by Nietzsche (as Trosman acknowledges Nietzsche's general pervasiveness ear-lier in the passage), could turn off that influence to pursue his own explorations in his own way. I believe there is some truth to this, but in an obviously limited way. One cannot very well say that

Freud was influenced by Nietzsche but then decided not to be influenced by him as he went his own way when the very foundational concepts of psychoanalysis are so similar to Nietzsche's own ideas in relation to which Freud decided not to be influenced.

On the other hand, Freud's genius was such that he absorbed and integrated an incredible array of influences—including of course that of the great scientists and medical practitioners with whom he had contact—made them his own and went on to utilize them in his own unique way in the service of his own discoveries and creations. It seems to me, contrary to Trosman, that the evidence points to Freud's use of Nietzsche as an impetus in the earlier as well as later phases of his work, but that he integrated that impetus and utilized it as one of the many factors that would enter into his creation of psychoanalysis.

Freud, who had a great need to see himself as one of the great disturbers of the peace of mankind, knew that his predecessor had been, among other things, just such a philosopher and psychologist. (In the ethical sphere, as early as 1896 George Simmel described Nietzsche as having accomplished "a Copernican deed."[8]) Freud created and discovered a great deal, but if psychoanalysis as a movement and community is to come to terms with its origins, recognition must be given to the fact that many of its foundational concepts come not from Freud's self analysis or his application of a new scientific instrument, the microscope of free association, and related methodologies, but from the explorations and insights developed by thinkers such as Nietzsche, Schopenhauer, Feuerbach and others (as well as, of course, from the ideas of Darwin and many other scientists and medical practitioners). I hope we can appreciate Freud's genius and also get beyond the idea that Freud was the lone scientist who brought laborious research, reason and objectivity where, with Nietzsche (and Schopenhauer and others), there had been only poetic intuition. Nietzsche highly valued science, rigorous logical thinking and scientific self-scrutiny as well as the disclosures and redeeming potential of art. He was a psychologist who developed a psychology of dynamic unconscious mental functioning.

# NOTES

## INTRODUCTION

1. Thomas Mann, "Freud's Position in the History of Modern Culture," in *Freud as We Knew Him*, ed. Hendrick M. Ruitenbeck (Detroit: Wayne State University Press, 1973), 84.

2. Thomas Mann quoted in Henri Ellenberger, *The Discovery of the Unconscious* (New York: Basic Books, 1970), 272.

3. For a discussion of Freud's complex and ambivalent relationship to philosophy see Patricia Herzog, "The Myth of Freud as Anti-philosopher," in *Freud: Appraisals and Reappraisals*, vol. 2, ed. Paul E. Stepansky (Hillsdale, New Jersey: The Analytic Press, 1988), 163–89.

4. Fritz Wittels, *Freud and His Time*, trans. Louise Brink (New York: Liveright Publishing Corporation, 1931), 318.

5. Ibid., 238. As we will see, this view is not correct.

6. Ibid., 399.

7. Maria Dorer, *Historische Grundlagen der Psychoanalyse* (Leipzig: Felix Meiner, 1932). Dorer's mention of Freud's debt to Nietzsche is noted by Edwin R. Wallace, "Freud and the Mind-Body Problem," in *Freud and the History of Psychoanalysis*, ed. Toby Gelfand and John Kerr (Hillsdale, NJ: The Analytic Press, 1992), 234.

8. Karl Jaspers, *General Psychopathology*, 7th ed. (Chicago: The University of Chicago Press, 1964), 360.

9. Ibid., 366.

10. Herman Nunberg and Ernst Federn, eds., *Minutes of the Vienna Psychoanalytic Society,* vol. 1, trans. M. Nunberg (New York: International Universities Press, 1962), 359.

11. See Ellenberger, *Discovery;* R. J. Hollingdale, *Nietzsche* (Boston: Routledge and Kegan Paul, 1973); Richard Waugaman, "The Intellectual Relationship between Nietzsche and Freud," *Psychiatry* 36 (November, 1973): 458–67; William J. McGrath, *Dionysian Art and Populist Politics in Austria* (New Haven: Yale University Press, 1974); Mitchell Ginsberg, "Nietzschean Psychiatry," in *Nietzsche: A Collection of Critical Essays,* ed. Robert C. Solomon (Notre Dame: University of Notre Dame Press, 1980), 293–315; Lorin Anderson, "Freud, Nietzsche," Salmagundi 47–48 (Winter-Spring, 1980): 3–29; Kim R. Holmes, "Freud, Evolution, and the Tragedy of Man," *Journal of the American Psychoanalytic Association* 31, no. 1 (1983): 187–210; Drew S. Nash, *Death or Power: A Reassessment of Human Aggression through an Analysis and Comparison of the Theories of Nietzsche and Freud* (Ph.D. dissertation, University of California at Berkeley, 1984); Ernest Gellner, *The Psychoanalytic Movement, or The Coming of Unreason* (London: Paladin Books, 1985); Peter L. Rudnytsky, *Freud and Oedipus* (New York: Columbia University Press, 1987); Paul Roazen, "Nietzsche and Freud: Two Voices from the Underground," *Psychohistory Review* 19, no. 3 (Spring, 1991): 327–48.

12. See Freud quoted in Herman Nunberg and Ernst Federn, eds., *Minutes of the Vienna Psychoanalytic Society,* vol. 2 (New York: International Universities Press, 1967), 32; Bruce Mazlish, "Freud and Nietzsche," *Psychoanalytic Review* 55, no. 3 (1968): 360–75; Peter Gay, *Freud: A Life for Our Time* (New York: W.W. Norton & Co., 1988), 45.

13. It is striking that as early as 1869, at the age of twenty-four, Nietzsche was interested in "the most diverse operations of the instinctive and the conscious" ("Homer and Classical Philology," in *The Complete Works of Friedrich Nietzsche,* ed. Oscar Levy vol. 3, trans. J. M. Kennedy [New York: Russel and Russel, 1964], 166).

14. Ernest Jones, *The Life and Work of Sigmund Freud,* 3 vols. (New York: Basic Books, 1953–1957), 3:283. Jones was familiar with Nietzsche's work at least as early as 1906 (see Vincent Brome, *Freud and His Early Circle* [New York: William Morrow and Co., 1968], 33).

15. Didier Anzieu, *Freud's Self-Analysis* (London: The Hogarth Press, 1986), 88–89. As Hollingdale points out, Nietzsche did not just use the word *sublimation* on several occasions. He seriously explored this concept; see R. J. Hollingdale, *Nietzsche* (Boston: Routledge and Kegan Paul, 1973), 110–115. Among the many other pertinent ideas that could be included are those pertaining to the unconscious resistance of an investiga-

tor into his or her area of inquiry, unconscious envy (*Zarathustra*, pt. 1, "On the Despisers of the Body"), and how unresolved dissonances in the personalities of parents go on echoing in the child's character. On this last point see Richard D. Chessick, "The Relevance of Nietzsche to the Study of Freud and Kohut," *Contemporary Psychoanalysis* 17, no. 3 (July 1981): 359–73. As we will see, Nietzsche also discussed issues pertaining to the nature of interpretation that are relevant to psychoanalytic theory and practice.

16. Edwin R. Wallace, *Freud and Anthropology: A History and Reappraisal* (New York: International Universities Press, 1983), 17.

17. Richard A. Shweder, *Thinking through Cultures* (Cambridge: Harvard University Press, 1991), 39.

18. Ronald Hayman, *Nietzsche: A Critical Life* (New York: Viking Penguin, 1980), 4.

19. Ibid., 2.

20. Ibid.

21. Gellner, *Psychoanalytic Movement*, 20–22.

22. Hans W. Loewald, *Papers on Psychoanalysis* (New Haven: Yale University Press, 1980), 71.

23. See Hans W. Loewald, *Sublimation* (New Haven: Yale University Press, 1988).

24. See Nunberg and Federn, *Minutes*, 2:32.

25. Nunberg and Federn, *Minutes*, 1:359–60.

26. See Jeffrey Moussaieff Masson, ed., *The Complete Letters of Sigmund Freud to Wilhelm Fliess, 1887–1904*, trans. Masson (Cambridge: The Belknap Press of Harvard University Press, 1985), 398.

27. Ernst Ticho, "The Influence of the German-Language Culture on Freud's Thought," *International Journal of Psycho-Analysis* 67 (1986): 232.

28. See Jones, *Life and Work*, 3:415.

29. Nunberg and Federn, *Minutes*, 2:31–32.

30. See Walter Boehlich, ed., *The Letters of Sigmund Freud to Eduard Silberstein, 1871–1881*, trans. A. J. Pomerans (Cambridge: The Belknap Press of Harvard University Press, 1990), 102.

31. See McGrath, *Dionysian Art;* Aldo Venturelli, "Nietzsche in der Berggasse 19. Über die erste Nietzsche—Rezeption in Wien," *Nietzsche-Studien* 13 (1984): 448–80.

32. See Harry Trosman, *Freud and the Imaginative World* (Hillsdale, New Jersey: The Analytic Press, 1985), 54–55.

33. See Ellenberger, *Discovery,* 271–78; McGrath, *Dionysian Art,* 53–83, and *Freud's Discovery of Psychoanalysis: The Politics of Hysteria* (Ithaca: Cornell University Press, 1986), 138–39; Arthur K. Berliner, *Psychoanalysis and Society: The Social Thought of Sigmund Freud* (Washington, D.C.: University Press of America, 1983), 19.

34. In 1931, the year after publication of *Civilization and Its Discontents,* Freud wrote in a letter: "I have rejected the study of Nietzsche although—no, because—it was plain that I would find insights in him very similar to psychoanalytic ones" (quoted in Gay, *Freud,* 46).

35. Franklin L. Baumer, *Modern European Thought: Continuity and Change in Ideas, 1600–1950* (New York: Macmillan Publishing Co., 1977), 305.

36. See Wallace, *Freud and Anthropology,* 17.

37. See David Thatcher, "Nietzsche's Debt to Lubbock," *Journal of the History of Ideas* 49, no. 2 (1983): 293–309.

38. Berliner, *Psychoanalysis and Society,* 19.

39. See Ellenberger, *Discovery,* 271.

40. Ibid., 273.

41. Berliner, *Psychoanalysis and Society,* 19.

42. Stephen Jay Gould, *Bully for Brontosaurus* (New York: W. W. Norton & Co., 1991), 57.

43. Nietzsche, *Human, All Too Human* (1878–1880), trans. R. J. Hollingdale (New York: Cambridge University Press, 1986), 1, sec. 162. For a discussion of the relationship of both Nietzsche and Freud to Spinoza, see Yirmiyahu Yoval, *Spinoza and Other Heretics* (Princeton: Princeton University Press, 1989), 104–66.

44. See Nunberg and Federn, *Minutes,* 1 and 2.

45. See Elisabeth Förster-Nietzsche, *Das Leben Friedrich Nietzsche,* 2 vols. (vol. 2 in 2 parts) (Leipzig: Nauman, 1895–1904); Richard Frank Krummel, "Dokumentation: Joseph Paneth über seine Begegnung mit

Nietzsche in der Zarathustra-Zeit," in *Nietzsche-Studien* 17 (1988): 478–95.

## CHAPTER 1. THE UNIVERSITY YEARS

1. Friedrich Nietzsche, "David Strauss, the Confessor and the Writer" (1873), in *Untimely Meditations*, trans. R. J. Hollingdale, intro. J. P. Stern (New York: Cambridge University Press, 1983), 1–55. Hereafter *UM*, 1.

2. Boehlich, *Letters*, 102. That the quote ("And thus we live, thus fortune guides our steps") derives from Goethe is noted by Boehlich (105n. 3).

3. See Jerry L. Jennings, "From Philology to Existential Psychology," *The Journal of Mind and Behavior* 9, no. 1 (Winter 1988): 57.

4. See Mark Warren, *Nietzsche and Political Thought* (Cambridge: The MIT Press, 1988), 211. For an overview of some of the more influential assessments of Nietzsche's relationship to Nazism (and one which takes Nietzshe's complicity very seriously), see Steven E. Aschheim, *The Nietzsche Legacy in Germany, 1890–1990* (Berkeley: University of California Press, 1992), 315–30. Aschheim does indicate that Nazi ideological appropriation of Nietzsche "entailed selective reading, casuistic interpretation, and even frequent suppression and expurgation of potentially embarassing material" (233).

5. See McGrath, *Dionysian Art*.

6. Ibid., ch. 2.

7. McGrath, *Freud's Discovery*, 138.

8. See McGrath, *Dionysian Art*, 62–64; Aschheim, *Nietzsche Legacy*, 93.

9. Boehlich, *Letters*, 166.

10. See Carl E. Shorske, *Fin-De-Siécle Vienna* (New York: Vintage Books, 1981), 189.

11. See McGrath, *Freud's Discovery*, 76–83.

12. See McGrath, *Dionysian Art*, 69–70.

13. Robert Pick, *The Last Days of Imperial Vienna* (London: Weidenfeld and Nicolson, 1975), 10.

14. See Shorske, *Vienna*, 195.

15. Ibid.

16. See McGrath, *Dionysian Art*, 62.

17. See Frederic Morton, *Thunder at Twilight: Vienna 1913/1914* (New York: Charles Scribner's Sons, 1989), 54–55.

18. Aschheim, *Nietzsche Legacy*, 167.

19. See Ernst L. Freud, Lucie Freud and Ilse Grübrich-Simitis, eds., *Sigmund Freud: His Life in Pictures and Words* (New York: W.W. Norton and Co., 1985), 326.

20. See Venturelli, "Nietzsche in der Berggasse 19"; Michael Molnar, *The Diary of Sigmund Freud, 1929–1939*, trans., annotated, with an introduction by Michael Molnar (New York: Charles Scribner and Sons, 1992), 191.

21. Sigmund Freud, *The Interpretation of Dreams* (1900), SE 5:423. Hereafter *ID*.

22. See Jones, *Life and Work*, 1:141; Albrecht Hirschmüller, *The Life and Work of Joseph Breuer* (New York: New York University Press, 1989 [1978]), 378.

23. See Boehlich, *Letters*, 70.

24. See McGrath, *Freud's Discovery*, 139.

25. See Boehlich, *Letters*, 70.

26. Ibid., 86.

27. Ibid., 70, 96.

28. See Ernst L. Freud, ed., *The Letters of Sigmund Freud and Arnold Zweig*, trans. Elaine and William Robson-Scott (New York: New York University Press, 1970), 78.

29. Freud quoted in Jones, *Life and Work*, 3:460.

30. E. Freud, *Letters of Freud and Zweig*, 78.

31. See Alexander Grinstein, *Freud at the Crossroads* (Madison: International Universities Press 1990), 208.

## CHAPTER 2. NIETZSCHE'S EARLY WRITINGS

1. Bernard Williams, *Shame and Necessity* (Berkeley: University of California Press, 1993), 9–10. See also Rudnytsky, *Freud and Oedipus*;

Johannes Irmscher, "Friedrich Nietzsche and Classical Philology Today," *History of European Ideas* 11 (1989): 963–66.

2. Nietzsche, *Human*, 2, Pt. 1, sec. 126. See Carl Pletsch, *Young Nietzsche* (New York: The Free Press, 1991), 126–158.

3. See Nietzsche, *The Birth of Tragedy* (1872), in *Basic Writings of Nietzsche*, ed. and trans. Walter Kaufmann (New York: Random House, 1968), sec. 10.

4. See David Adams Leeming, *The World of Myth: An Anthology* (New York: Oxford University Press, 1990), 108, 114.

5. See Bernhard Zimmermann, *Greek Tragedy: An Introduction*, trans. Thomas Marrier (Baltimore: The Johns Hopkins University Press, 1991), 76.

6. Friedrich Nietzsche, *The Will to Power* (1883–1888), ed. Walter Kaufmann, trans. Walter Kaufmann and R. J. Hollingdale (New York: Random House, 1967), n. 1050. Hereafter *WP*.

7. See Nietzsche, *Tragedy*, sec. 10.

8. Siegfried Mandel, Introduction to *Friedrich Nietzsche: The Man in His Work* by Lou Andreas-Salomé (Redding Ridge, CT: Black Swan Books, 1988 [1894]), xxiii. On Nietzsche's views of music see Anthony Storr, *Music and the Mind* (New York: The Free Press, 1992), 150-67. Storr writes that in his view "Nietzsche understood music better than any other modern philosopher" (167). He suggests that Nietzsche appreciated that while "conceptual thought demands the separation of thinking from feeling, of object from subject, of mind from body, . . . music may be one way of bridging this division" (165).

9. Nietzsche, *Tragedy*, sec. 2.

10. Ibid., sec. 4.

11. Ibid.

12. Ibid.

13. Ibid., sec. 1.

14. Julian Young, *Nietzsche's Philosophy of Art* (New York: Cambridge University Press, 1992), 33.

15. Ibid., 156 n. 9.

16. Nietzsche, *Tragedy*, sec. 4.

17. Ibid.

18. Ibid.

19. Ibid.

20. Ibid., sec. 15.

21. David Lenson, *"The Birth of Tragedy"*: *A Commentary* (Boston: Twayne Publishers, 1987), 72.

22. Nietzsche, *Tragedy*, sec. 15.

23. Ibid., sec. 5.

24. Ibid., sec. 18. For a discussion of the apparent contradiction on truth and illusion see Henry Staten, *Nietzsche's Voice* (Ithaca: Cornell University Press, 1990), 187–216. For a discussion of some related issues see Maudemarie Clark, "Language and Deconstruction: Nietzsche, de Man, and Postmodernism," in *Nietzsche as Postmodernist: Essays Pro and Contra*, ed. Clayton Koelb (Albany: State University of New York Press, 1990), 75–90.

25. Young, *Nietzsche's Philosophy of Art*, 62.

26. Nietzsche, *Tragedy*, sec. 9.

27. See Rudnytsky, *Freud and Oedipus*, 201–2.

28. See E. James Lieberman, "Why Oedipus Loved His Father," *The Harvard Mental Health Letter* 7, no. 6 (June 1991): 4–6. "In my youth I felt an overpowering need to understand something of the riddles of the world in which we live and perhaps even to contribute something to their solution" (Postscript to *The Question of Lay Analysis* [1927], SE 20:253).

29. See Stan Draenos, *Freud's Odyssey: Psychoanalysis and the End of Metaphysics* (New Haven: Yale University Press, 1982), 107.

30. See David Friedrich Strauss, *The Life of Jesus Critically Examined* (Philadelphia: Fortress Press, 1973 [1835]); *Der alte und der neue Glaube* (Leipzig: S. Hirzel, 1872). See Pletsch, *Young Nietzsche*, 165–66.

31. J. P. Stern, Introduction to *Untimely Meditations*, trans. R. J. Hollingdale (New York: Cambridge University Press, 1983), xi.

32. See Robert R. Holt, "Freud's Adolescent Reading: Some Possible Effects on His Work," in *Freud: Appraisals and Reappraisals*, vol. 3, ed. Paul E. Stepansky (Hillsdale, New Jersey: The Analytic Press, 1988), 186–87.

33. Nietzsche, *UM*, 1:29.

34. Ibid., 35.

35. Ibid.

36. Ibid., 49.

37. Ibid., 55.

38. In other words, the "not" is seen as defensive and betraying the true underlying intention.

39. Neitzsche, *UM*, 1:34–35.

40. Freud, *Group Psychology and the Analysis of the Ego* (1920), SE 18:116.

41. See Holt, "Freud's Adolescent Reading," 185–89.

42. See Stern, Introduction to *UM*, xiv.

43. Nietzsche quoted in Hayman, *Nietzsche*, 162.

44. Nietzsche, *Ecce Homo*, in *Basic Writings of Nietzsche*, trans. Walter Kaufmann (New York: Random House, 1968), "Why I Am So Wise," sec. 7. Hereafter *EH*.

45. See Pletsch, *Young Nietzsche*, 164–67.

46. See McGrath, *Dionysian Art*, 62.

47. Nietzsche, "On the Uses and Disadvantages of History for Life" (1874), in *UM*, 2:62.

48. Ibid., 63.

49. Nietzsche, *WP*, n.492.

50. *UM*, 2:67.

51. Nietzsche, *On the Genealogy of Morals*, in *Basic Writings*, 3, sec. 17.

52. Nietzsche, *UM*, 2:89.

53. Ibid., 94.

54. Ibid.

55. See McGrath, *Dionysian Art*, 70.

56. Ibid., 64.

57. Nietzsche, "Schopenhauer as Educator" (1874), in *UM*, 3:152.

58. See Rudnytsky, *Freud and Oedipus*, 9.

59. Ernst L. Freud, ed., *Letters of Sigmund Freud*, trans. Tania and James Stern (New York: Basic Books, 1960), 140–41.

60. Masson, *Letters*, 398.

61. Ibid.

## CHAPTER 3. 1878–1884

1. There is also a fourth essay in *Untimely Meditations*, "Richard Wagner in Bayreuth" (1876), which will not be discussed in this study.

2. According to Hollingdale, part 1 and part 2 were published in 1883, part 3 in 1884, part 4 issued privately in 1885 and publicly in 1892 as part of the first collected edition of Nietzsche's works. Parts 1, 2, and 3 were reissued as a single volume in 1887; see R. J. Hollingdale, *Nietzsche* (Boston: Ark Paperbacks, 1985), xi.

3. Nietzsche, *Human, All Too Human* (1878–1880), trans. R. J. Hollingdale (New York: Cambridge University Press, 1986), 1, sec. 1.

4. Ibid., 1, sec. 13.

5. Ibid., 1, sec. 57.

6. Ibid., 1, sec. 99.

7. Ibid., 1, sec. 107.

8. Ibid., 1, sec. 169.

9. Ibid., 2, pt. 1, sec. 37.

10. Ibid., sec. 76.

11. Ibid., pt. 2, sec. 52.

12. Ibid., sec. 194.

13. Ibid., sec. 297.

14. Nietzsche, *Daybreak* (1881), trans. R. J. Hollingdale (New York: Cambridge University Press, 1982), sec. 119.

15. Ibid., sec. 129.

16. Ibid., sec. 133.

17. Hollingdale states: "This theory of the emotions is not so much an anticipation as a complete statement of the well-known theory subsequently propounded by William James and Carl Lange: the theory that our emotions are our awareness of our physical reactions to events—that we

feel afraid, for instance, because we are trembling, and not the other way round" (Hollingdale, *Nietzsche* [1973], 183). Also, compare Nietzsche's statement with the definition offered by a prominent analyst and authority on empathy: "A given affective expression by a member of a particular species . . . This is done through the promotion of an unconscious, automatic, and in adults not necessarily obvious, imitation of the sender's bodily state and facial expression by the receiver. This then generates in the receiver the autonomic response associated with that bodily state and facial expression which is to say the receiver experiences an affect identical with that of the sender" (Michael Franz Basch, "Empathetic Understanding: A Review of the Concept and Some Theoretical Considerations," *Journal of the American Psychoanalytic Association* 31, no. 1 [1983]: 108).

18. Nietzsche, *Daybreak*, sec. 142.

19. Ibid., sec. 312.

20. Nietzsche, *The Gay Science* (1882; 2nd ed. 1887), trans. Walter Kaufmann (New York: Vintage Books, 1974), sec. 11.

21. Ibid., sec. 13.

22. Ibid., sec. 200.

23. Ibid., sec. 319.

24. Ibid., sec. 333.

25. Ibid., sec. 335.

26. Ibid., 2nd ed., 5, sec. 360.

27. Nietzsche, *Human*, 1, sec. 37.

28. Freud, "Recommendations to Physicians Practicing Psycho-Analysis" (1912), SE 12:115.

29. Ibid., 114.

30. See Trosman, *Freud*, 25–49.

31. Freud quoted in Jones, *Life and Work*, 3:41.

32. See Trosman, *Freud*, 25–49.

33. See Anzieu, *Freud's Self-Analysis*, 57.

34. See M. S. Silk and J. P. Stern, *Nietzsche on Tragedy* (New York: Cambridge University Press, 1981), 207, 415.

35. Ibid., 217, 415.

36. Ibid., 207.

37. Ibid., 105.

38. Jacob Bernays, *Die Heraklitischen Briefe: ein Beitrag zur philosophischen und religionsgeschichtlichen Litteratur* (Berlin: W. Hertz; London: Williams und Norgate, 1869).

39. Nietzsche, *Tragedy*, sec. 24.

40. See E. Freud, *Letters of Freud and Zweig*, 48.

41. Ibid., 33.

42. Ibid., 23.

43. Ibid., 52.

44. See Herschmüller, *Breuer*, 155–59; Yosef Hayim Yerushalmi, *Freud's Moses* (New Haven: Yale University Press, 1991), 47.

45. McGrath, *Freud's Discovery*, 145. For an important discussion of Freud's exposure to the ideas of Johann Friedrich Herbart (1776–1841) on repression and unconscious mental functioning, first through a text Freud read in his last year at the Gymnasium and later through the influence of Fechner and Griesinger on Meynert (and Breuer) see Jones, *Life and Work*, 1, 371–77.

46. Trosman, *Freud*, 43–44.

47. See R. K. Gupta, "Freud and Schopenhauer," *Journal of the History of Ideas* 36, no. 4 (October–December 1975): 721–28.

48. E. Freud, *Letters of Freud and Zweig*, 78. It was in early 1884 that Freud entered the hospital's Department of Nervous Diseases.

49. Förster-Nietzsche, *Nietzsche*, 2:481–93. There are two versions of these letters edited by Förster-Nietzsche. In a second printing of the volume in which they are included, also dated 1904 and spanning the same page numbers, Förster-Neitzsche modified what she originally included of the letters. It appears that in this second version the alterations may have been made in the service of enhancing the image of Nietzsche as a more exalted, prophetic figure and minimizing the simple, cordial and friendly relationship that seems to have developed between Paneth and Nietzsche.

50. Krummel, "Dokumentation: Joseph Paneth."

51. Ibid., 483.

52. See Sander L. Gilman, *Sexuality: An Illustrated History* (New York: John Wiley & Sons, 1989), 278.

53. Krummel, "Dokumentation: Joseph Paneth," 488.

54. Ibid., 482n. 9.

55. Ibid., 486.

56. Ibid., 495.

57. Förster-Nietzsche, *Nietzsche*, 2:474.

58. See Krummel, "Dokumentation: Joseph Paneth," 490.

59. Ibid., 486.

60. Ibid., 493.

61. Ibid., 490.

62. Ibid., 494.

63. Ibid., 481.

64. Ibid., 488.

65. Ibid., 495.

66. Paneth quoted in Walter Kaufmann, *From Shakespeare to Existentialism* (New York: Anchor Books, 1960), 324.

67. Freud, *ID*, SE 5:423, 425.

68. See E. Freud, *Letters of Freud and Zweig*, 78.

69. See Elizabeth Förster-Nietzsche, *The Life of Nietzsche*, 2 vols. (New York: Sturgis and Walton Co., 1915), 2:196.

70. See Gunter Godde, "Freuds philosophische Diskussionskreise in der Studentenzeit," *Jarbuch der Psychoanalyse*, 27 (1991): 73–113.

71. Freud, "Psychoanalytic Notes on an Autobiographical Account of a Case of Paranoia" (1911), SE 12:54.

72. Nietzsche, *Thus Spoke Zarathustra* (1883–1885), in *The Portable Nietzsche*, trans. Walter Kaufmann (New York: The Viking Press, 1954), 121–439.

73. Freud, "Some Character Types Met with in Psychoanalytic Work" (1916), SE 14:309–33.

74. See Nietzsche, *Zarathustra*, 1, "On the Despisers of the Body."

75. Nietzsche, *Daybreak*, sec. 128.

76. Rudnytsky, *Freud and Oedipus*, 204.

77. There are interesting implications to consider relating to the fact that Jocasta states that forbidden oedipal wishes directly expressed in dreams are not at all an uncommon occurrence.

78. See Zimmermann, *Greek Tragedy*, 72–73.

79. See Young, *Nietzsche's Philosophy of Art*, 66–67.

80. Nietzsche, *Human*, 1, sec. 1.

## CHAPTER 4. THE MID-1880S THROUGH THE MID-1890S

1. See Malcolm Macmillan, "The Sources of Freud's Methods for Gathering and Evaluating Clinical Data," in *Freud and the History of Psychoanalysis*, ed. Toby Gelfand and John Kerr (Hillsdale, New Jersey: The Analytic Press, 1992), 99–100, 108–9.

2. Freud, "On the Psychical Mechanism of Hysterical Phenomena. A Lecture" (1893), SE 3:35.

3. See Macmillan, "Sources of Freud's Methods," 116. In 1885 and 1886, when Freud was studying with Charcot, Nietzsche's writings were not widely known in France. The great interest in Nietzsche in France would begin in the early 1890s (see Christopher E. Forth, "Nietzsche, Decadence, and Regeneration in France, 1891–95," *Journal of the History of Ideas* 54, no. 1 (January 1993): 97–117.

4. Macmillan, "Sources of Freud's Methods," 131.

5. Ibid., 114.

6. Ibid., 121.

7. Ibid., 125. For a comprehensive examination of scientific influences on Freud during this period see Malcolm Macmillan, *Freud Evaluated: The Completed Arc* (Amsterdam: North-Holland, 1991), 10–231.

8. See Rosemarie Sand, "Pre-Freudian Discovery of Dream Meaning: The Achievements of Charcot, Janet, and Krafft-Ebing," in *Freud and the History of Psychoanalysis*, ed. Toby Gelfand and John Kerr (Hillsdale, New Jersey: The Analytic Press, 1992), 215–29.

9. Pierre Janet, *Psychological Healing: A Historical and Clinical*

*Study*, 2 vols., trans. Eden and Cedar Paul (New York: Ruskin House, The Macmillan Co., 1925), 1:606.

10. Ibid. See also Sulloway, *Freud*, 322–23. It should also be noted that in the 1880s and 1890s Janet wrote of the significance of traumatic memories and of how in certain psychopathological conditions mental processes could become subconscious, that is, split off from the mainstream or primary consciousness. There is a good deal in Janet's work that probably influenced Freud. See Campbell Perry and Jean-Roch Laurence, "Mental Processing Outside of Awareness," in *The Unconscious Reconsidered*, ed. Kenneth S. Bowers and Donald Meichenbaum (New York: John Wiley, 1984), 9–48; Ellenberger, *Discovery*, 372–74, 406–9, 385–90, 539–40.

11. Nietzsche, *Human*, 2, pt. 1, sec. 37. For a discussion of Nietzsche's views of the role of memory in the development of *ressentiment* see Claudia Crawford, "Nietzsche's Mnemotechnics, the Theory of Ressentiment, and Freud's Topographies," *Nietzsche-Studien* 14 (1985): 281–97. For Nietzsche "pain is the most powerful aid to mnemonics," "only that which never ceases to *hurt* stays in memory" (*Genealogy*, 2, sec. 3). Crawford points out that for Nietzsche "the slave, who is not able to act is also not able to forget" (288).

12. See Edwin R. Wallace IV, "Freud and the Mind-Body Problem," in *Freud and the History of Psychoanalysis*, ed. Toby Gelfand and John Kerr (Hillsdale, New Jersey: The Analytic Press, 1992), 231–69.

13. Freud, "Preface to the Translation of Bernheim's *Suggestion*" (1888), SE 1:75–85.

14. Wallace, "Freud, Mind-Body," 242.

15. Ibid., 250.

16. Nietzsche, *Gay Science*, sec. 127.

17. William J. McGrath, "Freud and the Force of History," in *Freud and the History of Psychoanalysis*, ed. Toby Gelfand and John Kerr (Hillsdale, New Jersey: The Analytic Press, 1992), 94–95.

18. See Ellenberger, *Discovery*, 271, 276–77.

19. Freud, "Some Points for a Comparative Study of Organic and Hysterical Motor Paralyses" (1893), SE 1:155–72.

20. Frederic Morton, *A Nervous Splendor: Vienna 1888/1889* (London: George Weidenfeld and Nicolson Limited, 1979), 203–5.

21. See Anzieu, *Freud's Self-Analysis*, 79–84.

22. See Richard Hinton Thomas, *Nietzsche in German Politics and Society, 1890–1918* (Manchester: Manchester University Press, 1983); Aschheim, *Nietzsche Legacy.*

23. See Hollingdale, *Nietzsche* (1985), xii.

24. Lou Andreas-Salomé, *Friedrich Nietzsche in seinen Werken* (Vienna: Carl Konegen, 1894); Förster-Nietzsche, *Nietzsche*, 1.

25. Nietzsche, *Beyond Good and Evil*, in *Basic Writings*, sec. 23. Hereafter *BGE.*

26. Ibid., sec. 32

27. Ibid., sec. 68. The "Rat Man" brought this passage to Freud's attention, and Freud expressed his admiration for Nietzsche's formulation; see Freud, "Notes upon a Case of Obsessional Neurosis (1909)," SE 10:184. See also Freud, *The Psychopathology of Everyday Life* (1901), SE 6:146.

28. Nietzsche, *BGE*, sec. 75.

29. Ibid., sec. 189.

30. Nietzsche, *Genealogy*, 2, sec. 1; Freud quoted in Perry and Laurence, "Mental Processing Outside Awareness," 22–23. Essay 2, sec. 1, of the *Genealogy* warrants careful reading for its relationship to psychoanalytic concerns. It is in line with the analyst Morris Eagle's comment that "in certain circumstances, repression of certain mental contents may be necessary in order to preserve the subjective experience of unity of consciousness and self" ("Psychoanalysis and the Personal," in *Mind Psychoanalysis and Science*, ed. Peter, Clark and Crispin Wright [New York: Basil Blackwell, 1988], 104).

31. Nietzsche, *Genealogy*, 2, sec. 16.

32. Ibid., sec. 17.

33. See Pletsch, *Young Nietzsche*, 202.

34. Nietzsche, *Gay Science*, sec. 99; Williams, *Shame and Necessity*, 9.

35. Nietzsche quoted in Mandel, Introduction to *Friedrich Nietzsche*, xxxiv.

36. Nietzsche, *Human*, 1, sec. 475.

37. See Nietzsche's letter to Overbeck in Kaufmann, *Portable Nietzsche*, 687.

38. Duffy and Mittelman examine Nietzsche's attitude towards Jews, noting his overall positive sentiments with the major exception of those developments leading to Christianity (see Michael F. Duffy and Willard Mittelman, "Nietzsche's Attitude towards the Jews," *Journal of the History of Ideas* 49, no. 2 [April-June 1988]: 301–17). Arnold M. Eisen finds in much of Nietzsche's writings a disturbing subtext hostile towards Jews. It appears that at the core of his belief and argument is the unfounded speculation that Nietzsche's "lavish praise of contemporary Jewry" is "compensation for his equally excessive condemnation of Judaism" ("Nietzsche and the Jews Reconsidered," *Jewish Social Studies* 48, no. 1 [Winter 1986]: 11). Sander Gilman also diminishes the genuiness of Nietzsche's appreciation and admiration of Jews and Judaism, referring to Nietzsche as not a philo-semite, but merely an anti-anti-semite who sees Jews in positive terms only to the extent that they are the target of Christian antisemitism ("Nietzsche, Heine, and the Otherness of the Jew," in *Studies in Nietzsche and the Judeo-Christian Tradition*, ed. James C. O'Flaherty, Timothy E. Sellner and Robert M. Helm [Chapel Hill: The University of North Carolina Press, 1985], 206–25). In a more recent work, Gilman's analysis of Nietzsche's attitude towards the Jews and Judaism ignores Nietzsche's comments on the positive contributions of European Jews to western civilization (*Freud, Race, and Gender* [Princeton: Princeton University Press, 1993], 150–52). Gilman's erudite works are filled with useful information and helpful insights on Nietzsche and Freud, but at times he attempts to utilize a few central ideas (such as the relationship to the "Other" and the mechanism of projection) to explain much more than they can account for and to greatly simplify material in an attempt to have it fit such constructs. No explaining away of Nietzsche's admiration of Jews is offered by Robert Wistrich in his history of antisemitism (*Antisemitism: The Longest Hatred* [New York: Pantheon Books, 1991], 54–65). On the ways in which Nietzsche's ideas were distorted by conservative German ideology see Fritz Stern, *The Politics of Cultural Despair: A Study in the Rise of the Germanic Ideology* (Berkeley: University of California Press, 1974), 283–89. For an overview which implicates Nietzsche in antisemitic ideology, see Aschheim, *Nietzsche Legacy*, 323–30.

39. Nietzsche, *BGE*, sec. 52.

40. Ibid., sec. 251.

41. Nietzsche, *Genealogy*, 3, sec. 22.

42. Nietzsche, *The Antichrist*, in *Portable Nietzsche*, sec. 45.

43. Sander L. Gilman, "Constructing the Image of the Appropriate Therapist: The Struggle of Psychiatry with Psychoanalysis," in *Freud in*

*Exile,* ed. Edward Timms and Naomi Segal (New Haven: Yale University Press, 1988), 22.

44. Nietzsche, *Gay Science,* sec. 348.

45. See Robert S. Wistrich, *The Jews of Vienna in the Age of Franz Joseph* (New York: Oxford Unversity Press, 1989), 554.

46. See Paul Lawrence Rose, *Revolutionary Antisemitism in Germany from Kant to Wagner* (Princeton: Princeton University Press, 1990); Aschheim, *Nietzsche Legacy,* 93–112.

47. See Nietzsche, *Twilight of the Idols,* in *Portable Nietzsche,* "Preface"; "Maxims and Arrows," sec. 35.

48. Ibid., "Morality as Anti-Nature," sec. 1.

49. Ibid., sec. 3.

50. Nietzsche, *Antichrist,* sec. 55.

51. Ibid., sec. 47.

52. Ibid.

53. Ibid.

54. Ibid., sec. 42. The biblical scholar Paula Fredriksen writes: "About Jesus of Nazareth Paul evinces little interest . . . Paul sees Jesus' significance and status as eschatological redeemer granted not in his biography . . . but in his resurrection" (Paula Fredriksen, *From Jesus to Christ* [New Haven: Yale University Press, 1988], 174). In a quite different context Alan F. Segal writes that "for Paul . . . the revelatory vision of Christ functions as a bid for power" (Alan F. Segal, *Paul the Convert* [New Haven: Yale University Press, 1990], 16). For a recent psychological analysis of Paul, see A. N. Wilson, *Jesus* (New York: W. W. Norton & Co., 1992), 17–43.

55. See Boehlich, *Letters,* 70, 96; Holt, "Freud's Adolescent Readings."

56. Nietzsche, *Nietzsche Contra Wagner,* in *Portable Nietzsche,* "We Antipodes."

57. See Paul C. Vitz, *Sigmund Freud's Christian Unconscious* (New York: The Guilford Press, 1988), 161–65.

58. See Harry Trosman and Roger Dennis Simmons, "The Freud Library," *Journal of the American Psychoanalytic Association* 21 (1973): 646–87.

59. See Lisa Appignanesi and John Forrester, *Freud's Women* (New York: Basic Books, 1992), 256; Ernst Pfeiffer, ed., *Sigmund Freud and Lou Andreas-Salomé: Letters*, trans. William and Elaine Robson-Scott (New York: W. W. Norton & Co., 1985), 211.

60. Anzieu, *Freud's Self-Analysis*, 118; Anna Freud, quoted in Appignanesi and Forrester, *Freud's Women*, 253.

61. Grinstein, *Freud at Crossroads*.

62. Ibid., 537–48.

63. Ibid., 431.

64. Ibid., 447.

65. Edith W. Clowes, "The Integration of Nietzsche's Ideas of History, Time and 'Higher Nature' in the Early Historical Novels of Dimitry Merezhkovsky," *Germano-Slavica: A Canadian Journal of Germanic and Slavic Comparative Studies* 3, no. 6 (Fall 1981): 401.

66. Merejkowski quoted by Clowes, "Integration of Nietzsche's Ideas," 403.

67. See Nietzsche, *Human*, 2, pt. 2, sec. 109.

68. See Nietzsche, *WP*, n. 1021.

69. See Krummel, "Dokumentation: Joseph Paneth," 490.

70. J. M. Lindsay, *Gottfried Keller: Life and Works* (Chester Springs, PA: Dufour Press, 1969), 88.

71. Grinstein, *Freud at Crossroads*, 318.

72. Freud, "The Neuro-Psychoses of Defense" (1894), SE 3:60.

73. See James Strachey, Appendix to "The Neuro-Psychoses of Defense," SE 3:62–68.

74. Ellenberger, *Discovery*, 273.

75. Nietzsche, *Gay Science*, sec. 360.

76. See Freud, "Neuro-Psychoses of Defense," SE 3:46–47.

77. Clement Rosset, *Joyful Cruelty* (New York: Oxford University Press, 1993), 59. For a discussion of the relationship of Nietzsche's ideas of *ressentiment* and bad conscience to Freud's neuro-psychological work of the mid-1890s, see Claudia Crawford, "Nietzsche's Mnemotechnics."

78. Rudnytsky points out the factual error: "In the *Odyssey*, Odysseus has his ears unsealed as, tied to the mast, he listens to the Siren's song. This slip [is] doubtless caused by an association of the Sirens with the character of Papageno in Mozart's *The Magic Flute*" (*Freud and Oedipus*, 210).

79. Nietzsche, *BGE*, sec. 230. For a discussion of Nietzsche's influence in Germany (and beyond) during the last decade of the nineteenth century and the first years of the twentiety century, see the first four chapters of Aschheim, *Nietzsche Legacy*.

CHAPTER 5. THE LATE 1890S: THE PERIOD OF
SELF-ANALYSIS AND *THE INTERPRETATION OF DREAMS*

1. Masson, *Letters*, 202.

2. See Chessick, "Nietzsche, Freud, Kohut," 361.

3. See Masson, *Letters*, 398.

4. See Grinstein, *Freud at Crossroads*, 135.

5. Masson, *Letters*, 252.

6. See Kim R. Holmes, "Freud, Evolution, and the Tragedy of Man," *Journal of the American Psychoanalytic Association* 31, no. 1 (1983): 193–97.

7. Nietzsche, *Genealogy*, 2, sec. 17.

8. Ibid., sec. 28.

9. Nietzsche, *Zarathustra*, 1, "On the Three Metamorphoses."

10. Masson, *Letters*, 239.

11. See Nietzsche, *Genealogy*, 3, sec. 8.

12. Walter Kaufmann, *Nietzsche: Philosopher, Psychologist, Antichrist*, 4th ed. (Princeton: Princeton University Press, 1974), 219.

13. Ibid., 223.

14. Masson, *Letters*, 249.

15. See Nunberg and Federn, *Minutes*, 1:359.

16. Freud, *Group Psychology*, SE 18:123.

17. See Alexander Nehamas, *Nietzsche: Life as Literature* (Cambridge: Harvard University Press, 1985), 111.

18. Nietzsche, *BGE*, sec. 260.

19. See Masson, *Letters*, 243.

20. Ibid., 266.

21. Jones, *Life and Work*, 1:356.

22. Nietzsche originally planned a four-volume work with the title *Revaluation of All Values* but completed only the preface and the first essay, *The Antichrist* (see Kaufmann, *Portable Nietzsche*, 565). Magnus, Stewart and Mileur point out that from November 1888 *The Antichrist* is conceived as the title of the planned major work (see Bernard Magnus, Stanley Stewart and Jean-Piere Mileur, *Nietzsche's Case* [New York: Routledge, 1993], 44).

23. Freud, *ID*, SE 4:330

24. Freud, *On Dreams* (1901), SE 5:655.

25. See Masson, *Letters*, 270–73. Two years earlier, on October 15, 1895, Freud announced to Fliess that "hysteria is a consequence of a presexual *sexual shock*. Obsessional neurosis is the consequence of a presexual *sexual pleasure*, which is later transformed into [self-] *reproach*. *'Presexual'* means actually before puberty . . . the relevant events become effective only as *memories*" (Masson, *Letters*, 144).

26. Ibid., 278–79.

27. Ibid., 281.

28. Ibid., 282n. 2.

29. Ibid., 279.

30. Ibid., 280.

31. Nietzsche, *Genealogy*, 2, sec. 7.

32. See Rudolph Binion, *Frau Lou* (Princeton: Princeton University Press, 1968); Lou Andreas-Salomé, "'Anal' and 'Sexual,'" *Imago* 4, no. 5 (1916): 249–73; Elizabeth Young-Bruehl, *Anna Freud* (New York: Summit Books, 1988), 27; Freud, "On Transformations of Instinct as Exemplified in Anal Eroticism" (1917), SE 17:125–39.

33. Nietzsche, *Genealogy*, 2, sec. 1.

34. See James Strachey, Preface to *Totem and Taboo* (1913), SE 13:x.

35. See Wallace, *Freud and Anthropology*, 5–57.

36. Masson, *Letters*, 325.

37. Theodor Lipps, *Grundtatsachen des Seelenlebens* (Bonn: Max Cohen, 1883).

38. See Trosman, *Freud*, 55–69.

39. See Jones, *Life and Work*, 3:131.

40. Masson, *Letters*, 365.

41. Nunberg and Federn, *Minutes*, 1, 359.

42. Freud quoted in Gay, *Freud*, 46.

43. Masson, *Letters*, 398.

44. Ibid. As I was completing this study, I came across these words of Carlo Strenger: "The moving moments of analyses are those in which the patient's experience of mute pain fuses with the words he never found" (*Between Hermeneutics and Science* [Madison CT: International Universities Press, 1991], 211).

45. Trosman and Simmons, *Freud Library*, 655.

46. Masson, *Letters*, 405.

47. Ibid., 406. In regard to Freud's use of Christian terms and imagery see Vitz, *Freud's Christian Unconscious*.

48. Masson, *Letters*, 406–7.

49. Georg Brandes, *Friedrich Nietzsche* (New York: Haskell House Publishers, 1972 [1889–1900]), 3.

50. See Ernst Pfeiffer, Notes to *Looking Back* by Lou Andreas-Salomé (New York: Paragon House, 1991), 178–79.

51. See Frank Field, *The Last Days of Mankind: Karl Kraus and His Vienna* (New York: St. Martin's Press, 1967), 22.

52. Brandes, *Nietzsche*, 103. Although Brandes did not have an appreciation of psychoanalysis, he was favorably impressed by Freud when the two met in 1925 (see Masson, *Letters*, 407n. 6). The young Martin Buber (1878–1965) was one of many Jews from a wide range of backgrounds and interests who were deeply influenced by Nietzsche. In his 1900 eulogy he

wrote of Nietzsche as one of the "apostles of life" who brought "the God of becoming, in whose development we may share" (quoted in Aschheim, *Nietzsche Legacy*, 106).

53. Freud, *ID*, SE 4:330.

54. Freud, *ID*, SE 5:608. In *On Dreams* Freud states that "what I have called dream-displacement might be described (in Nietzsche's phrase) as 'a transvaluation of values'" (SE 5:654–55).

55. Nietzsche, *Tragedy*, sec. 4. On Nietzsche's use of the two terms, *transvaluation of values* and *revaluation of values*, see Robert Solomon, *From Hegel to Existentialism* (New York: Oxford University Press, 1987), 92.

56. Nietzsche, *Human*, 1, sec. 13.

57. Nietzsche quoted in Leslie Paul Thiele, *Friedrich Nietzsche and the Politics of the Soul* (Princeton: Princeton University Press, 1990), 57.

58. Freud, *ID*, SE 5:608.

59. Ibid., 567.

60. Nietzsche, *Human*, 2, pt. 1, sec. 76.

61. Nietzsche, *Tragedy*, sec. 1.

62. Freud, *ID*, SE 5:513.

63. Nietzsche, *Human*, 1, sec. 13.

64. Jacob Golumb, *Nietzsche's Enticing Psychology of Power* (Ames: Iowa State University Press, 1987), 155.

65. See Freud, *ID*, SE 4:232.

66. Ibid., 279–304.

67. Ibid., 306.

68. Golumb, *Nietzsche's Psychology*, 152.

69. Nietzsche, *Human*, 1, sec. 12.

70. Ibid.

71. Ibid., II, pt. 1, sec. 76.

72. See Nietzsche, *Daybreak*, sec. 128.

73. See Golumb, *Nietzsche's Psychology*, 157.

74. Nietzsche, *Daybreak*, sec. 119.

75. Nietzsche, *Human*, 2, pt. 2, sec. 194.

76. Freud, *ID*, SE 5:599.

77. Ibid., SE 4:144. But see SE 23:169–70.

78. Nietzsche, *Gay Science*, sec. 8.

79. See Freud, *ID*, SE 5:598–604, 610–11.

80. J. Allen Hobson, quoted by Richard Restak, *The Brain Has a Mind of Its Own* (New York: Harmony Books, 1991), 79. But see SE 4:126–27.

81. Nietzsche, *Daybreak*, sec. 128.

82. See Freud, *ID*, SE 4:106–30.

83. See Adolf Grünbaum, *The Foundations of Psychoanalysis* (Berkeley: University of California Press, 1984), 220–31. Of course Freud was aware of other levels of interpretation of the dream. For a discussion of Freud's analysis of the dream that contrasts sharply with the approach of Grünbaum and argues for a "Freudian" approach to establishing causal linkages that differs from Grünbaum, see James Hopkins, "*The Interpretation of Dreams*," in *The Cambridge Companion to Freud*, ed. Jerome Neu (New York: Cambridge University Press, 1992), 86–135.

84. Nietzsche, *Daybreak*, sec. 312.

85. Freud, *ID*, SE 4:262.

86. Ibid., SE 5:548–49.

87. Nietzsche, *Human*, 1, sec. 147.

88. Nietzsche, *Daybreak*, sec. 119.

89. Ibid.

90. Masson, *Letters*, 365.

91. Ibid., 249.

92. Ibid., 239.

93. Ibid., 266, 278–81.

94. Ibid., 280.

95. Ibid., 272

96. Rudnytsky, *Freud and Oedipus*, 205; *The Merriam Webster Dictionary*, ed. Henry Bosley (New York: Pocket Books, 1974), 550.

97. Montague Ullman and Nan Zimmerman, *Working with Dreams* (Los Angeles: Jeremy P. Tarcher, Inc., 1979), 31.

98. Ibid., 29.

99. Ibid., 9.

100. Ibid., 12.

101. Ibid., 9.

102. Ibid., 31.

103. Ibid., 8.

104. Nietzsche, *Tragedy*, sec. 4.

105. Nietzsche, *Human*, 2, pt. 1, sec. 76.

106. Nietzsche, *Tragedy*, sec. 1.

107. Nietzsche, *Human*, 2, pt. 2, sec. 194.

108. Nietzsche, *Daybreak*, sec. 128.

109. Ibid., sec. 119.

110. Charles Rycroft, *The Innocence of Dreams* (New York: Pantheon Books, 1979).

111. Charles Rycroft, *Psychoanalysis and Beyond*, ed. Peter Fuller (Chicago: The University of Chicago Press, 1985), 90.

112. Rycroft, *Dreams*, 13, 71.

113. Ibid., 72.

114. Ibid., 19.

115. Ibid., 5.

116. Ibid., 48.

117. Ibid., 54.

118. Ibid., 7.

119. Ibid., 20.

120. See Freud, *The Ego and the Id* (1923), SE 19:23n. 3. See Nietzsche, *BGE*, sec. 17, on the "It" and the "I".

121. Nietzsche, *Zarathustra*, 1, "On the Despisers of the Body."

122. On the ancient idea of dreams as the voice of God, see Ullman and Zimmerman, *Dreams*, 36.

123. Nietzsche, *Zarathustra*, 1, "On the Despisers of the Body." See Alan White, *Within Nietzsche's Labyrinth* (New York: Routledge, 1990), 72–80.

124. Nietzsche, *UM*, 2:108.

125. See Freud, *ID*, SE 5:341.

126. See Nietzsche, *Daybreak*, sec. 119.

127. See Nietzsche, *Gay Science*, sec. 360.

128. Nietzsche, *Tragedy*, sec. 4.

129. Ibid., sec. 1.

130. Freud, *ID*, SE 5:507.

131. Ibid., 505–6.

132. Nietzsche, "On Truth and Lying in an Extra-Moral Sense" (1873), in *Friedrich Nietzsche on Rhetoric and Language*, ed. and trans. Sander L. Gilman, Carole Blair and David J. Parent (New York: Oxford University Press, 1989), 254–55.

133. Oliver Sacks, "The Last Hippie," *New York Review of Books*, 26 March 1992, 58n. 10.

134. Nietzsche, "Truth and Lying," 254.

CHAPTER 6. "NON VIXIT"

1. Freud, *ID*, SE 5:421.

2. Alexander Grinstein, *Sigmund Freud's Dreams*, 2nd ed. (New York: International Universities Press, 1980), 282–316; Anzieu, *Freud's Self-Analysis*, 375–88.

3. See Grinstein, *Freud's Dreams*, 311.

4. See Anzieu, *Freud's Self-Analysis*, 377.

5. See Lucille B. Ritvo, *Darwin's Influence on Freud* (New Haven: Yale University Press, 1990), 105–6.

6. See Anzieu, *Freud's Self-Analysis*, 377.

7. Freud, *ID*, SE 5:423. The correct word here was *publicae* rather than *patriae*. For a discussion of the word substitution see Grinstein, *Freud's Dreams*, 285-86.

8. See Grinstein, *Freud's Dreams*, 164–65; Anzieu, *Freud's Self-Analysis*, 367.

9. See Masson, *Letters*, 325–29.

10. Freud, *ID*, SE 5:485.

11. See Anzieu, *Freud's Self-Analysis*, 383. Freud's public portrayal of Paneth in this light (he was recognizable enough to some) led to "the termination of the friendship of a dear friend who felt hurt by the mention of her husband in the non vixit dream" (Masson, *Letters*, 383).

12. Ibid., 380.

13. Freud, *ID*, SE 5:425.

14. Ibid.

15. Ibid., 513.

16. Ibid., 484.

17. Ibid., 423

18. See Anzieu, *Freud's Self-Analysis*, 383.

19. See Freud, *ID*, SE 5:422.

20. In addition to "Non Vixit," there is another dream "Riding a Horse to a Chapel," dreamt around the same time, in which a Dr. "P" is seen riding high on his horse while Freud at first is riding timidly. A theme emerges of Freud feeling displaced by "P" who took over the treatment of a young woman Freud had been treating. There is no agreement on the identity of P, but the experts on these matters seem to think it is not Paneth.

21. Freud, *An Autobiographical Study* (1925), SE 20:9–10.

22. See E. Freud, *Letters*, 87.

23. See Jones, *Life and Work*, 1:140.

24. See Boehlich, *Letters*, 86. According to Grosskurth, with few exceptions, Freud never mentioned Silberstein in his work or correspondence after their correspondence ended (Phyllis Grosskurth, *The Secret Ring: Freud's Inner Circle and the Politics of Psychoanalysis* [Reading Massachusetts: Addison-Wesley, 1991], 3).

25. In fact Paneth would return. The letters regarding Nietzsche that Paneth wrote to his fiancé at the same time he was writing to Freud were published in Förster-Nietzsche's biography in 1904. It would be hard to imagine Freud not becoming aware of this fact. One would imagine that Freud would have been very interested to know how these letters compared with the ones he had received.

26. See Hayman, *Nietzsche,* 349.

27. See Sander L. Gilman, ed., *Conversations with Nietzsche,* trans. David J. Parent (New York: Oxford University Press, 1987), 245.

28. See Hayman, *Nietzsche,* 349. I have not looked into the extent to which such reports appeared specifically in the Vienna press. For useful bibliographies of works on Nietzsche see Richard Frank Krummel, *Nietzsche und der deutsche Geist,* 2 vols. (Berlin, New York: Walter de Gruyter, 1974/1983); Herbert W. Reichert and Karl Schlechta, *International Nietzsche Bibliography* (Chapel Hill: University of North Carolina Press, 1960). Krummel's work follows Nietzsche's reception in Germany through 1918.

29. Quoted in Hayman, *Nietzsche,* 25.

30. See Pletsch, *Young Nietzsche,* 103.

31. Quoted in Gilman, *Conversations,* 246.

32. See E. Freud, *Letters,* 103.

33. Andreas-Salomé quoted in Pfeiffer, Notes to *Looking Back,* 167, n. 47.

34. Mandel, Introduction to *Friedrich Nietzsche,* xliii.

35. Nietzsche, *Nietzsche Contra Wagner,* in *Portable Nietzsche,* 661–83.

36. Ibid., "Preface."

37. Ibid., "The Psychologist Speaks Up."

38. See Vitz, *Freud's Christian Unconscious,* 161–65.

39. See Trosmann and Simmons, *Freud Library,* 675.

40. See Masson, *Letters,* 159, 180.

41. Freud, *ID,* SE 4:212–13; see also SE 4:195–96.

42. McGrath, "Freud and the Force of History," 94.

43. See Godde, "Freuds philosophische Diskussionskreise."

44. William Beatty Warner, *Chance and the Text of Experience* (Ithaca: Cornell University Press, 1986), 106.

45. In 1927, after having met with Einstein the previous year, Freud wrote that Einstein "had had a much easier time than I have. He has had the support of a long series of predecessors from Newton onward while I have had to hack every step of my way through a tangled jungle alone" (quoted in Jones, 3:131).

46. See Freud, "On the History of the Psycho-Analytic Movement" (1914), SE 14:13; "Analysis Terminable and Interminable" (1937), SE 23:245; Nunberg and Federn, *Minutes*, 1:360.

47. Freud, *ID*, SE 5:485.

## CHAPTER 7. MEETINGS OF THE VIENNA PSYCHOANALYTIC SOCIETY

1. Nunberg and Federn, *Minutes*, 1:359. The minutes were taken by Otto Rank who at the time was quite close to and loyal to Freud.

2. See Kaufmann, Preface to *BGE*.

3. George Simmel, *Schopenhauer and Nietzsche*, trans. Helmut Loiskandl, Deena Weinstein and Michael Weinstein (Amherst: The University of Massachusetts Press, 1986 [1907]).

4. Nunberg and Federn, *Minutes*, 1:358.

5. Ibid.

6. Ibid.

7. Ibid., 356.

8. Ibid., 359.

9. Ibid., 361.

10. Ibid., 359–60.

11. Ibid., 360.

12. See *Gay Science*, sec. 360.

13. Nunberg and Federn, *Minutes*, 1:360.

14. Ibid.

15. See E. James Lieberman, *Acts of Will: The Life and Work of Otto Rank* (New York: The Free Press, 1985), 101.

16. Nunberg and Federn, *Minutes*, 1:359.

17. Nietzsche, *Genealogy*, 2, sec. 16.

18. Ibid., 3, sec. 28; I have drawn here upon Maudemarie Clark, *Nietzsche on Truth and Philosophy* (New York: Cambridge University Press, 1990), 159–203.

19. Nietzsche, *Genealogy*, 3, sec. 17.

20. Ibid., sec. 13.

21. Nietzsche, *BGE*, sec. 23.

22. Nietzsche, *Genealogy*, 3, sec. 15.

23. Ibid., sec. 20.

24. Ibid., sec. 19.

25. Ibid., 1, sec. 15n. 1.

26. See Alan White, *Within Nietzsche's Labyrinth* (New York: Routledge, 1990), 53; Nietzsche, *Genealogy*, 3, sec. 10.

27. Nietzsche, *BGE*, sec. 5.

28. Nietzsche, *Genealogy*, 3, sec. 23.

29. Ibid., sec. 24.

30. Ibid.

31. Martin Warner, *Philosophical Finesse: Studies in the Art of Rational Persuasion* (Oxford: Clarendon Press, 1989), 303.

32. Clark, *Nietzsche on Truth*, 272.

33. Ibid., 234.

34. Irwin Z. Hoffman, "Reply to Benjamin," *Psychoanalytic Dialogues* 1, no. 4 (1991): 541.

35. Ibid., 543.

36. Donnell B. Stern, "A Philosophy for the Embedded Analyst: Gadamer's Herneneutics and the Social Paradigm of Psychoanalysis," *Contemporary Psychoanalysis* 27, no. 1 (January 1991): 61.

37. Nietzsche, *Genealogy*, 3, sec. 24.

38. Freud, *New Introductory Lectures on Psychoanalysis* (1933), SE 22:113; Appendix to "Doestoevski and Parracide" (1928), SE 21:196.

39. Hoffman, "Reply," 537.

40. Nietzsche, *Genealogy*, 3, sec. 8.

41. See Young, *Nietzsche's Philosophy of Art*, 126–30.

42. Freud, "'Civilized' Sexual Morality and Modern Nervous Illness" (1908), SE 9:187.

43. See Kaufmann, *Nietzsche*, 222.

44. Nietzsche, *Twilight*, "What I Owe to the Ancients," sec. 4.

45. Nietzsche, *WP*, n.675.

46. See Hollingdale, *Nietzsche* (1973), 110–15.

47. Kaufmann, *Nietzsche*, 235.

48. Freud, "'Civilized' Morality," SE 9:186.

49. Nunberg and Federn, *Minutes*, 2:174.

50. Nietzsche, *Genealogy*, 2, sec. 16.

51. Ibid., sec. 18.

52. See Freud, *Three Essays on the Theory of Sexuality* (1905), SE 7:178, 239, 156, 238. Freud also wrote of sublimation in "Fragment of an Analysis of a Case of Hysteria" (1905 [1901]), SE 7.

53. Gregory Zilboorg, Introduction to *Beyond the Pleasure Principle* (New York: W. W. Norton & Co., 1961 [1920]), viii–ix.

54. Freud, "Instincts and Their Vicissitudes" (1915), SE 14:117–40.

55. Freud., *Three Essays*, SE 7:158.

56. Freud, *Jokes and their Relation to the Unconscious* (1905), SE 8:1–243.

57. Nietzsche, *Gay Science*, sec. 200.

58. Freud, *Jokes*, SE 8:199.

59. Nietzsche, *Human*, 1, sec. 169.

60. Freud, *Humour*, SE 21:162.

61. See Nunberg and Federn, *Minutes*, 1:365–66.

62. Nietzsche, *EH*, "Why I Am a Destiny," sec. 9.

63. See Emanual Rice, *Freud and Moses* (Albany: State University of New York, 1990), 135, 192. A typical family romance fantasy involves the notion that one is the child of parents other than those who are in fact one's parents. The fantasied parents are thought of as noble or exalted in rank or status. Rice's book is a rich resource on Freud's relationship to the figure of Moses.

64. See Nunberg and Federn, *Minutes*, 2:29.

65. Ibid., 30.

66. Ibid., 31.

67. Ibid., 31–32.

68. Ibid., 32.

69. See Jacob Golumb, "Freudian Uses and Misuses of Nietzsche," *American Imago* 37, no. 4 (Winter 1980): 371–85.

70. Ibid., 373–74.

71. Freud, "Notes upon a Case of Obsessional Neurosis" (1909), SE 10:184.

72. Carl Pletsch, "On the Autobiographical Life of Nietzsche," in *Psychoanalytic Studies of Biography*, ed. George Moraites and George H. Pollock (Madison: International Universities Press, 1987), 418.

73. Ibid., 421.

74. Ibid., 413–18.

75. Nietzsche, *EH*, "Why I Am a Destiny," sec. 6.

76. For a discussion of Freud's understanding of comedy and suffering that includes discussion of Nietzsche (although incorrectly reducing Nietzsche's laughter to laughter of the master directed at the slave), see Richard Keller Simon, "Freud's Concepts of Comedy and Suffering," *The Psychoanalytic Review* 64, no. 3 (1977): 391–407.

77. Nietzsche, *EH*, "Why I Write Such Good Books," sec. 5.

78. Nietzsche, *BGE*, sec. 236.

79. See Anzieu, *Freud's Self-Analysis*, 419.

80. Freud, *ID*, SE 5:453.

81. See Claudia Crawford, *"She,"* *Sub-stance* 29 (1981): 83–96.

82. Freud, *ID*, SE 5:454.

## CHAPTER 8. JUNG, ANDREAS-SALOMÉ AND *TOTEM AND TABOO*

1. Freud, *Totem and Taboo: Some Points of Agreement Between the Mental Lives of Savages and Neurotics* (1912–1913), SE 13:1–161.

2. William McGuire, ed., *The Freud/Jung Letters*, trans. Ralph Manheim and R. F. C. Hull (Princeton: Princeton University Press, 1974), 196–97.

3. Ibid., 168.

4. C. G. Jung, *The Psychology of Dementia Praecox* (1907), in *The Collected Works of C.C. Jung*, vol. 3, ed. Sir Herbert Read et al. (Princeton: Princeton University Press, 1972), 1–151.

5. See Herbert Lehman, "Jung Contra Freud/Nietzsche Contra Wagner," *International Review of Psychoanalysis* 13 (1986): 201–9.

6. Jung, "Cryptomnesia" (1905), in T*he Collected Works*, vol. 1, 95–106; see Lehman, *Jung Contra Freud*, 205.

7. See John Kerr, *A Most Dangerous Method. The Story of Jung, Freud, and Sabina Spielrein* (New York: Alfred A. Knopf, 1993), 590.

8. McGuire, *Letters*, 294. In 1907 Jung had also written to Freud of how the somewhat notorious analyst Otto Gross (Jung's patient at the time) linked Freud and Nietzsche on matters of "sexual immorality." Nietzsche had a great impact on Gross (McGuire, *Letters*, 90).

9. It will also be recalled that in *The Romance of Leonardo Da Vinci*, Merejkowski, who was influenced by Nietzsche, wrote of "Dionysus, the Galilaean" and of Christ and Antichrist being one (see Grinstein, *Freud at Crossroads*, 442–43).

10. See McGuire, *Letters*, 296.

11. Quoted in McGuire, *Letters*, 491.

12. Ibid., 492.

13. See Jacob Golumb, "Freudian Uses." On Rank's relationship to Nietzsche see Dennis B. Klein, *Jewish Origins of the Psychoanalytic Movement* (New York: Praeger Publishers, 1981), 103–37.

14. Ibid., 379n. 30.

15. McGuire, *Letters*, 477–80.

16. See Jones, *Life and Work*, 2:86.

17. See Mandel, Introduction to *Friedrich Nietzsche*, x.

18. See Andreas-Salomé, *Looking Back*, 103.

19. McGuire, *Letters*, 477.

20. Hilda C. Abraham and Ernst L. Freud, eds., *A Psycho-Analytic Dialogue: The Letters of Sigmund Freud and Karl Abraham, 1907–1926*, trans. Bernard Marsh and Hilda C. Abraham (New York: Basic Books, 1965), 114.

21. See Linda Donn, *Freud and Jung: Years of Friendship, Years of Loss* (New York: Charles Scribner's Sons, 1988), 162–68; Appignanesi and Forrester, *Freud's Women*, 261.

22. Ernst Pfeiffer, ed., *Sigmund Freud and Lou Andreas-Salomé: Letters*, trans. William and Elaine Robson-Scott (New York: W. W. Norton & Co., 1985 [1972]), 11.

23. Andreas-Salomé, *Looking Back*, 105.

24. See Estelle Roith, *The Riddle of Freud: Jewish Influences on His Theory of Female Sexuality* (New York: Tavistock Publications, 1987), 47–48.

25. Andreas-Salomé quoted in Binion, *Frau Lou*, 377.

26. See Roith, *Riddle*, 40.

27. Pfeiffer, *Freud and Lou*, 191.

28. See Groskurth, *Secret Ring*, 195.

29. See Appignanesi and Forrester, *Freud's Women*, 257.

30. Abram Kardiner, *My Analysis with Freud: Reminiscences* (New York: W. W. Norton & Co., 1977), 77.

31. Freud quoted in Young-Bruehl, *Anna Freud*, 110.

32. Ibid., 112, 117.

33. See Roith, *Riddle*, 42; Binion, *Lou*, 372–73.

34. Pfeiffer, *Freud and Lou*, 127.

35. Freud, "Postscript to the Case of Paranoia" (1911), SE 12:80–82.

36. Ibid., 82.

37. Ibid.

38. Nietzsche, *Human*, 1, sec. 13.

39. Nietzsche, *Daybreak*, sec. 312; see Gilman, *Freud, Race, and Gender*, 141–68.

40. See Freud, *ID*, SE 5:548–49.

41. Andreas-Salomé quoted in Donn, *Freud and Jung*, 166.

42. See Angela Livingstone, *Salomé: Her Life and Work* (Mt. Kisco, New York: Moyer Bell Limited, 1984), 152.

43. See Roith, *Riddle*, 41.

44. Livingstone, *Salomé*, 57.

45. Andreas-Salomé, *The Freud Journal of Lou Andreas-Salomé*, trans. Stanley A. Leavy (New York: Basic Books, 1964), 172.

46. Nietzsche, *WP*, n.639.

47. Nietzsche, *Gay Science*, "Preface for the Second Edition," sec. 2.

48. Andreas-Salomé, *Looking Back*, 53.

49. See Mandel, Introduction to *Nietzsche*, lx.

50. Freud, "The Moses of Michelangelo" (1914), SE 13:233; see Trosman, *Freud*, 188. The significance of the horns (rays of light) for understanding at what point we could see Moses, was brought to my attention by Rabbi Jerome Fishman of Boston (personal communication, 1992).

51. See Trosman, *Freud*, 100, 197–99.

52. Freud, "Moses," SE 13:221, 233.

53. Jung, "A Contribution to the Study of Psychological Types" (1913), *Collected Works*, vol. 6, *Psychological Types*, 499–509; see Golumb, "Freudian Uses," 375.

54. Freud, *Group Psychology*, SE 18:123.

55. See Nietzsche, *Zarathustra*, 4, "The Ass Festival."

56. Freud "On the History of the Psychoanalytic Movement," SE 14:15–16.

57. Freud, "The Theme of the Three Caskets" (1913), SE 12:297.

58. Wallace, *Freud and Anthropology*, 17.

59. Ibid.

60. See Nietzsche, *Daybreak*, sec. 312.

61. Wallace, *Freud and Anthropology*, 16.

62. See Jones, *Life and Work*, 3:283–84.

63. Wallace, *Freud and Anthropology*, 3.

64. See Wallace, *Freud and Anthropology*, 90–96; Ritvo, *Darwin's Influence*, 99–102.

65. See Freud, "A Special Type of Choice of Object Made by Men" (1910), SE 11:174; Bennett Simon and Rachel B. Blass, "The Development and Vicissitudes of Freud's Ideas on the Oedipus Complex," in *Cambridge Companion to Freud*, 163–64.

66. See Wallace, *Freud and Anthropology*, 97–98; Robert A. Paul, "Freud's Anthropology: A Reading of the 'Cultural Books,'" in *Cambridge Companion to Freud*, 267–86. For a summary of objections to Freud's theory of the Oedipus complex from the point of view of some evolutionary psychologists and anthropologists, see Bruce Bower, "Oedipus Wrecked," *Science News* 140 (October 19, 1991): 248–50. On Freud's use of phylogenetic theories see Stephen Jay Gould, "Freud's Phylogenetic Fantasy," *Natural History* 96 (December 1987): 13–19; Ritvo, *Darwin's Influence*, 74–98.

67. See Berliner, *Psychoanalysis and Society*, 68, chap. 6.

68. See Wallace, *Freud and Anthropology*, 102.

69. Freud, *Totem*, 158; Paul, "Freud's Anthropology," 282–83.

70. E. Freud, *Letters of Freud and Zweig*, 23.

71. Freud, *Totem*, SE 13:156.

72. Freud, *Moses and Monotheism*, SE 23:87.

73. Nietzsche quoted in John Sallis, *Crossings: Nietzsche and the Space of Tragedy* (Chicago: The University of Chicago Press, 1991), 89n. 7.

74. Nietzsche, *Tragedy*, sec. 10.

75. Ibid., sec. 17.

76. Ibid., sec. 18.

77. Sallis, *Crossings*, 40.

78. Lenson, "*Birth of Tragedy*," 84.

79. Paul, "Freud's Anthropology," 268.

80. Lawrence J. Hatab, *Myth and Philosophy: A Contest of Truths* (La Salle IL: Open Court, 1990), 136.

81. Nietzsche, *Genealogy*, 2, sec. 17.

82. See Lorin Anderson, "Freud, Nietzsche," *Salmagundi* 47–48 (Winter-Spring 1980): 24.

83. Nietzsche, *Genealogy*, 2, sec. 16.

84. Ibid., sec. 18.

85. Ibid., 3, sec. 11

86. Ibid., 1, sec. 7.

87. See Richard Schacht, "Nietzsche on Human Nature," *History of European Ideas* 11 (1989): 883–92

88. Nietzsche, *Genealogy*, 2, sec. 22.

89. Ibid., sec. 19.

90. Ibid.

91. Nietzsche, *Zarathustra*, 4, "The Ugliest Man."

92. Nietzsche, *Gay Science*, sec. 125.

## CHAPTER 9. "ON NARCISSISM" AND "INSTINCTS AND THEIR VICISSITUDES"

1. See Freud, "On Narcissism: An Introduction" (1914), SE 14: 73–102.

2. Ibid., 75, 100. For a Nietzschean amoeba see *WP*, n.653.

3. Nietzsche, *Human*, 1, sec. 57.

4. Freud, "On Narcissism," SE 14:91.

5. Marcia Cavell, *The Psychoanalytic Mind: From Freud to Philosophy* (Cambridge: Harvard University Press, 1993), 211.

6. Nietzsche, *BGE*, sec. 131.

7. Nietzsche quoted in Jean Graybeal, *Language and "the Feminine" in Nietzsche and Heidegger* (Bloomington: Indiana University Press, 1990), 48.

8. Ibid.

9. Freud, "On Narcissism," SE 14:89.

10. See Young-Bruehl, *Anna Freud*, 27.

11. Sarah Kofman, "Baubô: Theological Perversion and Fetishism," trans. T. Strong, in *Nietzsche's New Seas*, ed. Michael Allen Gillespie and Tracy B. Strong (Chicago: The University of Chicago Press, 1988), 190.

12. Ibid., 200n. 13.

13. Nietzsche, *BGE*, sec. 239.

14. See Sarah Kofman, *The Enigma of Woman: Woman in Freud's Writings*, trans. C. Porter (Ithaca: Cornell University Press, 1985), 52.

15. Jung quoted in Freud, "On Narcissism," SE 14:80.

16. Ibid.

17. See Nietzsche, *Genealogy*, 3, sec. 8.

18. Nietzsche, *Human*, 2, pt. 1, sec. 95.

19. Freud, "On Narcissism," SE 14:85.

20. Ibid., 96.

21. Ibid., 97.

22. See Nietzsche, *Tragedy*, sec. 4.

23. See Freud, *ID*, SE 5:505–6.

24. See Nietzsche, *Genealogy*, 2, sec. 16.

25. Freud, "Instincts and Their Vicissitudes," SE 14:117–40.

26. Freud, *Three Essays*, SE 7:158.

27. See Freud, "Instincts," SE 14:128–29.

28. Terry Eagleton, *The Ideology of the Aesthetic* (Cambridge: Basil Blackwell, 1990), 267.

29. Henry Staten, *Nietzsche's Voice* (Ithaca: Cornell University Press, 1990), 95.

30. Ibid., 98–99.

31. Nietzsche, *Daybreak*, sec. 133.

32. Nietzsche, Ibid.

33. Nietzsche, *Human*, 1, sec. 57.

34. Ibid., 2, pt. 1, sec. 37.

35. See Staten, *Nietzsche's Voice*, 98.

36. Nietzsche, *Daybreak*, sec. 113. A few pages after this passage Nietzsche writes: "We have expended so much labour on learning that external things are not as they appear to us to be—very well! the case is the same with the inner world!" (*Daybreak*, sec. 116). The context of this comment involves Nietzsche's idea that insight into an act does not suffice to ensure performance of the act.

37. Michel Hulin, "Nietzsche and the Suffering of the Indian Ascetic," trans. G. Parkes, in *Nietzsche and Asian Thought*, ed. Graham Parkes (Chicago: The University of Chicago Press, 1991), 65.

38. See Staten, *Nietzsche's Voice*, 99.

39. Freud, *Group Psychology*, SE 18:105.

40. Nietzsche, *WP*, n.657. See also *WP*, n.651.

41. Staten, *Nietzsche's Voice*, 100.

42. Andreas-Salomé, *Freud Journal*, 142–43.

## CHAPTER 10. THE PALE CRIMINAL

1. Freud, "Some Character Types," SE 14:311–33.

2. Ibid., 332.

3. Ibid., 333.

4. See Nietzsche, *Zarathustra*, 1, "On the Despisers of the Body."

5. Nietzsche, *Zarathustra*, 1, "On the Pale Criminal." All quotes from this section are from *The Portable Nietzsche*, 149–51. A useful introduction to "On the Pale Criminal," and upon which I have drawn, is provided by Timothy Gould, "What Makes the Pale Criminal Pale?" *Soundings: An Interdisciplinary Journal* 58, no. 4 (Winter 1985): 510–36.

6. Nietzsche, *WP*, n.234.

7. Nietzsche, *Twilight*, "Maxims and Arrows," sec. 10.

8. Freud, "Mourning and Melancholia" (1917), SE 14:248. A first draft of this paper was written in 1915.

9. Ibid., 251.

10. Ibid., 257.

11. Ibid.

12. Ibid.

13. Ellenberger, *Discovery*, 277.

14. Freud, "The Economic Problem of Masochism" (1924), SE 19:169.

15. Ibid.

16. Ibid., 170.

## CHAPTER 11. *BEYOND THE PLEASURE PRINCIPLE*

1. Freud quoted in Jones, *Life and Work*, 3:194.

2. Freud, "The Uncanny" (1919), SE 17:234.

3. Freud, *Beyond the Pleasure Principle* (1920), SE 18:22.

4. Freud, *ID*, SE 5:548–49. Otto Fenichel also published a Neitzschean-influenced article in 1919 (see Russell Jacoby, *The Repression of Psychoanalysis* [Chicago: The University of Chicago Press, 1986], 55).

5. Freud, *Three Essays*, SE 7:187n. 1.

6. Binion, *Frau Lou*, 353–54. See Andreas-Salomé's March and August 1913 journal entries (*Freud Journal*, 108–11, 163–65); see also her 1921 paper on narcissism ("The Dual Orientation of Narcissism," *The Psychoanalytic Quarterly* 31, no. 1 [January 1962 (1921)]: 3–30). Andreas-Salomé had a positive view of the state of narcissism as a good kind of self-love in which the self is loved along with the world of which it is a part or with which it is in union. She saw much constructive activity as being related to attempts to recreate this kind of relatedness to the world. She also wrote of the possibility of reaching this "guiltless and universal" realm with analysands (see Livingstone, *Salomé*, 159–63, 185–88).

7. See Livingstone, *Salomé*.

8. See Andreas-Salomé, *Freud Journal*, 143.

9. Andreas-Salomé, *Looking Back*, 53.

10. Pfeiffer, *Freud and Lou*, 99. In *Beyond the Pleasure Principle* Freud will write that "we have unwittingly steered our course into the harbor of Schopenhauer's philosophy. For him death is the 'true result and to that extent the purpose of life,' while the sexual instinct is the embodiment of the will to live" (49–50).

11. Gay, *Freud*, 397.

12. Freud, "Analysis of a Phobia in a Five-Year-Old-Boy" (1909), SE 10:140.

13. James Strachey, Introduction to *Civilization and Its Discontents* (1930), SE 21:62.

14. See Gay, *Freud*, 397.

15. Jung quoted in Patrick Mahoney, *Freud as a Writer* (New York: International Universities Press, 1982), 213.

16. Freud, *Beyond Pleasure*, SE 18:60n. 1.

17. Ibid., 52.

18. Ibid., 51.

19. Ibid., 52, 53.

20. Ibid., 60–61n. 1.

21. Ibid., 53.

22. Ibid., 54.

23. Kaufmann, *Nietzsche*, 278–79.

24. Ibid., 274.

25. Freud, "Masochism," SE 19:163.

26. Freud, *Beyond Pleasure*, 16.

27. Ibid., 17.

28. Ibid., 15, 39.

29. Ibid., 62.

30. Ibid., 62–63.

31. Nietzsche, *Twilight*, "What the Germans Lack," sec. 6.

32. Ibid., "Skirmishes of an Untimely Man," sec. 10.

33. On the various meanings of bound and unbound energy in Freud, see Robert Holt, *Freud Reappraised* (New York: The Guilford Press, 1989), 71–113.

34. Freud, *An Outline of Psychoanalysis* (1940 [1938]), SE 23:148.

35. Ibid., 148–49.

36. Freud, *Beyond Pleasure*, SE 18:55–56.

37. Ibid., 63.

38. Freud, "Masochism," SE 19:160.

39. Nietzsche, *Zarathustra*, 1, "On the Despisers of the Body."

40. Kaufmann, *Nietzsche*, 253.

41. Nietzsche, *Twilight*, "What I Owe to the Ancients," sec. 4.

42. Camille Paglia, *Sexual Personae* (New York: Vintage Books, 1991), 436. See also Nietzsche, *EH*, "Why I Write Such Good Books," sec. 5.

43. Ibid., 315.

44. Nietzsche, *Tragedy*, sec. 16.

45. Freud, *Beyond Pleasure*, SE 18:61, n. 1.

46. See Francois Lissarrague, "Figures of Women," in *A History of Women in the West*, vol. 1, *From Ancient Goddesses to Christian Saints*, ed. Pauline Schmitt Pontel, trans. Arthur Goldhammer (Cambridge: The Belknap Press of Harvard University Press, 1992), 193, 218–19.

47. Heraclitus quoted in Charles H. Kahn, *The Art and Thought of Heraclitus: An Edition of the Fragments with Translation and Commentary* (New York: Cambridge University Press, 1981), 263–64.

48. Ibid., 264.

49. See Leeming, *World of Myth*, 101.

50. Nietzsche, *Tragedy*, sec. 18.

51. Sallis, *Crossings*, 93.

52. See Lawrence J. Hatab, "Nietzsche on Woman," *Southern Journal of Philosophy* 19, no. 3 (1981): 333–45.

53. Freud, *Leonardo Da Vinci and a Memory of His Childhood* (1910), SE 11:94.

54. See Eli Sagan, *Freud, Women, and Morality: The Psychology of Good and Evil* (New York: Basic Books, 1988), 143.

55. Karen Horney, "The Dread of Women," *International Journal of Psycho-Analysis* 13 (1932): 353.

56. Freud, *Civilization*, SE 21:64.

57. Ibid., 66.

58. Ibid., 68.

59. Ibid.

60. Ibid., 72.

61. Ibid., 65.

62. Freud, "*Moses*," SE 13:211.

63. Freud quoted in Molnar, *Diary of Sigmund Freud*, 56.

64. See Cora L. Diaz de Chumaceiro, "Was Freud Really Tone Deaf? A Brief Commentary," *The American Journal of Psychoanalysis* 50, no. 2 (1990): 199–202.

65. See Nietzsche, *Daybreak*, sec. 215.

66. Ibid., sec. 50. See also *Twilight*, "The Four Great Errors," sec. 2.

67. Nietzsche, *Gay Science*, sec. 341. Daniel Chapelle suggests that Freud's writing on the compulsion to repeat in *Beyond the Pleasure Principle* alludes not only to eternal recurrence but also, in Freud's use of the term "daemonic," specifically to the demon who presents it (*Nietzsche and Psychoanalysis* [Albany: State University of New York Press, 1993], 97).

68. Heinz Lichtenstein, *The Dilemma of Human Identity* (New York: Jason Aronson, 1977), 30–31.

69. See Nietzsche, *Zarathustra*, 2, "On Redemption"; Clark, *Nietzsche on Truth*, 259.

70. Judith Butler, "The Pleasure of Repetition," in *Pleasure Beyond the Pleasure Principle*, ed. Robert A. Glick and Stanley Bone (New Haven: Yale University Press, 1990), 272.

71. Nietzsche, *Zarathustra*, 2, "On Redemption."

72. See Clark, *Nietzsche on Truth*, 259. Clark reviews the major interpretations of eternal recurrence. Her own interpretation emphasizes one's immediate, spontaneous, and emotional response to the demon's test. Logically one might very well have no special relationship to one's life lived over countless times if one lives it exactly the same, with no added memory or awareness outside of the current life as lived.

73. Nietzsche, *Twilight*, "Morality as Anti-nature;" *EH*, "Dawn," 2, "Birth of Tragedy," 2. See Clark, *Nietzsche on Truth*, 165.

74. See White, *Nietzsche's Labyrinth*, 102, 110, 115.

75. Nietzsche, *Zarathustra*, 2, "On Redemption."

76. Nehamas, *Nietzsche*, 191.

77. Young, *Nietzsche's Philosophy of Art*, 107.

78. Clark, *Nietzsche on Truth*, 262, 279.

79. See Bernard Magnus, Stanley Stewart and Jean-Pierre Mileur, *Nietzsche's Case* (New York: Routledge, 1993), 33–34, 29. We can also consider Neitzsche's description of his own experience of inspiration, revelation and rapture regarding *Zarathustra*: "Even what is most painful and gloomy does not seem something opposite but rather . . . a *necessary* color in such a superabundance of light" (*EH*, "Thus Spoke Zarathustra," 3).

80. Stephen Byrum, "The Concept of Child's Play in Nietzsche's 'Of the Three Metamorphoses,'" *Kinesis* 6 (1974): 129.

81. Nietzsche, *Zarathustra*, 1, "On the Three Metamorphoses"; Nietzsche quoted in Williams, *Shame and Necessity*, 172n. 14.

82. Byrum, "Child's Play," 131.

83. Maudemarie Clark, "Nietzsche's Misogyny," unpublished paper: 9.

84. George S. Moran, "Some Functions of Play and Playfulness," *The Psychoanalytic Study of the Child* 42 (1987): 12.

85. D. W. Winnicott, *Playing and Reality* (New York: Basic Books, 1971), 41.

86. See Mihai I. Spariosu, *Dionysus Reborn* (Ithaca: Cornell University Press, 1989), 176–90; Eugene Mahon, "Play, Pleasure, Reality," in *Pleasure Beyond the Pleasure Principle*, 26–37; Jerome Sachs, "Psychoanalysis and the Elements of Play," *The American Journal of Psychoanalysis* 51, no. 1 (1991): 39–53.

87. Loewald, *Sublimation*, 24.

88. Freud, "Remembering, Repeating and Working-Through (Further Recommendations on the Technique of Psycho-Analysis, 2)" (1914), SE 12:154.

## CHAPTER 12. 1921–1931: AN OVERVIEW

1. Freud, *Group Psychology*, SE 18:123.

2. See Eugen Biser, "The Critical Imitator of Jesus: A Contribution to the Interpretation of Nietzsche on the Basis of a Comparison," in *Studies in Nietzsche and the Judeo-Christian Tradition*, ed. James C. O'Flaherty, et al. (Chapel Hill: The University of North Carolina Press, 1985), 87.

3. Freud, *The Ego and the Id*, SE 19:23n. 3. Groddeck's relationship with and influence upon Sandor Ferenczi, one of the analysts closest to Freud, is mentioned by Grosskurth in *The Secret Ring*, 106–7.

4. Wittels, *Freud and His Time*, 54.

5. See Chessick, "Nietzsche, Freud, Kohut," 365; Ginsberg, "Nietzschean Psychiatry," 295.

6. Nietzsche, *Zarathustra*, 1, "On the Despisers of the Body."

7. Gregory Vlastos, *Socrates: Ironest and Moral Philosopher* (Ithaca: Cornell University Press, 1991), 39.

8. Nietzsche, *Zarathustra*, 1, "On the Despisers of the Body."

9. Nietzsche, *EH*, "Why I Write Such Good Books," sec. 5.

10. See Nietzsche, *Genealogy*, 3, sec. 21; *Daybreak*, sec. 39.

11. Robert Langs, *Decoding Your Dreams* (New York: Ballantine Books, 1988), 30–31, 58.

12. See Sebastion Gardiner, "The Unconscious," in *Cambridge Companion to Freud*, 152, 160; Clark Glymour, "Freud's Androids," in *Cambridge Companion*, 70–79. Of course there is the unconscious ego.

13. Freud, *Civilization*, SE 21:122.

14. Freud, *Ego and Id*, SE 19:25.

15. Nietzsche, *Gay Science*, 360.

16. Nietzsche, *Genealogy*, 3, sec. 20.

17. Freud, "Masochism," SE 19:160.

18. Ibid.

19. See Golumb, "Freudian Uses," 383.

20. E. Freud, *Letters*, 350.

21. Golumb, "Freudian Uses," 382. Claudia Crawford has also written that "in the *Genealogy of Morals*, we can find in the development of *ressentiment* and bad conscience, on the level of cultural evolution, the working out of a scene parallel to that which Freud describes as the development of the individual psyche" ("Nietzsche's Mnemotechnics," 293).

22. See Wittels, *Sigmund Freud: His Personality, His Teaching, and His School*, trans. Eden and Cedar Paul (Freeport, New York: Books for Libraries Press, 1971 [1924]), 11.

23. Ibid., 62.

24. Freud, *An Autobiographical Study*, SE 20:59–60.

25. See Frank J. Sulloway, *Freud: Biologist of the Mind* (New York: Basic Books, 1979), 467.

26. See Paul Roazen, *Freud and His Followers* (New York: New York University Press, 1984 [1974]), 412.

27. See Grosskurth, *Secret Ring*, 181.

28. Heinrich Meng and Ernst L. Freud, eds., *Psychoanalysis and Faith: The Letters of Sigmund Freud and Oskar Pfister*, trans. Eric Mosbacher (New York: Basic Books, 1963), 115.

29. See Freud, *The Future of an Illusion* (1927), SE 21:22.

30. Nietzsche, *Daybreak*, sec. 215.

31. Thatcher, "Nietzsche's Debt to Lubbock," 302–3; the quote from Nietzsche is from *The Will to Power*, note 1019. While not reading this note, Freud could have read related passages, such as *Daybreak*, sec. 215.

32. Freud, "Humour," SE 21:162.

33. Nietzsche, *Human*, 1, sec. 169.

34. Mann, "Freud's Position," 84.

35. Charles E. Maylan, *Freuds tragischer Komplex: Eine Analyse der Psychoanalyse* (Munich: Ernst Reinhardt, 1929).

36. See Yerushalmi, *Freud's Moses*, 58–59.

37. E. Freud, *Letters of Freud and Zweig*, 14.

38. See Michael Molnar, *Diary of Sigmund Freud*, 65.

39. Ibid.

40. See Anderson, "Freud, Nietzsche," 3–29.

41. Freud, *Civilization*, SE 21:123.

42. Ibid., 125–26.

43. Ibid., 127.

44. Ibid., 128.

45. Ibid., 134.

46. Ibid., 145.

47. Nietzsche, *Genealogy*, 2, sec. 16.

48. Ibid., sec. 17.

49. Ibid., sec. 16.

50. Jones, *Life and Work*, 3:283.

51. Nehamas, *Nietzsche*, 247n. 11.

52. See John Deigh, "Freud's Later Theory of Civilization: Changes and Implications," in *Cambridge Companion to Freud*, 287–308.

53. Simon, "Freud's Concepts of Comedy," 399.

54. Cavell, *Psychoanalytic Mind*, 208.

55. Gellner, *Psychoanalytic Movement*, 143, 145.

56. Nietzsche, *EH*, "*Genealogy of Morals:* A Polemic." We can recall that *Ecce Homo* was read and discussed at a society meeting in 1908.

57. Freud, *Civilization*, SE 21:65–66.

58. See Nietzsche, *Genealogy*, 2, sec. 16.

59. Loewald, *Papers*, 71.

60. Nietzsche, *Genealogy*, 2, sec. 16.

61. Ibid.

62. Ibid., sec. 19.

63. Loewald, *Papers,* 264, 318.

64. Wittels, *Freud and His Time,* 74, 54.

65. Freud quoted in Gay, *Freud,* 46.

66. Freud, *Future of an Illusion,* SE 21:35.

## CHAPTER 13. WOMAN, TRUTH AND PERSPECTIVISM

1. See Freud, *New Introductory Lectures on Psycho-Analysis,* SE 22:72. Freud suggests that readers might think they are reading not about natural science but "Schopenhauer's philosophy." His response: "But ladies and gentlemen, why should not a bold thinker have *guessed* something that is afterwards confirmed by *sober and painstaking research*" (SE 22:107, emphases added).

2. Ibid., 103–4.

3. Ibid., 182.

4. Ibid., 33, 31.

5. Ibid., 33.

6. Ibid., 36.

7. Ibid., 42.

8. Ibid., 34.

9. Ibid., 53.

10. Ibid., 160.

11. Ibid., 171.

12. Ibid.

13. See George J. Makari, "German Philosophy, Freud, and the Riddle of the Woman," *Journal of the American Psychoanalytic Association* 39, no. 1 (1991): 183–213. In his study of Freud's views on women, the psycho-analyst Samuel Slipp also briefly discusses Nietzsche and presents an overview that in essence reduces Nietzsche to being "profoundly antifemi-nist and phallocentric," as "elevating irrationality and subjectivism above reason," and as denouncing "the Jewish founders of Christianity" and the "Judeo-Christian culture [which] fostered a slave mentality" (*The Freudian*

*Mystique. Freud, Women, and Feminism* [New York: New York University Press, 1993], 45, 156). Whatever one's views of Nietzsche on women, truth and Jews, it is a wonder that this kind of overly simplified reduction continues in otherwise first-rate studies of Freud and psychoanalysis. Also, if it is true, as Slipp and others have pointed out, that during the time of Nietzsche and Freud, Jews and women were linked, then we can consider that Nietzsche's views on both were complex, ambivalent, and multi-layered. It would be every bit as great an error to see Nietzsche as "deeply, truly" denigrating Jews and women (and truth) as it would be to see him as truly and unambivalently elevating them. For a recent issue of a psychoanalytic journal in which Nietzsche plays a role see *Psychoanalytic Dialogues* 3, no. 2 (1993).

14. See Freud, *New Introductory Lectures,* 112–35.

15. Ibid., 134.

16. Ibid., 118.

17. Ibid., 116.

18. See Marianna Torgovnick, *Gone Primitive* (Chicago: The University of Chicago Press, 1990), 207.

19. See Freud, *New Introductory Lectures,* SE 22:117.

20. Ibid., 135.

21. Ibid., 113.

22. Nietzsche, *BGE,* secs. 231, 239, 86.

23. Ibid., secs. 231, 232. I was led to take another look at sections 231–39 after reading the opening paragraphs of Maudemarie Clark's unpublished paper, "Nietzsche's Misogyny." Clark's paper moves in an interesting and controversial direction, attributing to Nietzsche the intent in part 7 of *BGE* of "overcoming what he would like to believe about women, out of his commitment to truth" (9). She argues that Nietzsche's more negative statements refer to a "feminine essense, a social construction that individual woman need not exemplify" (5).

24. Nietzsche, *BGE,* sec. 239.

25. See Makari, "German Philosophy, Freud," 211.

26. See Roith, *The Riddle of Freud,* 85–88; Gilman, *Sexuality,* 266–67; Hannah S. Decker, *Freud, Dora, and Vienna 1900* [New York: The Free Press, 1991], 29–40.

27. Carolyn G. Heilbrun, *Hamlet's Mother* (New York: Columbia University Press, 1990), 37.

28. Nietzsche quoted in Graybeal, *Language and "the Feminine" in Nietzsche and Heidegger*, 53.

29. Ibid., 47.

30. Ibid. Such ideas and imagery of Nietzsche's were not lost on Andreas-Salomé (see Slipp, *Freudian Mystique*, 101–2).

31. Ibid., 53. Slipp is not alone in attributing this statement to Nietzsche and neglecting to mention that it is the advice to Zarathustra from a particular character (*Freudian Mystique*, 157).

32. Ibid., 76.

33. Nietzsche, *BGE*, sec. 239.

34. Hatab, "Nietzsche on Woman," 337, 340.

35. Ibid., 335.

36. See Louise Bruit Zaidman, "Pandora's Daughters and Rituals in Grecian Cities," in *A History of Women in the West*, vol. 1, *From Ancient Goddesses to Christian Saints*, 357.

37. Ibid., 358.

38. Robert John Ackerman, *Nietzsche: A Frenzied Look* (Amherst: University of Massachusetts Press, 1990), 126.

39. Nietzsche, *Human*, 1, sec. 425.

40. Nietzsche, *Gay Science*, sec. 68.

41. See Nancy Chodorow, "Freud on Women," in *Cambridge Companion to Freud*, 224–248.

42. See Gilman, *Sexuality*, 278.

43. See Freud, "A Mythological Parallel to a Visual Obsession" (1916), SE 14:338.

44. See Makari, "German Philosophy, Freud," 195.

45. See Mary Ann Doane, "Veiling Over Desire: Close-ups of the Women," in *Feminism and Psychoanalysis*, ed. Richard Feldstein and Judith Roof (Ithaca: Cornell University Press, 1989), 129–30.

46. Ibid., 130.

47. See Kofman, "Baubô," 191.

48. Nietzsche, quoted in Kofman, "Baubô," 189.

49. Kofman, "Baubô," 195.

50. Ibid., 197.

51. Doane, "Veiling Over Desire," 124.

52. Ibid., 125.

53. See Carol Diethe, "Nietzsche and the Woman Question," *History of European Ideas* 11 (1989): 865–75. For an understanding of Derrida's formulation which emphasizes the dialectical interplay of all three positions and views each position as potentially in the service of ascending life or declining life, see Kelly Oliver, "Woman as Truth in Nietzsche's Writings," *Social Theory and Practice* 10, no. 2 (Summer 1984): 185–99.

54. See Makari, "German Philosophy, Freud," 196.

55. Ibid., 195, 197.

56. Nietzsche, *Tragedy*, sec. 16.

57. Claudia Crawford, *"She,"* *Sub-stance* 29 (1981): 87; Nietzsche, *Twilight*, "Reason in Philosophy," sec. 2.

58. Schacht, *Nietzsche*, 62, 202.

59. Nietzsche, *WP*, n.569.

60. See Richard Schacht, *Nietzsche* (Boston: Routledge & Kegan Paul, 1983); Nehamas, *Nietzsche*; Martin Warner, *Philosophical Finesse: Studies in the Art of Rational Persuasion* (Oxford: Clarendon Press, 1989), 265–332; Clark, *Nietzsche on Truth*.

61. See Irwin Hoffman, "Discussion: Toward a Social-Constructivist View of the Psychoanalytic Situation," *Psychoanalytic Dialogues* 1, vol. 1 (1991): 74–105.

62. Makari, "German Philosophy, Freud," 210.

63. Nietzsche (*WP*, n.473) quoted in Mary Warnock, "Nietzsche's Conception of Truth," in *Nietzsche: Imagery and Thought*, ed. Malcolm Pasley (Berkeley: University of California Press, 1978), 42. See Nietzsche, *Twilight*, "How the 'True World' Finally Became a Fable." See also Warnock, "Nietzsche's Conception of Truth," 38; Schacht, *Nietzsche*, 202.

64. See W. J. Dannhauser, *Nietzsche's View of Socrates* (Ithaca: Cornell University Press 1974), 180.

65. Joseph Valente, "Beyond Truth and Freedom: The New Faith of Joyce and Nietzsche," *James Joyce Quarterly* 25, no. 1 (Fall 1987): 88–89.

66. Ibid., 88, 94.

67. Nietzsche, *WP*, n.608.

68. Nietzsche, *Genealogy*, 3, sec. 12.

69. Nietzsche, *WP*, n.1059.

70. Richard Rorty, Introduction to *Essays on Heidegger and Others* (New York: Cambridge University Press, 1991), 4.

71. Leszek Kolakowski, *Presence of Myth* (Chicago: The University of Chicago Press, 1989), 12.

72. Yovel, *Spinoza*, 180, 181.

73. Nietzsche, "Truth and Lying," 254.

74. Nietzsche, *WP*, n.616. Other apparently extreme notes (for example, notes 1059 and 1060) lend themselves to similar or related interpretations.

75. Ibid., n.625.

76. Popper quoted in Warner, *Philosophical Finesse*, 286.

77. Warnock quoted in Warner, *Philosophical Finesse*, 286.

78. Nietzsche, *Antichrist*, secs. 52, 47; *EH*, "The Birth of Tragedy," sec. 2; Nietzsche quoted in Aschheim, *Nietzsche Legacy*, 234n. 3.

79. Nietzsche, *Gay Science*, sec. 348.

80. Stephen Jay Gould, "Dinosaurs in the Haystack," *Natural History* (March 1992): 12.

81. Nietzsche, *Genealogy*, 3, sec. 23.

82. Nietzsche, *Twilight*, "Morality as Anti-Nature," sec. 4.

83. Nietzsche, *UM*, 3, sec. 1.

84. Nietzsche, *Genealogy*, 2, sec. 2.

85. Ibid., 3, sec. 12.

86. Nietzsche, *Antichrist*, sec. 50.

87. On Nietzsche's distinctions between appearance and reality see Schacht, *Nietzsche*, 188–93.

88. Nietzsche, *Antichrist*, sec. 55.

89. Linda Alcoff, "Continental Philosophy," in *A Companion to Epistemology*, ed. Jonathan Dancy and Ernest Sosa (Cambridge: Basil Blackwell, 1992), 77.

90. Nietzsche, *Genealogy*, 3, sec. 12.

91. Ibid.

92. Jacques Lacan, *Ecrits*, tr. A. Sheridan (London: Tavistock, 1977), 2.

93. Ellie Ragland-Sullivan, *Jacques Lacan and the Philosophy of Psychoanalysis* (Urbana: University of Illinois Press, 1986), 90.

94. Ibid., ix.

95. Rudnytsky, *Freud and Oedipus*, 205.

96. Stephen Frosh, *The Politics of Psychoanalysis* (New Haven: Yale University Press, 1987), 133.

97. Nietzsche, *WP*, n.518, n.561. For a discussion of homuncular explanations of agency and multiplicity in Freud that also has relevance for Nietzsche, see Clark Glymour, "Freud's Androids," in *Cambridge Companion to Freud*, 68–79.

98. Nietzsche, *WP*, n.485; see Nehamas, *Nietzsche*, chap. 6.

99. Warnock, "Nietzsche's Conception of Truth," 44. For a discussion of Nietzsche and Hume on self and identity see Nicholas Davey, "Nietzsche and Hume On Self and Identity," *Journal of the British Society for Phenomenology* 18, no. 1 (January 1987): 14–29.

100. See Macmillan, "Sources of Freud's Methods," 138–44.

101. Nietzsche quoted in Leslie Paul Thiele, *Friedrich Nietzsche and the Politics of the Soul* (Princeton: Princeton University Press, 1990), 59. Donna Haraway writes that "subjectivity is multidimensional; so, therefore, is vision." She also writes that the kind of objectivity that is possible requires that we accept a perspectivist approach to knowledge claims and abandon the idea "of seeing everything from nowhere . . . all eyes . . . are active perceptual systems, building on translations and specific *ways* of seeing, that is, ways of life . . . I am arguing for the view from a body,

always a complex, contradictory, structuring, and structured body, versus the view from above, from nowhere . . . situated knowledges are about communities not about isolated individuals" ("Situated Knowledges: The Science Question in Feminism and the Privilege of Partial Perspective," *Feminist Studies* 14, no. 3 [Fall 1988]: 581–91). Haraway's paper was brought to my attention by Professor Martha Ecker of Ramapo College.

102. Robert Holt, *Freud Reappraised* (New York: The Guilford Press, 1989), 285.

103. Gellner, *Psychoanalytic Movement*, 82–83.

104. Ibid., 85.

105. Ibid., 91.

106. Ibid., 93.

107. On the interrelationship of theory and observation, see Freud, "Instincts and Their Vicissitudes," SE 14:117. See also *Future of an Illusion*, SE 21:55–56. On Freud's sophisticated philosophical realism, see Nigel Mackay, *Motivation and Explanation* (Madison, CT: International Universities Press, 1987).

108. Freud, "The Unconscious" (1915), SE 14:171.

109. See Freud, *ID*, SE 5:611–15.

110. Freud, *Outline of Psycho-Analysis*, SE 23:196–97.

111. See Anthony O'Hear, *An Introduction to the Philosophy of Science* (New York: Oxford University Press, 1990), 91.

112. Freud, "On Narcissism," SE 14:77.

113. Freud, Appendix to "Doestoevski and Parracide" (1928), SE 21:196. There is the additional matter of the case histories and Freud's strange notions of the evidence that constitutes confirmation or conclusive proof of the validity of his interpretations and theories; see Allen Esterson, *Seductive Mirage: An Exploration of the Work of Sigmund Freud* (Chicago: Open Court, 1993).

114. Freud, *Future of an Illusion*, SE 21:31–32.

115. O'Hear, *Philosophy of Science*, 211, 215.

116. Stephen Jay Gould, "The Gift of New Questions," *Natural History* 102, no. 8 (August 1993): 4.

117. Freud, *Future of an Illusion*, SE 21:53–54. While authors such as

Grünbaum argue that Freud was quite open to evidence contradicting his theories and ready to make revisions based on such data, others strongly disagree; see Frank Cioffi, "'Exegetical Myth-Making in Grünbaum's Indictment of Popper and Exoneration of Freud," in *Mind, Psychoanalysis and Science*, 61–87, and A. A. Derksen, "Does the Tally Argument Make Freud a Sophisticated Methodologist?" *Philosophy of Science* 59, no. 1 (March 1992): 75–101.

118. See Freud, *Future of an Illusion*, SE 21:33.

119. Paul Davies, Review of *Dreams of a Final Theory* by Steven Weinberg and *The God Particle* by Leon Lederman with Dick Teresi. *The New York Times Book Review*, March 7, 1993, 11–12. On penis envy as a concept that could comfort and defend men, see Kofman, *Enigma of Woman*, 89. Towards the end of his life in "Analysis Terminable and Interminable," Freud concludes that "the female's wish for a penis . . . is the source of outbreaks of severe depression in her, owing to an integral conviction that the analysis will be of no use and that nothing can be done to help her. And we can only agree that she is right, when we learn that her strongest motive in coming for treatment was the hope that, after all, she might still obtain a male organ, the lack of which was so painful to her" (SE 23:252). There is also an important point to be made regarding Freud's distinction between the male coming to terms with the bedrock issue of fear of passivity "or a feminine attitude to another male" (and castration) and the female bedrock issue of coming to terms with "an *envy for the penis*" (SE 23:250). The female ideally is supposed to "abandon her wish for a penis on the ground of its being unrealizable." The male does not have to abandon any primal wish; he only has to recognize that his fear is unfounded, "that a passive attitude to men does not always signify castration and that it is indispensable in many relationships in life" (SE 23:252).

120. See Joseph Weiss, "Unconscious Mental Functioning," *Scientific American* (March 1990): 103–9.

121. Drew S. Nash, *Death or Power*, 158.

122. Ibid., 142; Steven J. Ellman, *Freud's Technique Papers: A Contemporary Perspective* (Northvale, NJ: Jason Aronson, 1991), 289.

123. John Passmore, *Recent Philosophers* (La Salle: Open Court Publishing Co., 1985), 88.

124. Ibid., 36, 144n. 17, 118.

125. Anthony Flew, *A Dictionary of Philosophy* (New York: St. Martin's Press, 1984), 247.

126. See Adolf Grünbaum, *The Foundations of Psychoanalysis* (Berkeley: University of California Press, 1984); "'Meaning' Connections and Causal Connections in the Human Sciences: The Poverty of Hermeneutic Philosophy," *Journal of the American Psychoanalytic Association* 38, no. 3 (1990): 559-77; Donald Spence, *The Freudian Metaphor: Toward Paradigm Change in Psychoanalysis* (New York: W. W. Norton & Co., 1987) and "The Rhetorical Voice of Psychoanalysis," *Journal of the American Psychoanalytic Association* 38, no. 3 (1990): 579–603; Edwin R. Wallace IV, "What Is 'Truth'? Some Philosophical Contributions to Psychiatric Issues," *The American Journal of Psychiatry* 145, no. 2 (February 1988): 137–47.

127. Spence, *Freudian Metaphor*, 15; see Nietzsche, *Truth and Lying*.

128. Spence, *Freudian Metaphor*, 56.

129. Ibid., 57.

130. Hayden White quoted by Spence, "Rhetorical Voice," 594. See also White, "Historiography as Narration," in *Telling Facts: Historiography and Narration in Psychoanalysis*, ed. Joseph H. Smith and Humphrey Morris (Baltimore: Johns Hopkins University Press, 1992), 284–99.

131. R. J. Bernstein quoted in Spence, "Rhetorical Voice," 591.

132. Flew, *Dictionary*, 248.

133. Rank quoted in Rudnytsky, *The Psychoanalytic Vocation* (New Haven: Yale University Press, 1991), 64; Nietzsche, *WP*, n.481; *BGE*, sec. 17.

134. Michael J. Mahoney, *Human Change Processes* (New York: Basic Books, 1991), 106.

135. Ibid., 394.

136. Ibid., 434.

137. Ibid., 432.

138. Ibid., 408, 412.

139. Ibid., 92.

140. Allan Megill, *Prophets of Extremity* (Berkeley: University of California Press, 1985), 23.

141. Hans-Georg Gadamer, *The Relevance of the Beautiful and Other Essays*, ed. Robert Bernasconi, trans. Nicholas Walker (Cambridge: Cambridge University Press, 1986), 46.

142. Ibid., 130. On Gadamer and psychoanalysis see Donnell B. Stern, "A Philosophy for the Embedded Analyst: Gadamer's Hermeneutics and the Social Paradigm of Psychoanalysis," *Contemporary Psychoanalysis* 27, no. 1 (January 1991): 51–80.

143. Arnold M. Cooper, "Changes in Psychoanalytic Ideas: Transference Interpretation," *Journal of the American Psychoanalytic Association* 31, no. 1 (1987): 77–98.

144. Milton Viederman, "The Real Person of the Analyst and His Role in the Process of Psychoanalytic Cure," *Journal of the American Psychoanalytic Association* 35 (1991): 467, 463.

145. Cavell, *Psychoanalytic Mind,* 191.

146. Rorty, "Freud and Moral Reflection," in *Essays,* 151.

147. Ibid., 152, 153. In a recent article, Rorty goes beyond anything compatible with Nietzsche's working in the service of truth when he writes that "I do not see much point in questions about whether the analyst discovers or invents the patient's unconscious"; "Centers of Moral Gravity: Commentary on Donald Spence's 'The Hermeneutic Turn,'" *Psychoanalytic Dialogues* 3, no. 1 (1993): 21. Daniel Conway argues that while narrative redescription figures prominently in the *Genealogy,* the master of narrative is the ascetic priest. And he suggests that Rorty's disembodied narrative self-creation is to some extent linked to world-denying asceticism. He emphasizes that for Nietzsche our perspectives are embodied, grounded in affect and will which anchor our perspectives in the world (see Daniel W. Conway, "Thus Spoke Rorty: The Perils of Narrative Self-Creation," *Philosophy and Literature* 15, no. 1 [April 1991]: 103–10).

148. Nietzsche, *Human,* 1, sec. 263.

149. See Stern, "Philosophy for the Embedded Analyst," 65.

150. Stephen A. Mitchell, *Relational Concepts in Psychoanalysis* (Cambridge: Harvard University Press, 1988).

151. Stephen A. Mitchell, "Editorial Philosophy," *Psychoanalytic Dialogues* 1, no. 1 (1991): 6.

152. Hoffman, "Discussion," 78.

153. Ibid., 77. On the other hand, the analyst and philosopher Charles Hanly continues to maintain that "pattern making by the analyst is not required so long as resistances and defenses are interpreted in such a way as to allow the intrinsic forces at work in the psychic life of the patient to make themselves known." Hanly appears to believe, in keeping with his

understanding of a correspondence theory of truth, that there is only one true description of the world (Charles Hanly, *The Problem of Truth in Applied Psychoanalysis* [New York: The Guilford Press, 1992], 20, 2). For a recent collection of papers on social constructionism as applied to the sociology of social problems see James A. Holstein and Gale Miller, eds., *Reconsidering Social Constructionism* (New York: Aldine De Gruyter, 1993).

154. Nehamas, *Nietzsche*, 243n. 20. On reflexivity in the sociology of scientific knowledge, see Malcolm Ashmore, *The Reflexive Thesis* (Chicago: The University of Chicago Press, 1989).

155. Schacht, *Nietzsche*, 10.

156. Nehamas, *Nietzsche*, 67.

157. Ibid., 68.

158. Ibid., 63.

159. Clark, *Nietzsche on Truth*, 155, 157.

160. Nehamas, "Nietzsche, Friedrich (1944–1900)," in *A Companion to Epistemology*, 305.

161. Clark, *Nietzsche on Truth*, 21.

162. Nietzsche, *Genealogy*, 3, sec. 24.

163. On theories of truth and justification see Richard L. Kirkham, *Theories of Truth* (Cambridge: MIT Press, 1992).

164. Nietzsche, *BGE*, sec. 6.

165. Nietzsche, *Antichrist*, sec. 52. For an excellent discussion of impairments in thinking about complex social problems see Charles E. Lindblom, *Inquiry and Change* (New Haven. Yale University Press, 1990).

166. Thomas S. Kuhn, "The Natural and the Human Sciences," in *The Interpretive Turn*, ed. David R. Hiley, James F. Bohman and Richart Shusterman (Ithaca: Cornell University Press, 1991), 21.

167. Clark, *Nietzsche on Truth*, 149.

168. See the discussion on Jacob Arlow's views on implications of infant and early childhood research in Ellman, *Freud's Technique Papers*, 271–81.

169. See Wagner Bridger, "Early Childhood and Its Effects," *The Harvard Mental Health Letter* 8, no. 2 (August 1991): 4–7; Julius R.

Bemporad, "Effects of Early Childhood Experience," *The Harvard Mental Health Letter* 8, no. 3 (September 1991): 4–6; Ellman, *Freud's Technique Papers.*

170. O'Hear, *Philosophy of Science,* 83. For a recent attempt to encourage such efforts and to strengthen psychoanalysis as a science see Leopold Bellak, *Psychoanalysis as a Science* (Boston: Allyn and Bacon, 1993). However, while Bellak mentions Grünbaum, he does not deal at all with the important issues and criticisms Grünbaum raises. See also the critical discussion of psychoanalysis, science and research in Macmillan, *Freud Evaluated,* 508–612.

171. See James Hopkins, *"The Interpretation of Dreams,"* in *Cambridge Companion to Freud,* 127–29n. 21; David Sachs, "In Fairness to Freud: A Critical Notice of *The Foundations of Psychoanalysis* by Adolf Grünbaum," in *Cambridge Companion to Freud,* 309–38. For Grünbaum's response to Hopkins, Sachs and other critics see his recent volume, *Validation in the Clinical Theory of Psychoanalysis* (Madison CT: International Universities Press, 1993).

172. Grünbaum, "'Meaning' Connections," 567.

173. See Eugene Gendlin, "Client-Centered: The Experiential Response," in *Use of Interpretation in Treatment,* ed. Emanual F. Hammer (New York: Grune & Stratton, Inc., 1968), 208–27.

174. Grünbaum, "'Meaning' Connections," 574.

175. Grünbaum, *Foundations,* 56.

176. Grünbaum's lecture was, I believe, presented at a conference of the American Psychoanalytic Association, New York City, 1988. I believe the lecture was recorded. Grünbaum was referring to Donald P. Spence, *Narrative Truth and Historical Truth: Meaning and Interpretation in Psychoanalysis* (New York: W. W. Norton & Co., 1982).

177. Ellman, *Freud's Technique Papers,* 279. Regarding the past as an actuality, Louis A. Sass writes that "distinctions . . . can separately be made on the grounds of accuracy or truth value . . . if such distinctions in terms of probable truth value can be made, then the way is open for rather more subtle distinctions, and there is no reason to reject entirely the possibility of adjudicating between more or less likely accounts of the past or the unconscious" ("Psychoanalysis as 'Conversation' and as 'Fiction'; Commentary on Charles Spezzano's 'A Relational Model of Inquiry and Truth' and Richard Geha's 'Transferred Fictions,'" *Psychoanalytic Dialogues* 3, no. 2 [1993]: 249). However, elsewhere Sass also makes it clear that such a valid and public knowledge is "based not on some kind of

timeless certainty, but on the relative persuasiveness, within a particular interpretive community, of the various interpretations offered" (quoted in Charles Spezzano, "Illusions of Candor: Reply to Sass," *Psychoanalytic Dialogues* 3, no. 2 [1993]: 267).

178. Nietzsche, *UM*, 2:62.

179. Gertrude Himmelfarb, "Supposing History Is a Woman—What Then?" *The American Scholar* 53, no. 4 (Fall 1984): 494–505.

180. Strenger, *Between Hermeneutics and Science*, 170.

181. Ibid., 171.

182. Ibid., 213.

183. Ibid., 172.

184. Ibid., 160.

185. Ibid., 169.

186. Ibid., 170.

187. Ibid., 172.

188. Nehamas, *Nietzsche*, 72.

189. For two recent influential volumes see Joseph Weiss, Harold Sampson, and the Mount Zion Psychotherapy Research Group, *The Psychoanalytic Process: Theory, Clinical Observations, and Empirical Research* (New York: The Guilford Press, 1986) and Lester Luborsky and Paul Crits-Christoph, *Understanding Transference: The CCRT Method* (New York: Basic Books, 1990). These two therapeutic approaches differ in substantial ways on theory and technique.

## CHAPTER 14. NIETZSCHE, LIPPS AND THE UNCONSCIOUS OF PHILOSOPHERS

1. Mann quoted in Jones, *Life and Work*, 3:205.

2. See Freud, *Lou Andreas-Salomé* (1937), SE 23:297.

3. Jones, *Life and Work*, 3:213.

4. Freud, "Analysis Terminable and Interminable," SE 23:245.

5. Ibid., 244.

6. Loewald, *Papers*, 318. Loewald's discussion of Nietzsche was brought to my attention by Professor Jeffrey Seinfeld of New York University. On the juxtaposition of the Nietzschean themes and cryptomnesia see Michael J. Scovio, Andrew Cooper and Pamela Scavio Clift, "Freud's Devaluation of Nietzsche," *The Psychohistory Review* 21, no. 3 (Spring 1993): 309. The article makes a number of interesting points, but there are also a number of important factual errors, such as mistaking what Arnold Zweig was working on in 1934.

7. Freud, "Analysis Terminable and Interminable," SE 23:242–43.

8. Freud, "Some Elementary Lessons in Psycho-Analysis" (1938), SE 23:286.

9. Freud, *ID*, SE 5:611–15.

10. Nietzsche, *Daybreak*, sec. 133.

11. Nietzsche, "Homer and Classical Philology," 166.

12. Nietzsche, quoted in Claudia Crawford, *The Beginning of Nietzsche's Philosophy of Language* (New York: Walter de Gruyter, 1988), 151. Nietzsche's meaning here, influenced by Hartmann, relates to making conscious the *ends* of the unconscious.

13. See Jörg Salaquarda, "Dionysus versus the Crucified One: Nietzsche's Understanding of the Apostle Paul," trans. Timothy F. Sellner, in *Studies in Nietzsche and the Judeo-Christian Tradition*, 100–29.

14. See Michael Goulder, "The Pauline Epistles," in *The Literary Guide to the Bible*, ed. Robert Alter and Frank Kermode (Cambridge: The Belknap Press of Harvard University Press, 1987), 479–502; Peter Brown, *The Body and Society* (New York: Columbia University Press, 1988), 44–57; Alan F. Segal, *Paul the Convert*.

15. Nietzsche, *Gay Science*, sec. 354.

16. Freud, *ID*, SE 5:616.

17. Ibid., 615.

18. Nietzsche, *Gay Science*, sec. 354.

19. Freud, *ID*, SE 5:613–14.

20. Ibid., 611 (note added in 1925); see also "The Unconscious," SE 14:201–3, on language as a condition for a "presentation" to enter consciousness.

21. Ibid., 574.

22. Ibid., 615.

23. Nietzsche, *Gay Science*, sec. 354. This question, "Why consciousness?", continues to be addressed by contemporary analysts and philosophers; see Eagle, "Psychoanalysis and the Personal"; John Haldane, "Psychoanalysis, Cognitive Psychology and Self-Consciousness," in *Mind, Psychoanalysis and Science*, 113–39.

24. Richard Schacht, "On Self-Becoming: Nietzsche and Nehamas's Nietzsche," *Nietzsche-Studien* 21 (1992): 266–80; Nietzsche, *Gay Science*, sec. 354. See Nina Jarmolych, "Nietzsche's Concept of Consciousness," *International Studies in Philosophy* 17, no. 2 (1985): 69–77.

25. E. Freud, *Letters of Freud and Zweig*, 77.

26. Freud quoted in Jones, *Life and Work*, 3:459.

## CHAPTER 15. *MOSES AND MONOTHEISM*

1. See Paul Roazen, *Freud: Political and Social Thought* (New York: Vintage Books, 1968); Michael P. Carroll, "*Moses and Monotheism* Revisited—Freud's 'Personal Myth?'", *American Imago* 44, no. 1 (Spring 1987): 15–35; Robert S. Wistrich, *The Jews of Vienna in the Age of Franz Joseph* (New York: Oxford Unviersity Press, 1989), chap. 16; Emanuel Rice, *Freud and Moses: The Long Journey Home* (Albany: State University of New York, 1990); Harold P. Blum, "Freud and the Figure of Moses: The Moses of Freud," *Journal of the American Psychoanalytic Association* 39, no. 2 (1991): 513–35; Yosef Hayim Yerushalmi, *Freud's Moses* (New Haven: Yale University Press, 1991).

2. Yerushalmi, "Freud on the 'Historical Novel': From the Manuscript Draft (1934) of *Moses and Monotheism*," *International Journal of Psychoanalysis* 70 (1989): 380.

3. See Wallace, *Freud and Anthropology*, 258.

4. Ibid., 258–59; Ritchie Robertson, "Freud's Testament: *Moses and Monotheism*," in *Freud in Exile*, 81.

5. See Gay, *Freud*, 647.

6. Blum, "The Moses of Freud," 530; see Rice, *Freud and Moses*, 201–5.

7. Pfeiffer, *Freud and Lou*, 205.

8. See Berliner, *Psychoanalysis and Society*, 131.

9. Ritchie Robertson, "Freud's Testament," 87.

10. Freud, *Moses and Monotheism: Three Essays*, SE 23:58.

11. See Graham Parkes, "The Dance from Mouth to Hand (Speaking Zarathustra's Write Foot ForeWord)," in *Nietzsche as Postmodernist*, 137.

12. See Freud, *Moses and Monotheism*, SE 23:114. On the significance of Freud's ignoring the sensual and bisexual aspects of the culture of Akhenaten see Carl E. Schorske, "Freud's Egyptian Dig," *The New York Review of Books* (27 May 1993): 35–40.

13. Richard B. Sewall, *The Vision of Tragedy* (New York: Paragon House, 1990), 26.

14. Zimmermann, *Greek Tragedy*, 52.

15. Freud, *Moses and Monotheism*, SE 23:114; Davies, Review of *Dreams of a Final Theory*, 12.

16. Ibid., 113.

17. Nietzsche, *Gay Science*, sec. 143.

18. Freud, *Moses and Monotheism*, SE 23:20.

19. Ernest Gellner, *Postmodernism, Reason and Religion* (New York: Routledge, 1992), 58.

20. Paglia, *Sexual Personae*, 34.

21. Rycroft, *Psychoanalysis and Beyond*, 264.

22. Paglia, *Sexual Personae*, 89.

23. Nietzsche, *Genealogy*, 2, sec. 3; see also Robertson, "Freud's Testament," 87.

24. Freud, *Moses and Monotheism*, SE 23:68.

25. Ibid., 43.

26. Ibid., 85.

27. See Wallace, *Freud and Anthropology*, 163.

28. Philip Reiff quoted in Wallace, *Freud and Anthropology*, 163.

29. Yerushalmi, *Freud's Moses*, 95.

30. E. Freud, *Letters of Freud and Zweig*, 23.

31. Ibid.

32. Ibid., 24.

33. Ibid., 25.

34. Ibid., 33.

35. For information on Freud's original draft see Yerushalmi, "Freud on the 'Historical Novel.'" In this article Yerushalmi discusses Freud's reaction to Zweig's Nietzsche project as it relates to Freud's own approach to his study of Moses (although Yerushalmi does not approach this at all along the lines of the present study). Yerushalmi's book *Freud's Moses* consists of lectures presented as they had been delivered orally. However, it has many notes added to it, but no discussion of the correspondence around Zweig's Nietzsche project.

36. See E. Freud, *Letters of Freud and Zweig*, 74.

37. Ibid.

38. Nietzsche, *Gay Science*, "Preface to the Second Edition," sec. 2.

39. See Nietzsche, *Zarathustra*, 4, "The Ass Festival."

40. Ibid., 3, "On Old and New Tablets."

41. Nietzsche, *BGE*, sec. 251.

42. Freud, Preface to *Totem and Taboo*, SE 13:xv.

43. Freud, *Moses and Monotheism*, SE 23:12.

44. Ibid., 18, 39.

45. Nietzsche, *Zarathustra*, 1, "On the Gift-giving Virtue."

46. E. Freud, *Letters of Freud and Zweig*, 76.

47. Ibid.

48. Ibid.

49. Ibid., 77.

50. Ibid.

51. Ibid., 77–78.

52. Ibid., 78.

53. Pfeiffer, *Freud and Lou*, 202.

54. Ibid., 203.

55. E. Freud, *Freud and Zweig*, 83.

56. Ibid., 84.

57. Ibid., 91. In his book *Freud, Race, and Gender*, Sander Gilman suggests that the antisemitic writings and characterization of Freud by Wilhelm Schmidt were important driving forces in Freud's formulations in *Moses and Monotheism*. He also regards the meaning of circumcision in this work as central to it. He believes that circumcision was the essential borrowing from Egypt, that it was a sign of a failed attempt to assimilate and become Egyptians (183–99).

58. E. Freud, *Freud and Zweig*, 88.

59. Ibid.

60. Ibid., 91.

61. Ibid.

62. Arnold Zweig, "Apollon bewältigit Dionysos, (Zum achtzigsten Geburtstag Siegmund Freuds, 6 Mai 1936.)," *Text und Kritik*, Heft 104 (Oktober 1989): 4; Karl Abraham, "Amenhotep IV: A Psycho-analytic Contribution towards the Understanding of His Personality and of the Monotheistic Cult of Aton," in *Clinical Papers and Essays on Psycho-analysis*, (London: Hogarth Press, 1955), 262–290; Leonard Shengold, "*The Boy Will Come to Nothing!*" (New Haven: Yale University Press, 1993), 59–94.

63. C. G. Jung, *Nietzsche's Zarathustra: Notes of the Seminar Given in 1934–1939*, 2 vols., ed. James L. Jarrett (Princeton: Princeton University Press, 1988).

64. See Yerushalmi, *Freud's Moses*, 29.

65. See Blum, "Freud and Moses," 520. Also, the god of this second Moses had the god of the first Moses "always at his back."

66. See Rice, *Freud and Moses*, 192.

67. Yerushalmi, *Freud's Moses*, 76.

68. Robert R. Holt, "Freud's Parental Identifications as a Source of Some Contradictions within Psychoanalysis," in *Freud and the History of Psychoanalysis*, ed. Toby Gelfand and John Kerr (Hillsdale, New Jersey: The Analytic Press, 1992), 3–4.

69. Freud, *Moses and Monotheism*, SE 23:59.

70. Ibid., 110.

71. Ibid., 88.

72. Ibid., 136.

73. Ibid., 90.

74. H. Meng and E. Freud, *Letters of Freud and Pfister*, 76.

75. Freud, *Moses and Monotheism*, SE 23:134.

76. Ibid., 135.

77. Ibid., 88.

78. Ibid., 133.

79. Ibid., 136.

80. Ibid., 88.

81. Nietzsche, *Genealogy*, 2, sec. 22.

82. Freud, *Moses and Monotheism*, 128.

83. Nietzsche, *Daybreak*, sec. 68.

84. See Trosman and Simmons, *Freud Library*, 655.

85. Nietzsche, *Daybreak*, sec. 68.

86. Ibid.

87. Terry Eagleton, *The Ideology of the Aesthetic* (Cambridge: Basil Blackwell, 1990), 272.

88. Salaquarda, "Dionysus versus the Crucified One," 127.

89. Segal, *Paul the Convert*, 287. Segal does not agree with this view of conversion.

90. See Salaquarda, "Dionysus versus the Crucified One," 128; Freud quoted in Molnar, *Diary of Sigmund Freud*, xxv. Nietzsche, like Paul, describes how he was shaken and thrown down by his revelatory experience (see Chapelle, *Nietzsche and Psychoanalysis*, 37).

91. Ibid., 109.

92. Nietzsche, *Genealogy*, 3, sec. 11.

93. Ibid., 2, sec. 18.

94. See Rorty, "Freud and Moral Reflection," in *Essays*, 143–63.

95. See Spariosu, *Dionysus Reborn*, 97.

96. Regarding childhood sexual desires, Rabbi Jerome Fishman of Boston (personal communication, 1992) has brought to my attention a Sephardic commentary on the Bible, the Ibn Ezra of Abraham Ben Meir (1092–1167), in which a discussion of Exodus 20:14 (Jewish Publication Society Bible) on the commandment to not covet includes the following as an example: "And one does not wish to lay with one's mother even though she is beautiful only because of training from childhood to know that she is forbidden to him" (Five Books of Torah, Mikraos Gedolos Edition [New York: Shulsinger Brothers Publishing Co., 1950], 318, freely translated by Rabbi Fishman).

97. Nietzsche, *Gay Science*, sec. 123.

## Chapter 16. Conclusion

1. See Anzieu, *Freud's Self-Analysis*, 88–89; Gellner, *Psychoanalytic Movement*.

2. Kerr, *A Most Dangerous Method*, 8.

3. Gellner, *Psychoanalytic Movement*, 26.

4. Ibid., 27. It should be noted that the title of Gellner's book was mistakenly printed and published as *The Psychoanalytic Movement, Or The Coming of Unreason*. The intended title was *The Psychoanalytic Movement, Or The Cunning of Unreason* (see Gellner, "Psychoanalysis as a Social Institution," in *Freud in Exile*, 223).

5. Peregrine Horden, "Thoughts of Freud," in *Freud and the Humanities*, ed. Peregrine Horden (New York: St. Martin's Press, 1985), 24.

6. See Erich Heller, "Observations about Psychoanalysis and Modern Literature," in *In the Age of Prose* (New York: Cambridge University Press, 1984), 177–91.

7. Trosman, *Freud's Imaginative World*, 54–55.

8. George Simmel, quoted in Aschheim, *Nietzsche Legacy*, 23.

# BIBLIOGRAPHY

Abraham, Hilda C., and Ernst L. Freud, eds. *A Psycho-Analytic Dialogue: The Letters of Sigmund Freud and Karl Abraham, 1907–1926*, trans. Bernard Marsh and Hilda C. Abraham. New York: Basic Books, 1965.

Abraham, Karl. "Amenhotep IV: A Psycho-analytic Contribution towards the Understanding of His Personality and of the Monotheistic Cult of Aton." In *Clinical Papers and Essays on Psychoanalysis*, trans. H. Abraham and D. Ellison, 262–90. London: Hogarth Press, 1955.

Ackerman, Robert John. *Nietzsche: A Frenzied Look*. Amherst: University of Massachusetts Press, 1990.

Alcoff, Linda. "Continental Philosophy." In *A Companion to Epistemology*, ed. Jonathan Dancy and Ernest Sosa, 76–81. Cambridge: Basil Blackwell, 1992.

Anderson, Lorin. "Freud, Nietzsche." *Salmagundi* 47-48 (Winter-Spring 1980): 3–29.

Andreas-Salomé, Lou. *Friedrich Nietzsche in seinen Werken*. Vienna: Carl Konegen, 1894.

———. *Friedrich Nietzsche: The Man in His Work*, ed. and trans. Siegfried Mandel. Redding Ridge, CT: Black Swan Books, 1988 (1894).

———. *Fenitschka. Eine Ausschweifung*. Stuttgart: J. C. Cotta, 1898.

———. "'Anal' and 'Sexual.'" *Imago* 4, no. 5 (1916): 249–73.

———. "The Dual Orientation of Narcissism." *The Psychoanalytic Quarterly* 31, no. 1 (January 1962 [1921]): 3–30.

——. *The Freud Journal of Lou Andreas-Salomé*, trans. Stanley A. Leavy. New York: Basic Books, 1964.

——. *Looking Back: Memoirs*, ed. Ernst Pfeiffer, trans. Breon Mitchell. New York: Paragon House, 1991.

Anzieu, Didier. *Freud's Self-Analysis*. London: The Hogarth Press, 1986.

Appignanesi, Lisa, and John Forrester. *Freud's Women*. New York: Basic Books, 1992.

Aschheim, Steven E. *The Nietzsche Legacy in Germany, 1890–1990*. Berkeley: University of California Press, 1992.

Ashmore, Malcolm. *The Reflexive Thesis*. Chicago: The University of Chicago Press, 1989.

Assoun, Paul Laurent. *Freud et Nietzsche*. Paris: Presses Universitaires de France, 1980.

Basch, Michael Franz. "Empathetic Understanding: A Review of the Concept and Some Theoretical Considerations." *Journal of the American Psychoanalytic Association* 31, no. 1 (1983): 101–25.

Baumer, Franklin L. *Modern European Thought: Continuity and Change in Ideas, 1600–1950*. New York: Macmillan Publishing Co., 1977.

Bellak, Leopold. *Psychoanalysis as a Science*. Boston: Allyn and Bacon, 1993.

Bemporad, Jules R. "Effects of Early Childhood Experience." *The Harvard Mental Health Letter* 8, no. 3 (September 1991): 4–6.

Berliner, Arthur K. *Psychoanalysis and Society: The Social Thought of Sigmund Freud*. Washington DC: University Press of America, 1983.

Bernays, Jacob. *Die Heraklitischen Briefe: ein Beitrag zur philosophischen und religionsgeschichtlichen Litteratur*. Berlin: W. Hertz; London: Williams und Norgate, 1869.

Binion, Rudolph. *Frau Lou*. Princeton: Princeton University Press, 1968.

Biser, Eugen. "The Critical Imitator of Jesus: A Contribution to the Interpretation of Nietzsche on the Basis of a Comparison."In *Studies in Nietzsche and the Judaeo-Christian Tradition*, ed. James C. O'Flaherty, Timothy F. Sellner and Robert M. Helm, 186–99. Chapel Hill: The University of North Carolina Press, 1985.

Blaire, Carole, and Sander L. Gilman. Introduction to *Friedrich Nietzsche on Rhetoric and Language*, ed. and trans. Sander L. Gilman, Carole

Blaire and David J. Parent, ix-xxvii. New York: Oxford University Press, 1989.

Blum, Harold P. "Freud and the Figure of Moses: The Moses of Freud." *Journal of the American Psychoanalytic Association* 39, no. 2 (1991): 513–35.

Boehlich, Walter, ed. *The Letters of Sigmund Freud to Eduard Silberstein, 1871–1881*, trans. A. J. Pomerans. Cambridge: The Belknap Press of Harvard University Press, 1990.

Bower, Bruce. "Oedipus Wrecked." *Science News* 140 (Oct. 19, 1991): 248–50.

Brandes, Georg. *Friedrich Nietzsche.* New York: Haskell House Publishers, 1972 (1889–1900).

Bridger, Wagner. "Early Childhood and Its Effects." *The Harvard Mental Health Letter* 8, no. 2 (August 1991): 4–7.

Brome, Vincent. *Freud and His Early Circle.* New York: William Morrow and Co., 1968.

Brown, Peter. *The Body and Society.* New York: Columbia University Press, 1988.

Butler, Judith. "The Pleasures of Repitition." In *Pleasure Beyond the Pleasure Principle,* ed. Robert A. Glick and Stanley Bone, 259–75. New Haven: Yale University Press, 1990.

Byrum, Stephen. "The Concept of Child's Play in Nietzsche's 'Of the Three Metamorphoses.'" *Kinesis* 6 (1974): 127–35.

Carroll, Michael P. "*Moses and Monotheism* Revisited—Freud's 'Personal Myth?'" *American Imago* 44, no. 1 (Spring 1987): 15–35.

Cavell, Marcia. *The Psychoanalytic Mind: From Freud to Philosophy.* Cambridge: Harvard University Press, 1993.

Chapelle, Daniel. *Nietzsche and Psychoanalysis.* Albany: State University of New York Press, 1993.

Chessick, Richard D. "The Relevance of Nietzsche to the Study of Freud and Kohut." *Contemporary Psychoanalysis* 17, no. 3 (July 1981): 359-73.

Chodorow, Nancy J. "Freud on Women." In *The Cambridge Companion to Freud,* ed. Jerome Neu, 224–48. New York: Cambridge University Press, 1991.

Cioffi, Frank. "'Exegetical Myth-Making' in Grunbaum's Indictment of Popper and Exoneration of Freud." In *Mind, Psychoanalysis and Science*, ed. Peter Clark and Crispin Wright, 61–87. New York: Basil Blackwell, Inc., 1988.

Clark, Maudemarie. "Language and Deconstruction: Nietzsche, de Man and Postmodernism." In *Nietzsche as Postmodernist: Essays Pro and Contra*, ed. Clayton Koelb, 75–90. Albany: State University of New York, 1990.

————. *Nietzsche on Truth and Philosophy*. New York: Cambridge University Press, 1990.

————. "Nietzsche's Misogyny." Unpublished paper.

Clowes, Edith W. "The Integration of Nietzsche's Ideas of History, Time and 'Higher Nature' in the Early Historical Novels of Dmitry Merezhkovsky." *Germano-Slavica: A Canadian Journal of Germanic and Slavic Comparative Studies* 3, no. 6 (Fall 1981): 401–16.

Conway, Daniel W. "Thus Spoke Rorty: The Perils of Narrative Self-Creation." *Philosophy and Literature* 15, no. 1 (April 1991): 103–10.

Cooper, Arnold, M. "Changes in Psychoanalytic Ideas: Transference Interpretation." *Journal of the American Psychoanalytic Association* 35, no. 1 (1987): 77–98.

Crawford, Claudia. "*She.*" *Sub-stance* 29 (1981): 83–96.

————. "Nietzsche's Mnemotechnics, the Theory of Ressentiment, and Freud's Topographies of the Psychic Apparatus." *Nietzsche-Studien* 14 (1985): 281–97.

————. *The Beginning of Nietzsche's Theory of Language*. New York: Walter de Gruyter, 1988.

Dancy, Jonathan, and Ernest Sosa, eds. *A Companion to Epistemology*. Cambridge: Basil Blackwell Ltd., 1992.

Dannhauser, W. J. *Nietzsche's View of Socrates*. Ithaca: Cornell University Press, 1974.

Davey, Nicholas. "Nietzsche and Hume on Self and Identity." *Journal of the British Society for Phenomenology* 18, no. 1 (January 1987): 14–29.

Davies, Paul. Review of *Dreams of a Final Theory* by Steven Weinberg and *The God Particle* by Leon Lederman with Dick Teresi. *The New York Times Book Review*, March 7, 1992, 11–12.

de Chumaceiro, Cora L. Diaz. "Was Freud Really Tone Deaf? A Brief Commentary." *The American Journal of Psychoanalysis* 50, no. 2 (1990): 199–202.

Decker, Hannah S. *Freud, Dora, and Vienna 1900.* New York: The Free Press, 1991.

Deigh, John. "Freud's Later Theory of Civilization: Changes and Implications." In *The Cambridge Companion to Freud,* ed. Jerome Neu, 287–308. New York: Cambridge University Press, 1991.

Derksen, A. A. "Does the Tally Argument Make Freud a Sophisticated Methodologist?" *Philosophy of Science* 59, no. 1 (March 1992): 75–101.

Diethe, Carol. "Nietzsche and the Woman Question." *History of European Ideas* 11 (1989): 865–75.

Doane, Mary Ann. "Veiling Over Desire: Close-ups of the Women." In *Feminism and Psychoanalysis,* ed. Richard Feldstein and Judith Roof, 105–41. Ithaca: Cornell University Press, 1989.

Donn, Linda. *Freud and Jung: Years of Friendship, Years of Loss.* New York: Charles Scribner's Sons, 1988.

Dorer, Maria. *Historische Grundlagen der Psychoanalyse.* Leipzig: Felix Meiner, 1932.

Draenos, Stan. *Freud's Odyssey: Psychoanalysis and the End of Metaphysics.* New Haven: Yale University Press, 1982.

Duffy, Michael F., and Willard Mittelman. "Nietzsche's Attitude toward the Jews." *Journal of the History of Ideas* 59, no. 2 (April-June 1988): 301–17.

Eagle, Morris. "Psychoanalysis and the Personal." In *Mind, Psychoanalysis and Science,* ed. Peter Clark and Crispin Wright, 91–111. New York: Basil Blackwell, Inc., 1988.

Eagleton, Terry. *The Ideology of the Aesthetic.* Cambridge: Basil Blackwell, 1990.

Eisen, Arnold M. "Nietzsche and the Jews Reconsidered." *Jewish Social Studies* 58, no. 1 (Winter 1986): 1–14.

Ellenberger, Henri. *The Discovery of the Unconscious.* New York: Basic Books, 1970.

Ellman, Steven J. *Freud's Technique Papers: A Contemporary Perspective.* Northvale, NJ: Jason Aronson, 1991.

Esterson, Allen. *Seductive Mirage: An Exploration of the Work of Sigmund Freud.* Chicago: Open Court, 1993.

Field, Frank. *The Last Days of Mankind: Karl Kraus and His Vienna.* New York: St. Martin's Press, 1967.

Fishman, Rabbi Jerome. Personal communication. Boston, Massachusetts, 1992.

Five Books of Torah, Mikroas Gedolos Edition. New York: Shulsinger Brothers Publishing Co., 1950.

Flew, Anthony. *A Dictionary of Philosophy.* New York: St. Martin's Press, 1984.

Förster-Nietzsche, Elisabeth. *Das Leben Friedrich Nietzsche,* 2 vols. Leipzig: Nauman, 1895–1904.

———. *The Life of Nietzsche,* 2 vols., trans. Anthony Ludovici (vol. 1) and Paul V. Cohn (vol. 2). New York: Sturgis and Walton Co., 1912–1915.

Forth, Christopher E. "Nietzsche, Decadence, and Regeneration in France, 1891–95." *Journal of the History of Ideas* 54, no. 1 (January 1993): 97–117.

Fredriksen, Paula. *From Jesus to Christ.* New Haven: Yale University Press, 1988.

Freud, Ernst L., ed. *Letters of Sigmund Freud,* trans. Tania and James Stern. New York: Basic Books, 1960.

———. *The Letters of Sigmund Freud and Arnold Zweig,* trans. Elaine and William Robson-Scott. New York: New York University Press, 1970.

Freud, Ernst L., Lucie Freud and Ilse Grübrich-Simitis, eds. *Sigmund Freud: His Life in Pictures and Words.* New York: W. W. Norton & Co., 1985.

Freud, Sigmund (1888–89). "Preface to the Translation of Bernheim's *Suggestion.*" SE 1:75–85.

——— (1893a). "On the Psychical Mechanism of Hysterical Phenomena: A Lecture." SE 3:25–39.

——— (1893b). "Some Points for a Comparative Study of Organic and Hysterical Motor Paralyses." SE 1:155–72.

——— (1894a). "The Neuro-Psychoses of Defense." SE 3:45–61.

—— (1900a). *The Interpretation of Dreams*. SE 4:1–338 and 5:339–621.

—— (1901a). *On Dreams*. SE 5:633–86.

—— (1901b). *The Psychopathology of Everyday Life*. SE 6:1–279.

—— (1905c). *Jokes and Their Relation to the Unconscious*. SE 8:1–243.

—— (1905d). *Three Essays on the Theory of Sexuality*. SE 7:135–243.

—— (1905e [1901]). "Fragments of an Analysis of a Case of Hysteria." SE 7:15–122.

—— (1908d). "'Civilized' Sexual Morality and Modern Nervous Illness." SE 9:177–204.

—— (1909b). "Analysis of a Phobia in a Five-Year-Old Boy." SE 10:5–147.

—— (1909d). "Notes upon a Case of Obsessional Neurosis." SE 10:153–318.

—— (1910c). *Leonardo Da Vinci and a Memory of His Childhood*. SE 11: 59–137.

—— (1910h). "A Special Type of Choice of Object Made by Men." SE 11:163–75.

—— (1911c). "Psycho-Analytic Notes on an Autobiographical Account of a Case of Paranoia (Dementia Paranoides)." SE 12:3–79.

—— (1912a). "Postscript to the Case of Paranoia." SE 12:80–82.

—— (1912e). "Recommendations to Physicians Practicing Psycho-Analysis." SE 12:109–20.

—— (1913f). "The Theme of the Three Caskets." SE 12:289–301.

—— (1912–1913). *Totem and Taboo: Some Points of Agreement between the Mental Lives of Savages and Neurotics*. SE 13:1–161.

—— (1914b). "The Moses of Michelangelo." SE 13:209–36.

—— (1914c). "On Narcissism: An Introduction." SE 14:73–102.

—— (1914d). "On the History of the Psycho-Analytic Movement." SE 14:3–66.

—— (1914g). "Remembering, Repeating and Working-Through." SE 12:147–56.

—— (1915c). "Instincts and Their Vicissitudes." SE 14:117–40.

—— (1915e). "The Unconscious." SE 14:161–204.

—— (1916b). "A Mythological Parallel to a Visual Obsession." SE 14:337–38.

—— (1916d). "Some Character-Types Met with in Psycho-Analytic Work." SE 14:311–33.

—— (1916–1917). *Introductory Lectures on Psycho-Analysis.* SE 15–16.

—— (1917c). "On Transformations of Instinct as Exemplified in Anal Eroticism." SE 17:125–39.

—— (1917e). "Mourning and Melancholia." SE 14:243–58.

—— (1919h). "The 'Uncanny.'" SE 17:217–52.

—— (1920g). *Beyond the Pleasure Principle.* SE 18:7–64.

—— (1921c). *Group Psychology and the Analysis of the Ego.* SE 18:69–143.

—— (1923b). *The Ego and the Id.* SE 19:12–66.

—— (1924c). "The Economic Problem of Masochism." SE 19:159–70.

—— (1925d). *An Autobiographical Study.* SE 20:7–70.

—— (1927c). *The Future of an Illusion.* SE 21:5–56.

—— (1927d). "Humour." SE 21:159–66.

—— (1928b). Appendix to "Doestoevski and Parracide." SE 21:195–96.

—— (1930a). *Civilization and Its Discontents.* SE 21:64–145.

—— (1933a). *New Introductory Lectures on Psycho-Analysis.* SE 22: 5–182.

—— (1937a). "Lou Andreas-Salomé." SE 23:297–98.

—— (1937c). "Analysis Terminable and Interminable." SE 23:216–53.

—— (1939a). *Moses and Monotheism: Three Essays.* SE 23:7–137.

—— (1940a [1938]). *An Outline of Psycho-Analysis.* SE 23:141–207.

—— (1940b [1938]). "Some Elementary Lessons in Psycho-Analysis." SE 23:279–86.

Frosh, Stephen. *The Politics of Psychoanalysis.* New Haven: Yale University Press, 1987.

Gadamer, Hans-Georg. *The Relevance of the Beautiful and Other Essays,* ed. Robert Bernasconi, trans. Nicholas Walker. Cambridge: Cambridge University Press, 1986.

Gardner, Sebastian. "The Unconscious." In *The Cambridge Companion to Freud,* ed. Jerome Neu, 136–60. New York: Cambridge University Press, 1991.

Gay, Peter. *Freud: A Life for Our Time.* New York: W. W. Norton & Co., 1988.

Gellner, Ernest. *The Psychoanalytic Movement, Or The Coming of Unreason.* London: Paladin Books, 1985.

———. "Psychoanalysis as a Social Institution: An Anthropological Perspective." In *Freud in Exile,* ed. Edward Timms and Naomi Segal, 223–29. New Haven: Yale University Press, 1988.

———. *Postmodernism, Reason and Religion.* New York: Routledge, 1992.

Gendlin, Eugene T. "Client-Centered: The Experiential Response." In *Use of Interpretation in Treatment,* ed. Emanual F. Hammer, 208–27. New York: Grune & Stratton, Inc., 1968.

Gilman, Sander L. "Nietzsche, Heine, and the Otherness of the Jew." In *Studies in Nietzsche and the Judeo-Christian Tradition,* ed. James C. O'Flaherty, Timothy E. Sellner and Robert M. Helm, 206-25. Chapel Hill: The University of North Carolina Press, 1985.

———. "Constructing the Image of the Appropriate Therapist: The Struggle of Psychiatry with Psychoanalysis." In *Freud in Exile,* ed. Edward Timms and Naomi Segal, 15–36. New Haven: Yale University Press 1988.

———. *Sexuality: An Illustrated History.* New York: John Wiley & Sons, 1989.

———. *Freud, Race, and Gender.* Princeton: Princeton University Press, 1993.

———, ed. *Conversations with Nietzsche: A Life in the Words of His Contemporaries,* trans. David J. Parent. New York: Oxford University Press, 1987.

Gilman, Sander L., Carole Blair and David J. Parent, eds. *Friedrich Nietzsche on Rhetoric and Language.* New York: Oxford University Press, 1989.

Ginsberg, Mitchell. "Nietzschean Psychiatry." In *Nietzsche: A Collection of Critical Essays*, ed. Robert C. Solomon, 293–315. Notre Dame, Indiana: University of Notre Dame Press, 1980.

Glymour, Clark. "Freud's Androids." In *The Cambridge Companion to Freud*, ed. Jerome Neu, 44–85. New York: Cambridge University Press, 1991.

Godde, Gunter. "Freuds philosophische Diskussionskreise in der Studentenzeit." *Jarbuch der Psychoanalyse* 27 (1991): 73–113.

Golumb, Jacob. "Freudian Uses and Misuses of Nietzsche." *American Imago* 37, no. 4 (Winter 1980): 371–85.

———. *Nietzsche's Enticing Psychology of Power*. Ames: Iowa State University Press, 1987.

Gould, Stephen Jay. "Freud's Phylogenetic Fantasy." *Natural History* 101 (December 1987): 13–19.

———. *Bully for Brontosaurus*. New York: W. W. Norton & Co., 1991.

———. "Dinosaurs in the Haystack." *Natural History* 106 (March 1992): 2–13.

———. "The Gift of New Questions." *Natural History* 108 (August 1993): 4–13.

Gould, Timothy. "What Makes the Pale Criminal Pale?" *Soundings: An Interdisciplinary Journal* 58, no. 4 (Winter 1985): 510–36.

Goulder, Michael. "The Pauline Epistles." In *The Literary Guide to the Bible*, ed. Robert Alter and Frank Kermode, 479–502. Cambridge: The Belknap Press of Harvard University Press, 1987.

Graybeal, Jean. *Language and "the Feminine" in Nietzsche and Heidegger*. Bloomington: Indiana University Press, 1990.

Grinstein, Alexander. *Sigmund Freud's Dreams*, 2d ed. New York: International Universities Press, 1980.

———. *Freud at the Crossroads*. Madison, CT: International Universities Press, 1990.

Grosskurth, Phyllis. *The Secret Ring: Freud's Inner Circle and the Politics of Psychoanalysis*. Reading, MA: Addison-Wesley, 1991.

Grünbaum, Adolf. *The Foundations of Psychoanalysis*. Berkeley: University of California Press, 1984.

————. "'Meaning' Connections and Causal Connections in the Human Sciences: The Poverty of Hermeneutic Philosophy." *Journal of the American Psychoanalytic Association* 38, no. 3 (1990): 559–77.

————. *Validation in the Clinical Theory of Psychoanalysis.* Madison, CT: International Universities Press, 1993.

Gupta, R. K. "Freud and Schopenhauer." *Journal of the History of Ideas* 36, no. 4 (Oct.-Dec. 1975): 721–28.

Haldane, John. "Psychoanalysis, Cognitive Psychology and Self-Consciousness." In *Mind, Psychoanalysis Science,* ed. Peter Clark and Crispin Wright, 113–39. New York: Basil Blackwell, Inc., 1988.

Hanly, Charles. *The Problem of Truth in Applied Psychoanalysis.* New York: The Guilford Press, 1992.

Haraway, Donna. "Situated Knowledges: The Science Question in Feminism and the Privilege of Partial Perspective." *Feminist Studies* 14, no. 3 (Fall 1988): 575–99.

Hatab, Lawrence J. "Nietzsche on Woman." *Southern Journal of Philosophy* 19, no. 3 (1981): 333–45.

————. *Myth and Philosophy: A Contest of Truths.* La Salle, IL: Open Court, 1990.

Hayman, Ronald. *Nietzsche: A Critical Life.* New York: Viking Penguin, 1980.

Heilbrun, Carolyn G. *Hamlet's Mother.* New York: Columbia University Press, 1990.

Heller, Erich. "Observations about Psychoanalysis and Modern Literature." In *In the Age of Prose,* 177–91. New York: Cambridge University Press, 1984.

Herzog, Patricia. "The Myth of Freud as Anti-philosopher." In *Freud: Appraisals and Reappraisals,* vol. 2, ed. Paul E. Stepansky. Hillsdale, New Jersey: The Analytic Press, 1988.

Himmelfarb, Gertrude. "Supposing History Is a Woman—What Then?" *The American Scholar* 53, no. 4 (Fall 1984): 494–505.

Hirschmüller, Albrecht. *The Life and Work of Joseph Breuer.* New York: New York University Press, 1989 (1978).

Hoffman, Irwin Z. "Discussion: Toward a Social-Constructivist View of the Psychoanalytic Situation." *Psychoanalytic Dialogues* 1, no. 1 (1991): 74–105.

———. "Reply to Benjamin." *Psychoanalytic Dialogues* 1, no. 4 (1991): 535–44.

Hollingdale, R. J. *Nietzsche.* Boston: Routledge and Kegan Paul, 1973.

———. *Nietzsche.* Boston: Ark Paperbacks, 1985.

Holmes, Kim R. "Freud, Evolution, and the Tragedy of Man." *Journal of the American Psychoanalytic Association* 31, no. 1 (1983): 187–210.

Holstein, James A., and Gale Miller, eds. *Reconsidering Social Constructionism.* New York: Aldine De Gruyter, 1993.

Holt, Robert R. "Freud's Adolescent Reading: Some Possible Effects on His Work." In *Freud: Appraisals and Reappraisals,* vol. 3, ed. Paul E. Stepansky, 167–92. Hillsdale, NJ: The Analytic Press, 1989.

———. *Freud Reappraised.* New York: The Guilford Press, 1989.

———. "Freud's Parental Identifications as a Source of Some Contradictions within Psychoanalysis." In *Freud and the History of Psychoanalysis,* ed. Toby Gelfand and John Kerr, 1–28. Hillsdale, New Jersey: The Analytic Press, 1992.

Hopkins, James. "*The Interpretation of Dreams.*" In *The Cambridge Companion to Freud,* ed. Jerome Neu, 86–135. New York: Cambridge University Press, 1991.

Horden, Peregrine. "Thoughts of Freud." In *Freud and the Humanities,* ed. Peregrine Horden, 1–25. New York: St. Martins Press, 1985.

Horney, Karen. "The Dread of Women." *International Journal of Psycho-Analysis* 13 (1932): 348–360.

Hulin, Michel. "Nietzsche and the Suffering of the Indian Ascetic," trans. Graham Parkes. In *Nietzsche and Asian Thought,* ed. Graham Parkes, 64–75. Chicago: The University of Chicago Press, 1991.

Irmscher, Johannes. "Freidrich Nietzsche and Classical Philology Today." *History of European Ideas* 11 (1984): 963–66.

Jacoby, Russell. *The Repression of Psychoanalysis.* Chicago: The University of Chicago Press, 1986.

Janet, Pierre. *Psychological Healing: A Historical and Clinical Study,* 2 vols., trans. Eden and Cedar Paul. New York: Ruskin House, 1925.

Jarmolych, Nina. "Nietzsche's Concept of Consciousness." *International Studies in Philosophy* 17, no. 2 (1985): 69–77.

Jaspers, Karl. *General Psychopathology*, 7th ed., trans. J. Hoenig and M. W. Hamilton. Chicago: The University of Chicago Press, 1964.

Jennings, Jerry L. "From Philology to Existential Psychology: The Significance of Nietzsche's Early Work." *The Journal of Mind and Behavior 9*, no. 1 (Winter 1988): 57–76.

Jones, Ernest. *The Life and Work of Sigmund Freud*, 3 vols. New York: Basic Books, 1953–1957.

Jung, C. G. "Cryptomnesia." *The Collected Works of C. G. Jung*, vol. 1, trans. R. F. C. Hull, ed. Sir Herbert Read, Michael Fordham, Gerhard Adler, and William McGuire, 95–106. Princeton: Princeton University Press, 1970 [1905].

———. "The Psychology of Dementia Praecox." *The Collected Works of C.G. Jung*, vol. 3, trans. R. F. C. Hull, ed. Sir Herbert Read, et al., 1–151. Princeton: Princeton University Press, 1972 [1907].

———. "A Contribution to the Study of Psychological Types." *The Collected Works of C.G. Jung*, vol. 6, *Psychological Types*, trans. H. G. Baynes (rev. R. F. C. Hull), ed. Sir Herbert Read et al., 499–509. Princeton: Princeton University Press, 1971 [1913].

———. *Nietzsche's Zarathustra: Notes of the Seminar Given in 1934–1939*, 2 vols., ed. James L. Jarrett. Princeton: Princeton University Press, 1988.

Kahn, Charles H. *The Art and Thought of Heraclitus: An Edition of the Fragments with Translation and Commentary*. New York: Cambridge University Press, 1981.

Kardiner, Abram. *My Analysis with Freud: Reminiscences*. New York: W. W. Norton & Co., 1977.

Kaufmann, Walter. *From Shakespeare to Existentialism*. New York: Anchor Books, 1960.

———. *Nietzsche: Philosopher, Psychologist, Antichrist*. Princeton: Princeton University Press, 1974.

———, ed. *The Portable Nietzsche*. New York: The Viking Press, 1954.

———, ed. *The Will to Power* by Friedrich Nietzsche, trans. Walter Kaufmann and R. J. Hollingdale. New York: Random House, 1967.

———, ed. *Basic Writings of Nietzsche*, trans. Walter Kaufmann. New York: Random House, 1968.

Kerr, John. *A Most Dangerous Method: The Story of Jung, Freud, and Sabina Spielrein.* New York: Alfred A. Knopf, 1993.

Kirkham, Richard L. *Theories of Truth.* Cambridge: The MIT Press, 1992.

Klein, Dennis B. *Jewish Origins of the Psychoanalytic Movement.* New York: Praeger Publishers, 1981.

Kofman, Sarah. *The Enigma of Woman: Woman in Freud's Writings,* trans. C. Porter. Ithaca: Cornell University Press, 1985.

———. "Baubô: Theological Perversion and Fetishism," trans. T. Strong. In *Nietzsche's New Seas,* ed. Michael Allen Gillespie and Tracy B. Strong, 175–202. Chicago: The University of Chicago Press, 1988.

Kolakowski, Leszek. *The Presence of Myth.* Chicago: The University of Chicago Press, 1989.

Krummel, Richard Frank. "Dokumentation: Joseph Paneth über seine Begegnung mit Nietzsche in der Zarathustra-Zeit." In *Nietzsche-Studien* 17 (1988): 478–95.

———. *Nietzsche und der deutsche Geist,* 2 vols. Berlin, New York: Walter de Gruyter, 1974/1983.

Kuhn, Thomas. S. "The Natural and the Human Sciences." In *The Interpretive Turn,* ed. David R. Hiley, James F. Bohman and Richard Shusterman, 17–24. Ithaca: Cornell University Press, 1991.

Lacan, Jacques. *Ecrits,* trans. A. Sheridan. London: Tavistock, 1977.

Lampert, Laurence. *Nietzsche's Teaching: An Interpretation of "Thus Spoke Zarathustra."* New Haven: Yale University Press, 1986.

Langs, Robert. *Decoding Your Dreams.* New York: Ballantine Books, 1988.

Leeming, David Adams. *The World of Myth: An Anthology.* New York: Oxford University Press, 1990.

Lehman, Herbert. "Jung Contra Freud/Nietzsche Contra Wagner." *International Review of Psychoanalysis* 13 (1986): 201–9.

Lenson, David. *"The Birth of Tragedy": A Commentary.* Boston: Twayne Publishers, 1987.

Lichtenstein, Heinz. *The Dilemma of Human Identity.* New York: Jason Aronson, 1977.

Lieberman, E. James. *Acts of Will: The Life and Work of Otto Rank.* New York: The Free Press, 1985.

————. "Why Oedipus Loved His Father." *The Harvard Mental Health Letter* 7, no. 6 (June 1991): 4–6.

Lindblom, Charles F. *Inquiry and Change.* New Haven: Yale University Press, 1990.

Lindsay, J. M. *Gottfried Keller: Life and Works.* Chester Springs, PA: Dufour Press, 1969.

Lipps, Theodor. *Grundtatsachen des Seelenlebens.* Bonn: Max Cohen, 1883.

Lissarrague, François. "Figures of Women." In *A History of Women in the West.* vol. 1, *From Ancient Goddesses to Christian Saints,* ed. Pauline Schmitt Pantel, trans. Arthur Goldhammer, 139–229. Cambridge: The Belknap Press of Harvard University Press, 1992.

Livingstone, Angela. *Salomé: Her Life and Work.* Mt. Kisco, NY: Moyer Bell Ltd., 1984.

Loewald, Hans W. *Papers on Psychoanalysis.* New Haven: Yale University Press, 1980.

————. *Sublimation.* New Haven: Yale University Press, 1988.

Luborsky, Lester, and Paul Crits-Christoph. *Understanding Transference: The CCRT Method.* New York: Basic Books, 1990.

Mackay, Nigel. *Motivation and Explanation.* Madison CT: International Universities Press, 1987.

Macmillan, Malcolm. *Freud Evaluated: The Completed Arc.* Amsterdam: North-Holland, 1991.

————. "The Sources of Freud's Methods for Gathering and Evaluating Clinical Data." In *Freud and the History of Psychoanalysis,* ed. Toby Gelfand and John Kerr, 99–151. Hillsdale, NJ: The Analytic Press, 1992.

Magnus, Bernard, Stanley Stewart and Jean-Pierre Mileur. *Nietzsche's Case.* New York: Routledge, 1993.

Mahon, Eugene. "Play, Pleasure, Reality." In *Pleasure Beyond the Pleasure Principle,* ed. Robert A. Glick and Stanley Bone, 26–37. New Haven: Yale University Press, 1990.

Mahoney, Michael J. *Human Change Processes.* New York: Basic Books, 1991.

Mahoney, Patrick. *Freud as a Writer.* New York: International Universities Press, 1982.

Makari, George J. "German Philosophy, Freud, and the Riddle of the Woman." *Journal of the American Psychoanalytic Association* 39, no. 1 (1991): 183–213.

Mandel, Siegfried. Introduction to *Friedrich Nietzsche: The Man in His Work* by Lou Andreas-Salomé, viii–lxii. Redding Ridge, CT: Black Swan Books, 1988.

Mann, Thomas. "Freud's Position in the History of Modern Culture." In *Freud As We Knew Him,* ed. Hendrick M. Ruitenbeck, 65–89. Detroit: Wayne State University Press, 1973 [1929].

Masson, Jeffrey Moussaieff, ed. *The Complete Letters of Sigmund Freud to Wilhelm Fliess,* 1887–1904, trans. Masson. Cambridge: The Belknap Press of Harvard University Press, 1985.

Maylan, Charles E. *Freuds tragischer Komplex: Eine Analyse der Psychoanalyse.* Munich: Ernst Reinhardt, 1929.

Mazlish, Bruce. "Freud and Nietzsche." *Psychoanalytic Review* 55, no. 3 (1968): 360–75.

McGrath, William J. *Dionysian Art and Populist Politics in Austria.* New Haven: Yale University Press, 1974.

———. *Freud's Discovery of Psychoanalysis: The Politics of Hysteria.* Ithaca: Cornell University Press, 1986.

———. "Freud and the Force of History." In *Freud and the History of Psychoanalysis,* ed. Toby Gelfand and John Kerr, 79–97. Hillsdale, NJ: The Analytic Press, 1992.

McGuire, William, ed. *The Freud/Jung Letters,* trans. Ralph Manheim and R. F. C. Hull. Princeton: Princeton University Press, 1974.

Megill, Allan. *Prophets of Extremity.* Berkeley: University of California Press, 1985.

Meng, Heinrich, and Ernst L. Freud, eds. *Psychoanalysis and Faith: The Letters of Sigmund Freud and Oskar Pfister,* trans. Eric Mosbacher. New York: Basic Books, 1963.

*The Merriam Webster Dictionary,* ed. Henry Bosley Woolf. New York: Pocket Books, 1974.

Mitchell, Stephen A. *Relational Concepts in Psychoanalysis.* Cambridge: Harvard University Press, 1988.

———. "Editorial Philosophy." *Psychoanalytic Dialogues* 1, no. 1 (1991): 1–7.

Molnar, Michael. *The Diary of Sigmund Freud, 1929–1939*, trans. and annotated by Molnar. New York: Charles Scribner's Sons, 1992.

Moran, George S. "Some Functions of Play and Playfulness: A Developmental Perspective." *The Psychoanalytic Study of the Child* 42 (1987): 11–29.

Morton, Frederic. *A Nervous Splendor: Vienna 1888/1889.* London: George Weidenfeld and Nicolson Ltd., 1979.

———. *Thunder at Twilight: Vienna 1913/1914.* New York: Charles Scribner's Sons, 1989.

Nash, Drew S. "Death or Power: A Reassessment of Human Aggression through an Analysis and Comparison of the Theories of Nietzsche and Freud." Ph.D. diss., University of California at Berkeley, 1984.

Nehamas, Alexander. *Nietzsche: Life as Literature.* Cambridge: Harvard University Press, 1985.

———. "Nietzsche, Freidrich (1844–1900)." In *A Companion to Epistemology*, ed. Jonathan Dancy and Ernest Sosa, 304–5. Cambridge: Basil Blackwell, 1992.

Nietzsche, Friedrich. "Homer and Classical Philology." In *The Complete Works*, ed. Oscar Levy, vol. 3, trans. J. M. Kennedy, 145-70. New York: Russell and Russell, 1964 (1869).

———. *The Birth of Tragedy.* In *Basic Writings of Nietzsche*, ed. and trans. Walter Kaufmann, 15-144. New York: Random House, 1968 (1872).

———. "On Truth and Lying in an Extra-Moral Sense." In *Friedrich Nietzsche on Rhetoric and Language*, ed. and trans. Sander L. Gilman, Carole Blair and David J. Parent, 246–57. New York: Oxford University Press, 1989 (1873).

———. *Philosophy in the Tragic Age of the Greeks*, trans. Marianne Cowan. Washington, DC: Regnery Gateway, Inc., 1962 (1873).

———. *Untimely Meditations*, trans. R. J. Hollingdale. New York: Cambridge University Press, 1983 (1873–76).

———. *Human, All Too Human*, trans. R. J. Hollingdale. New York: Cambridge University Press, 1986 (1878–80).

———. *Daybreak*, trans. R. J. Hollingdale. New York: Cambridge University Press, 1982 (1881).

————. *The Gay Science*, trans. Walter Kaufmann. New York: Vintage Books, 1974 (1882; 1887).

————. *Thus Spoke Zarathustra*. In *The Portable Nietzsche*, ed. and trans. Walter Kaufmann, 121–439. New York: The Viking Press, 1954 (1883–85).

————. *Beyond Good and Evil*. In *Basic Writings of Nietzsche*, ed. and trans. Walter Kaufmann, 191–427. New York: Random House, 1968 (1886).

————. *On the Genealogy of Morals*. In *Basic Writings of Nietzsche*, ed. and trans. Walter Kaufmann, 449–599. New York: Random House, 1968 (1887).

————. *Twilight of the Idols*. In *The Portable Nietzsche*, ed. and trans. Walter Kaufmann, 464–563. New York: The Viking Press, 1974 (1888).

————. *The Antichrist*. In *The Portable Nietzsche*, ed. and trans. Walter Kaufmann, 568–656. New York: The Viking Press, 1974 (1895 [1888]).

————. *Nietzsche Contra Wagner*. In *The Portable Nietzsche*, ed. and trans. Walter Kaufmann, 661–83. New York: The Viking Press, 1974 (1895 [1888]).

————. *Ecce Homo*. In *Basic Writings of Nietzsche*, ed. and trans. Walter Kaufmann, 671–791. New York: Random House, 1968 (1908 [1888]).

————. *The Will to Power*, ed. Walter Kaufmann, trans. Walter Kaufmann and R. J. Hollingdale. New York: Random House, 1967 (1883–1888).

Nunberg, Herman, and Ernst Federn, eds. *Minutes of the Vienna Psychoanalytic Society*, vols. 1–3, trans. M. Nunberg. New York: International University Press, 1962–1974.

O'Hear, Anthony. *An Introduction to the Philosophy of Science*. New York: Oxford University Press, 1990.

Oliver, Kelly. "Woman as Truth in Nietzsche's Writings." *Social Theory and Practice* 10, no. 2 (Summer 1984): 185–99.

Paglia, Camille. *Sexual Personae: Art and Decadence from Nefertiti to Emily Dickinson*. New York: Vintage Books, 1991.

Parkes, Graham. "The Dance from Mouth to Hand (Speaking Zarathustra's Write Foot ForeWord)." In *Nietzsche as Postmodernist: Essays Pro and Contra*, ed. Clayton Koelb, 127–41. Albany: State University of New York Press, 1990.

Passmore, John. *Recent Philosophers*. La Salle, Illinois: Open Court, 1985.

Paul, Robert A. "Freud's Anthropology: A Reading of the 'Cultural Books.'" In *The Cambridge Companion to Freud*, ed. Jerome Neu, 267–86. New York: Cambridge University Press, 1991.

Perry, Campbell, and Jean-Roch Laurence. "Mental Processing Outside of Awareness." In *The Unconscious Reconsidered*, ed. Kenneth S. Bowers and Donald Meichenbaum, 9–48. New York: John Wiley and Sons, 1984.

Peterfreund, Emanual. *The Process of Psychoanalytic Therapy*. Hillsdale, NJ: The Analytic Press, 1983.

Pfeiffer, Ernst. Notes to *Looking Back* by Lou Andreas-Salomé, 153–216. New York: Paragon House, 1991.

———, ed. *Sigmund Freud and Lou Andreas-Salomé: Letters*, trans. William and Elaine Robson-Scott. New York: W. W. Norton & Co., 1985.

Pick, Robert. *The Last Days of Imperial Vienna*. London: Weidenfeld and Nicolson, 1975.

Pletsch, Carl. "On the Autobiographical Life of Nietzsche." In *Psychoanalytic Studies of Biography*, ed. George Moraites and George H. Pollock, 405–34. Madison, CT: International Universities Press, 1987.

———. *Young Nietzsche*. New York: The Free Press, 1991.

Ragland-Sullivan, Ellie. *Jacques Lacan and the Philosophy of Psychoanalysis*. Urbana: University of Illinois Press, 1986.

Reichert, Herbert W., and Karl Schlechta. *International Nietzsche Bibliography*. Chapel Hill: University of North Carolina Press, 1960.

Restak, Richard. *The Brain Has a Mind of Its Own*. New York: Harmony Books, 1991.

Rice, Emanuel. *Freud and Moses: The Long Journey Home*. Albany: State University of New York Press, 1990.

Ritvo, Lucille B. *Darwin's Influence on Freud*. New Haven: Yale University Press, 1990.

Roazen, Paul. *Freud: Political and Social Thought.* New York: Vintage Books, 1968.

——. *Freud and His Followers.* New York: New York University Press, 1984 [1974].

——. "Nietzsche and Freud: Two Voices from the Underground." *Psychohistory Review* 19, no. 3 (Spring 1991): 327–48.

Robertson, Ritchie. "Freud's Testament: 'Moses and Monotheism.'" In *Freud in Exile,* ed. Edward Timms and Naomi Segal, 80-89. New Haven: Yale University Press, 1988.

Roith, Estelle. *The Riddle of Freud: Jewish Influences on His Theory of Female Sexuality.* New York: Tavistock Publications, 1987.

Rorty, Richard. "Freud and Moral Reflection." In *Essays on Heidegger and Others,* 143–63. New York: Cambridge University Press, 1991.

——. "Introduction: Pragmatism and Post-Nietzschean Philosophy." In *Essays on Heidegger and Others,* 1–6. New York: Cambridge Press, 1991.

——. "Centers of Moral Gravity: Commentary on Donald Spence's 'The Hermeneutic Turn.'" *Psychoanalytic Dialogues* 3, no. 1 (1993): 21–28.

Rose, Paul Lawrence. *Revolutionary Antisemitism in Germany from Kant to Wagner.* Princeton: Princeton University Press, 1990.

Rosset, Clement. *Joyful Cruelty,* ed. and trans. David F. Bell. New York: Oxford University Press, 1993.

Rudnytsky, Peter L. *Freud and Oedipus.* New York: Columbia University Press, 1987.

——. *The Psychoanalytic Vocation.* New Haven: Yale University Press, 1991.

Rycroft, Charles. *The Innocence of Dreams.* New York: Pantheon Books, 1979.

——. *Psychoanalysis and Beyond,* ed. Peter Fuller. Chicago: The University of Chicago Press, 1985.

Sachs, David. "In Fairness to Freud: A Critical Notice of *The Foundations of Psychoanalysis* by Adolf Grünbaum." In *The Cambridge Companion to Freud,* ed. Jerome Neu, 309–38. New York: Cambridge University Press, 1991.

Sachs, Jerome. "Psychoanalysis and the Elements of Play." *The American Journal of Psychoanalysis* 51, no. 1 (1991): 39–53.

Sacks, Oliver. "The Last Hippie." *The New York Review of Books* (March 26, 1992): 53–62.

Sagan, Eli. *Freud, Women, and Morality: The Psychology of Good and Evil.* New York: Basic Books, 1988.

Salaquarda, Jörg. "Dionysus versus the Crucified One: Nietzsche's Understanding of the Apostle Paul," trans. Timothy F. Sellner. In *Studies in Nietzsche and the Judaeo-Christian Tradition,* ed. James C. O'Flaherty, Timothy F. Sellner, and Robert M. Helm, 100–29. Chapel Hill: The University of North Carolina Press, 1985.

Sallis, John. *Crossings: Nietzsche and the Space of Tragedy.* Chicago: The University of Chicago Press, 1991.

Sand, Rosemarie. "Pre-Freudian Discovery of Dream Meaning: The Achievements of Charcot, Janet, and Krafft-Ebing." In *Freud and the History of Psychoanalysis,* ed. Toby Gelfand and John Kerr, 215–29. Hillsdale, NJ: The Analytic Press, 1992.

Sass, Louis A. "Psychoanalysis as 'Conversation' and as 'Fiction': Commentary on Charles Spezzano's 'A Relational Model of Inquiry and Truth' and Richard Geha's 'Transferred Fictions,'" *Psychoanalytic Dialogues* 3, no. 2 (1993): 245–53.

Scavio, Michael J., Andrew Cooper and Pamela Scavio Clift. "Freud's Devaluation of Nietzsche." *Psychohistory Review* 21, no. 3 (Spring 1993): 295–318.

Schacht, Richard. *Nietzsche.* Boston: Routledge & Kegan Paul, 1983.

———. "Nietzsche on Human Nature." *History of European Ideas* 11 (1989): 883–92.

———. "On Self-Becoming: Nietzsche and Nehamas's Nietzsche." *Nietzsche-Studien* 21 (1992): 266–80.

Schorske, Carl E. *Fin-De-Siécle Vienna.* New York: Vintage Books, 1981.

———. "Freud's Egyptian Dig." *The New York Review of Books* (May 27, 1993): 35–40.

Segal, Alan F. *Paul the Convert.* New Haven: Yale University Press, 1990.

Sewall, Richard B. *The Vision of Tragedy.* New York: Paragon House, 1990.

Shengold, Leonard. *"The Boy Will Come to Nothing!"* New Haven: Yale University Press, 1993.

Shweder, Richard A. *Thinking through Cultures.* Cambridge: Harvard University Press, 1991.

Silk, M. S., and J. P. Stern. *Nietzsche on Tragedy.* New York: Cambridge University Press, 1981.

Simmel, Georg. *Schopenhauer and Nietzsche,* trans. Helmut Loiskandl, Deana Weinstein and Michael Weinstein. Amherst: The University of Massachusetts, 1986 (1907).

Simon, Richard Keller. "Freud's Concepts of Comedy and Suffering." *The Psychoanalytic Review* 64, no. 3 (1977): 341–407.

Slipp, Samuel. *The Freudian Mystique: Freud, Women, and Feminism.* New York: New York University Press, 1993.

Solomon, Robert C., *From Hegel to Existentialism.* New York: Oxford University Press, 1987.

Solomon, Robert C., and Kathleen M. Higgins, eds. *Reading Nietzsche.* New York: Oxford University Press, 1988.

Spariosu, Mïhai I. *Dionysus Reborn.* Ithaca: Cornell University Press, 1989.

Spence, Donald P. *Narrative Truth and Historical Truth: Meaning and Interpretation in Psychoanalysis.* New York: W. W. Norton & Co., 1982.

———. *The Freudian Metaphor: Toward Paradigm Change in Psychoanalysis.* New York: W. W. Norton & Co., 1987.

———. "The Rhetorical Voice of Psychoanalysis." *Journal of the American Psychoanalytic Association* 38, no. 3 (1990): 579–603.

Spezzano, Charles. "Illusions of Candor: Reply to Sass." *Psychoanalytic Dialogues* 3, no. 2 (1993): 267–78.

Staten, Henry. *Nietzsche's Voice.* Ithaca: Cornell University Press, 1990.

Stern, Donnell B. "A Philosophy for the Embedded Analyst: Gadamer's Hermeneutics and the Social Paradigm of Psychoanalysis." *Contemporary Psychoanalysis* 27, no. 1 (January 1991): 51–80.

Stern, Fritz. *The Politics of Cultural Despair: A Study in the Rise of the Germanic Ideology.* Berkeley: University of California Press, 1974.

Stern, J. P. Introduction to *Untimely Meditations*, trans. R. J. Hollingdale, vii–xxxii. New York: Cambridge University Press, 1983.

Storr, Anthony. *Music and the Mind*. New York: The Free Press, 1992.

Strachey, James. Appendix to "The Neuro-Psychoses of Defense" (1894), SE 3:62–68.

―――. Preface to *Totem and Taboo* (1912–1913). SE 13:x–xii.

―――. Introduction to *Civilization and its Discontents* (1930), SE 21:59–63.

Strauss, David Friedrich. *The Life of Jesus Critically Examined*, trans. G. Elliot. Philadelphia: Fortress Press, 1973 (1835).

―――. *Der alte und der neue Glaube*. Leipzig: S. Hirzel, 1872.

Strenger, Carlo. *Between Hermeneutics and Science*. Madison, CT: International Universities Press, 1991.

Sulloway, Frank J. *Freud, Biologist of the Mind*. New York: Basic Books, 1979.

Thatcher, David. "Nietzsche's Debt to Lubbock." *Journal of the History of Ideas* 39, no. 2 (1983): 293–309.

Thiele, Leslie Paul. *Friedrich Nietzsche and the Politics of the Soul*. Princeton: Princeton University Press, 1990.

Thomas, Richard Hinton. *Nietzsche in German Politics and Society, 1890-1918*. Manchester: Manchester University Press, 1983.

Ticho, Ernst. "The Influence of the German-Language Culture on Freud's Thought." *International Journal of Psycho-Analysis* 67 (1986): 227–34.

Timms, Edwards, and Naomi Segal, eds. *Freud In Exile*. New Haven: Yale University Press, 1988.

Torgovnick, Marianna. *Gone Primitive*. Chicago: The University of Chicago Press, 1990.

Trosman, Harry. *Freud and the Imaginative World*. Hillsdale, NJ: The Analytic Press, 1985.

Trosman, Harry, and Roger Dennis Simmons. "The Freud Library." *Journal of the American Psychoanalytic Association* 21 (1973): 646–87.

Ullman, Montague, and Nan Zimmerman. *Working with Dreams.* Los Angeles: Jeremy P. Tarcher, Inc., 1979.

Valente, Joseph. "Beyond Truth and Freedom: The New Faith of Joyce and Nietzsche." *James Joyce Quarterly* 25, no. 1 (Fall 1987): 87–103.

Venturelli, Aldo. "Nietzsche in der Berggasse 19. Über die erste Nietzsche-Rezeption in Wien." *Nietzsche-Studien* 17 (1984): 448–80.

Viederman, Milton. "The Real Person of the Analyst and His Role in the Process of Psychoanalytic Cure." *Journal of the American Psychoanalytic Association* 35 (1991): 451–89.

Vitz, Paul C. *Sigmund Freud's Christian Unconscious.* New York: The Guilford Press, 1988.

Vlastos, Gregory. *Socrates: Ironist and Moral Philosopher.* Ithaca: Cornell University Press, 1991.

Wallace, Edwin R. *Freud and Anthropology: A History and Reappraisal.* New York: International Universities Press, 1983.

———. "What Is 'Truth'? Some Philosophical Contributions to Psychiatric Issues." *The American Journal of Psychiatry* 145, no. 2 (February 1988): 137–47.

———. "Freud and the Mind-Body Problem." In *Freud and the History of Psychoanalysis,* ed. Toby Gelfand and John Kerr, 231–69. Hillsdale, New Jersey: The Analytic Press, 1992.

Warner, Martin. *Philosophical Finesse: Studies in the Art of Rational Persuasion.* Oxford: Clarendon Press, 1989.

Warner, William Beatty. *Chance and the Text of Experience.* Ithaca: Cornell University Press, 1986.

Warnock, Mary. "Nietzsche's Conception of Truth." In *Nietzsche: Imagery and Thought,* ed. Malcolm Pasley, 33–65. Berkeley: University of California Press, 1978.

Warren, Mark. *Nietzsche and Political Thought.* Cambridge: The MIT Press, 1988.

Waugaman, Richard. "The Intellectual Relationship between Nietzsche and Freud." *Psychiatry* 36 (November 1973): 458–67.

Weiss, Joseph. "Unconscious Mental Functioning." *Scientific American* 262, no. 3 (March 1990): 103–9.

Weiss, Joseph, Harold Sampson, and the Mount Zion Psychotherapy Research Group. *The Psychoanalytic Process: Theory, Clinical Observations, and Empirical Research.* New York: The Guilford Press, 1986.

White, Alan. *Within Nietzsche's Labyrinth.* New York: Routledge, 1990.

White, Hayden. "Historiography as Narration." in *Telling Facts: Historiography and Narration in Psychoanalysis,* ed. Joseph H. Smith and Humphrey Morris, 284–99. Baltimore: Johns Hopkins University Press, 1992.

Williams, Bernard. *Shame and Necessity.* Berkeley: University of California Press, 1993.

Wilson, A. N. *Jesus.* New York: W. W. Norton & Company, 1992.

Winnicott, D. W. *Playing and Reality.* New York: Basic Books, 1971.

Wistrich, Robert S. *The Jews of Vienna in the Age of Franz Joseph.* New York: Oxford University Press, 1989.

———. *Antisemitism: The Longest Hatred.* New York: Pantheon Books, 1991.

Wittels, Fritz. *Sigmund Freud: His Personality, His Teaching and His School,* trans. Cedar Paul. London: George & Urwin, 1924.

———. *Freud and His Time,* trans. Louise Brink. New York: Liveright Publishing Corporation, 1931.

Yerushalmi, Yosef Hayim. "Freud on the 'Historical Novel': From the Manuscript Draft (1934) of *Moses and Monotheism.*" *International Journal of Psychoanalysis* 70 (1989): 375–95.

———. *Freud's Moses.* New Haven: Yale University Press, 1991.

Young, Julian. *Nietzsche's Philosophy of Art.* New York: Cambridge University Press, 1992.

Young-Bruehl, Elizabeth. *Anna Freud.* New York: Summit Books, 1988.

Yovel, Yirmiyahu. *Spinoza and Other Heretics.* Princeton: Princeton University Press, 1989.

Zaidman, Louise Bruit. "Pandora's Daughters and Rituals in Grecian Cities." In *A History of Women in the West.* vol. I, *From Ancient Goddesses to Christian Saints,* ed. Pauline Schmitt Pantel, trans.

Arthur Goldhammer, 338–76. Cambridge: The Belknap Press of Harvard University Press, 1992.

Zilboorg, Gregory. Introduction to *Beyond the Pleausre Principle* by Sigmund Freud, vii–xv. New York: W. W. Norton & Co., 1961 (1920).

Zimmermann, Bernhard. *Greek Tragedy: An Introduction,* trans. Thomas Marier. Baltimore: The Johns Hopkins University Press, 1991.

Zweig, Arnold. "Apollon bewältigit Dionysos (Zum achtzigsten Geburtstag Siegmund Freuds, 6 Mai 1936.)" *Text und Kritik,* Heft 104 (Oktober 1989): 3–8.